WITHDRAWN

The first comprehensive study of rituals in early modern Europe, this book argues that between about 1400 and 1700 a revolution in ritual theory took place that utterly transformed concepts about time, the body, and the presence of spiritual forces in the world. In this work of synthesis Professor Muir draws on the extensive anthropology-inspired historical research that has been published during the past twenty years, and emphasizes the persistence of traditional Christian ritual practices even as educated elites attempted to privilege reason over passion, textual interpretation over ritual action, and personal moral recitude over gaining access to supernatural powers. The themes discussed by Professor Muir are wide-ranging and include rites of passage, carnival-esque festivity, Protestant and Catholic Reformations, and the alleged anti-Christian rituals of Jews and witches.

NEW APPROACHES TO EUROPEAN HISTORY

Ritual in Early Modern Europe

NEW APPROACHES TO EUROPEAN HISTORY

Series editors
WILLIAM BEIK *Emory University*
T. C. W. BLANNING *Sidney Sussex College, Cambridge*
R. W. SCRIBNER *Harvard University*

New Approaches to European History is an important new textbook initiative, intended to provide concise but authoritative surveys of major themes and problems in European history since the Renaissance. Written at a level and length accessible to advanced school students and undergraduates, each book in the series will address topics or themes that students of European history encounter daily: the series will embrace both some of the more "traditional" subjects of study, and those cultural and social issues to which increasing numbers of school and college courses are devoted. A particular effort will be made to consider the wider international implications of the subject under scrutiny.

To aid the student reader scholarly apparatus and annotation will be light, but each work will have full supplementary bibliographies and notes for further reading: where appropriate, chronologies, maps, diagrams, and other illustrative material will also be provided.

The first titles in the series are

1 Merry E. Wiesner *Women and Gender in Early Modern Europe*

2 Jonathan Sperber *The European Revolutions, 1848–1851*

3 Charles Ingrao *The Habsburg Monarchy 1618–1815*

4 Robert Jütte *Poverty and Deviance in Early Modern Europe*

5 James B. Collins *The State in Early Modern France*

6 Charles G. Nauert, Jr. *Humanism and the Culture of Renaissance Europe*

7 Dorinda Outram *The Enlightenment*

8 Mack P. Holt *The French Wars of Religion, 1562–1629*

9 Jonathan Dewald *The European Nobility, 1400–1800*

10 Robert S. DuPlessis *Transitions to Capitalism in Early Modern Europe*

11 Edward Muir *Ritual in Early Modern Europe*

Ritual in Early
Modern Europe

EDWARD MUIR
Northwestern University

CAMBRIDGE
UNIVERSITY PRESS

PUBLISHED BY THE PRESS SYNDICATE OF THE UNIVERSITY OF CAMBRIDGE
The Pitt Building, Trumpington Street, Cambridge CB2 1RP, United Kingdom

CAMBRIDGE UNIVERSITY PRESS
The Edinburgh Building, Cambridge CB2 2RU, United Kingdom
40 West 20th Street, New York, NY 10011–4211, USA
10 Stamford Road, Oakleigh, Melbourne 3166, Australia

First published 1997

Printed in the United Kingdom at the University Press, Cambridge

Typeset in 10/12 Plantin

A catalogue record for this book is available from the British Library

Library of Congress cataloguing in publication data
Muir, Edward, 1946–
Ritual in early modern Europe / Edward Muir.
    p.   cm. – (New approaches to European history: 11)
Includes index.
ISBN 0 521 40169 0 (hb). – ISBN 0 521 40967 5 (pb)
1. Ritual.   2. Rites and ceremonies.   3. Ritualism.
4. Europe – Church history.   I. Title.   II. Series.
BL600.M85   1997
291.3′8′094 – dc21   96–50034   CIP

ISBN 0 521 40169 0 hardback
ISBN 0 521 40967 5 paperback

CE

To
Edward Wallace Muir
and
Mary Margaret Muir

Contents

List of figures	*page* x
Acknowledgments	xi
Introduction: what is a ritual?	1
Part I: The ritual moment	13
1. Rites of passage	19
2. The ritual calendar	55
Part II: Rituals of the body	81
3. Carnival and the lower body	85
4. Manners and the upper body	117
Part III: Ritual and representation	147
5. The Reformation as a revolution in ritual theory	155
6. The Reformation as a ritual process	185
7. Government as a ritual process	229
Epilogue: mere ritual	269
Glossary	276
Index	284

Figures

1 Pieter Brueghel the Elder, *The Peasants' Wedding*,
Kunsthistorisches Museum, Vienna, Austria. Foto Marburg/
Art Resource, N.Y.   *page* 36
2 Scene from the *Ars Moriendi* from Lionel Henry Cust,
*The Master E. S. and the "Ars Moriendi": A Chapter in the
History of Engraving During the XVth Century*. Oxford:
Clarendon Press, 1898. Photo courtesy of the Newberry Library.   47
3 The Christian liturgical calendar   59
4 Elevation of the host, from Andrea da Bologna, initial to the
prayer "Deus qui" of the Corpus Christi mass. Vatican,
Archivio San Pietro B 63, fol. 227v.   68
5 Pieter Brueghel the Elder, *Battle between Carnival and
Lent*, Kunsthistorisches Museum, Vienna. Foto Marburg/
Art Resource, N.Y.   82
6 Fra Angelico, *Marriage of the Virgin*, Museo di San Marco,
Florence, Italy. Alinari/Art Resource, N.Y.   100
7 Witch kisses the devil's ass, from Francesco Maria
Guazzo, *Compendium Maleficarum*. Milan: Apud Haeredes
August. Tradati, 1608. Photo courtesy of the Newberry Library.   219
8 Witches sacrifice babies, from Francesco Maria Guazzo
Compendium Maleficarum. Milan: Apud Haeredes August.
Tradati, 1608. Photo courtesy of the Newberry Library.   221
9 Gentile Bellini, *Procession in Piazza San Marco*, Accademia,
Venice, Italy. Alinari/Art Resource, N.Y.   236

Acknowledgments

Most of this book was written while I was an Associate Fellow at the National Humanities Center in Research Triangle Park, North Carolina, during a sabbatical year made possible by a leave from Louisiana State University and a Fellowship for Independent Study and Research from the National Endowment for the Humanities. During that year I enjoyed the opportunity to explore ideas with the remarkably congenial and stimulating community of scholars who gathered there and especially with the members of the seminar on ritual.

I first presented some of the views found in this book in a lecture at the Center, which was published as "Gaze and Touch: Ritual in the Renaissance and Reformation," *Ideas from the National Humanities Center* 2 (Summer 1993): 4–14. While finishing the book, I was particularly fortunate to try out some of the more controversial ideas at various meetings, including the biannual Conference on Medieval and Renaissance Studies at New College, Sarasota, Florida; the annual Conference of the American Academy of Religion; the annual Sixteenth-Century Studies Conference; a conference on "Spectacle, Monument and Memory" at York University, Ontario; and one on "La ville à la Renaissance: espaces – représentations – pouvoirs" at the Centre d'Etudes Supérieures de la Renaissance, Université François-Rabelais, Tours, France. I was also granted the opportunity for extended discussions on various issues found in this book at lectures and seminars at Northwestern, Dartmouth, Harvard, the Graduate School of the City University of New York, and the University of California at Santa Barbara. The many scholars from various disciplines who commented on and criticized my work have altered the book in so many ways that it would be impossible for me to thank everyone individually. If I have failed always to follow their advice, it is not because I was disinclined to listen but because I am relapsed in my errors.

My colleague at Northwestern and master prose stylist, James Campbell, made some very judicious recommendations for the Introduction. Susan C. Karant-Nunn and Matteo Casini kindly allowed me to see their forthcoming books in advance of publication. Bob Scribner, who first invited me to write this book, has read the entire manuscript to its considerable benefit. The influence of his scholarship and superb critical sense hovers over the entire book. I especially wish to thank him. In thinking through many of the issues discussed here, I have especially profited from frequent conversations with Regina Schwartz, who has been engaged in her own forthcoming study of the Eucharist. My chapter 5, particularly the discussion of representation as a consequence of the Eucharist debates and the connections between communion and community, is indebted to draft chapters of her book, which were first delivered as the following conference talks: "George Herbert and the Matter of the Eucharist," Modern Language Association Convention (1992); "*Hoc Est Corpus Meum*: Signification and Donne," The John Donne Society Meeting (1993); "'All in All': Communion and Community in Milton," International Milton Conference (1994). Her insights remain as a powerful presence in this book.

Introduction: what is a ritual?

"Each generation must inevitably play on the dead whatever tricks it finds necessary for its own peace of mind."   Carl Becker

"[History] is a kind of respect for the dead."   Carlo Ginzburg

When I was sixteen, I became a priest in the lay hierarchy of the Mormon church. One of our tasks as teenage priests was to read a prayer from a little card that blessed *the* sacrament, a bloodless vestige of the ancient Eucharistic rites by which Catholic priests had changed the substance of bread and wine into the flesh and blood of Christ. For us there were only homely pieces of white sandwich bread and small paper cups of water, which we had been taught were nothing more than *reminders* of Christ's last supper with his apostles.

Usually three of us sat at the sacrament table, and when our moment in the service arrived, we stood up, and the two of us at the ends of the table lifted a white cloth that had covered stainless-steel trays (no silver or gold for us) of bread and water. As the two of us faced each other, we tried to communicate with little clandestine gestures how we were going to fold the large cloth and who would hold the corners while the other reached down to make the final crease. This simple process seemed immensely solemn to us. We were concerned to make the folds neatly and never to drop the cloth, because we were intensely aware of the gaze, not of God so much as of the congregation. We were quite unlike young man Luther stumbling over the words of his first mass in dread of his human and divine fathers. We were boys trying to impress the girls.

It has been decades since I performed this simple activity, but I retain a persistent feeling of awe, less about the meaning of the ceremony than about folding that large cloth. One might call this feeling the "fear of the sacred." I have wondered where the fear comes from, and I suspect that it is a product of the gaze, the voyeurism of the congregation, intensified by sensual memories of other sheet-like foldings and prolonged gazes

1

going back to early childhood, by long histories of commonplace actions performed under watchful eyes until they are no longer common but so exquisite, so appropriate to the moment, so precise in their details that they become precarious to execute. They have become a ritual.

Although words may often be affixed to the ritual, like those completely forgotten sentences we read so many times off a little card, the awe seems to spring from the appeal to the senses rather than from an understanding of the text. Rituals give access to emotional states that resist expression in language, which is why they have become so desired and yet distrusted in our logo-centric culture. The repetition of everyday gestures within the confines of a special place and time rouses emotional responses – of fear or joy, hate or love, alienation or communion. In that emotional evocation lies the work of the ritual. As Ernst Cassirer put it, to share in a ritual performance means to live "a life of emotion, not of thoughts."[1]

Both the gazed upon and the gazers participate in the creation of a ritual, but sight is not the only sense enlisted in the performance. The feeling I experienced in folding the sacramental cloth also came from the sense of touch, the odd sensual pleasure of crisp, clean cloth skimming the skin. Other times the feeling came from pure sound, the congregation singing "Come, Come Ye Saints" or "A Mighty Fortress Is Our God," the melodies of which seem to have outlasted the verses in my memory.

Precisely because rituals conjure emotional responses, they are extremely difficult to define. They exist in the transience of the moment, and when they fail to summon the expected response, they are empty, dead, "mere rituals." Recognizing their stunning power, religious and political authorities strive to create them, manipulate them, embellish them, regulate them, even abolish them, without ever quite succeeding to do any of these things because authority can never fully blot out the gaze or glove the touch. A satisfactory definition of the word "ritual" must take account to this process of emotional evocation.

My remembered emotion, however, only accounts for a fragment of the ritual experience. The folded sacramental cloth may have only derived its affective force from repetition in a compulsive return to a defining moment of pleasure or pain. Repetitions can create order out of chaos, but rituals seem to involve more than just repetition. The neurologist Oliver Sacks discussed an amnesiac patient who, lacking the cohesion of memory, held himself together by attending mass or

---

[1] Ernst Cassirer, *The Myth of the State* (New Haven: Yale University Press, 1946), 24 as quoted in David I. Kertzer, *Ritual, Politics, and Power* (New Haven: Yale University Press, 1988), 67.

listening to music. Sacks hypothesized that it was precisely the organic unity of these recitations, in which each part led to another, that produced the salutary effect: "such structures cannot be perceived, or remembered, in part – they are perceived and remembered, if at all, as wholes."[2] A ritual must do more than just recall an emotion through repetition. It must be experienced as a unified performance.

Most theorists would accept that a ritual is a formalized, collective, institutionalized kind of repetitive action, but there is still a bewildering range of answers to the question, "what is a ritual?" One is tempted to take refuge in the famous quip of the United States Supreme Court justice who, when asked to define pornography, replied he could not define it but he knew it when he saw it. The same could be said for ritual. The possibilities range from a narrow definition that restricts ritual to religious practices that attempt to gain access to the super-natural to a broad one that sees ritual in nearly any form of repeated, formalized human activity. The touchstone of the modern analysis of ritual has been the critical distinction between the profane and sacred in Emile Durkheim's *Elementary Forms of the Religious Life* (1912):

All known religious beliefs, whether simple or complex, present one common characteristic: they presuppose a classification of all things, real and ideal, of which men think, into two classes or opposed groups, generally designated by two distinct terms which are translated well enough by the words *profane* and *sacred*.[3]

From this point of view, rituals function as "rules of conduct" that guide the behavior of men and women in the presence of the sacred.

More recently scholars have been less certain that ritual should be understood as exclusively related to religion or as a way of enforcing a classification scheme. Ritual behavior seems to be nearly as ubiquitous in the domain of the profane as the sacred. Nevertheless, as David Kertzer has pointed out, Durkheim's understanding of religion did not just involve gaining access to the supernatural:

For Durkheim, worship of a god is the symbolic means by which people worship their own society, their own mutual dependency. Thus, the sacred ultimately refers not to a supernatural entity, but rather to people's emotionally charged interdependence, their societal arrangements. What is important about rituals, then, is not that they deal with supernatural beings, but rather that they provide a powerful way in which people's social dependence can be expressed.[4]

From this point of view rituals produced and maintained community

[2] Oliver Sacks, "The Last Hippie," *New York Review of Books*, vol. 39, no. 6 (March 26, 1992), p. 59, n. 13.

[3] Emile Durkheim, *The Elementary Forms of the Religious Life: A Study in Religious Sociology*, trans. Joseph Ward Swain (Glencoe, Ill.: Free Press, 1947), 37.

[4] Kertzer, *Ritual, Politics, and Power*, 9.

solidarity: "it is by uttering the same cry, pronouncing the same word, or performing the same gesture in regard to some object that they become and feel themselves to be in unison."[5] Public rituals in this sense become the necessary way for achieving group cohesion.

The problem with this view of rituals is that many societies struggle with seemingly interminable conflicts, and sometimes the very performance of a ritual seems to incite strife. There have been several possible solutions to this problem. For Max Gluckman and Victor Turner rituals do not unify all divisions but create solidarity in the few parts of society shared by all. For David Kertzer the crucial function of rituals is not to get people to agree to things but to create the *experience* of solidarity in the absence of consensus. It is precisely the fact that people cannot agree that makes rituals of solidarity necessary. For Clifford Geertz the problem must be solved in an entirely different way. He argues that rituals do not function to create social solidarity at all but provide enacted narratives that allow people to interpret their own experience. In Geertz's famous formula, rituals produce a story people tell themselves about themselves. The value of studying rituals for him is not that they reveal universal laws about how societies function but that they help us discover the native's point-of-view – that idiosyncratic perspective that differentiates one culture from another.

But even Geertz's elegant solution creates new problems in defining what a ritual does. As Don Handelman points out, rituals – or what he calls "public events" – may not reveal social codes any better than other kinds of activities, and they may not reveal just one social code but many. In other words, they can open up a labyrinth of dissonance rather than a neatly unified vision of society. The identification of differences in rituals can potentially undermine any vision of collectivity. Claude Lévi-Strauss identified the process of "parcelling-out" as an essential procedure of ritual, a process that classifies objects and gestures to make infinite distinctions and to give value to the slightest shades of difference. The result is what Lévi-Strauss called *bricolage*, the amalgamation of pre-existing elements into playful or ritual assemblies: a simple wafer of bread is utterly transformed in the rite of the mass or the simple gesture of dropping a glove takes on a dire significance when it is a challenge to a duel.

Perhaps the best solution to the confusing problem of what rituals do is to make a distinction between what Handelman calls "models" and "mirrors." We commonly understand the word "model" in two ways. First, a model can be useful for thinking in the sense that it provides a

---

[5] Ibid., 61–62.

standard to follow. A model of comportment, for example, might be a book of manners that defines proper behavior in a variety of difficult social situations. A model might be a "how to" book that explains how to solve a calculus problem, repair a car, or bake a cake. To follow such a model means to think certain thoughts or perform certain actions in accord with the rules the model presents. Second, a model might consist of a miniature of something. Before a building is constructed or an automobile made, the architect or designer fashions a miniature model of it so that the relationship of the parts to the whole can be visualized. The miniature model presents a simplified and closed example that parallels the confusing complexity of the thing it models, but also a model anticipates the future in some way: it allows one to imagine creating something in its image, which is perhaps why so many children's toys are models in this second sense.

Many rituals work like models. They present a standard or a simplified miniature for society to follow. When churchgoers exchange handshakes, they enact a model of goodwill that the ritual encourages people to carry into their daily lives. When public officials calmly walk in an ordered procession they model the behavior expected of them in the conduct of the affairs of state.

Mirrors, on the other hand, present the world as it is understood to be. They have a declarative character: *I* am the king in a coronation, *you* are my enemy in a challenge to a duel, *she* is my wife in a wedding. Rituals that make statements and that present persons or things to the world may constitute the most common examples of rituals. When the Lord Mayor and guard paraded through the streets of London, they were showing themselves to be in charge of the city. In effect, rituals that mirror *re*-present someone or something in a public way. Such rituals can inform and incite emotions, clarify a situation, and even enact a passage from one status to another, but unlike a model they do not offer an alternative for the future constitution of society. A king who performs the rituals of rulership without challenge becomes, in effect, the king whether he is entitled to be or not.

The distinction between models and mirrors is useful for understanding the different kinds of things rituals do, but in practice it is often tricky to determine whether a specific ritual performance is modeling or mirroring. Rituals tend to blur these two processes, which is perhaps the very source of the creative tension in rituals, the tension between a conservative mirroring of what is and the utopian modeling of what might be. Rituals are inherently ambiguous in their function and meaning. They speak with many voices. The sense of disturbance created by the odd juxtapositions that rituals make is also one of the sources of their power, because anyone who can successfully pull off a ritual performance is playing with danger, and those who survive dangerous situations are feared and followed. Speaking of the Aztecs, Inga Clendinnen summarizes the point eloquently.

Heavenly powers rarely merely mirror the formal relations of those below, the earthly light being more commonly refracted than reflected. It is the points of stress and abrasion in men's own social experiences, the hidden, obsessive themes in the dialogues they have with one another, which lend urgency and structure to their imagined engagement with the sacred.[6]

The consequence of the engagement in rituals is what Pierre Bourdieu calls *habitus*, those deeply held beliefs and assumptions expressed through gestures and repeated actions, those inner dispositions that integrate past experiences and function at every moment in every perception, appreciation, and action. From this point of view, ritual helps to form and reform all social life, or to put it another way, "we are what we do, not what we think."[7]

Ritual then is basically a social activity that is repetitive, standardized, a model or a mirror, and its meaning is inherently ambiguous. Some scholars place greater emphasis on it as a form of behavior, either as an enactment that creates social solidarity or forms social identities; others focus on ritual as a kind of communication that allows people to tell stories about themselves; and still others see ritual as a collectively created performance, a specific kind of practice that constructs, maintains, and modifies society itself. The question, however, is not what is the true definition, but how can the concept be framed so that it is useful for analysis – so that it has *heuristic* value. A heuristic procedure helps us to discover things, and it might be useful to borrow from several different perspectives to understand how rituals worked in the early modern period of European history.

The task of this book is not to explain ritual in a universally applicable way but to examine rites in the particular historical situation of Christian Europe from about 1400 to 1700. Some historians call this period the "long Reformation" because of the intensity with which religious controversies dominated public affairs and private sentiment. The age begins during the late fourteenth and early fifteenth centuries when the ecclesiastical hierarchy struggled to recover from the long papal residency in Avignon and the Great Schism of the church, and new heresies broke out in England and Bohemia that challenged the sacramental privileges of the clergy. At the same time laymen and

[6] Inga Clendinnen, *Aztecs: An Interpretation* (Cambridge: Cambridge University Press, 1991), 68.
[7] Kertzer, *Ritual, Politics, and Power*, 68.

women in cities across Europe experienced an unprecedented spiritual reawakening manifest in new pious practices and which spread doubt about the usefulness of sacramental rituals for promoting ethical behavior. During the fifteenth-century Renaissance a few intellectuals began to reconsider Christian practice by reinvestigating Hebrew and pagan learning. During the sixteenth century the Protestant Reformation permanently divided Christian society into mutually suspicious and hostile camps, each led by powerful monarchs who made claims to special authority derived from God.

The early modern period was also the most crucial moment in history for ritual theory. It was during the Reformation that the generalized concept of *ritual* as a distinct kind of activity came into being. The practice of what we would recognize as rites had, of course, always been an essential component of Western culture, and medieval Latin employed the term *ritus* for the liturgical practices of the church, but the invention of the idea of "ritual" belongs to the sixteenth century. The term was originally employed in a pejorative sense to describe the disreputable practices of somebody else: what I do was ordained by God and is "true religion"; what you do is "mere ritual," at best useless, at worst profoundly evil. The appearance of the word "ritual," moreover, indicates a major intellectual shift in the understanding of the relationship between human behavior and meaning.

That shift, which precipitated a historical revolution in ritual theory, anticipated some of the modern definitions of ritual discussed above. The Reformation debate derived from a deceptively simple question: "what do rites do?" The range of answers, some of which betrayed remarkable ingenuity, stretched across a wide spectrum. To simplify the situation, at one extreme was what might be called the traditional position, *the doctrine of presence.* From this point of view, which came to be associated with dogmatic Catholicism, rites made something "present." The most obvious and ubiquitous example derived from the Eucharistic rites of the mass, when at the moment of consecration Christ became physically present in the host. Rituals also had the ability to enact, to bring something into being: when an infant was baptized original sin disappeared, when a couple said "I do" they passed into the married state, when a crown was placed on a man's head he became king. The doctrine of presence implied a certain understanding of time and space: something is "present" by being here, now, and "not present" by not being here, now. According to this view, what was present in rituals was usually a body, whether the body of an infant at the baptismal font, the body of Christ in the Eucharist, or the body of the king as he progressed in triumph into a city.

The first part of this book will explore how this doctrine influenced concepts of time. The attributes of time in traditional rituals might be called the "ritual moment," which included rites of passage, such as those of baptism, transition to a new social status, marriage, and death. The ritual moment can also be seen in the passage of calendrical or liturgical time in annual, weekly, daily, and hourly cycles.

A second part will examine the rituals that specifically pertain to the human body. These both borrowed from and helped create the vocabulary of gestures that constituted the *habitus* of traditional Christian practice. During the early modern period, the rituals of the body came to be bifurcated into those associated with the passionate lower body and those with the rational upper body, providing a radical division of body parts that signified contrasting social values and has had striking implications for modern consciousness.

The opposite extreme from the doctrine of presence in the Reformation debate was *the theory of representation*. According to the humanists and Protestant reformers who espoused some form of this theory, rituals should not be understood as a kind of behavior that created presences and enacted states of being but as an aspect of language that communicated meaning. The Eucharist reminded believers of Christ's sacrifice rather than offering up his actual physical body. The coronation of a king merely represented his accession to the throne, which had actually taken place at the moment of his predecessor's death.

The third part of the book will examine the genesis of this theory of representation and its implications for the religious practices of Protestants, the Eastern Orthodox, and Counter Reformation Catholics. The heightened sensitivity toward ritual behavior stimulated by the theoretical debate about presence and representation also intensified the allegations against Jews and supposed witches of practicing anti-Christian rituals. Finally, both civic and royal rituals reveal a struggle between concepts of presence and representation, especially in modeling the critical concept of the "body politic," whether understood to be the body of citizens or the body of the king.

The theory of representation has a long and distinguished intellectual pedigree, stretching from Plato to contemporary literary theory, and many scholars today would agree with the axiom that "everything is representation." It is vital to recognize, however, that this hermeneutic conception of ritual only became widespread at a certain moment in history as the product, not just of a conceptual revolution, but also of an immense religious and political struggle over issues of authority and freedom. Espousing one view of ritual over another was not just an intellectual exercise but a way of establishing, rejecting, or reforming authority. All answers to the question, "what do rites do?", were inevitably tainted by the vicissitudes of politics and power.

Part of the task in any historical investigation is to adjudicate between, on the one hand, the need to explain the past in the terms of the present – the temptation to play tricks on the dead, as Carl Becker put it – and, on the other, the noble wish to preserve past ways of thinking and acting – to respect the dead, as Carlo Ginzburg urged. In our post-modernist era of indeterminate meaning it may be instructive, as we play our inevitable tricks on the dead, to pay a little respect to them as well by engaging in a thought experiment: imagine returning to a world of mysterious presences. What was it like to believe that supernatural beings, whether divine or demonic, could be brought into the here and now through a simple gesture? What was it like to conceive of the city as a body, the state as a body, God as a body? What was it like to assume that certain days and times were malevolent, others benevolent? To pursue this thought experiment, one has to ask what did it feel like to witness or participate in a ritual, not just what did people think the ritual meant. One must pay as much attention to the body as to the mind, as much to the power of the gaze and the touch as to the meaning of words. One must be willing to respect the dead, to honor how different they were from us rather than to celebrate their ability to anticipate us or our ability to surpass them.

BIBLIOGRAPHY

Entries marked with a * designate recommended readings for new students of the subject.

Bell, Catherine. *Ritual Theory, Ritual Practice*. Oxford: Oxford University Press, 1992. Although difficult for beginners to the subject, this very stimulating book makes a critical appraisal of the theoretical literature on ritual, arguing that ritual should be seen as a special kind of practical activity.

*Biller, Peter. "Medieval Notions of Religion." *Journal of Ecclesiastical History* 36 (1985): 351–69. A stimulating beginning for understanding the differences between modern and medieval conceptions.

*Bossy, John. "Some Elementary Forms of Durkheim." *Past and Present* 95 (1982): 3–18. A useful examination of the applicability of Durkheim's views to the history of Christianity.

Bourdieu, Pierre. *Outline of a Theory of Practice*. Translated by Richard Nice. Cambridge: Cambridge University Press, 1977. A brilliantly stimulating theoretical work that enables us to see rituals as a form of practice.

*Chartier, Roger. *Cultural History: Between Practices and Representations*. Ithaca: Cornell University Press, 1988. Contains many acute observations on the historical study of ritual.

Clendinnen, Inga. *Aztecs: An Interpretation.* Cambridge: Cambridge University Press, 1991. Although about a very different society from those discussed here, Clendinnen's approach to the historical study of ritual is exemplary, especially in laying out the problems of making interpretations based on fragments of evidence.

Connerton, Paul. *How Societies Remember.* Cambridge: Cambridge University Press, 1989. A highly influential work, which examines the relationship between ritual performances and collective memory.

Coppet, Daniel de, ed. *Understanding Rituals.* London: Routledge, 1992. See especially the Introduction for an analysis of the current issues in ritual studies.

Darnton, Robert. "The Symbolic Element in History." *The Journal of Modern History* 58 (1986): 218–34. A good survey of how historians working in the new cultural history have treated the problem of symbolism and ritual.

*Durkheim, Emile. *The Elementary Forms of the Religious Life: A Study in Religious Sociology.* Translated by Joseph Ward Swain. Glencoe, Ill.: Free Press, 1947. The classic study in the sociology of religion and the beginning point for a serious study of ritual. For a discussion of the usefulness of Durkheim for historians, see John Bossy, "Some Elementary Forms of Durkheim," *Past and Present* 95 (1982): 3– 18. For a critique of Bossy's views, see Peter Biller, "Medieval Notions of Religion," *Journal of Ecclesiastical History* 36 (1985): 351–69.

*Geertz, Clifford. *The Interpretation of Cultures: Selected Essays.* New York: Basic Books, 1973. Introducing the concept of "thick description," Geertz's work has been at the center of the revival of interest in ritual during the past generation.

Local Knowledge: Further Essays in Interpretive Anthropology. New York: Basic Books, 1983. An important evolution of concepts presented in *The Interpretation of Cultures,* especially the idea that rituals represent a form of "blurred genres."

* *Negara: The Theatre State in Nineteenth-Century Bali.* Princeton: Princeton University Press, 1980. The brilliantly influential study of the Balinese "theater state," which argues that public rituals constitute a story people tell themselves about themselves.

Goody, Jack. "Religion and Ritual: The Definitional Problem." *The British Journal of Sociology* 12 (1961): 142–64. A useful though dated analysis of the problem of defining ritual.

Grimes, Ronald L. *Beginnings in Ritual Studies.* Washington: University Press of America, 1982. An academic contribution to the attempt to revitalize ritual in modern life.

Research in Ritual Studies: A Programmatic Essay and Bibliography. Chicago: American Theological Library Association, 1985. A helpful analysis of the issues with a comprehensive bibliography.

Handelman, Don. *Models and Mirrors: Towards an Anthropology of Public Events.* Cambridge: Cambridge University Press, 1990. Introduces the concept of ritual as a proto-event.

*Kertzer, David I. *Ritual, Politics, and Power.* New Haven: Yale University Press, 1988. A lucid analysis of ritual in politics that provides the best discussion of current ritual theories and their implications.

Lévi-Strauss, Claude. *The Savage Mind*. Chicago: University of Chicago Press, 1970. See pp. 16–33 for a discussion of *bricolage*.

*Lincoln, Bruce. *Discourse and the Construction of Society: Comparative Studies of Myth, Ritual, and Classification*. New York: Oxford University Press, 1989. A lively and often gripping book that offers a theory of ritual as a form of communication and social construction.

Moore, Sally F. and Myerhoff, Barbara G., eds. *Secular Ritual*. Assen: Van Gorcum, 1977. A collection of studies that have been especially influential in expanding the definition of what constitutes ritual and the forms of ritual practice in non-religious settings.

Nora, Pierre. "Between Memory and History: *Les Lieux de Mémoire*." *Representations* 26 (Spring 1989): 7–25. A discussion of the differences between historical and ritual forms of memory.

Parkin, David. "Ritual as Spatial Direction and Bodily Division." In *Understanding Rituals*. Edited by Daniel de Coppet. London: Routledge, 1992. Pp. 11–25. Argues that "ritual is fundamentally made up of physical action, with words often only optional or arbitrarily replaceable, that it can be regarded as having a distinctive potential for performative imagination that is not reducible to verbal assertations" (11–12.) Parkin's insight into how some anthropologists have treated ritual provides a basis for the approach taken in this book.

Rappaport, Roy A. "The Obvious Aspects of Ritual." In *Ecology, Meaning, and Religion*. Richmond, Calif.: North Atlantic, 1979. Pp. 173–221. A survey of definitions of ritual.

Smith, Jonathan Z. "The Bare Facts of Ritual." *History of Religions* 20 (1980–81): 112–27. Looking at the roots of ritual in hunting, Smith analyzes why rituals do not match the way society actually functions.

    To Take Place: Toward Theory in Ritual. Chicago: University of Chicago Press, 1987. A crucial study in helping develop a theory of presentation in explaining rituals.

Staal, Frits. *Rules Without Meaning: Ritual, Mantras, and the Human Sciences*. New York: Peter Lang, 1990. A powerful argument about the impossibility of attributing meaning to ritual performances.

Tambiah, S. J. *A Performative Approach to Ritual*. London: Oxford University Press, 1979. Links ritual studies to performance theory.

Turner, Victor. *From Ritual to Theater: The Human Seriousness of Play*. New York: Performing Arts Publications, 1982. An important late work by one of the greatest modern theorists of ritual.

    The Ritual Process: Structure and Anti-Structure. Chicago: Aldine, 1969. Perhaps the most influential work in the last half of the twentieth century creating a model for the analysis of ritual. Widely copied and borrowed, Turner's model was refined in his later works, especially *From Ritual to Theater*.

Turner, Victor and Turner, Edith. *Image and Pilgrimage in Christian Culture: Anthropological Perspectives*. New York: Columbia University Press, 1978. Based on anthropological fieldwork in Mexico, this study also examines the historical tradition of pilgrimage.

Part I

The ritual moment

In 1393 an ambitious, fledgling businessman, a twenty-two-year-old Florentine named Giovanni Morelli, began to write a "memory book," a combined family history and personal diary that he kept for most of the rest of his life. This revealing little book opens a window into the passions and even psychological quirks of a man who entered adulthood 600 years ago.

Despite his background of privilege, disappointment and tragedy seemed to stalk him at every stage of his life. When he was two his father died, and soon afterward his mother abandoned him. Raised by his grandparents until his grandfather died, Giovanni spent his teenage years kicked about among various relatives, including his elder sister who also abandoned him by dying in childbirth when Giovanni was sixteen.

By the time he began his memory book, however, the young merchant had grounds for optimism about his future, a feeling encouraged by his ardent love for a woman he wanted to marry. His optimism was unwarranted. When he asked for her hand, her father refused, leaving the disappointed Giovanni to marry a woman he did not love. This marriage of convenience enmeshed him in the political troubles of her family and ruined his own chances for public office. His business began to flounder, confiscatory taxes almost ruined him, he found no comfort in his marriage: by the age of thirty-one he felt like a complete failure. In compensation he concentrated his hopes on his sons, trying to give them the love and guidance he had never enjoyed from his own father.

Again tragedy ruined his search for happiness. In May 1406, his eldest son became sick with a chronic nose bleed, the first sign of a mysterious fatal illness. Nine-year-old Alberto was in constant, sleepless agony for seventeen days, his only solace the succor of his family and the consolatory rituals of the church:

He commended himself repeatedly to God and His mother the Virgin Mary, had the *tavola* [a small painting] of the Lady brought, and embraced it with so many expressions of penitence and with so many prayers and vows, that no heart is so hard not to be moved to great pity to see him.[1]

Pain-ravaged Alberto, repentant of whatever puckish sins he might have committed, finally died amidst the loving circle of his relatives. The deathbed scene followed the conventional ritual, called at the time the "art of dying," save for one critical omission. No priest arrived in time to administer the last rites.

Giovanni's grief overwhelmed him. He described the unrelenting emotional pain as like the stab of a knife or the torments of a thousand lances, and he began to suspect that his agony was caused by the unquiet soul of little Alberto himself who was wandering in the darkness of purgatory because Giovanni had failed to provide his son with the proper death ritual by neglecting to call a priest in time. Abandoned by his own father, now by his son, Giovanni felt as if he were at fault for his own suffering, but the religious practices of his time provided him with a ready solution for his disquieting feelings of guilt.

To liberate little Alberto's restless soul and to give himself some inner peace, Giovanni conducted an elaborate private ritual of propitiation, timed according to astrological calculations to take place exactly one year to the hour after Alberto had died. Dressed in his nightgown with a halter around his neck to signify his abject contrition, Giovanni contemplated for hours with a fixed stare images of Christ, Mary, and John the Evangelist (his namesake and the patron of Florence); the consequence of the gazing was a prolonged bout of tears; and after this intense outpouring of emotion, he zealously prayed, according to the standard formulas, imploring the saints to save Alberto's soul. There followed a wild, sleepless night during which his whole doleful life tumbled through his mind, and he felt the temptations of the devil. Finally, in a half-sleep he was blessed with a stunning vision in which little Alberto appeared to assure his father that God had answered Giovanni's prayers and accepted Alberto into heaven. Giovanni's ritual had worked. Giovanni felt an immense sense of relief.

Giovanni Morelli probably never met Margherita Datini, who lived at the same time in the nearby town of Prato, but he may have run across her irascible, sullen husband who was also a member of the small circle of Florentine merchants. Like Giovanni's, her marriage was an unhappy one, and she lived for many years apart from her husband, Francesco. The couple kept in touch through daily letters, which were found in the nineteenth century underneath a stairway and which give us rare

---

[1] Quoted and translated in Richard C. Trexler, *Public Life in Renaissance Florence* (New York: Academic Press, 1980), 173.

glimpses into the life of a woman in the early Renaissance. Although Margherita Datini never suffered from the death of a child as did Giovanni Morelli, she had to live with a different sort of personal tragedy. She was sterile. Her inability to conceive a baby was clearly her problem since in the course of the marriage Francesco managed to father by a slave an illegitimate daughter whom Margherita adopted as her own.

For Margherita barrenness constituted a devastating assault on her womanhood, making her the object of ridicule by her female relatives and justifying Francesco's long absences from home. After the prescriptions of medical men failed, she resorted to the fertility lore of other women. A business associate of her husband sent Margherita his own wife's remedy, a magical belt.

> She says it is to be girded on by a boy who is still a virgin, saying first three Our Fathers and Hail Marys in honour of God and the Holy Trinity and St. Catherine; and the letters written on the belt are to be placed on the belly, on the naked flesh . . . but I, Niccolò, think it would be better, in order to obtain what she wishes, if she fed three beggars on three Fridays, and did not hearken to women's chatter.[2]

Unfortunately, these ritual solutions failed to cure Margherita's medical problems as successfully as other rituals had helped Giovanni with his psychological ones.

Giovanni Morelli and Margherita Datini suffered the recurrent sorrows of life typical of the era before modern medicine. The prevalence of epidemic diseases (especially in crowded cities), the lack of hygiene or accurate medical knowledge, the volatility of the economy, the ubiquity of war, the vagaries of unstable political regimes, the unquiet enmities of vendetta – in short, the terrible insecurity of daily life created an unquenchable demand for ritual, for rituals that assisted fertility, succored the afflicted, eased grief. As the great French historian Jean Delumeau has argued, the period from the fourteenth to the seventeenth century was notably obsessed with sin and fear. Both the legitimate rituals provided by the clergy and the unauthorized incantations of cunning women and wizened sorcerers helped people compensate for the deep-seated sense of sin and assuaged the endemic fears that plagued everyone, king and peasant, merchant and monk, wife and nun. Rituals provided rightfully directed actions that enmeshed humans in a vast support system of socially prescribed activities that helped them through difficult transitions, especially those involving life and death.

---

[2] Quoted in Iris Origo, *The Merchant of Prato: Francesco di Marco Datini* (London: Jonathan Cape, 1957), 161.

Although Margherita's prayers and magic belt did not work for her, they gave her the assurance that she had done what she could. Giovanni's private ritual, which he certainly did not invent but was prescribed by a repertoire of religious practices, unstopped his own emotional grief, giving him the freedom to cry his heart out and to release his loving grip on his lost son. These rituals licensed the expression of deep emotions, encouraging unfathomed psychological effects.

The many little and grand rituals that punctuated the lives of Giovanni and Margherita were attached to problems of biological reproduction and to maintaining social connections, both among the living and between the living and the dead. These rituals were performed in two forms: the first consisted of *rites of passage* that marked and assisted the biological and social transitions of birth, elevation in social status, marriage, procreation, and death; the second comprised *calendrical rites* that marked out the cardinal points in the year, ensnaring the Christian story in the apparently natural cycle of the seasons.

The chaos of life meant that sterility, bankruptcy, or death could strike anyone at any time, but rituals provided a countervailing principle of order, what has been called a "cosmic order." Rituals brought the cosmic order into daily life by giving persons access to divine power. Margherita cared less to understand the cause of her infertility than to employ whatever supernatural power was available to make a pregnancy possible.

Understood in this way as a summoning of breathtaking powers, ritual practice revealed certain traits typical of traditional lay Christianity. First, in contrast to what Durkheim had imagined was fundamental to all religion, lay ritual practice blurred the distinction between the sacred and the profane, because people experienced the sacred within the profane world through their need to attract a lover, heal the sick, or calm deep anxieties. Most people came into contact with the sacred through the effects they believed it had on their bodies and in their social relationships. Second, no matter what the priests said or the canons of the church decreed, the laity seemed to have had a very pragmatic attitude toward ritual that led them to try whatever worked best, making few distinctions between the august rites of the liturgy and the more humble practices they could perform themselves. Third, rituals were comprehensible to observers simply because they relied upon a common vocabulary of gestures performed in both the liturgy and in daily life. Even at a pre-verbal stage children were taught or imitated these gestures. A child learned to genuflect and fold her hands in prayer before she learned to speak and relied on these and other gestures to communicate her deepest feelings throughout her life. Everyone could read this elaborate vocabulary of gestures: merchants, for example, conveyed trust by employing them in negotiations, and Christians distinguished themselves from Jews and Moslems more by recognizing these outward signs of behavior than by professing coherent beliefs or by reciting scripture. People in the early modern period exhibited a highly sophisticated sensitivity to rituals. As the English jurist, John Selden (1584–1654) put it in his *Table Talk* (London, 1689), "to know what was generally believed in all ages the way is to consult the liturgies." That is what we are about to do.

1   Rites of passage

The cardinal biological or social changes in the lives of all Europeans were marked by what are called "rites of passage." An examination of rites of this sort must begin with a look at the famous anthropological study by Arnold van Gennep, *Les rites de passage*, first published in 1908.

According to van Gennep a rite of passage consists of a sequence of rituals performed at a special time and in a special space. The sequence unfolds in three distinct phases: (1) the rites of separation (preliminary), which displace the individual from his or her previous station; (2) the rites of transition (liminary), which temporarily suspend the subject betwixt and between his or her old and new state, providing an experience of the sacred or a utopian vision of an alternative social world; and (3) the rites of aggregation or incorporation (postliminary), which bring the person into the embrace of the new community.

The meaning of a particular gesture in a rite of passage derives from its position in the sequence and from the context in which the rite takes place. A sprinkling in a baptism purifies the baby, but in a wedding it might allude to fertility. Or to put it more graphically, even though the action is similar kissing your grandmother means something different from kissing your lover, and the significance of the lovers' kisses depends a great deal on where they lead. Specific phases of the sequence might be differently accentuated according to the kind of passage being recognized: rites of dying might stress the separation of the deceased from the living, but a baptism would emphasize the incorporation of the baby within the living community of kin and protectors.

In most cases the transitional or liminal phase creates a special state, a moment when there is a "pivoting of the sacred," whereby the participant, ceremoniously and often physically separated from others, sees the rest of society from the outside, as if society itself were sacred and thus prohibited. In the transitional phase the individual crosses a threshold into another level of existence, a sacred or inverted world or sometimes a world of pure feeling. In Latin the word for threshold is *limen*, the basis for such terms as the liminal phase, liminal states, liminal moments, and liminality. Van Gennep emphasized the significance of an actual physical transition in a rite of passage, the literal crossing over a threshold, accomplished in many rites by walking through a doorway. The passage is not just symbolic but a physical movement from one place to another, often from a profane to a sacred space.

The anthropologist Victor W. Turner has analyzed extensively the liminal phase of various rituals, showing how important an experience of the liminal is for sustaining and reforming normal social life. Liminal experiences sometimes appear to be anarchic, moments when the normal rules governing sexual urges and inhibitions about abusive or obscene language break down. Since liminal moments are separated from normal times, they provide an abnormal experience of a world without social structure or one in which the usual structures are turned upside down. Liminal states offer an experience of what is potential but unrealized in normal life, a brief but intoxicating whiff of utopia or heaven. During liminal phases in European rites of passage, loyal subjects stripped their new king of his rich robes, good Christians looted the dead pope's palace, and old lechers kissed the virginal young bride. Most often these brief moments of social inversion helped to enforce the usual rules of normal life in which subjects deferred to kings, revered the pope, and respected virgins, but the very experience of the liminal suggests the possibility of alternatives. Although rituals often appear to be conservative, preserving the most ancient traditions of a society, through liminality they also make change possible and can even become the instrument of dramatic social reform.

Birth and baptism

All societies demarcate birth in some ritual fashion. Infant baptism was the characteristic ritual for traditional Christians, and even after the Reformation most Protestants retained this fundamental rite of passage. Among the radical Protestants, the Anabaptists transformed the rite into the central act confirming their faith but displaced its performance to adulthood when believers could obtain the spiritual knowledge to be "born again" and baptized into spiritual maturity.

Initiated by the purification rituals performed by St. John the Baptist, baptism became the necessary ritual for incorporation into the body of the church. St. Paul reserved baptismal rites for a spiritual elite as a repetition of the death and rebirth of Christ, signified by total immersion of the body in water. By the fourth century, however, as a result of a shift of emphasis toward the absolution of original sin, baptism was performed immediately after birth, replacing the Jewish circumcision rite for males and becoming an exorcism that provided the soul with the gift of the holy spirit. By the tenth century aspersion or a sprinkling of water on the baby's head began to replace immersion, but some regions retained bodily immersion until as late as the thirteenth century. Radical Protestant sects revived the practice of immersion in the sixteenth.

Baptism evolved during the late Middle Ages into a powerful rite of passage that can be conveniently broken down into van Gennep's three phases. The first, the rite of separation, involved a striking exorcism carried out at the door of the church, the threshold that separated the realm of the devil from the blessings of God. The infant, far from innocent, had been brought into the suffering world because of Adam and Eve's primal sin of disobedience, the disobedience that brought lust, shame, pain, and death to God's creation, the disobedience induced by the arch-deceiver, Satan. The sexual congress of the infant's parents compounded the sin, and the shivering little boy or girl brought to the font was, in fact, a corrupted piece of flesh and a dangerous emissary of the devil. To expel the evil and make salvation possible, the priest had to act quickly after birth. Standing on the threshold of the church, the priest intoned, "I exorcise thee, unclean spirit . . ., accursed one, damned and to be damned . . ." The ritual promulgated the opinion that original sin was a form of bewitchment, and as long as the infant remained unbaptized the living themselves were endangered by a demonic presence.

After the exorcism the parents carried their infant into the baptistery or church where the second phase took place. The rite of transition, that slipping into a betwixt and between state, began when the priest took the child from his or her parents, physically separating him or her from the natal kin. According to the prescribed ritual the baby should be dipped face-down into the water, but one can well imagine the cries that procedure induced in the babies and the fears it invoked in parents; most priests instead resorted to the practice of merely sprinkling the water on the child's forehead. Sometimes a pinch of salt was placed in the infant's mouth and his back was rubbed with oil, probably to counter the effects of the cold water.

In the final phase of aggregation the priest passed the infant into the arms of the godparents who raised him from the font, incorporating the child into the Christian community. The godparents answered on the child's behalf, recited the Credo for him, said a paternoster, and vowed to educate him in the faith of Christ. John Bossy has pointed out that the role of the godparents was the most elaborate in the entire ritual, the key to the act of aggregation. Besides providing the child with a network of spiritual kindred, who would supplement and could even replace the natural kin, the godparents became god kin to the child's whole family. Thus, incest prohibitions against inter-marriage applied to all the relatives on both sides. The godparents brought gifts, paid the priest, and usually solidified the new alliances made through the child by providing a banquet. The creation of *god sibs* linked natural and spiritual kindred, creating friends and allies in a society that was always full of real and potential enemies.

The institution of godparentage became one of the most important social institutions in traditional Christian Europe. In the North godparentage arrangements seem to have been egalitarian. For example, in France godparents were usually close blood relatives, selected from among the immediate kin of the mother and father. But in the South, especially in the Balkans and Italy, godparents were suspended in the webs of elaborate patronage networks. Despite legal prohibitions to the contrary, Venetian nobles might ask 150 godparents to crowd around the font for the baptism of a son. These included both men and women and usually some of the worthy poor, often an old widow, but most were well-placed godfathers, who supplied vital political connections for the family. In the Italian countryside godparents habitually came from the same social level as the parents, but social climbers might try to employ Christian charity to create connections above themselves. Powerful men found themselves frequently in demand for baptismal duties, and the choice of godparents required careful considerations of politics and local power. For example, in the town of Novello, just north of the Italian Riviera, a notary named Malacria was for more than forty years the most popular choice to act as godfather, but when in the 1680s a feud broke out in the region, the requests for his spiritual services suddenly ceased. In Europe the hierarchic tendencies of godparentage never reached the levels of colonial Brazil where local strong men served as the godfathers of everyone in the town, slave and free alike.

Baptism became the essential rite in establishing a child's social identity. It publicly confirmed his parentage, incorporated him into the Christian community, gave him surrogate "spiritual" parents, and expanded his range of potential patrons. Most important of all, it gave him or her a name, that marker by which individuals identify themselves throughout life. Everywhere the name of the saint on whose feast day the child was born provided a potential source for a name, especially since it was believed that employing such a name would induce in the child the particular virtues of the saint.

Northern and southern Europe again differed in the other sources for given names. In the North children were often given the name of one of the godparents, and it was considered proper to try to maintain a rough balance between names supplied from the father's and the mother's lineages. In the more patriarchal South, there was greater emphasis on choosing names from the father's side. In fifteenth-century Florence, with its almost obsessive concern for sustaining the fragile patriarchic lineages, given names were quite often attempts to "remake" a dead ancestor or sometimes an older sibling who had died young. Such naming practices constituted a kind of "reincarnation," revealing a belief that the loss of a member had impoverished the family, and that this could be offset by the revival of his and, less frequently, her name. This traditional practice of choosing names from among departed ancestors reveals a belief that the spirits of the dead were present among their descendants and that by naming an infant after a deceased relative the dead man was reincarnated among his kin. A child in Renaissance Italy was born into an identity supplied by kin. The modern idea that one makes one's own identity through discovering and developing natural talents hardly existed.

Even the location of the baptism created powerful associations. In Florence, for example, every new-born baby had the right to be baptized in the magnificent Romanesque baptistery of St. John, the patron of the city, and Florentines understood the baptism as a rite of passage into citizenship in their city, a place where a sense of civic consciousness and loyalty was especially intense. Giovanni Morelli and his son Alberto were both baptized there.

Baptism seems to have generated particularly strong associations in the Mediterranean countries. Many Italian cities built magnificent baptisteries that were separate from the cathedral or main church. These baptisteries became an important focus of civic life, housing the city's flag, serving as the meeting hall for the town council, and even becoming mausolea for distinguished churchmen and citizens. In Serbia before the Turkish occupation, an elaborate procession of a ruler from the baptistery to the church proper relied upon an explicit comparison with the transitional phase of the rite of baptism. The procession was understood to symbolize the role of the ruler in leading his people toward true knowledge of God.

The tremendous ritual potency of baptism helped parents to cope emotionally and practically with the dreadful realities of childbirth and infancy at a time when many babies were still-born and as many as two out of three children died during the first years of life. So efficacious was baptism that the unbaptized child produced tremendous anxieties. Despite St. Augustine's belief that unbaptized children went straight to hell, medieval Christians imagined a separate realm of limbo, a special place where the only suffering of the unbaptized came from being deprived of the light of God.

Canon law made special provisions for the child who was unlikely to survive long enough to be brought to the baptismal font. Although only the priest could exorcize the infant, anyone could baptize: fathers were enjoined to baptize the sickly and midwives the still-born or even just the protruding limb of a dying child.

The formula was simple. The person baptizing sprinkled water on any part of the body and pronounced in their own language the words, "God's creature, I hereby baptize thee in the name of the Father, the Son, and the Holy Ghost." If the mother died in labor, then the mid-wife was to deliver the child by caesarean to save and baptize it. If both the mother and child died before the birth, then the mother could not be buried in church unless the fetus were removed from the womb because the unbaptized flesh polluted the mother, and some priests went beyond official teachings by refusing Christian burial to any woman who died in pregnancy or childbirth. Even in the best of circumstances, the new mother was obligated to be "churched" after the birth, a ceremony through which she was cleansed of the impurities of child bearing, received a blessing, and was accepted back into the embrace of the parish and church.

Baptism had a quasi-magical efficacy in the imagination of many. Before the eleventh century and even later in some remote regions, an unbaptized child was sometimes buried with a stake driven into its heart to prevent its unquiet soul from haunting the living, and a properly baptized one was entombed with a chalice in one hand and the host in the other, a physical proof of its Christianity to take to the world beyond. Not only were unbaptized babies thought to be more vulnerable to disease than baptized ones, but peasants in France believed that such a child was liable to be replaced by a diabolical changeling, a pixie child put there by fairies who stole human babies. People generally believed that baptism gave infants a better chance for survival, cured sick babies, and made handicapped ones whole.

Fears of the unbaptized even led to strange abuses of the sacrament itself. In 1681 the Inquisitor of the Holy Office in Udine, the regional center of Friuli, reported that

In the village of Trava . . . there are some wicked women who for many years, with the consent of the parish priest, have abused the sacrament of baptism and, taking advantage of the ignorance of the faithful, pretend to resuscitate the dead. These women are brought the babies who came out of their mother's wombs dead, and they display them before the altar of the Madonna and have the Holy Mass celebrated. Saying particular prayers, all of a sudden they shout that the

Madonna has performed a miracle, that the baby has given signs of life, opened an eye, shed a tear, moved an arm, urinated; and immediately with the water they have ready they baptize it; then, having baptized it, they say that it again has returned to death and they bury it, taking so much from the baby's parents, or, to be more accurate, from the parents of the corpse that emerged inanimate from the maternal womb.[1]

The Friulan practice of temporarily resurrecting dead babies for baptism was apparently not all that unusual, and church authorities found the ritual extremely difficult to stamp out, a difficulty that illustrates the ways in which the laity transformed church rituals to serve their own deep emotional needs.

Perhaps more than any other, the cult of St. Guinefort, popular in France, exemplifies the nexus of fears and dangers that surrounded birth and infancy. St. Guinefort was a dog of flawless loyalty. When, after administering to the sick, St. Roch contracted the plague and went into the forest to die, the dog Guinefort brought food to him until he recovered. Later, after Roch died in prison, Guinefort was slaughtered by a father who came upon the overturned crib of his child and assumed the dog had killed the baby when in fact Guinefort had been protecting the infant from a venomous snake. St. Guinefort became the center of a cult for the curing of sick babies, the dog having been more faithful to humankind than it to him. Although this cult of a saintly dog would later be ridiculed by the Protestants and discreetly suppressed by educated Catholic authorities, the hagiography of Guinefort represented the anxious feelings humans had that babies needed all the help – medical, magical, spiritual, and canine – they could get.

So obviously vital for the survival of the family and community, births were surrounded not only by the official rituals of the church but by a body of magical beliefs that did not come under serious attack until the Protestant and Catholic Reformations. Mothers gave their babies amulets and pronounced incantations to protect them from harm, especially from witches who it was believed sought to kill and dismember infants to be used in their own rituals. Unusual birth marks were interpreted as dire portents for the future. Siamese twins or a baby with a birth defect promised ill for the whole community and could defile an entire household in the eyes of neighbors. Even normal, healthy twins in their ambiguous duality prognosticated either great good or evil fortune. And an infant born feet first was seen as possessing a certain gift.

No birth sign, however, matched the marvelous omen of the caul.

---

[1] Quoted in Silvano Cavazza, "Double Death: Resurrection and Baptism in a Seventeenth-Century Rite," in Edward Muir and Guido Ruggiero, eds., *History from Crime* (Baltimore: Johns Hopkins University Press, 1994), 1.

Enclosing the fetus is an inner membrane, the amnion or caul, part of which is occasionally found around the child's head at birth. When this happened, often with the appearance that the baby was wearing a hood and cloak, the child was understood to have visionary powers, to be able to "see" into the world of spirits. From Iceland to Russia and Sweden to Serbia the caul was understood to be the seat of the "external soul," a guardian spirit that could take the form of an animal and could appear to a person in his or her sleep. By keeping the caul after birth, the mother guaranteed that her offspring would retain direct contact with the external soul and was the bearer of good fortune. So prevalent was the fascination with cauls that St. Bernardino of Siena (1370–1444) even preached against the practice of baptizing them.

Beliefs about the powers of the caul spread widely. In Ireland if the caul was preserved the child would have good luck but the mother was to suffer one year of poor health; when the child reached the age of fourteen or the age of sexual maturation the mother sewed the caul into a sack, which was worn with the clothes. The sexual connection could also be found in Serbia where a young woman carried her caul on her person as an amulet. If she managed to put it next to the skin of her beloved, he would fall in love with her. By contrast in Ruthenia if the caul was kept and worn among the clothing, the child would become a bishop. In Iceland and Italy possession of the caul gave the person the ability to combat evil spirits. The most famous examples of this type were the *benandanti* or "do-gooders" of Friuli, who had ecstatic visions in which they did battle at night against the "army of the dead" who sought to destroy the crops. Communicating with spirits was a typical attribute of those born with the caul: in Serbia, England, New England, and the Low Countries such people were considered clairvoyants. In Dalmatia if a preserved caul was placed under the head of a dying person, the passage into the other would be made easier. As late as the nineteenth century in England, there was a substantial trade in cauls sold through newspaper advertisements to sailors or persons contemplating long sea voyages, as a protection from drowning. The symbolic logic seems to have been that since before birth the caul had permitted the fetus to live within fluid, it could prevent drowning in water for adults.

The mysterious excitements and dangers of birth created an enormous demand for ritual protection for both the physical and social survival of the infant. Baptism succeeded remarkably in filling this demand, establishing itself more than any other as the Christian ritual that captured the imagination of the common lay believers and that survived the critique of the most radical Protestant reformers. Firm in its biblical foundation, baptism, especially infant baptism, became the archetypical Christian rite of passage.

Passages of status

Most rites of passage pointed to changes in biological states, but other transformations, especially the elevation to a new social status, also called for ritual demarcation. In many incidents the correct public performance of ritual acts legally sanctioned a new social position.

Most women in traditional Europe experienced changes in social status only through changes in their sexual status, typically through the transitions of marriage, motherhood, and widowhood. Although marriage represented sexual maturity for women, most did not achieve full social maturity at marriage because they moved from subordination to fathers or guardians to subordination to husbands. Although in many parts of Europe marriage brought a woman her dowry, she had no rights to it until her husband died, and thus only widowhood, the end of normal sexual life, brought some measure of social independence. Besides the normal wifely rites of passage, a few permanently celibate women experienced the drama of marriage to Christ, the rite of passage provided for nuns, and many more permanently uncelibate women suffered the indignity of prostitution with its attendant rituals of public shame.

The transitions in status for males were much more varied, given the greater range of public roles afforded them. In villages and especially cities, adult men often tolerated or even encouraged adolescent boys from the artisan classes to form aggressive gangs, variously called youth-abbeys, youth-kingdoms, or brigades. These were especially prominent in France, Italy, Switzerland, Germany, Hungary, and Romania. The evidence for the prevalence of similar gangs is less clear for England, Scotland, and Spain. Where they existed, the youth-abbeys structured what might be seen as a period of prolonged liminality during the transition between puberty and marriage, what is now called adolescence.

The activities of youth-abbeys could be highly ambiguous. Providing a rite of passage through the "dangerous" years that licensed rowdiness and even legitimated certain forms of violence, the abbeys also enforced community moral standards (especially with regard to sexual behavior) on others. In France they performed ritual charivaris and in Italy *mattinate* that humiliated couples whose marriages somehow failed to measure up to the community's standards (see chapter 3). In the mountains of Liguria they managed vendetta street fights, thereby serving as apprenticeships in the factions that dominated local politics.

Certainly the most extraordinary way in which youth-abbeys ritualized a passage of status for young males was through participation in a gang rape. The phenomenon is best documented for south-east France. In towns such as Dijon and Arles youth gangs, mostly made up of journeymen and the sons of artisans from the same or similar trades, roamed the walled cities at night, looking for a fight, annoying the night guards, or planning a rape. Neither the choice of rape victim nor the occasion for the act was random since her public reputation, the proximity of male protectors for her, and the pressures of local vendettas came into play in selecting her. The assault constituted a kind of rite of passage for both the rapists and their victim.

By participating in the gang rape, the boys acquired their manhood. Especially in Mediterranean societies, masculinity had to be publicly demonstrated through acts of aggression against other males and by maintaining a tough demeanor. Men also felt obliged to show their mastery over women: as a Lyons merchant wrote to his son in 1460, "when woman has mastery over man, he is not worth much; the good cock masters the hen."[2] Given this concept of masculinity as requiring a performance, the gang rape initiated the boys into manhood and membership into the local gang. Jacques Rossiaud has estimated that in Dijon about half of the youths participated at least once in the gang rape of a young woman.

The young female victims of such cruelty underwent a rite of passage of a rather different sort. The rapists and, unless they had mistakenly chosen their victim without proper sensitivity to public opinion, the rest of the community considered her to be the guilty party. Typically, she had broken or appeared to break the normal rules of sexual behavior: she was a servant kept as a concubine by her master, the mistress of a priest, an "abandoned" wife. The boys acted, therefore, as enforcers of the habitual misogyny of the community, collectively marking a woman who in the community's eyes had already shamed herself. The consequence of the marking for her was often tragic. For most victims of a gang rape, the only alternative to becoming a beggar or vagabond was to enter the communal brothel. The rape constituted the characteristic initiation into prostitution.

Enjoying the fruits of gender solidarity denied to females, the members of the male gangs or youth-abbeys exercised a ritual jurisdiction over sexual behavior, proving themselves to be one-of-the-boys through calculated acts of violence and enforcing the implicit rules of sexual behavior on vulnerable women. The honored leader of a gang

[2] Letter by François Garin quoted in Jacques Rossiaud, *Medieval Prostitution*, trans. Lydia G. Cochrane (Oxford: Basil Blackwell, 1988), 21n.

was called an "abbot" and the madam in charge of the municipal bawdy house was its "abbess," terms that reveal the close relationship between these two forms of youth associations, voluntary for the males, involuntary for the females. The world of youth-abbeys and public bordellos formed a temporary alternative to the state of marriage, a culture of illicit sexuality that provided sexual access to females for unmarried men and enforced a cruel double morality. Eventually most of these boys would marry, as would many of their female victims turned temporary prostitutes. When prostitutes retired from the bordello in their late twenties or thirties, in effect after having served a term of punishment for their own misfortune, they could marry without retaining any particular mark of infamy. The experiences of these young women formed a prolonged rite of passage: the gang rape separated them from the larger community, their service as prostitutes put them in a liminal position as neither maidens nor wives, and through their retirement and subsequent marriage they were reaggregated into the community.

For the journeyman artisans in the youth-abbeys, the transition to adulthood was completed when they finally married and passed the examination for master guildsman. Ideally, masters were married and journeymen were not, so that a journeyman's wedding denoted the final rite of passage into both marital and professional maturity. The groom could now sit with the adult masters in the guild hall, and at his wedding his former companions as journeymen and gang members sat at a separate table, segregated from their friend who now had a legitimate sexual partner. When economic conditions made it more difficult for young men to stand for the master's exam and therefore prolonged the time before they could marry, the sexual violence of the gangs served as a kind of protest about the delay in the transition to adulthood.

In contrast to these artisan gang members, aristocratic youths entered the hierarchy of chivalry. The medieval ritual of vassalage provided the archetype for defining a relationship between a social superior and inferior throughout the early modern period. The formidable rite, which had developed between the eighth and tenth centuries, provided the essential ritual linkage between the social hierarchy and the political authority of princes and kings.

A vassal was someone who voluntarily (at least in theory) offered his services and loyalty to a lord who, in return, engaged to protect the vassal and to provide him with an income in the form of a fief. The relationship was one of dependency (for his survival the vassal depended upon the good favor of the lord) and reciprocity (each party had obligations to the other). Although lawyers expended vast quantities of ink and parchment trying to clarify the exact nature of vassalage, the vassalage ritual was the starting point for any interpretation of the relationship.

The ritual had three essential phases. The first was called the *homage*, which consisted of two distinct acts. The verbal part comprised a formal declaration by the vassal of his willingness to become the *man* of the lord, a necessary act of acceptance that paralleled the verbal consent essential to a marriage. In the next part the lord grasped the clasped hands of the vassal, the "mixing of the hands" or "hand ceremony." In the Spanish variant of the ritual, the vassal's gesture was much more humble: instead of offering his hands to be grasped, he kissed his lord's right hand.

In the normal version of the ritual, however, the kiss belonged to the second phase, the *oath of fealty*. The vassal and lord promised ("gave their faith") by exchanging a kiss on the mouth. At this stage of the ritual, the vassal became the lord's "man of mouth and hand," an expression that reveals how basic the symbolism of the body was in providing a vocabulary for ritual performances. Just as in engagements and weddings where the binding force of the rites came from the physical contact between parties made by clasping hands, kissing, and putting on the ring, in the vassalage ritual two adult men intermixed their hands and exchanged breath and saliva, thereby becoming one. The rituals that physically joined or merged bodies compelled obedience to the verbal oath because the parties offered their bodies as surety of their word.

In the third phase, the *investiture of the fief*, the lord gave a symbolic object to his new vassal. Although less important in many respects than the first two phases, the investiture made the arrangement a legal and property issue by transferring some possession from the one to the other. The actual fief was typically a landed estate from which the vassal could enjoy the income. In the ritual an enormous variety of objects, such as a clod of earth, branch, stick, knife, sword, helmet, cup, or horn, could symbolize the fief. In fact, Du Cange discovered some ninety-nine different objects used in investiture ceremonies.

It would be fairly easy to interpret the ritual of vassalage in light of the three stages of rites of passage as defined by van Gennep. The homage separated the vassal from his fellows in an act that publicly represented the inferiority of the vassal to the lord. In the oath of fealty phase, however, the reciprocal exchange of kisses represented the two as equal allies in a utopian moment of social equality. Finally, with the investiture of the fief the vassal was assimilated into a new relationship and a new social status as a man loyal to this particular lord.

The vassalage ritual represented a system of reciprocities established through the homage, which was enforced by the kiss and sealed by the investiture. At the core of the system, as Jacques Le Goff has shown, was the idea of mutual obligation. The vassalage ritual became a powerful means of representing obligation because of its affinity to the kinship systems of Europe that defined family relationships in terms of such obligations. Like the betrothal kiss, the kiss of faith denoted admission into a new family, for the vassal entered into the artificial family of the followers of the lord. Likewise, the lord's and the vassal's hands enacted the ritual: the hands grasped and were grasped, they were placed on a relic or the Bible to confirm the kiss of fealty, they gave or received the symbolic token of the investiture. In fact in Roman law the word for hand, *manus*, stood for the power of the head of a family, and medieval Christian paintings often depicted the hand of God as the instrument of divine action.

In the ritual of vassalage the words of consent and faith did not suffice unto themselves. Only the physical involvement of the body made the vassal a "man of mouth and hands." In the youthful rites of passage, most tragically exemplified in the gang rapes of the French youth-abbeys, words played no role whatsoever. The physical act alone accomplished the transition. This demand for bodily involvement characterized all rites of passage, indeed all rituals in traditional Europe.

Sex and marriage

In contrast to birth rites, Christian authorities had much greater difficulty imposing on the laity a sacramental view of marriage. Given the fact that in traditional Europe it was assumed that any two unrelated families were potential enemies, a marriage became a kind of peace pact between them. More than anything about the couple *per se*, marriage rituals publicly demonstrated a new alliance between families, and clerical involvement only obscured what the laity considered to be the essentials. In fact, the general hostility toward clerical interference in wedding rites certainly encouraged the Protestant reformers, such as Ulrich Zwingli and Martin Luther, who eliminated the sacramental status of marriage.

Rather than the divine sanction of the union, marriage rituals emphasized the essential human commitments: the obligation of the couple to procreate and the pledge of their respective kin to exchange property. The wedding ceremony itself did not become a sacrament until 1439, and only after 1563 did Catholic marriages absolutely require the intervention of a priest. Until the sixteenth century in most places, the role of the church in marriage was more legal than sacramental, consisting of a responsibility to define the prohibited degrees of incest, to judge the legitimacy of disputed unions, and to dissolve unsuccessful ones. Church law merely required the mutual consent of both parties for a marriage to be valid. Although the wedding ceremonies should demonstrate consent, no particular ritual formula was required, and the church tolerated an enormous variety of local customs.

Among the lower classes marriage rites might be quite informal. In Wales the groom and then the bride merely jumped across a birch-broom that had been set aslant across the open door of the bridal cottage. Witnesses had to be present, and sensitivities to the magical potentialities of the act required that neither partner touch the broom or door post. It is telling that this rite of passage focused so completely on the threshold and the potential dangers evoked in crossing it.

With the possible exception of Spain, it appears that most weddings in the fifteenth century took place outside of a church: 73 percent in a court book from Ely, 92 percent in one from Canterbury, and 98 percent in notarial registers from Toulouse. The example of how John married Marjory in a private house in York in 1372 was probably typical of many lower-class marriages:

John Beke, saddler, sitting down on a bench of that house . . . called the said Marjory to him and said to her, "Sit with me." Acquiescing in this, she sat down. John said to her, "Marjory, do you wish to be my wife?" And she replied, "I will if you wish." And taking at once the said Marjory's right hand, John said, "Marjory, here I take you as my wife, for better or worse, to have and to hold until the end of my life; and of this I give you my faith." The said Marjory replied to him, "Here I take you John as my husband, to have and to hold until the end of my life, and of this I give you my faith." And then the said John kissed the said Marjory through a wreath of flowers, in English "Garland."[3]

In a celebrated Florentine bigamy case, a lower-class widow, Lusanna, who had been kept for many years by a prominent gentleman, Giovanni Della Casa, sued him in the church courts when he married a younger woman. Lusanna asserted and was backed by witnesses that she married Giovanni in a private ceremony in which mutual promises were made and he gave her a ring. The case hinged on the credibility of the witnesses and Giovanni's political influence, but the saintly archbishop who heard the case never even hinted that the absence of a church wedding had any relevance to the legitimacy of the disputed marriage.

The exotic variety of marriage rites in Europe represented, in the

[3] Quoted in Christopher N. L. Brooke, *The Medieval Idea of Marriage* (Oxford: Oxford University Press, 1989), 251–52.

words of one historian, "a kind of museum of the history of marriage."[4] Nevertheless, certain typical, if not universal, features can be discerned. (1) Ceremonies were often performed at a door or, as we saw in the Welsh case, on the threshold of a house or church, reinforcing the importance of the transitional or liminal phase of the rites. (2) Gifts and symbolic tokens were exchanged. The father gave the bride and a dowry to the groom in return for a ring or some other token. (3) Both parties spoke words stating the intention to marry and promising mutual support. (4) The words were sealed by the joining of hands and, in some places, by a kiss, derived from the kiss of peace used in the liturgy of the mass.

The varieties of marriage rites can be illustrated by looking at the differences between two prominent and exceptionally wealthy banking cities – Florence in the fifteenth century and Augsburg in the sixteenth. These cities offer special opportunities for understanding marriage rituals since in both cases the educated and pious citizens were unusually introspective and self-revealing.

Italian marriage rituals were notably archaic, remaining strongly tied to ancient Roman and Lombard practices and resisting attempts by the church to alter deeply ingrained habits. Christiane Klapisch-Zuber has examined the peculiar qualities of Florentine marriage rituals, the very kinds of marriage ceremonies experienced by Giovanni Morelli and Margherita Datini. Two things are particularly striking about Florentine marriage ceremonies. One is the wide age gap between the typical bride and groom – she was usually eighteen or younger, he over thirty. The second is that each of the three essential marriage ceremonies took place in a different location. A preliminary phase involved the initial negotiations, carried out in the presence of a marriage broker between the senior males of the two families, typically the fathers or guardians of the prospective bride and groom. When these men finally came to terms over the dowry arrangements, they sanctioned their assent with a kiss on the mouth that duplicated the gesture of trust in the vassalage ceremony.

The decisions made in the initial negotiations were then formalized in the first of the ceremonies, the engagement, to which the future bride was not even invited. The party was for men only, including as many male kin from both sides as could be assembled. The young bride's father or male guardian promised to give her away and to obtain her consent while the future groom pledged to marry her within a certain period of time. Since typically the groom was more than ten years older than the bride, she might have still been a little girl at this stage, and the

[4] John Bossy, *Christianity in the West, 1400–1700* (Oxford: Oxford University Press, 1985), 21.

actual wedding could be years away. The principal men again kissed on the mouth to declare publicly their assent, and a notary carefully and with great attention to form wrote up on a parchment the agreement that spelled out the exact size of the dowry and other financial conditions. The marriage contract had the full force of custom and the law behind it. To break it risked a feud between the families.

What is most remarkable about these early stages in Florence is the complete invisibility of the prospective bride, whose name is not even mentioned in the oldest contracts. Sisters were almost interchangeable as future brides. Marriage was an alliance between two lineages, arranged by the male leaders, and involving the exchange of a woman and property. Who the bride was, how delightful her personality, or beautiful her looks, mattered far less than who her male kin were. In fact, there is no reason to assume that the bride and groom had even had a glimpse of each other yet.

Only later did the bride join the ceremonies, which took place at her house on what the Florentines called the "ring day." Her father or male guardian was in charge, but this time he invited both the men and women from each family, their kin and friends. A notary, significantly *not* a priest, asked the groom and bride if each consented to the union, and then drew the right hand of the woman toward the groom who placed a ring on her finger. The notary drew up the whole procedure in another highly formalized parchment document. Typically, the ceremony ended with the groom and his relatives offering gifts to his new in-laws, and the bride's family provided as elaborate a feast as they could afford.

Although the couple were now called husband and wife, the marriage ritual remained incomplete until they publicized the union in a final phase, the wedding proper. Again there might be long delays between the ring day and the wedding because, in part, custom required that the dowry be paid before the wedding, and inflated dowries could be difficult to put together. The wedding, a bit of an anti-climax by this time, consisted of a procession to the house of the husband, whose family and friends welcomed the new bride with feasts that could last for days. Only then was it proper for the newlyweds to sleep together. The final banquet completed the rite of passage with the incorporation of the bride into the kin group of her husband. In Florence most couples never even entered a church as a part of their marriage rites, let alone received the blessing of a priest, although elsewhere in Italy it was more common for the couple to stop at a church during the wedding procession. Ironically, Sunday was the day most often chosen for each of the three ceremonies, but the reason seems to be that on Sunday the ceremonies were less likely to be subject to meddling by churchmen. In the occasional Florentine marriage when the blessing of the church was sought, it was almost always on the ring day, when the consent of the couple could be solemnized.

Couples and their families by and large successfully resisted the attempts of the Catholic church to impose a sacramental order on the multiplicity of local marriage customs. Partly in accord with this resistance, the Protestant reformers rejected the idea that marriage should have been declared a sacrament in the first place. With his usual crusty directness, Martin Luther professed, "nowhere in Scripture do we read that anyone would receive the grace of God by getting married, nor does the rite of matrimony contain any hint that the ceremony is of divine institution."[5] After declaring in his denunciation of the papists that the clergy should not meddle in the private matters of married life, Luther went right ahead and meddled. He introduced a new wedding liturgy in 1529. By negating the sacramental status of marriage, however, he and the other reformers assisted an ironic transformation in which the marriage bond between husband and wife began to have a religious significance completely absent in traditional Christianity. The reformers insisted that marriage was a secular matter, but they tried very hard to Christianize it by rejecting many of the more profane traditions, such as the clamorous processions and horde of tipsy guests who invaded the church on the wedding day.

As in Florence, the townspeople of Augsburg, as Lyndal Roper has described them, saw the rite of passage into married life as requiring the participation of a large group of witnesses and relatives, not just the couple themselves. The series of formal rites was similar to those in Florence, if not so exclusively male-dominated. After the hopeful groom approached the bride's parents with his proposal and obtained their assent, negotiations opened over the property and inheritance arrangements. Once all was agreed a formal engagement ceremony took place about a week later, after which the couple were known as a bride and groom.

Some months later the actual wedding took place, lasting for several days and consisting of parties and dances. The day of the wedding began with the *Morgensuppe*, or wedding breakfast, during which guests consumed enough wine and chickens to make them thoroughly rowdy and liable to arrive late to the church. After the breakfast the "wedding-inviters," who were young patricians or hired professionals among the artisan classes, emanated out to invite others to join the wedding

[5] Martin Luther, "The Pagan Servitude of the Church," in *Martin Luther: Selections from His Writings*, ed. and trans. John Dillenberger (New York: Doubleday, 1958), 326.

Figure 1   Pieter Brueghel the Elder, *The Peasants' Wedding*.

procession. The most important rite in proving the legitimacy of a marriage was the noisy public wedding procession to the church and to the house of the couple, called "going to church and street." The steady beating of the drummers, the piercing music of the pipers, the fancy clothes, and rowdy relatives brought as much attention as possible to the procession, which constituted a declaration to the couple's neighbors of their vows. Rather than some church or state document, witnesses to a wedding procession provided proof of the legitimacy of the marriage. Although private ceremonies were legally possible, and after the Reformation popular among those who remained Catholic in dominantly Protestant towns, the Protestant reformers emphasized the need for the community, defined as the members of the parish church, to witness the wedding.

There usually was a ceremony at that most liminal of locations, the door of the church, where the couple exchanged vows and received the priest's blessing, but these religious rites were not essential for establishing the couple as married in the eyes of the community. Overwhelming the bridal mass itself was the distribution of St. John's wine, a barely Christianized version of the ancient Germanic love-drink, shared by warriors at the beginning of a journey to provide mutual protection through prophylactic magic. The incorporation of the love-drink into the wedding ceremonies emphasized the transition that was about to occur in the lives of the couple. Although the priest blessed the wine and gave it to the newlyweds to drink, it was often taken away to the wedding banquet and distributed among the guests. The "love" signified by the drinking of St. John's wine was as much the mutual obligations of the members of the same community as the conjugal love of marital intimacy.

After the wedding proper the couple, their relatives, and guests retired to the wedding feast. The opulence of these banquets, of course, depended on the means of the family. The poor might just dine in a tavern where each of the guests was asked to pay for his or her own meal (see figure 1). But the rich burghers took the opportunity of wedding banquets to display their wealth and status by throwing extravagant parties with entertainment supplied by clowns, musicians, acrobats, and even prostitutes who would steal the groom and demand a ransom from the bride. The carnivalesque atmosphere evoked by the reciting of obscene poems and the wild dancing in which the men would swing young women about so lifting their skirts (underwear had not yet been invented) annoyed grave city officials and pious reformers who tried to abolish wild wedding parties.

The imagery of sexual union permeated each stage of this series of rites. The most important of these images for the bride was the wreath, which symbolized her virginity. At the engagement party and at the wedding, she gave her groom a wreath, and during the all-important wedding procession she wore one over her loose hair. The virginity symbolism became even more explicit in the late sixteenth century, when in both the Catholic and Protestant parts of Germany, brides who had lost their virginity before their wedding day were forced to wear a wreath that was open at the back to declare their shame to the entire community. Other practices symbolized the union of the couple through the mutual exchange of gifts and through sharing. During the banquets each drank from the same cup, ate off the same plate, joined hands. Even the official manuals for clergy emphasized how the ring symbolized the emotional and sexual union of the couple.

The bedding of the couple on their wedding night finally brought forth the explicitly sexual nature of the relationship. The priest entered the bedchamber first, censing it and sprinkling holy water and salt on the bed, exorcizing it against dangers of male impotence or female infertility. After the couple had retired to bed, the guests celebrated the *Ansingwein*, a rowdy drinking party during which they sang suggestive songs, told dirty jokes, and men and women alternately lampooned the opposite sex. Needless to say, the Protestants eliminated the priest's role in all these sexual fertility rites but were far less successful in ending the popular *Ansingwein*. As a substitute for the bawdy tradition of drinking the newlyweds to bed, one reform minister recommended that the couple kneel first in prayer beside the bed. It is not hard to see why clerical interference, whether Catholic or Protestant, met with so much resistance.

Both in Florence and Augsburg the public presentation of the couple to the community and the assembling of kin and friends dominated the rites. Behind this almost obsessive publicity lay a deep fear shared by parents all over Europe – the possibility of clandestine marriage. Church law, which defined a valid marriage as the mutual expression of consent by two people capable of sexual relations, made seductions and elopement possible, an event that might be disastrous for the interests of the larger kin group. The Protestants, with the exception of the Lutherans, solved the problem by treating marriage as a civil contract, leaving it up to the communities themselves to establish the relevant legal criteria. In the decrees of the Council of Trent in 1563, the Catholic church essentially compromised between the demands of the laity for public weddings and the canon law tradition that focused on the issue of the personal consent of the couple. Henceforth, valid marriages required the posting of three bans or announcements of the intent to marry, which were duly registered by the parish priest. The reform made all marriages, perforce, public events, substituting the priest for the notary and emphasizing the publicity over the actual sacramental ritual. Eventually the Catholic liturgy moved the site of the marriage from the church door to the altar, reducing the liminal character of the transition.

In one respect, however, the rituals of the church provided something no civil contract or public procession ever could – protection against infertility and sexual impotence. Unblessed couples, like unbaptized infants, flirted with danger, especially from magic performed by those who through envy desired to ruin the marriage and prevent the birth of babies. The widespread modern wish to prevent births through contraception and abortion contrasts with the concerns of couples in earlier times who worried more about the opposite problem of infertility. In the early modern period abortion and perhaps even infanticide were certainly practiced, and techniques such as primogeniture and restricted marriage protected aristocratic property by limiting the number of sons who could inherit or marry in each generation, but none of these practices were significant in comparison with the near-universal longing for children.

Although couples certainly understood the basics of procreation, they did not consider fertility so much a natural process as the product of a series of ritual interventions performed from conception through gestation to birth. Just as modern mothers seek continuous medical care during pregnancy, early modern women employed ritual precautions that were part of women's lore. Recipe books, sex manuals, almanacs, medical treatises, and most of all women's folklore provided information on the subject. *The Ten Pleasures of Matrimony*, attributed to Aphra Behn, advised barren wives to ask the advice of women knowledgeable and experienced in the rituals of sex. When a previously infertile wife did become pregnant the community of women prided themselves on the power of their wisdom about such matters.

In England alone the range of ritual and magical customs was vast. There were aphrodisiacs, such as the one created by the woman who kneaded dough between her thighs, then baked it into bread which she gave to her lover. The principle of sympathetic magic appeared in many forms: one remedy advised the young bride to make an amulet of sweet potato, which has an obviously phallic appearance, and to walk in the shadow of a lusty woman of proven fecundity to attract the latter's fertility. Other solutions included charms, prayers, and herbs collected at certain propitious times such as during a full moon. Once a woman became pregnant she had to protect herself against miscarriage.

Recommendations included wearing a girdle containing wax or quinces or hanging a dried toad around the waist.

The most widespread fertility fear was that someone might employ castration magic against the groom. The earliest description of the forms of the ligature can be found in the writings of Albertus Magnus, the great thirteenth-century theologian, who described the following procedure: "take the penis of a newly killed wolf, go to the door of him you wish to bind and call him forth by name. As soon as he answers, tie the penis with a length of white thread and immediately the poor man will become impotent."[6] Based on the methods for castrating animals, tying a string or cord was the operative ritual act in human castration magic.

It is a revealing commentary on the psychological conditions of the age that this fear spread particularly among the peasantry during the sixteenth and seventeenth centuries. The French called the formidable practice the *aiguillette*, named after a cord with metal tips on the ends like a shoelace. Jean Bodin reported that at a judicial session held in Poitiers during the French Wars of Religion when paranoid fears gripped so many, he witnessed a young woman of good reputation demonstrate some fifty different ways of tying the *aiguillette*. The variations determined which partner would be affected and for how long; some created a horribly frustrating breach between the couple, others permitted intercourse but prevented conception. Swellings supposedly appeared on the cord, each of which signified a baby that was not conceived. Unborn children were the real victims of tying the *aiguillette*, a belief that made it akin to abortion or infanticide. In Languedoc the knotting took place at the moment when the priest intoned, "whom God has joined together, let no man put asunder"; at that exact point in the liturgy the evil-doer whispered, "but let the devil do it," and tossed a small coin over his or her shoulder. Unless the coin was found, the marriage was lost. The notion of demonic influence spread with the great witch craze, which had strongly sexual overtones since it was believed that the only parts of the human body Satan could influence were the sex organs, a belief justified by referring to how the serpent in the Garden of Eden had been made in the image of a penis.

One simple way to avoid the *aiguillette* was to marry in secret, but such an expedient violated the traditions of public display associated with weddings and constituted a clandestine marriage, which was outlawed in the mid-sixteenth century by King Henry II. What was caused by magic, however, could be prevented or cured by counter magic. To frustrate

---

[6] Cited in Emmanuel Le Roy Ladurie, "The Aiguillette: Castration by Magic," in *The Mind and Method of the Historian*, trans. Siân Reynolds and Ben Reynolds (Chicago: University of Chicago Press, 1981), 92–93.

the magical binding of his member, a husband put marked coins in his shoes, and to prevent her frigidity the bride put a ring in her shoe. The analogous logic of sympathetic magic equated the coins with his testicles and the ring with her vagina, each hidden away from malevolent magic through this practice. (Grooms and brides in modern times have continued similar practices without knowing the reason.) Once a man discovered his impotence, he had several remedies he could employ: one was to tap a full barrel of wine and direct the initial stream through his wife's wedding ring, a second required him to urinate through her ring, and a third had him piss through the keyhole of the church in which he was married.

Gradually the blessings of the priest or minister came to replace these more overtly magical solutions. In Germany and Scandinavia the blessing of the bed and couple sufficed to prevent castration magic, and in the south of France the priest's blessing of the wedding ring just before it was placed on the bride's finger became the most effective talisman for fertility. In a case involving a couple from the Terra d'Otranto in the south of Italy, the couple and their parents tried a series of remedies, both magical and ecclesiastical, in a desperate search for a solution. First they sought out the *magara* or cunning woman who they suspected had tied the impotence-making ligature in the first place. When the amulet she gave them to hang over the couple's bed failed to reverse the magic, they consulted a Capuchin friar who repeatedly read the gospels over the afflicted pair, and when this produced no results a cunning man gave both husband and wife a pouch to wear. They finally went back to the original suspected *magara* but decided that her advice was sinful and eventually resorted to denouncing her to the church courts. Their pragmatic approach to find anything that would work revealed a willingness to mix popular magic and religious ritual.

Needless to say, all the rituals of folk magic and the church could not guarantee the compatibility and happiness of the couple. Then as now some husbands and wives separated after marriage. Since it was only in some Protestant countries that divorce became a realistic legal option and since the Catholic and Anglican churches did not authorize an annulment unless there had been some defect in the original marriage, such as the absence of consent, couples usually just split up without legal or ritual sanction.

But in some places the dissolution of a marriage required more publicity. In Wales the broomstick wedding ceremony could be reversed by a dissatisfied spouse who in the presence of witnesses merely jumped back over a broom placed across the threshold, still making sure that neither the broom nor the doorjamb was touched in the process. In Scotland and Ireland there were several ritual variations for reversing the marriage compact: in the Orkneys divorcing couples went to a church near the Ring of Brodgar where they had previously married by clasping each other's hands through a hole in the stone. After hearing a service they left by separate doors, which divorced them in the eyes of the public. On the island of Skye before the seventeenth century, trial marriages of one year were permitted after which a disaffected spouse could divorce but retained custody of any children. More common were divorces achieved when a wife simply removed and returned her wedding ring, an act with powerful magical overtones since, as we have seen, the ring had great symbolic powers. A woman who lost her ring was in danger of losing her chastity or her husband. Any mishap involving a wedding ring offered evil omens about the fate of the marriage. Perhaps most common of all were divorces achieved by a seven-year separation, which was popularly believed to permit remarriage.

More problematic to interpret are the known cases of the ritual sale of wives, best known from English examples. Although there are scattered reports of the practice from the sixteenth and seventeenth centuries, wife sale may not have been employed as a ritualized form of divorce much before the 1770s when the frequency of reported cases increases. Rather than an ancient peasant custom for sanctioning divorce, Edward Thompson sees ritual wife sale as an "invented tradition" employed by the growing class of displaced workers in the eighteenth century. In any case the custom reflected the spreading market mentality of the early modern period and the psychological requirements of people who needed a ritual unloosening of the solemn oath made at marriage.

The undiluted form of wife sale required that she be brought with a halter around her neck or waist to the market-place for public "sale." In most cases it appears that she consented to the sale, and in many examples the "buyer" was actually a lover with whom she had been having an affair. The ritual had many potential purposes: renouncing publicly the marriage promise, compensating a cuckolded husband for the loss of his wife, shaming a wayward wife, and authorizing a new union, but most of all it demonstrated the essentially powerless position of wives in a society in which the law, religion, and custom employed the language of ownership to represent the authority of adult males over women, children, and servants. A woman presented to her neighbors in the guise of a haltered mare or cow suffered humiliation and degradation, whether she had "consented" or not.

The ritual had several requirements. (1) It must take place in an acknowledged market-place. (2) It had to be public and was often preceded by an advertisement or announcement. (3) It required the use of a halter, even if it were only a vestigial one made of ribbons. More than just a symbol for comparing the wife to a domestic animal, the halter authenticated the sale since it was a sign of ownership, which indicated that the wife had been "delivered" over to the new owner. Without the humiliating halter public report might not recognize the change in marital status it conveyed. (4) Someone had to take on the role of auctioneer, who went through the charade of an auction, even if the buyer had been determined beforehand. (5) Money should change hands. Sometimes this was a paltry sum, perhaps only a shilling, and a certain quantity of drink was often included in the price. In many cases the husband-seller returned the money as a token of good luck to the new couple. (6) At the moment of the transfer of the halter, words were sometimes exchanged that made new promises clearly derived from wedding ceremonies. The sold wife and the purchaser might openly consent to the deal and even promise to treat each other as man and wife. If the seller and buyer were on congenial terms, all three might repair to a tavern to solemnize the sale with drinks; if bad feelings and a lack of trust prevailed, they might resort to drawing up a written record of the transaction. When fully followed the ritual "legalized" the divorce and remarriage in the eyes of the community.

Although ritual wife sales may only belong to the end of the early modern period, they exemplify the assimilation of ritual practices into the cultural practices of the market-place. In the early market economy of Renaissance Italy, the exchange of women and property between two patriarchal lineages so dominated the rituals of the rich that girls were not even invited to their own engagement parties. In late eighteenth-century England, poor workers found the rituals of market transactions the most meaningful way to represent the exchange of a wife between a man who had been her husband and the one who would become it. The great symbolic power of the market-place came from the fact that it was there that men learned to trust one another and to represent their mutual confidence in the little rituals of striking a deal, such as the kiss on the mouth or standing for drinks in a tavern. The rituals of marriage, procreation, and divorce looked in two directions, toward other people and toward God, with the emphasis on the former. As these rituals demonstrate, God's role was largely to authenticate and guarantee the hard-won and potentially dangerous trust in others implied by the marriage bond. Although some of these rituals suggested divine sanctions for violating oaths, the people who employed these rituals were realists who recognized their value for attracting the attention of the community and who understood that the sanction of public opprobrium held greater immediate terror for potential violators than divine wrath.

Dying and death

On February 18, 1546, Martin Luther lay dying in an obscure inn far from home. As his final moments approached, his devoted disciple Justus Jonas quickly summoned witnesses and shook poor Martin to rouse him for the performance of his final scene. The father of the Protestant Reformation could not be allowed to die in peaceful solitude because the character of his dying would reveal whether God or Satan claimed his soul, and the accounts of his death would portend the future course of the reform movement.

For centuries Christians had believed that the ability to face death without fear through a calm fading away, a "good death," was an intimation of salvation. To die suddenly from a heart attack, in writhing fits from extreme pain, or in delirium pointed to a direct passage into hell. The devil's plan was to cut off the life of those he claimed without warning, leaving the soul deprived of the final rites of the church. Even though Martin Luther had begun his epic religious adventure by objecting to indulgence doctrines that were part of the church's scheme for assisting dead souls and even though his reforms led to the dismantling of much of the church's vast ritual apparatus of death, *he* still needed to die well. The old ideas persisted too powerfully. Luther's loving flock insisted on portraying his death as a slow ebbing of the life force accompanied by Martin's simple commendation of his spirit to God's care. Martin had a good death.

During the later Middle Ages an elaborate ritual script assisted Christians through the final rite of passage. These rites as well as the vast accoutrements of the cult of death – the funerals, tombs, commemorative masses – have been studied extensively in recent years, in large part due to the inspiration of the brilliantly evocative work of Philippe Ariès. A great deal is now known about dying and death in France, Italy, and England.

Although there were earlier indications of a morbid preoccupation with death in Christian countries, after the extreme mortality produced by the Black Death in 1348, during which some one-third or more of all Europeans died, a profound sense of pessimism and guilt permeated the sensibilities of the living. The Black Death and other epidemic diseases kept coming back, quite often at least once in each generation, persisting throughout the early modern period. Unlike the modern world where we do our best to ignore death, hide it from children, speak of it in hushed tones, and consider it pathological for someone to be overly concerned with it, during the fifteenth through seventeenth centuries death could be said to be the central concern of life. Michel de Montaigne epitomized the sentiment with the aphorism, "men must be taught to die in order that they may learn to live."

For survivors a death did not so much create a sense of absence as a recognition that their association with the dead person would henceforth take a different form. Their attitude contrasts in many ways with ours in that they seem remarkably without compassion for the sufferings of the dying but extremely familiar with those already dead. The callous, laughing crowds who witnessed the torture and execution of criminals testifies to the first trait while the most famous example of the second might be the Cemetery of the Innocents in Paris, which during the seventeenth century served as a popular shopping center, complete with tailors and book stalls, where customers walked among the dead, stepped around open graves, and witnessed daily burials and exhumations without any sense of horror or revulsion. Philippe Ariès called this attitude, "the tame death": "It has by now been so obliterated from our culture that it is hard for us to imagine or understand it. The ancient attitude in which death is close and familiar yet diminished and desensitized is too different from our own view, in which it is so terrifying that we no longer dare say its name."[7]

Two of the governing qualities of the tame death were the sense of resignation on the part of the dying person, that is the calm attitude depicted in the accounts of Martin Luther's death, and the public nature of the deathbed scene, exemplified in the report of the death of Louis XIV's mistress, Madame de Montespan, who kept waking up the women holding vigil around her bed to make certain that she would not die alone. The rituals of death sustained the social community of the living to such a degree that the historian Sharon Strocchia has proposed the concept of the "ritual family." By this she means that the actual gathering of witnesses to a death and the participants in the funeral rites constituted the family as much as do blood ties or common residence. Although in the fifteenth century humanists argued that the public display of mourning was unseemly and that death ought to be a private affair, they had little influence on actual practice. A proper death was just as much a public event as a proper marriage.

The rituals of dying and death can be grouped into three general categories. First, the last rites and the "art of dying" (*ars moriendi*)

[7] Philippe Ariès, *The Hour of Our Death*, trans. Helen Weaver (New York: Alfred A. Knopf, 1981), 28.

served to assist souls in their final test before God and to separate the
departed from their kin. Second, the funeral rites reasserted the ties of
kinship among the survivors and the obligations the living had to the
dead. Third, prayers and masses for the dead and the All Souls holiday
reaffirmed the collective claims the dead had upon the living.

According to the art of dying, which was prescribed in numerous
advice books and illustrations, the sick or injured person was to die in
bed, surrounded by a room full of people. However, the living were
unable to see the real drama faced by the dying person who watched a
supernatural spectacle visible to him alone. On one side of the bed
appeared a heavenly host including the members of the Trinity, the
Virgin Mary, saints, angels, and prominently the dying person's
guardian angel. On the other side Satan and his demon minions
clamored for attention (see figure 2). At this critical moment as Satan
made his final pitch, the dying man faced the greatest temptation of his
life, the temptation of the desperate to deny the faith. Surrounded by a
cosmic battle between what Alberto Tenenti calls "two supernatural
societies," the angelic legions versus the hordes of hell, the suffering
Christian could not hide and could barely choose among such powerful
forces. Nevertheless, he could act upon his only hope, which was to
appeal to the intercession of the Virgin, whose prayers would be passed
through Christ to God the Father. Less a judge than a kind of referee in
the cosmic contest, God finally released the man from his spiritual and
physical agonies by shooting him with the dart of death, allowing him to
give up the ghost to its fate.

This final moment determined all. The Dominican Friar Girolamo
Savonarola compared the deathbed contest to a horrific game of chess in
which the devil did all he could to trap the dying person into a
checkmate just at the moment of death. Although only the dying
witnessed the supernatural scene, he was not without human assistance.
In the best of circumstances, the priest arrived in time to hear a
confession, offer words of consolation, encourage him to forgive his
enemies and redress any wrongs, anoint the body with the rites of
extreme unction, and slip the holy wafer into the man's mouth in the
viaticum. Then he could die.

The art of dying separated the individual from the living by
emphasizing a supernatural battle that only he could witness and by
providing liturgical assistance for the salvation of his soul. Although his
family members gathered around, the rites gave them no role and did
little at this stage to succor them in their grief. By the sixteenth century,
in the eyes of many the heavy involvement of the priest in these rites
produced more burdens than provided solace. Just like the sacrament of

Figure 2   Scene of the *Ars Moriendi* from Lionel Henry Cust,
*The Master E. S. and the "Ars Moriendi": A Chapter in the History
of Engraving During the XVth Century.*

marriage, the last rites came under attack. Desiderius Erasmus's brilliant parody exemplifies this critical attitude.

When the last hour finally comes, certain ceremonies for the occasion are already prepared. The dying man makes his general confession. He is given Extreme Unction and the last sacrament. The candles and the holy water are there. No chance of forgetting the indulgences! A papal bull is unrolled before the dying man's eyes; if necessary, it is even sold to him. Then arrangements are made for the elaborate funeral service. A last solemn promise is extracted from the dying man. Someone shouts in his ear and hastens his end, as often happens, either by excessive noise, or by a breath that reeks of wine.[8]

At the Council of Trent, Catholics reaffirmed the rites but trans-formed them from a last-chance sacramental aid for the remission of the sins to an anointing of the sick. Objecting to the impression that a deathbed confession could compensate for a reprobate life, the Protes-tants eliminated the sacramental value of the rites altogether, left confession to the initiative of the dying person, and substituted the support of godly friends for the priest.

If analyzed as a rite of passage, the last rites constituted the phase of separation while the moment of death was the transitional or liminal phase. As a biological transition only birth and death represented a clear crossing over a threshold. The numerous social and ritual events that followed the death assisted in reaggregating the community of kin and friends centered on the deceased and in incorporating him into the community of the dead.

A vast range of practices stretched out this final phase to last days, months, even years. As soon as the priest returned to his parish after the death, he had the death bell rung, which informed the neighbors to stop their work to offer prayers. Typically, female relatives laid out the body in the house and in Languedoc cut its nails and hair, carefully guarding the cuttings to prevent them from falling into the hands of witches. The mourning and wailing were also usually in the domain of women, as was crying out for revenge in the case of a murder. The Irish considered attendance at the wake one of the principal obligations of religion and followed an established series of intensely emotional phases of weeping, joking, insulting the cadaver, drinking, and eating. Domestic rites of mourning such as these were sufficiently curative for the emotional health of the survivors that the liturgical requirement to transport the corpse immediately to the church was widely ignored.

From the dead person's home, the corpse was transported in a procession to the church for the funeral mass. In Florence where the city

8 Ibid., 303.

fathers wanted to maintain public decorum, women were banned from funeral processions to prevent unseemly displays of grief. Florentine men feared that the wild emotions of women would provoke vendettas and undermine the very social order that the funeral rites helped to reaffirm. Major increases in death rates, such as happened in Avignon about 1330 and Florence after 1348, led to flamboyant funerals, especially among the aristocracy: teams of horses pulled the funeral wagon, blazons and heraldic banners decorated the church, and numerous expensive candles blazed on the altar. Like marriage processions, spectacles such as these became fantastic public manifestations of the solidarity and power of the great patrician families, especially during times when the vagaries of high mortality threatened the very survival of all families.

The priest intoned the funerary rites, read the office of the dead over the body, and led a final procession to the place of burial in the churchyard for the modest classes or in a tomb near an altar in the church for the select few who could afford to buy a space close to God and the saints. From the place of burial the cortege returned to the home of the deceased for a funeral supper.

Many of the distinctive post-funerary practices can be linked to the doctrine of purgatory. The idea that there was some intermediary world, neither heaven nor hell, in which most of the dead would be subject to a term of punishment for their sins, gradually spread through the Middle Ages, receiving its definitive formulation in Dante's poem, *The Divine Comedy*. Based on the central Christian tenets of immortality and resurrection, the doctrine of purgatory explained how sinners might receive a second chance at eternal life by paying for their sins before the last judgment. The payment need not be exclusively theirs to make because the living could contribute to a reduction in the term of punishment through prayers and intercessory masses. In the fourteenth and fifteenth centuries, a vast enterprise of holy support bloomed to assist souls in purgatory.

Purgatory was, in effect, a remarkable example of human projection, of extending human institutions into another dimension. According to Jacques Le Goff, the projection took two forms, the "spatialization" of purgatory and the stretching of the ritualistic penitential system of the church beyond life. Spatialization refers to the widespread belief that purgatory occupied a specific space, the antipodes in Dante's poem, the churchyard in popular belief. The common attitude left the souls of the dead in close proximity to their buried bodies and near their living relatives and neighbors in the parish. The graveyard became a magnificently evocative spectral theater where the living and dead interacted.

For example, it was a sanctuary, a place of necessary peace that would be polluted by the shedding of blood. When the powerful Friulan aristocrat, Antonio Savorgnan, was murdered in a church graveyard in Villach, Austria, in 1512, the defilement caused an uproar among the local citizenry. A few days after the murder when a great storm appeared the locals were convinced that it was caused by the churchyard dead, angered to a fury by the violent invasion of their space.

In most places in Europe before the Reformation, people were buried collectively rather than individually. Most tombs were not marked with names, and after an appropriate wait of seven or eight years the bones were dug up and mixed with those of others in the charnel-house. This practice seems to have been tied to the idea that the soul hovered close to the body for as long as the flesh remained, a macabre aspect of popular biology that correlated with the belief in the proximity of the dead and the spatiality of purgatory. Most people chose to be buried in their parish churchyard, but in Italy where confraternities supplied the necessary services for the cult of the dead, many sought the alternative of burial among their confrères. In places where the parish system was weak, such as the growing cities, the mendicant orders provided the dead with shelter. Only the very rich or very saintly obtained a permanent tomb of their own, marked with an inscription detailing their accomplishments in life and sometimes capped with an effigy. Burial was truly an extension of the society of the living with all its discriminations of status, rank, and gender into the community of the dead.

Only after the Reformation did the pattern created in the later Middle Ages by the aristocracy of establishing familial turf in a chapel or complex of tombs trickle down to other classes, who tried to segment the churchyards into family plots, obliterating the collective character of the old graveyards.

The second form of the projection of human institutions onto the dead assembled penitential rituals to assist the dead in purgatory. By praying and having masses said, it was believed, the amount of time the dead spent in purgatory would be reduced. Maintaining a constant round of ritual supplications became the principal means by which the living sustained obligations to ancestors and provided for their own comfort in the afterlife. The nobility endowed chantries, the urban classes joined confraternities, and the poor paid for anniversary commemorations and single masses as their resources allowed. By increasing the demand for the service of priests, assisting the dead in purgatory provided a significant dividend for the church, greatly expanding its wealth and influence during the fourteenth and fifteenth centuries. Particularly after the ravages of the plague magnified the number of persons taken in the prime of life, endowments for perpetual masses increased dramatically. The animosities aroused by this expensive ritual bureaucracy provoked some of the most vehement protests of the sixteenth-century reformers.

The masses for the dead also provided insurance against molestation by ghosts. Ghosts were understood to be dead relatives who visited their kin to rectify wrongs committed against them while alive and to enforce the obligations of kinship. Hauntings were very personal, an expression of family piety and a manifestation of the survivors' residual guilt or the fear of retaliation. Ghosts were those souls lurking in the graveyard. It was best to placate them as much as possible, and the institution of masses for the dead offered a kind of prophylactic magic against hauntings.

Certainly the most emphatic expression of the intimacy between the living and the dead can be found in the dance of death. With the dance the cult of the dead was transformed from ritual to theater and art. Often performed as a masque on All Souls' Day, November 2, and frequently represented in paintings and engravings, the dance of death reversed the process of projection by representing the society of the dead as a model for the society of the living. The paintings show a circle of dancers in the graveyard, holding hands, with the dead intermixed with the living. The dead lead the agitated, manic dance, almost dragging the living along. Depicted as naked skeletons or mummies, the dead are sexless and without any signs of status. They represent death as the great equalizer. In contrast to their partners, the living are dressed according to their station in life and their gender. They represent the social inequalities of the living. Unlike the art of dying, which presents the idealized scene of death as a gradual fading away, the dance of death warns that death can take anyone at any time, evincing a great fear of sudden death.

More than the other rites of the dead, the dance created a truly liminal situation by representing death as radically different from life with its many social distinctions, dramatic contrasts of wealth, petty preoccupations. Liminal states are fantasy states that provide a useful index of the deepest desires of a period, and they are volatile because fantasies change. Liminal states are inevitably unstable. In the fifteenth century the dance projected a utopian vision of a world without rank and privilege. By the sixteenth century the dance had become violent and erotic. Death then came not as a beckoning dancer but as one of the Four Horsemen of the Apocalypse, the grim reaper ready to cut down the living. He no longer quietly drew away his female victims but violently marked them, plunging his fingers into their sex to emphasize their vulnerability. Death had become a lecherous predator.

The Reformation, particularly in its early phases, can be seen as a forceful rejection of the ritual industry of death with all its expensive commitments to priestly intervention. Through his attack on the abusive selling of special indulgences that were advertised to release the dear departed from purgatory, Luther opened the way for a systematic re-examination of the role of ritual. As psychologically necessary as the rites of passage had been in assisting in the essential transformations of life, for many they had become more of a burden than a solace.

BIBLIOGRAPHY

Entries marked with a * designate recommended readings for new students of the subject.

*Ariès, Philippe. *The Hour of Our Death*. Translated by Helen Weaver. New York: Alfred A. Knopf, 1981. A highly influential book that posits that there has been a major shift in attitudes about dying and death since the late Middle Ages.

Belmont, Nicole. *Les signes de la naissance: études des représentations symboliques associées aux naissances singulières*. Paris: Plon, 1971. An analysis of the meaning of births with the caul.

Bossy, John. "Blood and Baptism: Kinship, Community and Christianity in Western Europe From the Fourteenth to the Seventeenth Centuries." In *Sanctity and Secularity: The Church and the World*. Edited by Derek Baker. Oxford: Basil Blackwell, 1973. Pp. 129–43.

  Christianity in the West, 1400–1700. Oxford: Oxford University Press, 1985. An excellent, concise discussion of practice as well as belief. Especially useful on baptism, marriage, and death.

Brooke, Christopher N. L. *The Medieval Idea of Marriage*. Oxford: Oxford University Press, 1989.

Cavazza, Silvano. "Double Death: Resurrection and Baptism in a Seventeenth-Century Rite." In *History from Crime*. Edited by Edward Muir and Guido Ruggiero. Baltimore: Johns Hopkins University Press, 1994. Pp. 1–31. A fascinating account of a resurrection cult devoted to quieting the restless souls of unbaptised infants.

Davis, Natalie Zemon. "The Reasons of Misrule." In *Society and Culture in Early Modern France*. Stanford: Stanford University Press, 1975. Pp. 97–123. The best discussion of youth-abbeys and their violence.

Delumeau, Jean. *Sin and Fear: The Emergence of a Western Guilt Culture – Thirteenth–Eighteenth Centuries*. Translated by Eric Nicholson. New York: St. Martin's Press, 1983.

Duby, Georges. *The Knight, the Lady, and the Priest: The Making of Modern Marriage in Medieval France*. New York: Pantheon Books, 1985.

*Gennep, Arnold van. *The Rites of Passage*. Translated by Monika B. Vizedom and Gabrielle L. Caffee. Chicago: University of Chicago Press, 1960. Still readable and stimulating, it is the beginning point for any examination of rites of passage.

Gittings, Clare. *Death, Burial and the Individual in Early Modern England*. London: Croom Helm, 1984.

Gluckman, Max. "Les rites de passage." In *Essays on the Ritual of Social Relations*. Edited by Max Gluckman. Manchester: Manchester University Press, 1962. An argument that one of the functions of ritual is to cloak conflict.

Houlbrooke, Ralph. "Death, Church, and Family in England between the Late Fifteenth and the Early Eighteenth Centuries." In *Death, Ritual, and Bereavement*. Edited by Ralph Houlbrooke. London: Routledge, 1989. Pp. 25–42.

Klapisch-Zuber, Christiane. *Women, Family, and Ritual in Renaissance Italy*. Translated by Lydia G. Cochrane. Chicago: University of Chicago Press, 1985. A brilliantly evocative social history of Florence. On marriage rites, see chapters 9 through 12.

Le Goff, Jacques. "The Symbolic Ritual of Vassalage." In *Time, Work, & Culture in the Middle Ages*. Translated by Arthur Goldhammer. Chicago: University of Chicago Press, 1980. Pp. 237–87.

Le Roy Ladurie, Emmanuel. "The Aiguillette: Castration by Magic." In *The Mind and Method of the Historian*. Translated by Siân Reynolds and Ben Reynolds. Chicago: University of Chicago Press, 1981. Pp. 84–96. Examines rituals of castration magic and their cures in France.

Llewellyn, Nigel. *The Art of Death: Visual Culture in the English Death Ritual, c. 1500–c. 1800*. Seattle: University of Washington Press, 1992.

McLaren, Angus. *Reproductive Rituals: The Perception of Fertility in England from the Sixteenth to the Nineteenth Century*. London: Methuen, 1984. Discusses attempts to induce and prevent fertility through magical means.

Menefee, Samuel Pyeatt. *Wives for Sale: An Ethnographic Study of British Popular Divorce*. Oxford: Basil Blackwell, 1981. Describes the ritual of wife sale but should only be used in conjunction with E. P. Thompson's study, cited below.

Paxton, Frederick S. *Christianizing Death: The Creation of a Ritual Process in Early Medieval Europe*. Ithaca: Cornell University Press, 1990.

Roper, Lyndal. "'Going to Church and Street': Weddings in Reformation Augsburg." *Past and Present* 106 (1985): 62–101.

Rossiaud, Jacques. *Medieval Prostitution*. Translated by Lydia G. Cochrane. Oxford: Basil Blackwell, 1988. For youth-abbeys and the rite of gang rape, see chapter 2.

Shahar, Shulamith. *Childhood in the Middle Ages*. New York: Routledge, 1990. The most comprehensive study of attitudes toward children. It includes a good discussion of baptism.

Strocchia, Sharon T. *Death and Ritual in Renaissance Florence*. Baltimore: Johns Hopkins University Press, 1992.

Thompson, E. P. "The Sale of Wives." In *Customs in Common*. London: Merlin Press, 1991. Pp. 404–66.

Trexler, Richard C. *Public Life in Renaissance Florence*. New York: Academic Press, 1980. A brilliant, evocative portrait of the city from the point of view of its public rituals. Chapter 5 tells the story of Giovanni Morelli.

*Turner, Victor W. *The Ritual Process: Structure and Anti-Structure*. Chicago: Aldine, 1969. Outlines Turner's highly influential theories about liminality.
Weissman, Ronald F. E. *Ritual Brotherhood in Renaissance Florence*. New York: Academic Press, 1982. A highly stimulating study of male confraternities that organized collective worship among young men.

2 The ritual calendar

In the fourteenth and fifteenth centuries, many Florentine businessmen kept "memory books." Most neither agonized over a dead son nor described elaborate rituals quite like Giovanni Morelli did in his. More typical of his class might be Goro Dati, who is a study in the stolid complacency of the cautious businessman. Utterly unimaginative, without evident passions or dramatic impulses, Dati's comments might be a measure of "normal" behavior. Even in such a private document as his diary, Dati seems to have voiced only the most conventional sentiments.

When he reached the age of forty, Dati took stock of his life, not so much because of what we might now term a mid-life crisis as because good Christians were supposed to evaluate their progress toward salvation at cardinal moments in their lives. He recognized that in the past he had allowed business concerns to interfere with his religious obligations.

Distrusting my own power to reform, but hoping to advance by degrees along the path of virtue, I resolve from this day forward to refrain from going to the shop or conducting business on solemn church holidays, or from permitting others to work for me or seek temporal gain on such days. Whenever I make exceptions in cases of extreme necessity, I promise, on the following day, to distribute alms of one gold florin to God's poor. I have written this down so that I may remember my promise and be ashamed if I should chance to break it.[1]

It is evident that Goro Dati saw himself being pulled in opposite directions by two different conceptions of time, merchant time and church time.

Jacques Le Goff has pointed to the fundamental opposition between these two conceptions of time. For example, churchmen condemned merchants for lending money at interest, offering as justification a reason that demonstrates more than anything else a sensitivity to the value of time. During the fourteenth century a lector-general of the Franciscan

---

[1] Gregorio Dati, *Two Memoirs of Renaissance Florence: The Diaries of Buonaccorso Pitti and Gregorio Dati*, ed. Gene Brucker (New York: Harper & Row, 1967), 124.

order asserted that businessmen cannot legitimately charge interest on overdue bills because to do so would be to *sell time,* a usurious activity because they would be selling something they did not own.

Dati sensed this incompatibility between the two kinds of time when he confessed that unlike his ordinary earnings money obtained on holy days somehow contained an alloy of sin. To him "the path of virtue" could be followed simply by changing his activities on certain days, those red-letter days of the church. Dati's vow embodies a notion of the power invested in certain days. He could only take advantage of that super-natural power by performing the appropriate ritual activities prescribed by the church.

Both the merchant's time and the church's time established forms of what Eviatar Zerubavel calls "hidden rhythms," ways in which calendars and beliefs in the special qualities of certain units of time establish temporal regularity. Some of these rhythms have astronomical corre-lates: the year in the rotation of the earth about the sun, the seasons in the tilt of the earth on its axis, the month loosely in the phases of the moon, and the day in the rotation of the earth on its axis. Others, such as the week, the distinction between feast and ferial days, and the institution of the hour have no relationship at all to astronomical cycles and are completely arbitrary creations of culture. The intertwining of the superficially astronomical and the cultural gave the tempo of the calendrical system the illusion of naturalness, an illusion that be-queathed enormous power over people's lives, becoming so habitual that even the most radical modern revolutions have failed to abolish the institution of the week or the mechanical despotism of the hour clock.

In traditional Europe, these rhythms were established, celebrated, promulgated, and altered through rituals – the rituals of work and the rituals of festivity. Those rituals related to the passage of the seasons were particularly akin to rites of passage in that they included sympathetic rites guarding against the dangers of winter and promoting spring fertility. The rational ordering of time expressed in calendrical rituals established routines and schedules, which worked against individual spontaneity. The implicit message was that everyone should be doing the same thing at the same time, and if they did so, the community would be stronger for it. Each individual had to ignore his or her private inclinations and personal rhythms in response to the collective demand.

The heritage of the ritual calendar of traditional Europe has been momentous for modern civilization in the West. Although most of us no longer tune our daily routine to the bells of the nearest monastery or exhibit Goro Dati's obsessive concern about keeping feast days pure from the taint of business, practically everyone has a little mechanical time tyrant attached to his or her wrist and an appointment calendar near the telephone. Weekly cycles are especially pervasive. What is acceptable on any other day of the week, such as a morning phone call, seems an intrusive violation of proper behavior on a Sunday, whether one is preparing for church or nursing a hangover.

The ritual calendar of traditional Europe operated on four levels. The first, the church's cycles of jubilee years, the liturgical year, and liturgical seasons, found its origins in a blending of ancient Roman solar calculations and Jewish lunar holidays. The second, the institution of the week, derived from the peculiarly Hebrew conception of the sabbath, an extremely powerful idea that has spread to much of the world through Christianity, Islam, and modern business practices. The third temporal unit, the day, had multiple roots, given its obvious astronomical regularity, but its distinguishing ritual characteristic was the singling out of some days as more sacred than others. The fourth aspect of time, the hour, had peculiarly Christian origins in the rule of the Benedictine Order, which called monks to prayer at prescribed intervals.

Liturgical cycles: years and seasons

The liturgical calendar determined what kinds of ritual celebrations would be performed on special days. In effect, the church organized group worship around this calendar and defined what special additions or modifications might be made to the central rite of the liturgy, the Eucharist or lord's supper. In so doing the church structured years and seasons by creating feast days that acted as temporal borders between one segment of time and the next.

The broadest liturgical grouping consisted of the holy year, first established in 1300. The idea of the holy year found biblical justification in the Judaic institution of the Jubilee every fifty years, during which debts were pardoned and Hebrew slaves freed. Pope Boniface VIII determined that every 100 years the faithful could earn a plenary indulgence for the remission of time to be spent in purgatory by visiting certain designated basilicas in Rome. Later modifications reduced the prescribed time between holy years to twenty-five. Although the desire to promote the holy tourist trade to Rome certainly provided one of the initial motivations for holy years, Boniface was also responding to a widely held belief that the first year of every century was especially propitious, even though technically speaking 1300 was the last year of the old century rather than the first of the new.

Behind this belief in the efficacy of centennial years prowls a compelling belief in the power of certain numbers. There is, of course, no inherent reason why 100 should be a more auspicious interval than 99 or 104, other than the fact that we use a base-ten number system that provides a gratifying enumerate regularity to multiples of ten. Vestiges of other non-base-ten number systems, such as the sixty-minute hour, survive in our cultural consciousness with continued vigor. The liturgical calendar, thus, expresses the mysterious power of numbers, a wonder that especially fascinated medieval and Renaissance thinkers. The liturgical calendar gave all Christians, not just prophets and magicians, access to that magnificent power.

The broad outlines of the Christian liturgical calendar were established in the second half of the fourth century with the superimposition of the pre-agrarian lunar calendar of the Hebrews onto the solar calendar of the Romans. The result created the two distinct cycles of the Christian liturgy: the Easter cycle of movable feasts, derived from the lunar dating of the Hebrew Passover; and the Nativity cycle of fixed feasts, reckoned from the dating of Christ's birth on the twenty-fifth day of the tenth month of the Julian solar year (see figure 3). From the very beginnings of officially sanctioned Christianity, the celebration of these feast days was opposed to work days, as can be seen in the Edict of Thessaloniki of 380, which determined the days of the sun (*dies solis*), or Sundays, when peasants were exempt from agricultural work.

The ritual commemoration of the life of Christ in the liturgy kept time with the passing of the seasons, creating a festive counterpoint to work, making the mission of Christ, relived each year in the church's feasts, as much a part of the universal order as the waning and waxing of the moon or the apparent movements of the planets. Every year the most momentous events in the story of the New Testament were retold and recelebrated in the liturgical seasons of Advent, Christmas, Epiphany, Lent, Easter, Ascension, and Pentecost. The marvelous narrative of Christ's singular life, confined in historical time to thirty-three years, replayed itself each year through the liturgy. As Edward Thompson has put it, "to the degree that the ritual calendar year chimes in with the agrarian calendar, the authority of the Church is strengthened."[2] As a result the moments of emphasis in the liturgical calendar often varied according to local agricultural or climatic conditions. In Coventry, for example, the year seems to have begun on Candlemas, February 2, the day when the city's pastures were opened for private use; in Venice the beginning of the year corresponded to the reopening of the sailing season.

As a consequence of the great power of calendars to regulate life, they

---

[2] Thompson, "Anthropology and the Discipline of Historical Context,' *Midland History* 1 (1972): 51.

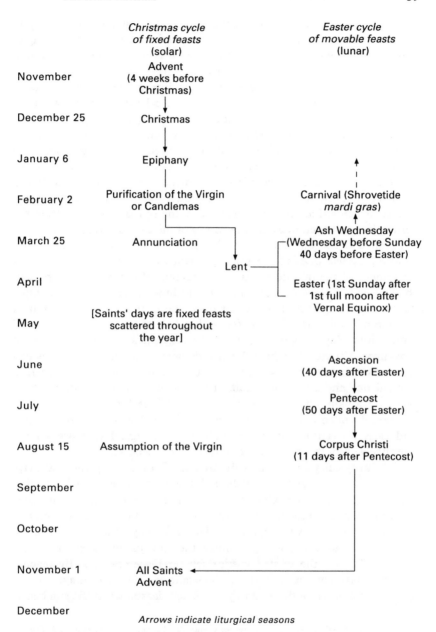

Figure 3   The Christian liturgical calendar

have always been an object of contention. The Eastern Orthodox and Roman Catholic churches have never been able to agree on the dating of Easter, which was one of the most divisive issues in the early church. Whatever the churchmen did, governments have always had the final say in legislating calendars, and everywhere in Europe there were vast local variations in practice. The official liturgical calendar became a framework for the disputation of meanings, the expression of regal ambitions, and the preservation of local idiosyncrasies, but the seemingly arbitrary differences among calendars should not obscure their significance for the conduct of all forms of collective life. There was no alternative to the liturgical calendar for reckoning time, which meant that all activities followed its periodization: business contracts were marked by it, leases and rents came due on certain feast days, the schedule of courses at the universities followed it, as did the chores of the agricultural season.

In most of Europe the liturgical year, including both the fixed and movable cycles, divided the year approximately in half. The ritual reenactment of the life, death, and resurrection of Christ densely packed the first half of the year from December to June, a period adorned with a special festive quality that accompanied the critical growing season of the agricultural year. The less festive last half of the year was scattered with saints' days, many of merely local significance. In his study of Coventry, Charles Phythian-Adams depicted the difference between these two halves of the year as an absolute contrast between a "ritualistic" and a "secular" half, but this seems an exaggeration, based more on looking at the crowded calendar of the first half than on the perceptions of contemporaries. As Eamon Duffy has put it, "to fifteenth- and early sixteenth-century sensibilities the liturgical year was spread over twelve months, not six, and none of it was secular."[3]

The liturgical year began with Advent. Commencing four Sundays before Christmas, Advent celebrated the incarnation of Christ, that singular moment when God became a man. The dating of Christmas derived from the Emperor Constantine's adaptation of Christianity to the sun cult that was popular in late antiquity among the Roman aristocracy and bureaucracy. Under the old Julian calendar of the Roman Empire, the winter solstice fell on December 25. By placing Christ's birthday on that date, Constantine took advantage of the symbolic potential of this first day of the new season when the sun began

---

[3] Cf. Charles Phythian-Adams, "Ceremony and the Citizen: The Communal Year at Coventry 1450–1550,' in P. Clark and P. Slack, eds., *Crisis and Order in English Towns, 1500–1700: Essays in Urban History* (Toronto: University of Toronto Press, 1972), 57–85. Quote from Eamon Duffy, *The Stripping of the Altars: Traditional Religion in England, c.1400–c.1580* (New Haven: Yale University Press, 1992), 47.

to shine longer each day. According to the symbolism created by this dating, Christ became the Sun of Justice, who arrived at midnight on the longest night of the year in the depths of a cave. To complete the symbolism the annunciation, the moment when Christ entered Mary's womb, was celebrated exactly nine months earlier at midday on March 25, the day of the vernal equinox in the old Julian calendar.

The liturgy placed Christ's birth at the center of time, making it the event from which years were numbered backward to the creation and forward to the second coming; he was born in the middle of the centuries, in the depth of the year and of the earth, at a moment when time itself stopped, creating such a breathtaking stillness that, according to the medieval *Golden Legend*, the entire created universe from stones to angels instantly perceived it. To the fifth-century saint, Paulinus of Nola, the connection between the birth of Christ and the solar year was not just a metaphor but a historic truth:

For it is after the solstice, when Christ was born in the body of a man and changed the freezing season of winter with the new sun. Promising mortals a life-saving dawn, he advanced the length of the day and commanded the nights to decrease with his coming.[4]

The Christmas season lasted twelve days from December 25 to January 6, the feast of the Epiphany, commemorating the recognition and adoration of the Christ child by the three kings or Magi as they were known in the Middle Ages. In the middle of the Christmas season, on December 28, fell the day of the Massacre of the Holy Innocents, out of order from the chronology in the Bible. By the fifteenth century the Christ child and holy family had become the evocative focus of the season, which celebrated birth, childhood, innocence, and family life in a way quite alien to the early church and most of the Middle Ages. Perhaps the high childhood mortality of the age stimulated a heightened recognition of the Christ child through the celebration of Christmas. According to legend St. Francis introduced the creche as a dramatic representation of the cult of the holy infant, which spread with the success of Franciscan preachers in the fourteenth and fifteenth centuries. The first examples of carol singing also appeared in the fifteenth century, and Christmas gradually evolved to replace other days as one of the principal holidays of the year although it remained far behind Holy Week and Easter in popularity until about a century ago.

The second liturgical season lasted from January 20 to February 14, centering on the feast of the Purification of the Virgin, or Candlemas, on

---

[4] St. Paulinus, bishop of Nola, *Poema*, xiv, 15–19 in *Opera*, ed. William Hartel (Vienna: F. Tempsky, G. Freytag, 1894).

February 2. This season connected the pure fertility of the Virgin, who gave birth to the light of the world, to the onset of spring (at least in the Mediterranean) with its promise of the regeneration of nature. In some ways an amalgam of the pagan Feast of Lights (February 1) and the Roman Lupercalia (February 15), the Christian purification rituals retained associations with lustration, fire symbolism, and fertility. The central images of the season involved the rising of sap in plants and the lengthening of the day, symbolized by the blessing of candles at Candlemas, an appropriate image since the seasonal work now shifted from indoor tasks to the first outdoor ones. In Germany the feast of Fabian and Sebastian, January 20, marked the last day on which trees could be pruned since about then the sap begins to rise. The next day, St. Agnes' day, the priest introduced a new-born lamb into church to symbolize the coming spring, and on the 22nd peasants tapped the vines in their vineyards to estimate by the level of the sap when the grape harvest would be.

Depending on the locale, several feasts during this period, especially St. Paul's on January 25, were notable moments when the prospects for springtime weather could be determined. In the United States popular tradition still holds that if a groundhog sees his shadow on February 2 there will be six more weeks of bad weather, but if the day is cloudy, it is an omen of an early spring. The tradition derives from English lore about Candlemas:

> If Candlemas be fair and bright,
> Come, Winter, have another flight;
> If Candlemas bring clouds and rain,
> Go, Winter, and come not again.

On Candlemas candles were blessed to symbolize the Purification of the Virgin. The blessed candles were then used throughout the year for private devotions, such as the house candle that burned at a sick bed, and for protective magic. In Germany candles were lit during bad storms, the smoke from an extinguished Candlemas taper expelled the devil from a house, women in childbirth had red candles burn near their hands and feet to assist them, and crosses made of melted candle wax were placed over stalls or on wagons and plows for protection.

The most revealing association between fertility and the Purification of the Virgin festival can be found in the Festival of the Twelve Marys, celebrated in Venice until the late fourteenth century and in a reduced form long after that. In the festival twelve wooden effigies, dressed in jewels and crowns provided by the city government and called the Marys, were paraded in an elaborate gondola procession along the canals of the city. There was a dramatic re-enactment of the annunciation by some priests, a formal homage by young bachelors to the eligible women of each neighborhood, and several days of gluttonous banquets and lusty drinking, in short a barely Christianized fertility rite. Local legend associated the celebration with an ancient practice whereby the city gave dowries to twelve poor but deserving young girls every year on January 31. One year a gang of pirates from Trieste, tempted by the virgins, their dowries, and the gems with which they were adorned on the occasion broke up the ceremony, abducted the brides, and stole their dowry boxes. A group of Venetian carpenters chased after the pirates, saved the women, and recovered all the riches.

Both ritual and legend of the Festival of the Twelve Marys projected a defensive view of sexuality and the community's obligation to protect its women. The Triestines, the Venetians' competitors in the Adriatic, were imagined to be dangerous predators and potential rapists of Venetian women. In such ways religious rites helped form community identities around the powerful emotions of sexual jealousy. Such identities were constructed at the expense of some imagined alien. As in the case of the Venetians and Triestines or more recently the Croats and the Serbs, groups that sought to demonize each other were often culturally very similar. Liturgical rituals assisted in the dangerous process of identifying and intensifying minor differences.

Several other feast days in the following two weeks sustained these associations with fertility and survival. On St. Blasius' day (February 3) horses and cattle drank blessed water to protect against future maladies, St. Agatha's day (February 5) saw the distribution of her health-providing bread, and the hagiography of St. Dorothea (February 6) told how she protected the delicate young plants from frost. St. Valentine's day (February 14) was, and still is, the festival celebrating sexual love, and finally the season ended with the feast of the Chair of St. Peter (February 22), which was the occasion for the priest to bless oats for cattle and the last day for gathering dead winter wood to be used in spring and summer fires.

The cycle of movable feasts often overlapped the Candlemas season as a consequence of the variable dating of Easter. The Carnival season (discussed in the next chapter) of gaiety and rule breaking, which preceded the Easter cycle, could even intrude into the Christmas season. The Easter cycle proper began on Ash Wednesday, forty days before Easter itself. As Easter could fall on any Sunday from March 22 to April 25, Ash Wednesday could occur as early as February 4. Ash Wednesday began the season of Lent, a period of prayer, penance, and fasting in preparation for Easter. The last of the Lenten Sundays, Palm Sunday, itself initiated Holy Week, which gradually built up the intensity of ritual observances leading to the dramatic climax on Easter Sunday.

In the modern world Holy Week has lost much of its emotional intensity, but for most of Christian history it was by far the most important moment of the year. The rituals of the week brought to memory the history of Christ's arrest, torture, and crucifixion, a commemoration of great suffering that gave believers an opportunity to express their own personal anxieties through identification with Christ. Especially in Spain men voluntarily submitted themselves to severe bodily pain, often induced by self-flagellation in imitation of the suffering Christ experienced through his humiliating scourging at the hands of the soldiers of Pontius Pilate. In many towns the streets filled with moaning and screaming supplicants, their backs lacerated by knotted whips, their clothing flecked with their own blood. These otherwise respectable patricians and artisans indulged themselves in a vast collective release of psychic energy in what Maureen Flynn has called a "spectacle of suffering." Through such rituals the purifying blood of Christ mixed with the blood offerings of the assembled penitents, an act that cleansed the community while it assisted individual salvation.

Sacred performances dramatized the principal liturgical events of the week. On Holy Thursday, for example, a priest washed the feet of twelve parishioners in imitation of Christ washing the feet of his apostles. Everywhere powerful men sought to humble themselves through a similar ritual: the pope washed the feet of his cardinals and pious kings those of beggars, propitiatory acts that inverted the usual social and political hierarchy. On Good Friday the performance of "laying Christ in the grave" took place, during which an image of the crucified Jesus or a crucifix itself was placed in a sepulcher and guarded until Easter morning. In Venice this performance became a vast public funeral for the savior. Bells were muted, churches were draped with mourning cloths, and citizens wore black. One of the civic confraternities carried a coffin containing the body of Christ in the form of the consecrated host, which was later buried in a tabernacle in the great basilica of St. Mark, and the little symbolic tomb was officially sealed by the doge, who was the head of the republic.

The scene on Easter morning contrasted with the somberness of Good Friday. Participants now appeared in golden robes rather than black mourning, the greatest treasures of the basilica – golden chalices and jeweled reliquaries – were placed out on the high altar, and, in what is still a stunning spectacle to see, the brilliant ruby- and emerald-decorated altar panel, itself hammered out of gold and normally hidden from the eyes of the vulgar, was turned around to gleam upon the assembled officials and ecclesiastics. The drama included a chanted re-enactment of the discovery of the empty tomb of Christ: knocking at the door a priest asked to see the crucified Jesus of Nazareth, but a choir of singers impersonating the angel replied, "He is not here; for he has risen, just as he said. So proclaim the news again and again, for he is risen." Breaking the official seal on the tabernacle, a priest found the box empty and intoned, "Christ has risen."

The desire to create verisimilitude to the biblical account was never more systematic than during Holy Week, one of the cradles of the European theatrical tradition. Dramatic realism was particularly pronounced in Germany. Priests in Bamberg and Nuremberg rolled a stone across the door of the tomb in literal imitation of the biblical narrative. In Essen at the point where the priest read the passage, "they divided my garments among them," two canons tore an altar cloth in half. On Wednesday, Thursday, and Friday evenings Judas became a particular object of contempt in the popular custom of driving his spirit from the churches by employing rattles, hammers, flails, clappers, clubs, and other noise-makers to scare him away in a barely controlled performance involving the entire congregation. In Leipzig an early morning procession of children and a day-long tumult mocked the betrayer of the savior. Many towns re-enacted the discovery of the empty tomb, often displaying a cloth representing the holy shroud in which Christ's body had been wrapped during his short death.

Whether through systematic flagellation or sacred performances, Holy Week rituals attempted to stimulate believers to an intense emotional pitch. In many places we read how many actually experienced the blackest grief and most horrible apprehension from witnessing the symbolic nailing of Christ to a cross, imagining his cries, acknowledging the moment of his death. On Sunday morning their mood shifted to delirious joy, a foretaste of the joys of salvation. Before the late sixteenth century, in fact, most Catholics took communion only once a year on Easter Sunday: the whole liturgical cycle reached its fulfillment on Easter at the moment when each communicant ate the flesh of the resurrected Christ. The disciplining during Lent of their sinful physical bodies prepared Christians to ingest the perfected body of God in a moment of dramatic personal and often collective catharsis. Although the emotions of lay believers might have been cleverly manipulated by these rituals, there is no reason to doubt the authenticity and force of the response.

The Easter liturgical season, which stretched beyond Easter Sunday to Pentecost in June, completed the cycle of movable feasts and the busy festive half of the year. Just as Easter was preceded by forty days of penance during Lent, so it was followed by forty days of rejoicing, leading up to the feast of the Ascension. Whereas the liturgical season before Easter marked Christ's life and mission as a man on earth, the period after commemorated the events that followed his singular resurrection. Ascension, which marked the moment when Christ's resurrected body ascended to heaven, completed the liturgical re-enactment of Christ's life on earth that began at Christmas, and there was a neat symbolic symmetry in these two feasts since the former enshrined the birth of God in a man while the latter evoked the mysterious elevation of Christ's human body, given to him by the Virgin, into the embrace of God. The cataclysmic breaking of the hard physical laws of procreation and death, evoked by these events, constituted the dogmatic and spiritual core of Christianity, its essential claim to absolute, exclusive, final truth. One of the great sources of the church's authority derived from its ability to conflate various aspects of time: into the perpetually repetitive cycle of seasons was inserted a commemoration of a particular moment in history, a moment that revealed in its marvelous completeness the wholeness of history, the significance of all previous and all future events. The liturgy brought together the cyclical patterns of the seasons, the linear course of recorded biblical history, and the unmoving stillness of eternity, the truths in the mind of God that existed beyond time.

The week of Ascension, called the Rogation Days or in Germany *Kreuzwoche*, attracted a wide range of supplicatory appeals designed to protect the crops and community from natural misfortunes. In much of Europe these rites appeared at a critical agricultural moment when the spring buds were still vulnerable to freezes and tempests. The typical procedure after the celebration of a morning mass was for the priest to lead a procession out to the fields to beat the bounds, invoking divine protection for the crops and livestock. The sacrament was carried in a monstrance or pyx hung about the neck of the priest who aspersed the fields with holy water. Acolytes or members of the local confraternities typically carried the most prized relics in the procession. In Venice the Rogation ceremonies, elsewhere dedicated to defending the fecundity of crops, were adapted to the needs of a seafaring community in the ritual of the marriage of the sea, which was performed on Ascension Day. Similar to the agrarian ceremony of beating the bounds, the Venetian maritime ceremony assembled the entire community in a flotilla of boats that proceeded to the boundaries of the lagoon, the rich fishing ground and harbor that nurtured the city. As was the case with most liturgical rites, Rogation Days could be adapted to a wide variety of local conditions, which meant that its significance was highly pliable. In many respects, the rituals were merely containers into which people poured the meanings that were vital to them.

Rogation processions were theologically a form of collective prayer, an invocation for divine assistance, but the rituals themselves could easily be misinterpreted. They became the archetype for other weather or plague processions that were organized on special occasions during a drought or epidemic because Rogation processions created the impression that beating the bounds with the consecrated host constituted a form of prophylactic magic. Although it appears that such quasi-magical practices derived from pre-Christian fertility rites, they were mutable in their local function and significance. As John Bossy has pointed out, by the fifteenth century they were often not so much magical in orientation as an attempt to conjure up the spirit of mutual cooperation necessary for collective survival. As a result of their ability to elicit community spirit, the Rogation rites of beating the bounds even survived the Protestant Reformation's antipathy toward all things magical, especially in parts of England.

Three final feasts, Pentecost (Whitsun) falling ten days after Ascension, Trinity Sunday coming a week later, and Corpus Christi on the Thursday after Trinity Sunday, completed the sequence of celebrations that had begun with Advent. These three feasts fell into a tight festive sub-cycle that lasted ten days.

Based on the Jewish Feast of Weeks, which was a harvest celebration, Pentecost fell too early in most of Europe to be associated with agricultural harvests. Instead, it commemorated the gift of the holy spirit to the apostles, employing the agricultural image of "gathering in" as a metaphor for the assembly of the apostles in one place. The idea of a gathering of the followers of Christ came to be seen as the foundation day for the establishment of the church, which was also known as the mystical body of Christ, a living body that carried on Christ's authority in contrast to the "dead letter" of scripture.

Despite its theological significance, Pentecost was symbolically and ritually impoverished in comparison to the more popular Corpus Christi, which in the fourteenth and fifteenth centuries became one of the most important feasts of the year. The Eucharistic visions of a thirteenth-century nun, Juliana of Liège, inspired Pope Urban IV to authorize the feast of Corpus Christi, which he did in a bull issued in 1264. In part because the mass came to be seen as a dramatization of the passion of Christ, the late medieval cult of the Eucharist often emphasized seeing the host rather than eating it through taking communion. Crowds were known to rush from one church to another on important feast days in the hopes of witnessing the elevation of the host several different times (see figure 4). The intensity of the public's visual adoration of the host was surpassed only by the private, deeply sensual Eucharistic devotions of female religious who gazed upon,

Figure 4   Elevation of the host, from Andrea da Bologna, initial to the prayer "Deus qui" of the Corpus Christi mass.

touched, and ingested the exquisite sweetness of the physical body of Christ. Miri Rubin has described the peculiarly female attachment to the Eucharist: "Christ was apprehended in it as a man, a husband, a son, resplendent in vulnerable humanity, in the feminine principle, not as a judge, or as paternal, majestic or lordly."[5]

The demand for visual gratification favored the development of the out-of-doors Corpus Christi procession, which became the centerpiece for vast public spectacles and dramatic performances. Encouraged at first by the bishops, Corpus Christi processions soon took on a life of their own, becoming one of the most important occasions to connect governmental authority to the supernatural power of the Eucharist. In Germany the assembled peasants with their mayor and priest would beat

[5] Miri Rubin, *Corpus Christi: The Eucharist in Late Medieval Culture* (Cambridge: Cambridge University Press, 1991), 168.

the boundaries of the village to bless vital locations, such as mills, bridges, or orchards. In many cities confraternities and guilds devoted themselves to organizing and paying for sacred pageants in association with the Corpus Christi procession. The enormous explosion in the number of confraternities during the late fourteenth century may have been the consequence of a surge in lay piety, or the need for solidarity to face the Black Death, or a by-product of increased bureaucratic cohesion and civic consciousness of the urban centers, but whatever the impulse in establishing them, confraternities gave a great number of lay persons an active role in the liturgical life of their communities. The processions can be read as a commentary on urban society.

The great Corpus Christi processions often included tableaux vivants, consisting of paraders dressed in costumes who stood on floats that were decorated with painted scenes, statuary, and sometimes inscriptions explaining what was depicted or drawing a lesson from it. Such tableaux provided the archetype for modern parade floats and were typically used to represent scenes for religious edification. The power of these processions to engage the interest of the crowds was such that city governments and princes found them useful for propaganda purposes. For example, during the papal interdict against the republic of Venice in 1606, the city government insisted that all the city's religious participate in a vast demonstration of anti-papal propaganda. Several tableaux proclaimed the idea of the separation of ecclesiastical and political authorities: in one a confraternity member dressed as Christ stood above a sign citing the scriptural passage, "Render to Caesar the things that are Caesar's, and to God the things that are God's"; on another Christ admonished his apostles not to meddle in the affairs of princes. In this case the forms of a religious procession and scripture itself served local interests against the universalizing claims of the popes.

In France, Germany, Spain, Italy, and especially England, plays were performed on Corpus Christi that acted out stories from the Bible, Apocrypha, or lives of the saints. Guilds or confraternities typically supplied the actors, who declaimed in the vernacular language of the people and mounted play cycles that in England could take four or five days to perform with each guild taking responsibility for one section of the cycle. The Corpus Christi feast became one of the most important occasions for the transformation of ritual into drama. The transformation had several distinctive characteristics: lay actors replaced priest cele-brants as the focus of activity; the rigid script of the liturgy yielded to more flexible, evocative, and elaborate verbal performances; the location of the performance was transferred in some places from a mobile procession to fixed stages; the center of attention moved from the literal mystical body of Christ to representations of his life and legacy; and there was a subtle yet extremely compelling shift in emphasis from creating an aura of mystery through singing in the strange Latin of the church, incensing, wearing rich robes, and displaying opulently bejeweled reliquaries to creating narrative clarity through miming and declaiming.

Because Corpus Christi was the paramount feast celebrating the transubstantiation of the Eucharist, Protestants tried hard to abolish its celebration, but, particularly in England where the play cycles were so widely popular, there was considerable resistance. Although the Corpus Christi plays at York were eliminated in 1558, within three years they were back on the stage. For several years reform-minded Protestants and traditionalists in York struggled over eliminating Corpus Christi from the liturgical calendar or retaining it. Part of the dispute came from the fact that the organization of the feast had long been the responsibility of the social hierarchy of magistrates and guilds, which invested liturgical reforms with potent social overtones. The abolition of Corpus Christi threatened these established interest groups.

In northern Europe, especially the British Isles, the final festive season that liturgically ended with Corpus Christi extended a few weeks to Midsummer Day, which celebrated the summer solstice when in the upper latitudes the sun never set. Liturgically the day supposedly commemorated the nativity of St. John the Baptist, but in the North there was little explicitly Christian content to the activities, which had obvious pagan origins. Until the middle of the sixteenth century and later in some places, Midsummer was marked by decorations of floral garlands, morris dances, and especially bonfires. King Henry VII regularly paid for some of the bonfires out of his own funds, but the custom died out among his successors. Protestants attacked the bonfires as somehow an invention of popery, but they were too much fun to abandon entirely. Long after the Reformation, in Herefordshire and Somerset, bonfires continued to be set on Midsummer, justified with the explanation that the purpose was to bless the apples. The semi-paganism of the festival permeated even the pageants mounted at Midsummer in Chester, Coventry, Oxford, and London, which highlighted giants, dragons, and hobby horses. When the puritanical mayor of Chester had the paganistic Midsummer images of giants, devils, and dragons broken up in 1599 he caused considerable animosity among the populace who found his pallid substitute of a white knight on horseback thoroughly disappointing.

The second half of the year from late June to December contrasted with the first half, as full as it was with numerous holy days and liturgical seasons. The last half was almost exclusively devoted to normal work activities, the only interruptions being the feast days of various saints and the All Saints and All Souls feasts in early November. Five of the seven feasts of the Virgin appeared in this period as did those of the individual apostles, and the fourteen auxiliary saints. Nevertheless, in most places the local patron saint's feast day could be of considerably greater significance than those of the higher saints. The last half of the year can be viewed as a ritual retreat into the local and particular, the world of work and village or town life, in contrast to the focus of the first half on the church's systematic representation of the universal.

The one significant exception to the particularist character of the second half of the liturgical year was the Feast of All Saints (November 1) and All Souls' Day (November 2). Both days can be closely associated with a fixation on the needs of the dead, who seemed especially close to the living at this time of year. Both had a catch-all character: All Saints honored all the martyrs and saints of the church, whereas on All Souls the office for the dead and requiem masses were celebrated for all the Christian dead still in purgatory. Probably the Irish first celebrated All Saints on November 1, the date for the beginning of winter in the ancient Celtic calendar, and the combination of these two days produced a morbid sensibility, anticipating how the approaching winter would bring greater contact with death and the dead, a sensibility best exemplified in the observances of All Hallows' Eve or Halloween, a barely Christianized survival in Ireland and Scotland of the Celtic festival of Samhain. Persisting into the Christian era was the belief that on these days the souls of the dead revisited their homes as ghosts, hobgoblins, black cats, fairies, or demons and would appear to persons who had wronged them in life. The attempts to Christianize these dark propitiatory rites hardly concealed the sense that demonic powers and vengeance-minded souls hovered close at hand at this time, menacing the living who needed ritual protection.

Although the proximity of the dead seemed most threatening in Celtic lands, All Souls' Day services elsewhere displayed a similar awareness of death. In fifteenth-century Spain the Dominicans began the custom of having each priest celebrate three masses on November 2, creating a marathon of requiem masses that spread to Portugal, Latin American, and in modern times to much of the Catholic world. All Souls was one of the busiest days of the year for lay confraternities and private chantries who provided for the dead. In France, for example, the burial fraternities were especially active in decorating the churchyard, and everywhere priests led a procession around the graveyard and blessed the graves. The intensity of these masses and prayers for the dead in purgatory provided an officially sanctioned substitute or supplement for more popular practices that were ubiquitous in the late medieval period. In some places the church bells rang all night in an attempt to ward off demonic spirits; in Germany children lit candles and put out cakes on the graves to feed the dead ancestors who would return to visit; in England and Germany bonfires were lit in the churchyard, a practice that had once been employed to drive away malevolent spirits but as the dead became less threatening in the eyes of the laity, the fires were explained as welcoming – they warmed the dead souls who had been shivering in their graves. At home food was put out for dead relatives and hot surfaces were covered so that the naked dead would not burn themselves. These seemingly quaint details, explained by the sixteenth century as examples of Christian charity, bespoke a deep primordial awareness of the proximity of the dead.

The week

Unlike the liturgical seasons, the week has remained an unchallenged institution in the secularized, modern world. The secret of the seven-day week hides in the observance of a single day, the sabbath. Jews invented the institution, although the ancient Romans and others attempted to impose a similar cyclical order on the passage of linear time. Even though Jews, Christians, and Moslems distinguish themselves by celebrating their holy day on different days of the week, the biblical institution of the sabbath bequeathed to all three religions their most deeply felt and powerful conception of time.

Regina Schwartz has argued that "repeating is linked to remembering in the Bible, where both assume the sacred context of ritual commemoration. Such commemoration does not begin after an event; rather, ritual repetition becomes part of the event itself." She notes how the exodus was still in progress when God commanded the Israelites to commemorate it in the Passover. More momentously Genesis provides for the sabbath celebration of the creation as part of the process of creation itself: "So God blessed the seventh day and hallowed it, because on it God rested from all his work which he had done in creation" (Genesis 2:30). And God required humankind to *remember* his work in ritual: "Remember the sabbath day, to keep it holy. Six days you shall labor, and do all your work; but the seventh day is a sabbath to the Lord our God" (Exodus 20:8). "And it was good" incants the creation text again and again with the repetitive insistence of a liturgy.[6] The ritual of sabbath and the ritual of work required each other.

[6] Regina M. Schwartz, *Remembering and Repeating: On Milton's Theology and Poetics* (Chicago: University of Chicago Press, 1993), 3.

In his *Elementary Forms of the Religious Life*, Emile Durkheim points out how religion requires the segregation of time into profane times and sacred times, a characteristic that is particularly true of Judaism and Christianity, both of which have transportable rituals that do not require the occupation of sacred sites. For the Jews the institution of a holy day rigidly celebrated fifty-two times per year, may in fact be the consequence of the specific historical circumstances of exile, creating a compensation in time for the loss of a homeland. Although the segregation of sacred from profane times may not be as powerful as it once was, the surviving classification of work and non-work days has remained fundamental to all modern social life.

Eviatar Zerubavel has examined in a brilliant study the implications of the sabbath. The underlying principle behind the sabbath and the week is one of discontinuity. The undifferentiated flow of time has been segmented according to a rhythmic structure, separating the weekly holy day from the profane work days. The seventh holy day becomes, in effect, a liminal moment betwixt and between the "normal" days, a moment that is somehow out of time. Whereas profane time is linear – a continuous sequence of equal days, equal years, equal centuries – sacred time is cyclical, a continuous return to the same place, a sameness guaranteed by the rituals repeated on the sabbath. Jews, in particular, had a moral obligation to enjoy themselves on the sabbath: husbands were even directed to have sex with their wives on the sabbath eve, and the freedom from work meant a freedom from tension and anxiety. Emotions were structured according to weekly rhythms. The notion is so deep in Judaism that it was believed that God gave every Jew a second soul on the sabbath. Saturday for Jews and Sunday for Christians required special food served at a different time on special plates. Sabbath or Sunday best clothing was distinct from work clothing.

The seven-day week established by the Hebrews constituted an artificial rhythm that was utterly unconnected with any other temporal cycle: only February in a non-leap year contains exactly four weeks and the year comprises fifty-two weeks with 1.2422 days left over. It is perhaps this incommensurate rhythm that provides the week with its enormous power to step outside of normal time and to assist memory, to bring mythical events into what Mircea Eliade called, the "eternal present."

The Christian origins of Sunday worship reside in the sabbath legacy of the Hebrew Bible combined with the Emperor Constantine's flirtations with the sun cult. The idea of a rest from labor on the day of the sun gradually spread throughout the Roman Empire, and by the sixth century, Saturday sabbath worship had been formally transferred to Sunday, further distinguishing Christians from Jews. Moslems later distinguished themselves from both Jews and Christians by adopting Friday as the day of prayer.

Even though it is completely independent from seasonal and celestial harmonies, the deep structure of the seven-day week has been remarkably resilient. When Pope Gregory XIII reformed the Julian calendar in 1582, he had ten days dropped from the calendar, which meant that a whole host of saints had to miss their annual commemoration that year. But he did not dare modify the week: thus, Thursday, October 4, was followed by Friday, October 15 (not Monday as it would have been if the dropping of ten days included eliminating the days of the week to which the dates belonged). In later centuries there have been numerous attempts to secularize and rationalize the calendar, as in the French and Russian Revolutions and the International Fixed and the World Calendars, but none of these revisions succeeded in eliminating the week.

The day

The creation of the calendrical rhythms of liturgical seasons and weeks, in fact, hinged upon the definition of certain days as different than others. The notion of differences, which underlay the entire arbitrary structure of the calendar, resided in distinctions among days, which created borders between the seasons and the weeks and which provided the reference points for the two major cycles of movable and fixed feasts. Some days were thought to possess certain mysteriously distinctive qualities.

Richard Trexler has examined the conceptions of time among fifteenth-century Florentines. One of the most obvious patterns was the animosity of the clergy toward the laity's attitude toward days, which did not entirely correspond to the religious distinction between feast days and normal days. Florentine laymen and -women considered Mondays, Tuesdays, Fridays, and Saturdays to be unlucky. Saturday was particularly profane: it was the day on which criminals were executed, and it was apparently widely believed that sins committed on Saturday did not count on God's ledger. The feasts of the decapitation of St. John the Baptist and especially Good Friday were days of notably ill omen. In contrast, Wednesdays and Sundays brought good fortune, so that prayers said on those days were thought to be more efficacious than those said on other less propitious days.

The famous preachers, St. Bernardino of Siena and Fra Girolamo Savonarola, criticized these beliefs as symptoms of superstition. Their criticism was in some ways disingenuous because the church itself had long encouraged the reverential observance of feast days and the sabbath, a practice that sustained the mental habit of distinguishing special sacred or lucky qualities in certain days. Bernardino, himself, harbored a contradictory attitude toward the character of certain days, labelling as a demonic illusion the belief that certain activities such as taking out a loan, writing a letter, starting a new enterprise, or buying cloth should be undertaken only on certain days of the week but also asserting that acts of charity performed on certain days were more rewarding than on others and that sins committed on feast days had a greater taint. Although he considered many popular attitudes toward days to be superstitious, Bernardino nevertheless thought that by believing in the unluckiness of certain days people could make them so. Others argued that the host should be taken only on certain solemn days when it would not be polluted by the sins of daily life.

Even though preachers and laymen might not have agreed about which days were special and why, the attitude about distinctions among days was so widespread that governments felt obliged to regulate behavior by setting aside the rules of normal life for feast days and prohibiting certain sinful activities permitted on other occasions. The sumptuary laws that regulated excessive expenditures on dress and the collection of debts were suspended on feast days. On the vigils of the sabbath and of other solemn feast days the streets were swept, prostitutes were driven from public view, and usurers had to close their shops. Crimes committed on such days received double the normal punishment, since, as well as the public order, the crime had offended the saint on whose day it had taken place.

The definition of what was to be commemorated on a particular feast day rested as much with the local authorities as with the universal church or the authority of the Bible. The control of the shape and character of the calendar was a highly charged political matter, which meant that the decision to honor some saints over others was often the product of a regal decree or civic legislation. In England the feast of St. George spread as a manifestation of the power of the monarchy. When the royal party visited Coventry in 1474, a belated St. George Day tableau was presented that showed the king and queen witnessing a mounted St. George saving their daughter from a dragon. Florence sponsored special processions on the feast of St. John the Baptist as did Milan for St. Ambrose, Venice for St. Mark, and Naples for St. Janarius. The specifically political uses of saints' days will be discussed in later chapters, but here it should be noted how throughout Europe people interpreted local history and contemporary events with an eye toward the saint who controlled the day of the event. When the combined Catholic fleets defeated the Turkish Armada at the battle of Lepanto on October 7, 1571, St. Justina, who had heretofore been considered a minor martyr, saw her day transformed into a major commemorative holiday in the cities and countries that had sent ships and men to the battle. On the other hand, when unfortunate events took place in Florence on the feast of the decapitation of St. John the Baptist in both 1433 and 1434, the city changed its own official liturgical calendar to prevent future mishaps.

The pattern of designating special days occurred at all levels of authority from the pope in Rome to the most humble parish church. On the neighborhood or village level the patron of the local parish was honored on his or her own saint's day by an elaborate feast, called in England a church-ale, in which the entire congregation gathered together in an attempt to create feelings of solidarity in contrast to the usual quarrels and animosities of daily life.

The designation of special days fulfilled certain deeply felt needs in the social psychology of traditional European life. The rhythms of work themselves created a sense of periodicity that demanded a respite from labor, restrictive rules, and habitual antagonisms. Just as the God of Genesis built the commemoration of his creative labor into the labor itself, so did normal human work produce repetitive patterns in the straight furrows of the plow, the spinning of the potter's wheel, or the throw of the shuttle across the warp – patterns that assumed other patterns, the ritual patterns of the days of rest. The opposition between work days and feast days came from their distinctive rhythms that demanded the counterpoint of the other. The designation of ferial and festive days became a source of mastery over life, and it is no accident that governments and religious reformers took the matter so seriously.

The modification of the liturgical calendar of feast days was one of the most disputed goals of Protestant reformers, who by and large succeeded in wiping out the established rhythms by which the liturgy had ceremonialized the agricultural cycle and structured urban life. England provides an especially instructive example because throughout the sixteenth and seventeenth centuries persons of very different religious persuasions contested the shape of the calendar. On the eve of the Reformation there were nearly seventy fast days in the English liturgical calendar, most appearing during Lent. In addition to the official fasts, pious persons established their own private fasts to occur on the day of a favored saint or on one particular day of the week. These were penitential fasts that limited the devotee to bread and water. Fast days were supplemented on the calendar by feast days that required the complete or partial refraining from all forms of labor and a full round of religious observances including a fast on the eve of the feast and attendance the next day at matins, mass, and evensong. In England there were between forty and fifty of these feast days, depending on the region and the ability of the local workers to extend the number of holidays and the landowners to limit them.

During the sixteenth-century Reformation, Protestants concerned themselves with eliminating certain Roman Catholic practices, especially the surfeit of saints' days, and the pagan elements that had survived in the structure of the Christian year. In its early stages the Reformation in England concentrated on reducing the number of saints' days, which was damaging both for the economy and for the sense of the sacred, so diluted had it become through such excessive display. Protestants presented calendar reform as an aspect of social discipline, an attempt to reduce drunkenness and idleness, the perverse by-products of the church of Rome. In 1536 King Henry VIII ordered that all local parish feasts be consolidated on one day, the first Sunday in October. The key provision in his reforms was the elimination of religious customs that interrupted the work routine, especially during the harvest season from July 1 to September 29. Any saint whose day fell during that period had to be content with a token observance involving only the clergy. These reforms came from the top down and met with extensive organized resistance called the Pilgrimage of Grace. On the village level the old holidays had been very popular, not just because they provided farmers and artisans with a day free from work but because they had been a stimulus to commerce at country fairs. Moreover, the reforms demanded that the common people abandon what was most important to them in the entire calendar, the celebrations of the local patron saints who provided protection and comfort, even miracles.

After the Elizabethan settlement, which allowed traditionalists to continue to follow most of the old Catholic calendar, radicals – later called Puritans – demanded a more thorough purge. To them the battle was not just a theoretical one: the persistence of the old festivals preserved superstition, licentiousness, and disorder. The struggle was carried out in a pamphlet war, from the pulpit, and in the streets, each festival becoming an arena for a confrontation among puritanical, moderate, and traditional forces, a confrontation that could turn violent. Although the church calendar was eventually cleansed of many of its supernumerary feasts, the outlines of the calendar survived in such lay venues as the terms of the Westminster law courts and the academic year at Oxford and Cambridge.

Although the notion that some days were holy survived the Reformation and industrialization, the grand liturgical passage of the seasons did not, and the modern world has lost a sensitivity to a calendar defined by mysteries rather than by the demands of work. The loss was useful for industry, discipline, and social control, but the result has been the rigidification of human lives in accord with the mechanics of production and clocks. Despite the many legacies of church time, merchant time has been relentlessly victorious: the modern holidays now celebrate important historical events for the state or work itself, as in the European May Day or the American Labor Day.

The hour

The origins of the daily schedules that govern all modern life can be found in the ritual time of the medieval monasteries. Because he organized his time according to a precise schedule, the medieval monk was, in the words of Zerubavel, the "first professional," forming the first class of persons to subject themselves to a rigid routine of temporal regularity by assigning tasks to discrete parts of the day. Just as the liturgical calendar established ritual seasons and Sunday worship fixed the cycle of weeks, the rhythm of the day followed its subdivision into twenty-four hours.

St. Benedict of Nursia, the abbot of Monte Cassino, composed his highly influential rule sometime between 530 and 540. The Benedictine Rule outlined the routine of work and worship required of all monks so that each task – working, praying, sleeping, eating, and even visiting the latrine – occurred at a fixed time. As part of the rule the canonical hours established the divine offices of psalms and prayers to be sung or said at eight fixed points during a twenty-four hour period. These offices were called matins, lauds, prime, terce, sext, none, vespers, and compline. At each of these hours the monastery bell was rung calling the monks to the chapel to perform the office, creating markers of sound that divided up the day and that could be heard in the villages that often grew up around great monasteries.

The celebration of the divine offices at the appointed hours established one of the fundamental principles of orderly life in the West, punctuality. According to the rule, "as soon as the signal for the Divine Office has been heard, let them abandon what they have in hand and assemble with the greatest speed," and Benedict precisely defined the moment in the office after which arriving monks were considered tardy. Now, from the first days of schooling all children are trained according to the ancient monastic rules of punctuality.

At least until the end of the fourteenth century, monks and everyone else interested in keeping time followed the ancient Egyptian and Roman method of reckoning in which the intervals between sunrise and sunset and between sunset and sunrise were always divided into twelve equal hours. As a result of this system, the length of the hour varied with the season and whether it was a daylight or night-time hour. This system began to change with the introduction of mechanical clocks that divided the entire day into twenty-four equal segments, creating a different conception of the hour because of the mechanical laws of weight-driven ratchet gears. The earliest mechanical clocks seem to have been an alarm system for sacristans to alert them to ring the bell and call the monks to prayer. The first public clock that struck the hour appeared in Milan in 1335, and similar clocks soon appeared in other cities, making the regularity that had once characterized the lives of monks alone the domain of all. Public clocks meant that not just ritual life but business negotiations and civic affairs could be structured according to an ethic of punctuality. With the spread of clocks, merchant time and church time merged, creating a tenacious hold on daily life.

The spread of the monastic sense of ritual time has had indelible consequences for the modern world. First, it spread the principle of discipline, the subjection of the individual to the structures of time that followed mechanical laws rather than seasonal and diurnal cycles. Second, it helped to build social solidarity, coordinating the activities of all members of a community according to the same schedule. In the monastery the intention was to create a sense of community among the monks by having each of them perform the same task at the same time. As the synchronization of tasks spread from the monasteries to the villages and towns, establishing schedules in which everyone ate, worked, and slept at the same times, the solidarity of the monastery has become an attribute of modern citizenship.

Although the theologians demanded a strict separation of sacred time and profane time, each, in fact, generated the other. The liturgical seasons helped coordinate the cycles of agricultural work, and monastic clocks assisted the regimentation of the merchant's daily routine. The ritual calendar intertwined with the most elemental sources of power – economic production, community solidarity, the inculcation of disci-pline – becoming an object of contention, manipulation, and resistance according to the needs of ecclesiastical and political authorities. Perhaps one of the most striking aspects of the ritual calendar was the way in which it structured the expression of the deep emotions of grief, love, and hope according to a seasonal and weekly, even hourly pattern. The expanding control of ritual structures of time over the lives of people created the need for less-structured outlets, for liminal moments entirely outside of the normal rules of time. Such outlets were provided by Carnival and carnivalesque festivals, to which we now turn.

BIBLIOGRAPHY

Entries marked with a * designate recommended readings for new students of the subject.

*Cressy, David. *Bonfires and Bells: National Memory and the Protestant Calendar in Elizabethan and Stuart England.* Berkeley and Los Angeles: University of California Press, 1989. A highly readable examination of the implications of calendar reform in England.

Flynn, Maureen. "The Spectacle of Suffering in Spanish Streets." In *City and Spectacle in Medieval Europe.* Edited by Barbara A. Hanawalt and Kathryn L. Reyerson. Minneapolis: University of Minnesota Press, 1994. Pp. 153–68. A disturbing account of the religious value of ritualized suffering in Spanish society.

*Harper, John. *The Forms and Orders of Western Liturgy from the Tenth to the Eighteenth Century: A Historical Introduction and Guide for Students and Musicians.* Oxford: Clarendon Press, 1991. An excellent introduction to the sometimes arcane field of liturgical studies.

*Le Goff, Jacques. "Merchant's Time and Church's Time in the Middle Ages." In *Time, Work, & Culture in the Middle Ages.* Translated by Arthur Goldhammer. Chicago: University of Chicago Press, 1980. Pp. 29–42. A classic essay that provides an essential beginning point for understanding medieval conceptions of time.

Muir, Edward. *Civic Ritual in Renaissance Venice.* Princeton: Princeton University Press, 1981. An analysis of the relationship between local myths and ritual performances.

Pfaff, Richard W. *Medieval Latin Liturgy: A Select Bibliography.* Toronto: University of Toronto Press, 1982. The best work of its kind.

Phythian-Adams, Charles. "Ceremony and the Citizen: The Communal Year at Coventry 1450–1500." In *Crisis and Order in English Towns, 1500–1700: Essays in Urban History.* Edited by Peter Clark and Paul Slack. Toronto: University of Toronto Press, 1972. Pp. 57–85. Although conceptually dated, a still useful examination of the role of ritual in assisting civic order.

Rubin, Miri. *Corpus Christi: The Eucharist in Late Medieval Culture.* Cambridge: Cambridge University Press, 1991. A sometimes difficult but comprehensive and detailed account of the spread of the cult of the Eucharist.

*Scribner, R. W. "Ritual and Popular Religion in Catholic Germany at the Time of the Reformation." In *Popular Culture and Popular Movements in Reformation Germany.* London: Hambledon Press, 1987. Pp. 17–48. A very influential article that demonstrates how ritualized the Protestant Reformation really was.

Trexler, Richard C. *Public Life in Renaissance Florence.* New York: Academic Press, 1980. See chapter 2 for his discussion of time.

*Watts, Alan W. *Myth and Ritual in Christianity.* Boston: Beacon Press, 1968. A useful explanation of the mythology behind the liturgical calendar, but the account is notably ahistorical and should be consulted with caution.

Zerubavel, Eviatar. *Hidden Rhythms: Schedules and Calendars in Social Life.* Chicago: University of Chicago Press, 1981. A masterful sociological examination of calendrical time that is especially strong working out the legacy of the Hebrew calendar.

   The Seven Day Circle: The History and Meaning of the Week. New York: Free Press, 1985.

Part II

Rituals of the body

Some of the most compelling glimpses into the lives of peasants and common people during the Renaissance can be found in the paintings of the Flemish artist, Pieter Brueghel the Elder. His *Battle between Carnival and Lent* (1559) not only depicts a wide variety of popular games, but it also allegorizes a cosmic struggle between the two festive seasons that represent contrasting aspects of human life (see figure 5) – Carnival, the pleasures of the flesh, and Lent, the constraints of piety and reason. Falling just before Lent, Carnival comprises as much as a week of wild self-indulgence and gluttony, culminating with a drunken day of play on Fat Tuesday (Shrove Tuesday, *mardi gras*, *Fastnacht*). Beginning the next day on Ash Wednesday, Lent embraces the forty-day period of abstinence and penance that precedes Easter.

In the foreground of Brueghel's painting are two ill-formed processions led by personifications of Carnival and Lent who are about to joust with makeshift spears. A grossly fat man riding a wine barrel represents the King of Carnival. Crowning his head is a crow-meat pie, from which someone has taken a bite, and for a spear he wields a roasting spit that skewers a pig's head, a chicken, and sausage links. Affixed to the wine barrel is a large ham, which serves as his coat-of-arms, and the followers in his train carry or wear food or cooking utensils: one man wears a kettle for a helmet and a "nun" has a huge tray on her head bearing waffles, pancakes, and a roll. Behind the procession a woman cooks waffles over an open fire, and to the far left is a tavern. As the first of its attributes Carnival celebrates drinking and eating, especially the consumption of rich, delicious meats and sweets.

The King of Carnival sports a huge codpiece and wears on his belt a long knife which hangs suggestively between his legs. As a second attribute, then, Carnival connotes phallic pleasure and fertility.

Next to the wine barrel playing cards are scattered on the ground. At the bottom left two men throw dice and above them others dance and frolic in a farce. In the background others can be seen playing a variety of games, sports, and pantomimes. Carnival's third attribute acclaims

81

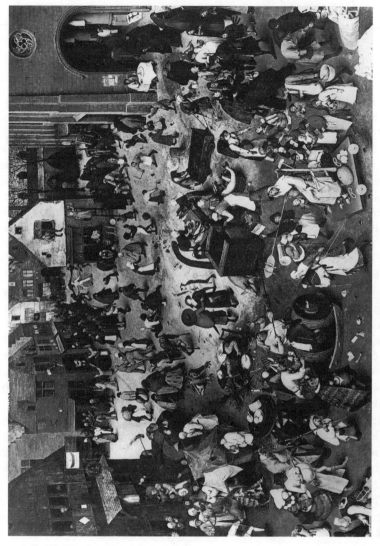

Figure 5   Pieter Brueghel the Elder, *Battle between Carnival and Lent.*

play itself – the desire for risky, competitive, and theatrical entertainment. The play of Carnival is located in the town square, the marketplace where neighbors contracted business deals, made friends and enemies, flirted, arranged marriages, and argued – in short where they lived the life of the community.

Food, sex, and play comprise the bodily pleasures, and Carnival celebrates, in particular, the desires and drives associated with the belly and genitals, what might be called the lower body. Eating food and having sex may be understood as bodily functions, ways in which the borders of the human body are breached through ingestion and phallic penetration. The orientation toward the lower body means that as a commentary on social life, Carnival denigrates pretensions, formality, and authority: the Carnival King replaces the symbol of regal authority with a humble symbol by wearing a crow-meat pie for his crown. To the triad of food, sex, and play should be added a fourth attribute of violence, which is suggested by the representation of a mock joust or battle. Centered as it is on the body, Carnival invokes not only bodily pleasure but also violent social conflict and protest. Throughout the early modern period, Carnival and carnivalesque festivals were often the occasions for violence, and the forms the violence took sometimes borrowed from Carnival motifs. For example, eating can be a playful experience as Brueghel's painting depicts, but the meat on the table is the result of violence against an animal. Carnival festivity served as a reminder of this paradox.

The right side of the painting is devoted to the motifs of Lent. The emaciated personification of Lent sits on a meager throne, which is perched on a wheeled cart, pulled by a monk and nun. For his sword Lent wields a long-handled paddle, adorned with two bony fish. At his feet are pieces of unleavened bread and pretzels. In contrast to Carnival's gluttony, Lenten food is spare and plain, as befits an extended period of fasting. Fish displaces meat, the water from a well substitutes for wine. In the parade following the figure of Lent, persons offer alms to beggars and cripples, and others reverently proceed from a church in the right background. Lent does not represent so much starvation as abstinence and pious self control, the triumph over the desires of the lower body by the intellect and spirit, understood to be located in the head and upper body.

The figurative battle between the lower and upper body, between sensual pleasure and temperance, became a major festive, literary, and theatrical theme during the Renaissance. On the one hand, Carnival and carnivalesque festivals, such as May Day and Midsummer's Eve, played a central role in the culture of everyday life that was shared by all the classes, while on the other, inculcating self-restraint increasingly concerned religious reformers, governmental magistrates, and aristo-cratic proponents of courtly manners. At the most rudimentary level the dichotomy between the lower and upper body was represented through competing ritual behavior and formalized gestures of the body as in the etiquette of dining, courting, playing games, and fighting.

3   Carnival and the lower body

In 1580 in Romans, France, a peculiar event took place. During Carnival, as Emmanuel Le Roy Ladurie has reconstructed the events, the lively festivities degenerated into a confrontation between members of the popular faction of craftsmen and the local notables. On Candlemas, which fell during the Carnival season that year, the leader of the artisans showed up to a meeting of the town council dressed as a bear and proceeded to take a seat above his station, a mocking action typical of Carnival season. The judge who led the opposing elite faction, however, chose to interpret this gesture as a threatening demand for power. On the following day, 600 working men from the cloth trades marched through the streets fully armed in a demonstration, which heightened the climate of suspicion that a popular rebellion was at hand. For several days there were dances in the streets, including some involving the swinging of naked swords or the carrying of rakes, brooms, and flails for threshing wheat, all emblems of violence. The flail bearers wore death shrouds, which had traditionally signified their role in beating grain to death, that is acting out the death of the old growing season so that the new one could flourish.

On this occasion the flail bearers introduced an ominous new chant to their usual dance. As they marched through the streets swinging their flails, they called out that within three days the flesh of Christians would be on sale for six *deniers* a pound, and with a macabre sense of humor the marchers offered what they said was the flesh of corpses for the bystanders to eat. Although this cannibalistic offering could have been interpreted as a traditional reference to how the living were nourished by the dead, the notables of the town took it as an act of intimidation, which it probably was. By *mardi gras* proper the elite, organized in their Partridge Club, ambushed members of the popular faction, who were masquerading as sheep and capons. Several of the artisans were killed or imprisoned.

To modern eyes the events that took place in Romans during Carnival in 1580 look quite bizarre. Why should an episode of violent civil strife take place during the most fun-filled holiday of the year? Why would threats and even political ambitions be encoded in festive images? The episode looks even stranger when one discovers that the Carnival ambush was part of the struggle between Catholics and Protestants that comprises the French Wars of Religion, even though on the surface there hardly seems to be any religious content at all to the event.

When observed in the context of time, however, the Carnival in Romans appears rather typical of the ways in which people represented their hopes and desires through festive performances. Festivity, Carnival in particular, provided the occasion for public gatherings and supplied a ritual vocabulary and syntax for communicating ideas. To understand what was going on, one must learn to read the language of festivity. Carnival language derived its vocabulary from the human body and its processes, which meant that the image of cannibalism, of eating another human being, helped express anger and encoded the desire for revenge. Understanding the syntax of the body as it was constructed in Carnival helps explain how a festival could dramatically shift from creating a sense of community to destroying it through violence. Samuel Kinser has pointed out how festive representations "embodied" both the psyche of the individual and the structures and processes of society. The key to unraveling the language of the body is in paying careful attention to the sensory nature of Carnival imagery. As Caroline Walker Bynum put it, "however we construct it and whatever it stands for to us, body is what we've got."[1]

Carnival

Among all the popular lay festivals Carnival presents the archetypical form against which others can be measured. It produced the richest symbolic imagery; had the greatest influence on European culture, especially on comic drama; and celebrated the materiality of everyday life, the realm of the body. Carnivals varied enormously from place to place and time to time, following local interests and traditions on the one hand and responding to changing political and economic circum-stances on the other. Christian Carnival paralleled Jewish Purim, and in areas where the two communities lived in close proximity to one another, such as Spain, Provence, or Rome, each influenced the other. Carnival proper was more popular in southern than in northern Europe, probably because in Sweden or Scotland February is not a pleasant time to frolic outside, but Carnival-like festivals were celebrated in the North

[1] Caroline Walker Bynum, *Fragmentation and Redemption: Essays on Gender and the Human Body in Medieval Religion* (New York: Zone Books, 1991), 19.

during the spring and summer. No particular Carnival can represent all others, but certain themes reoccurred widely and frequently enough to be seen as characteristic.

Many Carnival rites concerning fertility, death, and the arrival of spring seem to echo agrarian rituals, but most of the information about Carnival comes from cities, especially German, French, Spanish, and Italian cities. In those cities the Carnival season began in January, sometimes in late December as an extension of the Christmas season, and gradually intensified until Fat Tuesday itself, the day before Ash Wednesday. In many locales there were both official celebrations – such as processions or parades, competitions, and plays – and unofficial ones, such as neighborhood sports and private balls or banquets. Nuremberg, Rome, Florence, Naples, Montpellier, Seville, Barcelona, and many other cities had well-documented, highly popular Carnivals, but none were as famous as those of Venice, which by the seventeenth century attracted tourists from all over Europe.

The centerpiece of the official rituals of Carnival in Venice consisted of the ritualized chase and slaughter of twelve pigs and a bull in the small square next to the Palace of the Doges. Although the butchering of pigs to make sausages and chitterlings was a seasonal chore attached to Carnival throughout much of Europe, in Venice it became ritualized into an elaborate allegory of justice and domination. The animals underwent a formal judicial sentencing procedure carried out in a mock serious manner. After being herded into the courtroom and condemned to death, they were taken to a pen at the usual place of execution, where the "executioners" (who were actually blacksmiths) had to chase and capture them before they were beheaded. Later a group of octogenarian senators retired to their meeting hall to smash with cudgels miniature wooden castles, said to be reminders of Friulan fortresses destroyed by Venetian armies in the twelfth century. After a visiting bishop laughed himself silly at what he thought was an absurd practice, the government tried to abolish the ritual, but the pig slaughter was so popular that it persisted despite the hostility of many high officials. The official embarrassment, which intensified during the sixteenth century, provides a useful indicator of the ways in which the upper classes in sophisticated Venice began to separate themselves from the kinds of mass amusements that only a century before they had enjoyed with the same evident pleasure as youthful carpenters and fishermen. The interest of the Venetian Carnival ritual lies in the way in which the peculiarly carnivalesque preoccupation with eating and violence, presented by the public execution of pigs and bulls, came to be interpreted in ways useful to the regime.

Other entertainments proliferated around the pig slaughter: fireworks displays, acrobatic shows, and daredevil high-wire acts. In the neighborhoods there were bull chases and boat races, balls and pageants, which consisted of mimed shows on themes such as the battle between civilization and wildness, the temptations of the Goddess of Love, the fall of Troy, and the pursuit of nymphs by giants. During the early sixteenth century, festival clubs for aristocratic youths, called Companies of the Hose from the distinctively colored tights they wore, organized the production of comedies. At first they resurrected the classical comedies of Plautus and Terence, but during the 1520s several of the clubs commissioned plays by Ruzante, a brilliant dramatist who employed peasant characters to satirize and sometimes bitterly criticize the pretensions of the upper classes. Linda Carroll has shown that until his satire went too far and he disappeared from the Venetian stage, Ruzante explored more fully than anyone else the tense knot of social animosities at the core of Carnival culture. His depictions of the persistent hunger of the peasants, who would sell their bodies and their honor for a piece of bread, added a bitter taste to the gluttonous banquets that the upper classes enjoyed during Carnival. Later in the century the *commedia dell'arte* introduced a repertoire of masked characters who appeared in plays and were widely imitated by casual maskers in the streets. The boastful Captain, pedantic Gratiano, and the clever servants Harlequin and Pulcinella turned up everywhere during Carnival. By the seventeenth century Venetian Carnival had become a major tourist attraction, transforming Venice into a city of pleasure and leisure, full of courtesans, gaming houses, and a vast range of theatrical entertainments. This was the environment that gave birth to grand opera, the ultimate blending of theater, music, ballet, and set-design. In the seventeenth and eighteenth centuries, at least 1,632 different operas were performed in Venice. Even though Venetian Carnival evolved into the centerpiece of the tourism and entertainment industries, it never seems to have lost its significance for the local people during the early modern period.

The word "Carnival" is apparently derived from *carne*, which means "flesh," and *levare*, which means "to take away"; hence Carnival literally means "the taking away of flesh," which could be understood in the double sense of giving up the meat of animals and abstaining from sexual intercourse. Lent required that Christians abstain from meat and sex during the forty-day fast, making Carnival in its most obvious form a final fling before a period of self denial. As the Venetian example conveys, however, Carnival could become far more than a moment of indulgence: it was a vast celebratory commentary on the material aspects of life.

Meat and sweets provided the symbolic framework for Carnival: in

1583 at Koenigsberg butchers carried a 440 lb. sausage in procession, in the renowned Nuremberg *Schembartlauf* Carnival the butchers' guild played a central role in organizing festivities, and everywhere the King of Carnival looked something like the corpulent gourmand in Brueghel's painting. Along with eating came excessive drinking. The people of Moscow were especially famous for their Carnival drunks, which made the city a very dangerous place during the holiday.

Not only did the symbolism of sexual indulgence pervade Carnival, but it appears that a great deal of it was going on during the season. Jean-Louis Flandrin has shown that in France the Carnival season produced more conceptions than any other period except the late spring period of May and June. Carnival was a preferred occasion for weddings, and in the early Middle Ages in Venice all weddings apparently were solemnized at that time. The prominent, long nose common on many masks was widely understood to represent the phallus, and bawdy jokes about sausages explicitly connected food and sex. Peter Burke has translated a typical Florentine Carnival song sung by a group of "key-makers" to the women who witnessed their parade:

> Our tools are fine, new and useful;
> We always carry them with us;
> They are good for anything,
> If you want to touch them you can.[2]

Street slang in modern Italian still employs the word *chiave* (key) for the penis. Sexual imagery during Carnival took many forms: in Germany unmarried girls and spinsters had to pull a plow through the streets while men cracked whips about their heads, in many Italian cities prostitutes held foot races (in Venice they had a regatta), in mock weddings men who cross-dressed as women formed the bridal party and the groom might be a dog or bear, and masked men and women in Italy and Spain enjoyed anonymity and considerable license in what they said and did.

In the processions, pantomimes, and plays that characterized Carnival in the big cities, the theme of the *world turned upside down* (variously called, the land of Cockaigne, *Die verkehrte Welt, le monde renversé, il mondo alla rovescia*), an extremely widespread trope in the later Middle Ages, unified Carnival festivity. The very battle between Carnival and Lent introduced the idea of a world in which the normal rules of social order and the pieties of Christian life were disputed and mocked. These Carnival inversions of normal life came in an extraordinary variety of forms – peasants imitating kings, artisans masquerading as bishops,

[2] Peter Burke, *Popular Culture in Early Modern Europe* (London: T. Smith, 1978), 186.

servants giving orders to their masters, poor men offering alms to the rich, boys beating their fathers, and women parading about in armor. Carnival was an especially attractive venue for giving voice to subordinate groups. The ironic Christian text, the "Sermon of the Jews" from Carpentras, portrayed the reversal of fortunes for the Jews forced to live among Christians by depicting young David's victory over the giant Goliath. During the Protestant Reformation in Germany, *Fastnacht* occasioned satirical attacks on the Catholics. In Zwickau in 1525, for example, a group of citizens and youths held a mock hunt of monks and nuns driving them through the streets into nets as in a hunt.

How are we to understand the great variety and paradoxical nature of Carnival? Obviously no single answer would be sufficient. Even those who witnessed and participated in Renaissance Carnivals did not agree about what was going on, its effects, or its meaning. There was often something to scandalize the prudish, such as the rectors of the University of Padua who in 1507 foolishly ordered that the usual Carnival vacation be suspended for the moral good of the students, who in turn rebelled by smashing the furniture in their classrooms and beating up professors who dared to continue lecturing. On the other hand, many otherwise pious individuals thought that Carnival helped make obedient subjects. Stephen of Bourbon observed that in Rome after Carnival all seven deadly sins evaporated making for peaceful relations between the pope and his flock.

During recent decades scholars from many disciplines and backgrounds have extensively investigated and theorized about Carnival. One common thesis sees Carnival as acting as a "safety valve" for the tensions that build up in any hierarchic, highly structured society. The metaphor comes from a valve on a steam boiler that releases excess steam when the pressure builds too high. From this point of view, Carnival is merely an interlude in normal life, a cyclic release of social pressures, or what the social anthropologist Max Gluckman called rituals of rebellion. Such rituals allow subjects to express their resentment of authority but do not change anything and, in fact, strengthen the established government and social order. In a variation of this thesis, Gluckman's student, Victor Turner, emphasized the *liminal* character (see chapter 1) of such rituals. The absurdity, paradox, extravagance, and illicit behavior of rituals of rebellion provide an emotional release, but since such behavior is set apart from everyday life by the ritual calendar, the ritual rebellion actually demonstrates the coherence of the social order as it is. A young Venetian artisan who parodied the doge, in fact, demonstrated the inevitability of the political inferiority of all artisans. Turner, however, recognized that the liminal moment of Carnivals could have certain positive effects, especially in promoting artistic creativity and pointing to alternative models for social organization.

The various versions of the "safety valve" thesis see Carnival as a kind of subplot to regular daily life. In contrast, the Russian literary theorist, Mikhail Bakhtin, argued that Carnival possesses a life and logic of its own; it is a kind of separate reality that is independent of the world of hierarchy and authority. Carnival offers alternatives to the normal world, even an experience of utopia. To Bakhtin Carnival liberated human consciousness and permitted a new outlook by allowing common people to organize themselves "in their own way" as a Carnival crowd.

According to Bakhtin, the basic mechanism by which Carnival achieved its liberating effects was through turning the world upside down, especially by privileging images from the earthly underworld and the lower body, what Bakhtin called the "material bodily lower stratum" represented through "grotesque realism." Carnival images of food, defecation, sex, and violence elaborate in a comic way processes associated with the lower body. Even fights, blows, curses, and insults bring the adversary down either literally to the ground or figuratively in public esteem. Bakhtin's powerful style evokes this topsy-turvy world of Carnival:

This downward movement is also inherent in all forms of popular–festive merriment and grotesque realism. Down, inside out, vice versa, upside down, such is the direction of all these movements. All of them thrust down, turn over, push headfirst, transfer top to bottom, and bottom to top, both in the literal sense of space, and in the metaphorical meaning of the image.[3]

To Bakhtin and his followers, Carnival opens up the underworld of festive laughter and market-place language. This underworld has three characteristics: (1) *ambivalence*, the tendency to combine praise and abuse, as when a fat glutton is crowned King of Carnival; (2) *duality of the body*, the distinction between, on the one hand, the material bodily lower stratum of ingestion and secretions and, on the other, the ascetic upper stratum of reason and piety; and (3) *incompleteness*, the idea that nature is never finished and perpetually requires the old to die in order to make way for the new. In fact, the dominant participation of youth in the festivities, the positive emphasis on youthfulness in Carnival images, and the negative depictions of the old and authoritarian in Carnival lampoons conveyed the sense that the work of nature is always in the process of replacing the old with the young. Bakhtin's theory has been

---

[3] Mikhail Bakhtin, *Rabelais and His World* (Cambridge, Mass.: MIT Press, 1968), 370.

particularly useful for unraveling images in Carnival pageants, for analyzing the peculiar combinations of insult and laughter in masquerades, and for explicating the influences of Carnival on theater and literature, but it is less successful in explaining the complexity of crowd behavior in a wide variety of historical situations.

Social historians who have studied Carnival during the early modern period have tended to agree with Bakhtin's emphasis on the elements of popular culture in Carnival but have shown that the consequences of Carnival behavior for society and politics are not predictable. As Natalie Zemon Davis puts it, "rather than being a mere 'safety valve,' deflecting attention from social reality, festive life can on the one hand perpetuate certain values of the community (even guarantee its survival), and on the other hand, criticize political order. Misrule can have its own rigor and can also decipher king and state."[4] During the Protestant Reformation Carnival players who turned the values of the world upside down during a time of intense religious conflict saw themselves as liberating rather than destroying. What religious conservatives and public authorities might see as criminal behavior was, in the eyes of Carnival revelers, an expression of deeply felt beliefs.

Carnival might best be understood in dramatic terms. The festival provided an occasion, the week or so before the beginning of Lent, and a stage, usually the market square and the streets of the town. It supplied some of the characters, mimed by average citizens who dressed in costumes as wild men, giants, kings, peasants, Turks, or peacocks, in short, something other than what they were in daily life. There was, however, a great deal of ambiguity about who was on stage and who was in the audience; in fact, the roles could be completely interchangeable. There was considerable ambiguity about what a particular Carnival character or motif meant; it may be futile to try to determine the meaning of performances that had the unpredictability of all forms of play. Finally, there was absolute ambiguity about the function of Carnival; what started out as mere satire could easily slip into violence, what one year brought neighbors together in collective laughter could the next divide them in a bloody confrontation. Something like that happened in Romans in 1580. In Carnivals the drama of representation and the experience of real life cannot be easily separated.

There can be no universal interpretation of Carnival that successfully explains all the variations. Carnival employed a set of images of its own that were independent of any particular social function they performed. By pulling down the established, the old, the authoritarian, turning the

---

[4] Natalie Zemon Davis, "The Reasons of Misrule," in *Society and Culture in Early Modern France* (Stanford: Stanford University Press, 1975), 97.

world upside down and making prominent the functions of the lower body, Carnival stimulated creativity, especially in theatrical productions, as well as music and dance, social commentary, and even rebellion. Through the inspiration of Carnival, numerous writers and artists created the forms of comedy that keep us amused to this day. Erasmus, Rabelais, Cervantes, and Shakespeare all employed motifs of grotesque realism to create comic effects in their work.

During the Renaissance in the great cities of Europe, Carnival came to be transformed from a truly universal festival with mass participation to one in which different forms of entertainment proliferated. In the fifteenth century street masquerades by average citizens presented gluttony, lust, and aggression as in Nuremberg where butchers organized dances and music in the streets. By the seventeenth century, however, many town dwellers had learned to enjoy theatrical comedies that employed the old Carnival themes and that were performed by actors, some of whom had become professionals. Now Carnival was not so much *presented* as *represented*. Commercial entertainment in the form of theatrical performances and spectator sports supplanted collective festive participation.

The carnivalesque

In northern Europe, especially in Scandinavia and the British Isles, other festivals took on the characteristics of Carnival proper. In those places the seeds of Carnival scattered beyond its normal space in the ritual calendar, sprouting forth in the grotesque realism of the carnivalesque.

Carnivalesque blossomings were particularly apparent in the North during the late spring months of May and June. Although officially sanctioned by the church as the feast of Saints Philip and James, May Day celebrations in England smothered religious veneration with fertility rites suggested by flowers and fires. The notorious lecher, King Henry VIII, took great pleasure in his court's floral masquerades and the sexual license of Mayings. The common people had fun with setting up maypoles, lighting bonfires, playing football, running races, morris dancing, and flirting. Villagers went into the woods where they would cut down a maypole (that most obviously phallic symbol) to erect in front of the parish church, and many young couples, it appears, got "lost" for the night in the woods to enjoy semi-clandestine love. The historical demographers of England can demonstrate that the months of May and June produced more conceptions than any other time of year.

Like the bell towers of Italy, the maypoles of English villages and towns became emblems of community pride. Parishes put up the money to acquire them, and village elders facilitated setting them up. In 1610 the town of Woodstock in Oxfordshire paid for musicians to accompany the bringing in of a giant elm to be used as a maypole. In the same year in the parish of Bisley in Gloucestershire a maypole was set up near the local church, and the youth of the parish spent the day dancing around the pole. The great maypole of London, called "Undershaft," so overshadowed the nearby church of St. Andrew that puritanical authorities insisted that it be taken down in 1644. During the Reformation maypoles and May Day merriments offended Protestant radicals who described the festival as pagan, superstitious, and wicked, but the popularity of the occasion, especially among the young, kept the traditions alive.

Rogation week, which as we have seen was linked to the Easter cycle of movable feasts, frequently overlapped with Maytide. As a result it harbored carnivalesque games as well as rites of propitiation, described in the previous chapter. In Oxford in 1598,

the inhabitants assembled on the two Sundays before Ascension day, and on that day, with drum and shot and other weapons, and men attired in women's apparel, brought into the town a woman bedecked with garlands and flowers, named by them the queen of May. They also had morris dances and other disordered and unseemly sports, and intended the next Sunday to continue the same abuses.[5]

Male cross-dressing and ribald merriment infiltrated an otherwise holy occasion, a situation that was not unusual, despite the earnest efforts of religious authorities to keep the carnivalesque and the Lenten distinct. The beating of the bounds, which was one of the religious rituals of Rogationtide, could also become a springtime caper for children. When they accompanied the parish priest on his rounds of the fields, even though they should have been singing solemn litanies, the boys often went "roguing," as it was called, and ran amuck.

During June there were several carnivalesque feasts. In many English parishes, Whitsuntide or Pentecost, which officially commemorated the descent of the holy ghost, became the occasion for church-ales, parish festivals designed to make money through the sale of ample supplies of alcohol and rich foods. The rowdiness of the occasion provoked zealous complaints from the puritans. St. John's Eve, Midsummer, which fell on June 24, celebrated the summer solstice with bonfires and massive quantities of beer. In many parts of England, Midsummer included

---

[5] H.M.C., *Calendar of Cecil MSS. at Hatfield House* (London, 1899), vol. 8, p. 201, as quoted in David Cressy, *Bonfires and Bells: National Memory and the Protestant Calendar in Elizabethan and Stuart England* (Berkeley and Los Angeles: University of California Press, 1989), 23.

displays of martial valor, typically through a march of the watch and cannon firings. The image of fire in Chaumont, France, took the form of masqueraders dressed as devils running about the town throwing firecrackers into the crowd. Throughout northern and eastern Europe, the solstice festival of Midsummer celebrated the sun through solar symbols of bonfires, fireworks, and cannon shots. Baltasar Russow, a Lutheran pastor in Estonia, complained about the survival of "pagan religion" and "papal idolatry" at Midsummer at the Pirita cloister near Tallinn:

It is not possible to tell even briefly what a dreadful thing happened here around the holy fire of St. John . . . Nothing was to be seen in any city, town, estate, or village, not excepting a single one, but flames of joy over the whole country. Around these bonfires people danced, sang and leapt with great pleasure . . . People gathered in great masses along distant roads at that time, both nobles and peasants . . . Then also many loads of beer were brought there from the city of Tallinn and from all the taverns and villages in the surrounding area . . . What a great epicurean feast . . . there started by boozing, carousing, singing, leaping, and dancing, and what great skirling from large bagpipes, which had been brought there from the whole country, and what untidiness, whoring, fighting, and killing and great, dreadful idolatry took place there; this no human being is capable of believing sufficiently.[6]

Although one should allow for some exaggeration from a pastor who suspected to find the work of the devil everywhere, these celebrations were certainly Bacchanalian.

In the late summer and autumn, harvest festivals included carnival-esque elements of riotous drinking and eating. In Bologna at the St. Bartholomew's Day festival (August 25) a pig was carried in triumph through the city before it was slaughtered and butchered, a practice that paralleled the ritual killing of pigs in Venetian Carnival. In the country-side the end of the harvest was celebrated with barn dances and rites of thanksgiving, which took many forms. In Romania and Sicily harvest dances centered around a young woman dressed in pure white to whom men paid ritual homage.

No festival, however, generated misrule as stirringly as All Fools' Day, held on various dates in December. In England it was called the Day of the Boy Bishop, an appellation that reveals the irony of performing a carnivalesque feast in churches. Often associated with the Feast of the Holy Innocents (December 28), which commemorated the children massacred by King Herod, the Feast of Fools was organized by the young clergy, much like the youth-abbeys who planned Carnival

[6] I. Paulson, *The Old Estonian Folk Religion* (Bloomington, Ind.: Research Center for the Language Sciences, Indiana University, 1971), 103.

pageants and parties. The young clerks mocked the behavior and speech of the priests during the celebration of the mass. Led by one of their number who was elected Bishop of the Fools, the boys put on their vestments backwards, held the missal upside down, danced and drank in the church, masqueraded (even as women), sang obscene songs, brought donkeys into church, and insulted the congregation. The boy bishop wore the bishop's own robes, miter, and ring; all his companions and even the cathedral canons bowed to him; he led nonsense prayers, delivered a gibberish sermon, marched backwards in procession. In the choir stalls the boys sat on benches usually reserved for the canons, who in turn were obliged to sit where the boys normally did. The boy bishop traveled throughout the town asking for donations. Despite numerous attempts to curtail the riotous behavior encouraged by the occasion, the Feast of Fools survived until the middle of the sixteenth century in England, France, Germany, and parts of Spain.

The Feast of Fools enacted a role reversal of age groups, with the boys performing adult functions, while the adults were encouraged to emulate the innocence of the boys. There was certainly an element of protest against the rules inflicted on the young: the boy bishop characteristically preached against the use of the lash to punish the boys and even declared his hope that all the teachers be hung from a tree. The feast could be rowdy and was always irreverent, which made it a particular object of attack by both Protestant and Catholic reformers who were appalled by the license it granted to youth and the encouragement it gave to profanity. Given the fact that more than any other carnivalesque holiday it was a festival of the weak, the Feast of Fools was much easier to abolish than May Day or Midsummer.

Migrations of motifs from Carnival proper into other holidays "Carnivalized" much of Renaissance festivity, which in many places thrived on the mixings of sacred and profane images. Giants were especially popular in great public processions, notably in Iberia, Italy, the Low Countries, England, France, and Germany. The earliest reported festive giant comes from 1265 in a procession in Alenquer, Portugal, and by the fifteenth century, giants could be found in many Portuguese processions. The most popular subjects for these huge mannequins were St. George and the dragon, which were paraded about in many towns on the patron saint's day. Even though these were sacred holidays, vital to civic pride and communal spirit, a carnivalesque atmosphere of licensed play permeated the celebrations. Giants such as Goliath and Gargantua appeared in many folk tales, which were suggested by the mere display of a gigantic statue in a procession. Such displays associated the townsfolk with the deeds of the giant, some of which were heroic but more often carnivalesque by virtue of the fact that giants had enormous bodies with enormous physical needs. Gargantua ate entire herds of cattle, drank barrels of wine, and pissed floods. Giants became one of the most translatable motifs of Carnival.

The carnivalesque constituted a kind of ritual language that could be employed outside the calendrical series of holidays to serve a variety of festive purposes. It gave persons access to the forms for taboo-breaking, creating a liminal moment when new associations or alternative ideas could be asserted, in part through turning the usual values of normal life upside down. By bringing the private parts of the lower body into public recognition, carnivalesque and rule-breaking behavior made certain experiences stand out in memory and prepared persons for radical changes in their public loyalties. Certain religious sects in Russia employed sexual license to incorporate new members into an exclusive, tightly bound group. After initiation ceremonies, there was a period during which men and women copulated together according to their choice or chance, an experience that attempted to transform the sect into an artificial family. In Albania pacts of friendship among men were sometimes solidified by a rite of homosexual union. Similar customs in Dalmatia allegedly involved bestiality.

During the Protestant Reformation in Germany and France, there were numerous occasions when carnivalesque travesty was employed to mock Catholicism. Some of the most famous examples of the world turned upside down occurred in Wittenberg at critical moments of Martin Luther's defiance of the pope. On December 10, 1520, in the presence of the assembled university administration, Professor Luther burned both the papal bull condemning his writings and the university library's copies of the books of canon law. Even though it was outside the Carnival season, in the afternoon Luther's students staged a Carnival procession that included a float with a sail made out of a giant facsimile of the papal bull and a trumpeter with another bull affixed to his sword. As the satirical float passed through the streets, the citizens reacted with laughter and offered firewood to the students for another great bonfire. In the rekindled fire they burned the mock bulls and copies of the books of Professor Luther's academic enemies. One of the maskers dressed as the pope threw his tiara into the flames. Two months later during *Fastnacht* proper the Wittenberg students staged another Carnival travesty. After a sham pope paraded through the streets, he was pelted with dung in the market square; then he and a whole Curia of cardinals and bishops were hunted through the streets. The Wittenbergers apparently found these satirical Carnival lampoons of the highest church authorities tremendously funny.

In June 1524 the bones of an eleventh-century bishop who had recently been canonized were disinterred for public veneration in Meissen. Later the same month miners from the rival town of Buchholz staged a parody of this heavily ritualized event. A satirical procession boasted banners made of rags and participants who wore bathing caps in place of the berets of cathedral canons and who sang while holding gaming boards instead of song books. A sham bishop had a fish basket on his head in place of a miter, wore vestments of straw, had a dirty cloth carried over his head as a canopy, used dung forks for candles, and aspersed unholy water from an old kettle. After marching out to an abandoned mine, the carnivalesque clerics raised a horse's head, the jawbone of a cow, and two horse legs out of the shaft to serve as relics, which were thrown on a manure cart. In his parody sermon, the bishop identified the bones as coming from the ass of the good Meissen saint.

The ritual vocabulary of the carnivalesque had the powerful potential to be translated from the calendar of festivities to many other situations. Social satire, reform, and even rebellion were offshoots from carnivalesque rites, which provided a model for social creativity. The creativity of the carnivalesque required collective improvisations upon a theme using stock images more than individual acts of genius: carnivalesque scenes adapted the principle of grotesque realism to new applications, new objects of ridicule, new twists of meaning.

Charivari

Practiced in various forms all across Europe – in England, Scotland, Portugal, Spain, France, Germany, Italy, Hungary, and Rumania – charivari was a ritual of popular judgment typically employed in cases involving some apparent violation of the community's standards for proper sexual or marital behavior. At its simplest it involved the defamation of a couple or individual in public by means of mocking songs and a noise made by beating pots and pans (rough music, *Katzenmusik*, *mattinata*). Usually the jesters formed a procession, sometimes in costume or masks, and subjected their victims to a dunking in water, a humiliating serenade, or a parade backwards on an ass. The mood was usually carnivalesque, full of laughter and rough parody, and if all went according to the typical ritual script, the charivari ended with a payoff from the victims, a round of drinks, and an evening of revelry. If the ritual took a different turn, it could end in quarrels, fist fights, even murder.

The kinds of people likely to find themselves victims of a charivari varied according to their reputation in the community and local views about what was proper. Anyone marrying for a second or third time produced an attractive target as did an old man marrying a young woman or vice versa. A girl who married a stranger or a boy who came courting from outside the village could be victimized; dominated husbands, adulterers, and childless couples were all potentially subject to the defamation of a charivari. For example, in Lyons in 1668 when the widow Florie Nallo, who had inherited a carting business from her husband and was the mother of a teenage daughter, married a younger man who may have been one of her employees, the couple suffered a "grand chirivary" outside their door on their wedding night. Unmarried journeymen, including three who worked in the saddle shop next door, organized the ridicule. In Geneva in 1669 a master craftsman of lace-trimming was paraded through the streets on an ass because he had been repeatedly beaten by his wife. In the late sixteenth century, the young peasant Martin Guerre, whose impotence and indifference to his wife Bertrande were widely known suffered a personally devastating charivari during which he was forced to dress up as a bear while his young neighbors beat him. Although charivaris were most commonly practiced among artisans and peasants, even the highborn were not exempt. When in 1502 the infamous Lucrezia Borgia, who had considerable experience in the marriage bed, wedded her third husband, Alfonso d'Este, who had also been married before, the couple called off the usual *mattinata*, which was to take place after they arose from their first night in bed, because they apparently dreaded the offensive derision they were likely to receive.

The ritual of the charivari might best be seen as an enforcement mechanism employed by the youth-abbeys, which claimed jurisdiction over carnivalesque festivities and the behavior of marriageable girls, other youths, and aberrant married couples. The youth-abbeys included young male peasants or artisans who had passed the age of puberty but were not yet married. We have already seen one manifestation of the French youth-abbeys' sexual jurisdiction through their collective rape of vulnerable young women who were then drawn into prostitution. In more benign situations, the youth-abbeys planted a smelly bush on May Day in front of the house of a girl whose morals were questionable and beat up strangers who attempted to court one of the girls in their village. At the very least, an outsider who wanted to see a local woman would be forced to pay a fine or treat the members of the youth-abbey to drinks. Even at normal weddings, they might try to obstruct the wedding procession or burst into the marital chamber in the middle of the night under some ridiculous pretext. Without wives of their own and jealously defensive of access to the pool of available mates, the young men

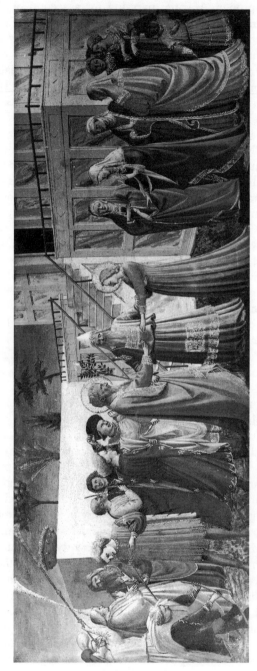

Figure 6 Fra Angelico, *Marriage of the Virgin*.

attempted to regulate sexual access to the young women in their community through ritual and force. Although girls and unmarried women often had special ritual functions, especially on May Day, they did not have a parallel form of youth-abbey for themselves.

The charivari ritual extended the sexual jurisdiction of the youth-abbeys into the bedrooms of married couples. As in all carnivalesque rituals, charivari commented on the social realities of the community, serving to enforce proper behavior through mockery of the improper, but it also attempted to resolve dangerous tensions created by irregular marriages. In the case of second marriages, as Natalie Zemon Davis has argued, charivari helped to placate the dead spouse whose spirit might be tempted to cause trouble. From this point of view, charivari was a form of prophylactic magic. Such a belief was indicated by the masks typically worn in French and Piedmontese charivaris, which besides representing animals and harlequins included demons and the souls of the dead, what were called *larvae*. In addition, there might be children from the first marriage who were threatened, both psychologically and economically, by the arrival of a step-parent. In such cases the perpetrators of a charivari enforced the claims of children on their parents. Male adolescents collectively exercised power on behalf of all children and youths who had not yet found a place in society.

Perhaps the most important problem with second marriages, however, was the resentment of the unmarried young men that a woman had been inappropriately removed from the marriage market by an older man who had already had a chance at nuptial joy. Marriages that included an older partner meant that the number of children to be produced from the union might be limited, a fact that threatened the survival of the entire community in an age of high mortality. So widespread was the animosity toward old men marrying young women that in fifteenth-century Tuscany religious paintings of the marriage of the Virgin Mary to gray-haired Joseph reflected popular ideas of charivari: in Fra Angelico's version of the scene young men stand behind Joseph, raising their fists against him, their faces contorted in anger, with some holding sticks as if they were about to hit the saint (see figure 6).

In Italy charivari practices were closely associated with the *mattinata* tradition of lovers serenading their beloved, as Romeo serenaded Juliet outside her window in Shakespeare's famous play. An obligatory rite of courtship, serenading was often parodied in *cantilene*, which were songs full of obscene innuendoes and insulting words. Towns in northern and central Italy passed numerous laws against such songs, even absolving in advance any father who assaulted a man singing dirty songs to his daughter outside the house at night. In the seventeenth century a priest,

Abramo Russo, composed a scandalous *cantilena* of some eighteen stanzas that questioned the honor of several of the city fathers of Carmiano in the south of Italy. Russo was brought to court by the offended parties on the charge of libel, and from the evidence presented it became clear how effectively a catchy song could smear someone: a witness stated that "When I went into the country to gather olives with my father I would hear, from near and far, a new song sung by the other women."[7] In some situations a *mattinata* serenade would bring honor to a beautiful young girl and her family, but in others the same ritual form produced a *cantilena* of abuse that embarrassed and shamed the entire household, leading to court cases and violent retaliation.

Given the high charge of sexual matters in the closely packed atmosphere of villages and urban neighborhoods where everyone knew everyone else and where personal privacy was unknown, a charivari always played with danger. Like other aspects of the carnivalesque, charivari provided the occasion and a structure for violence when ridicule crossed the boundary to assault or the ridiculed attempted revenge. One of the most powerful symbolic devices of charivari consisted of the use of effigies, which were originally employed as stand-ins for the dead spouse in the case of second marriages. Charivari effigies were borrowed for other rites of abuse against tax-collectors, landlords, mayors, or members of an opposing religious group. Unpopular figures – Guy Fawkes, the Turk, the Pope, Cardinal Mazarin – were hanged or burned in effigy during popular demonstrations. Charivari became a school in which young men learned how to shame in a ritual fashion anyone they did not like.

The case of Florie Nallo, the Lyonnaise widow mentioned above who married one of her servants, illustrates how a charivari could turn dangerously sour. After parading around the newlyweds' house and raising a racket for about an hour, the journeymen performing the charivari broke in the door. Etienne Tisserand, the servant who had become a master by marrying his mistress, tried to bribe the revelers with a paltry sum that was insufficient to supply drinks for the several dozen men in the group. Dismissing the bribe with contempt, they promised to return the next evening. The following day Tisserand publicly insulted the master of the journeymen who had organized the charivari, and when a small group again showed up outside Tisserand's house that night, he met them armed with a stick and supported by some friends. The journeymen responded by arming themselves with tools and weapons, and in the ensuing exchange Tisserand was mortally

---

[7] Quoted in David Gentilcore, *From Bishop to Witch: The System of the Sacred in Early Modern Terra d'Otranto* (Manchester: Manchester University Press, 1992), 59.

wounded from a pistol shot. Although the ritual forms were initially observed, personal animosities and miscalculations allowed violence to take over.

Although the Tisserand murder seems exceptional, there may be no such thing as a normal non-violent charivari, but rather charivari provided a ritual form that could be employed for many different purposes and produced different levels of punishment. Moreover, charivari was a process with an open-ended outcome: it could be employed both to reintegrate a non-conformist couple into the community or to force them out; it could chide them or kill them; and the perpetrators may have neither known exactly what they wanted to achieve nor anticipated the outcome. Charivari constituted a ritual challenge to the honor of the victims, which could be answered in various ways: the victims could negotiate their way out by paying a fine that was sufficient to placate their tormentors, and having done so they might then be accepted back into the community; but they could refuse to pay the usual bribe and challenge the charivari revelers, who would then be obliged to defend their own honor. Charivari was a model for working out social and value conflicts through rituals of challenge and response, the course and results of which were unpredictable.

During periods of more widespread discord, as sometimes happened in the towns of France that had both Catholic and Protestant residents, charivari ritual went far beyond sexual and marital matters. In 1642 in the dominantly Catholic St.-Rambert-sur-Loire, the sole Calvinist family, the Peyretiers, suffered what on the surface appears to have been a traditional charivari. On the evening of the dinner to celebrate the signing of the marriage contract between Ysabeau Peyretier and Pierre de Montmain, a Protestant clock maker from Lyons, a crowd of young men surrounded the Peyretier house, beating drums, blowing trumpets, and parading about. After investigating the racket, the wedding party retreated into the house and bolted the door against the rowdy crowd that rapidly increased in size. Hurling blasphemous threats against the Huguenot faith and stones against the door, the crowd besieged the house. Assaults were repeated for several nights, while the magistrate coolly ignored the victims' complaints, and continued until the wedding couple were secreted out of town in the dead of night under the cover of decoys who were caught and beaten by the crowd. In the Peyretier case the traditional situation that might have called for a charivari – the marriage of a local woman to an outsider – was mixed up with religious animosities and the refusal of a Protestant family to recognize the legitimacy of the charivari, which they considered contrary to their faith.

Charivari provided ambivalent but powerful ritual forms not only for controlling marriage behavior but for ridiculing non-conformists of various kinds because it was basically a rite of intolerance employed in communities that were deeply threatened by any manifestation of difference. Charivari resolved conflict and furthered it, adapting to different functions depending on the situation and the position of the victims and participants in the community. In many ways, the ambivalent nature of charivari violence provided a bridge between the rowdy but usually peaceful carnivalesque and the rites of violence, which created a ritual frame around violent contests, feuding, punishments, and rebellions.

Rites of violence

Most of the time in most places, Carnival, carnivalesque festivities, and charivari expressed the habitual social conflicts of normal life, provided outlets for those conflicts, and stimulated creative solutions to dangerous situations that were fraught with the potential for violence. These rituals typically contained discontent through play and ridicule, but they did not always function that way. The rituals of the lower body, which brought aggression into play, created the occasions for acts of violence. They also became associated with violence by virtue of the fact that the carnivalesque shared a common repertoire of bodily images with the rituals of vendetta and justice, exhibiting a continuum of behavior that makes it impossible to distinguish precisely between rituals that merely poked fun and those that led to killing.

The youth-abbeys that conducted charivaris also had jurisdiction over street fights among rival gangs. Daily life for young working-class men in many European towns was burdened with the constant potential for violent conflict, a situation similar to conditions today in the poorest sections of Los Angeles, Belfast, and Liverpool. Then and now, joining a gang provided some measure of security and solidarity in a dangerous, hostile world. In the seventeenth century in the Langhe region near Genoa, a son of one of the town's elite usually served as "abbot" of the youth-abbey and organized his fellows both for carnivalesque lampoons of authority and for fights with other gangs. In the big cities, gangs of youths roamed the streets at night, getting themselves into brawls and attacking defenseless bystanders. For example, in 1494 a fight between some young Venetian nobles, backed up by their artisan friends, on one side and the retainers of the ambassador of the Duke of Milan on the other left one man dead in the streets and created a major diplomatic incident.

The activities of the youth-abbeys might be seen as a manifestation of

traditional ideals of masculinity, which the anthropologist David
Gilmore has characterized as striving for "performative excellence." A
man who was "good at being a man" followed a script that involved him
in public displays of physical risk, which he met with decision and useful
action. The "good" man was neither a saint nor a bully but someone
who employed aggressiveness to deter challenges and was above all loyal
to his own family and friends. Establishing a masculine identity, thus,
required public performances of aggression that often took ritual forms.

The streets of daily life became the stage for proving manhood
through "performative excellence." Ritual combats and dangerous
sports provided the most obvious venue. These included the rough
French and English versions of football, Spanish bull chases, and
Sienese horse races (the *palio*). In Venice an elaborate culture evolved
around "bridge battles," recurrent ritual combats held to gain possession of a bridge. Staged several times a year during the sixteenth and
seventeenth centuries by fishermen, arsenal workers, and other laborers,
the bridge battles consisted of several distinct phases: for several weeks
in advance of the battle young boys, apprentices in violence, made forays
into the neighborhoods of the rival faction, hurling insults and making
challenges; on the day appointed for the battle individual champions
first met on the designated bridge for individual fist fights; in the final
phase general mayhem broke out between the two sides with combatants
fighting with fists and sticks to drive their opponents off the bridge, some
falling off the sides into the canal below, some retiring with serious
injuries. There were frequent deaths. When a battle was staged for his
entertainment in 1574, the future King of France, Henri III, observed
that it was too small a combat to be a real war but too cruel an
entertainment to be a game. The bridge battles serve as a useful example
of how rites of violence often worked: they opened through a highly
formalized series of rituals that gradually escalated the scale and intensity
of the confrontation, moving from rule-laden boxing matches between
individuals to a general disarray during which rules quickly changed or
were abandoned. Rites of violence created an opening to disorder, the
outcome of which could not be entirely contained by ritual or controlled
by single leaders, characteristics shared by modern sports in which rules
limit the nature of the competition but make it impossible to predict
exactly the result.

The vast complex of behaviors associated with feuding shared with
Carnival a ritual language of the body and of insult. Extremely
widespread throughout the later Middle Ages, feuding persisted into the
early modern period, especially in mountainous areas, regions distant
from the political center of the country, and along borders between

states, including such famous epicenters as Iceland, the Highlands of Scotland, Gévaudan in France, the island of Corsica, Liguria and Friuli in Italy, Albania and Montenegro in the Balkans. In many parts of the Mediterranean feuding constituted the principal framework for all social relationships.

The ritual nature of feuding is strikingly evident in the most famous Italian vendetta of the fifteenth and sixteenth centuries, the 200-year-long struggle between the Zambarlano and Strumiero factions in Friuli, which served as the historical prototype for the *Tragedy of Romeo and Juliet*, first penned by a participant named Alvise Da Porto, whose story was later adapted by William Shakespeare into a play.

Every year at Carnival time tensions between the two sides escalated, in part because the partisans of both factions gathered in the town of Udine to celebrate and in part because insulting enemies and contests of arms were appropriate to the occasion. The "Cruel Carnival" of 1511 was bloodiest of all. Late on the morning of February 27, which was Fat Thursday, a party of militiamen stumbled back through the gates of Udine after searching since dawn for a raiding party of German mercenaries rumored to be in the vicinity. The men were tired, hungry, and angry enough to blame the members of the town's aristocratic faction for their troubles. Instead of organizing the usual satirical pantomimes and drunken sports, the men became the nucleus of a huge crowd that looted and burned more than twenty great palaces. During three days of rioting they killed nearly fifty nobles and their retainers. The Carnival violence spread to the countryside where peasants attacked the castles of their feudal lords, resulting in the most extensive and most damaging popular revolt in Renaissance Italy.

Much of the violence toyed with the usual Carnival themes of social inversion and the butchering of animals. The leader of the victimized Strumieri, Alvise Della Torre, was forced to his knees to beg for his life in an inversion of the normal gesture of respect accorded a man of his rank. After the massacre the Zambarlani masqueraded in the clothing of their victims and reveled in wearing the hats of the dead aristocrats, the most obvious insignia of rank. The looters justified their actions by mimicking the customs of official justice. As one eyewitness observed, "I saw the goods taken in that sacking sold at the stands in the piazza of the city, as if such confiscations had been against rebels . . . and the property sold by commission of the [government]."[8]

The Cruel Carnival rioters most graphically displayed the connection between carnivalesque mockery and vendetta vengeance through the

[8] Luigi Da Porto, *Lettere storiche dall'anno 1509 al 1528* (Florence: F. Le Monnier, 1857), 279.

disposal of the corpses of their victims. Some people were thrown into
latrines or wells. Several of the corpses were purposely left in the street
for days, and relatives were blocked from retrieving their dead so that
the bodies would be eaten in a final degradation by roaming herds of
pigs and packs of dogs. To make someone "dog meat" is not just a
modern taunt but an ancient vendetta practice. Other victims were
systematically dismembered in an imitation of the seasonal butchering of
pigs that took place during the Carnival season. One witness described
how "bloody butchers" carved up their victims "like cattle." Dismemberment deprived the victim of his body, the very source of masculine
identity and social honor, just as a refusal to bury him denied salvation
to his soul.

The leader of the faction of the Zambarlani, which did most of the
killing at the Cruel Carnival, was a powerful if controversial aristocrat
named Antonio Savorgnan. Despite the successes of his partisans in
Udine, some six months later events turned against him and he was
forced into exile, across the border in Villach, Austria. His assassination
by the relatives of his Cruel Carnival victims included a moment of
supreme carnivalesque degradation, described here by a brother of one
of the assassins.

It was by divine miracle that Antonio Savorgnan was wounded: his head opened,
he fell down, and he never spoke another word. But before he died, a giant dog
came there and ate all his brains, and one cannot possibly deny that his brains
were eaten. His servant did nothing about it . . . Since I am a priest . . . I did not
want to participate in that homicide, so I stayed at home.[9]

The macabre detail of a dog eating Antonio's brains became for
contemporaries the most revealing point of the whole assassination, one
that most subsequent accounts included or embellished. Vendetta
murders shared with Carnival and hunting practices a ritual language
that established the forms for killing prey, both animals and men.
During the Cruel Carnival of Udine human victims were strung up and
slaughtered as if they were Carnival pigs or cattle, and Antonio
Savorgnan had his head fed to a dog in an inversion of hunting rituals,
which prescribed that the least valued parts of the prey would go to the

---

[9] Agostino di Colloredo, "Chroniche friulane, 1508–18," *Pagine friulane* 2 (1889): 6.

hunting hounds. By such means Antonio's head, which had master-minded the Cruel Carnival slaughter, was symbolically lowered and compared to the guts of a boar or deer killed in the hunt. Vendetta ritual inverted the upper and lower bodies in a decidedly dramatic fashion.

Just as the combats and killings of vendetta took place within a ritual frame, so did the peace pacts among feuding families require suitable ritual solemnity. Beginning around the year 1000 the Peace of God movement in the church attempted to suppress the violence of feuding through the mediation of the parish priests and the insertion of formal peace rituals into the liturgy. In the mass the paternoster text, "forgive us our trespasses as we forgive them that trespass against us," was followed by an exchange of the kiss of peace. In England in the thirteenth century the actual exchange of kisses was replaced by passing around a wooden *pax-board*, which was kissed by each member of the congregation in turn. So strong were the impulses toward conflict that quarrels habitually broke out over the order of the kissing, and English puritans attacked the use of the *pax-board* as conducive to dissension.

Extracted from the paternoster liturgy, the kiss of peace was adapted to the ritual of truce making. As was the case with the rite of vassalage or marriage compacts, the kiss worked as a physical warranty whereby men joined mouths to pledge their bodies as an assurance that they would forswear future assaults. By performing the ritual in the presence of holy relics or the host, the disputants faced the possibility of supernatural punishment if anyone violated their solemn oath. Nevertheless, peace pacts were frequently violated, a fact that reveals the limits of ritual solutions to grave social antagonisms.

Official judicial punishments attained legitimacy in many ways by emulating rituals of personal retaliation, that is the "divine vendetta" of public justice attempted to supplant the human vendetta of private justice. Until the later Middle Ages, judicial duels and trial by ordeal survived from Germanic law. These procedures put an official ritual frame around what was essentially private combat to resolve disputes or to call upon divine intervention to establish guilt or innocence. Even in business-minded Siena in the thirteenth century a suit over bank fraud was resolved through a judicial duel. Many official punishments retained a measure of popular participation, such as *la scopa* penalty for adulteresses or prostitutes in Italian towns. The offender had to "run the town," naked or barely clothed, while citizens pelted her with rotten vegetables and other garbage; in Ferrara even members of the duke's court joined in hurling filth at the woman.

In contrast to the modern world in which the decisions of justice are public and the punishment of criminals is hidden, in early modern justice the determination of guilt was often done in secret while the punishment was very public. Judicial penalties branded the guilty person, either in reputation or with a physical mark. Culprits might suffer public exposure, often bound or in a stock, usually with symbols of the crime, such as a knife, prominently displayed alongside; there were whippings, brandings, and mutilations, such as blinding and severing ears, tongues, or hands. Sometimes the logic behind mutilation involved a kind of purifying magic: the tongue of a blasphemer would be pierced, the hand of a thief cut off. Some criminal statutes required different punishments for each sex: for a man judicial mutilation was to deprive him of earning a living by chopping off his hands whereas for a woman it was to deprive her of attracting a man by scarring her face or cutting off her nose. Capital punishments produced a gory variety of forms of execution, including death by hanging, beheading, garroting, breaking on the wheel, drowning, and burning at the stake.

When governments attempted to replace private vengeance with public executions, which produced the most powerful symbols of state authority, magistrates paid considerable attention to presenting the punishment as a kind of quasi-liturgical drama. These "awesome ceremonies," as an Amsterdam magistrate described them, surrounded the killing of a criminal with an elaborate ritual that justified the execution, deflected the taint of killing from the regime itself onto the despised hangman, and produced a spectacular warning about the consequences of crime. At first, executions took place at the scene of the crime, providing a warning to the neighborhood and a ritual cleansing of the location through the shedding of blood. As governments became more secure and centralized, executions were removed to a permanent site – Tyburn in London, Place de Grève in Paris, the columns of Justice in Venice. Scaffolds were erected at such places both to remove the criminal from direct abuse from the crowd and to elevate him on a stage to make the execution visible to the public. The condemned was typically conducted to the place of execution in a procession through the streets of the city: in Venice the procession usually returned to the scene of the crime where the sentence was publicly read and the condemned mutilated; in London the criminal walked or was carted three miles through the center of the city from Newgate prison to the gallows; in Paris the hangman and a priest accompanied the culprit in a chariot from prison to the town hall; in Seville an execution procession might involve as many as 200 people and include a series of elaborately staged dialogues between the condemned and Jesuit priests about the honor of a justly deserved death; and sober Amsterdam avoided gallows processions altogether.

The representations that surrounded executions might be read as documents of official notions of justice. In chivalric fifteenth-century Burgundy, hierarchic rank was strictly observed during executions: the Constable of Saint-Pol had silver-embroidered lilies on his scaffold, and the prayer cushions and blindfold were made of crimson velvet. When the notorious Cesare Borgia, whose legal status as the prince of Cesena was highly tenuous, had Ramiro de Lorqua killed, the body appeared cut in two pieces one morning in the town square with a piece of wood and bloody knife carefully placed alongside. Although the people were reportedly satisfied by the execution, they were puzzled by the meaning of the objects placed alongside the severed body. It was suggested that the wood symbolized the chopping block and the knife the tools of a butcher, implying that Ramiro had been butchered like an animal rather than executed like a man. In this case official justice was made more acceptable by connecting it symbolically to vendetta justice.

In times of public hysteria, such as during anti-Semitic pogroms and the witch craze, the rituals of execution took especially macabre forms as officials sought to exterminate a polluting presence in the community. Three Jewish brothers from Endingen in Breisgau, accused of the ritual murder of Christians, were stripped naked, encased in dry cowhides, then dragged by horses to the place of execution where they were burnt. Particularly degrading punishments were reserved for Jews. A convicted thief in Dortmund, Michael the Jew, was hung at the gallows between two dogs.

The most widespread public hysteria, however, about an imagined malevolent enemy within the community was associated with the great witch craze of the late sixteenth and early seventeenth centuries. In 1600 in Bavaria the Pappenheimer family and a few supposed confederates were convicted of having killed and dismembered children for the purposes of witchcraft. It is now clear that these poor innocent vagrants were caught up in an official campaign of exemplary justice, which led them to a horrific execution that epitomized the most extreme forms of judicial ritual. In front of the Munich town hall, charcoal braziers were set up to heat large iron pincers. The prisoners were stripped to the waist, and the executioner drew the fire-hot pincers from the brazier and cut six smoking wounds on the arms and body of each of the condemned. The only woman, Anna Pappenheimer, had her breasts sliced off and the bloody remains rubbed over her mouth and the mouths of her two sons who were also among the condemned. Her eleven-year-old son, Hänsel, was forced to watch everything. There followed a long and elaborate procession led by judges and constables, soldiers, civic and ducal officials, and two carts carrying the condemned chained to benches. At the town gate the convicts descended from the carts to pray at a wooden cross and to receive a few gulps of wine offered by two municipal officials in the only act of charity in the execution rite. On gallows hill each of the men were in turn tied to a grate to have their arms broken by a heavy wheel, but the executioner was careful not to go too far at this stage since he did not want any of the alleged witches or warlocks to die before they had suffered the full range of torments planned for them. The supposed ringleader, Paulus Pappenheimer, suffered the rarely employed, especially excruciating torture of anal impalement after which he and the others were dragged to the top of an enormous pile of brush wood that was set aflame. As Anna writhed in agony amid the flames, the little involuntary witness Hänsel screamed out, "My mother is squirming."

The Pappenheimer execution brought together in one appalling event many of the basic assumptions about public justice. The bodies of the convicted had to be utterly degraded and broken, certainly to cause excruciating pain and to warn others against similar deeds but also to eliminate an individual corrupted body to keep the body politic healthy. The rituals circumscribed a dangerously polluting body with an aura of purifying pain, and many executed persons served as scapegoats, as certainly did the Pappenheimers, for the fear and guilt of the spectators. The atmosphere at public executions was decidedly carnivalesque. Huge crowds of men, women, and children showed up to watch; hawkers sold refreshments and souvenirs; people laughed at the degradation, screamed in horror at the pain inflicted, and vicariously participated in a vast ritual display, identifying in some cases with the forces of justice, in others with the victims, often perhaps with both.

The rituals of feuding and those of judicial punishments shared a common vocabulary of gestures and images derived from how the human body can be degraded through corporeal abuse and dismemberment. Notions of private and public justice cannot always be carefully distinguished, and together they provided an abundant store of techniques employed in other forms of violence. Rebels, for example, could shroud their actions with an aura of legitimacy by imitating the rituals of justice. The violence of rebellious crowds who demanded a share of the power or an end to corruption or merely a better bread supply was often framed by rituals that included dismembering and even cannibalizing hated public officials.

During a period of serious fiscal crisis in 1342, the Florentine republic experimented with the expedient of bringing in a lord to dictate policy. Walter of Brienne, who as a soldier of fortune had acquired the fancy title of the Duke of Athens, was granted the position of lord for life, but within months his relentless attempts to collect taxes fairly so enraged many wealthy families, who were used to avoiding taxes through loopholes in the law and bribes, that they organized a revolt against him. After staging a sham brawl in the market-place to divert the duke's forces, they besieged the duke in the Palazzo della Signoria and refused to allow him to leave Florence unless he turned over his chief henchmen to their justice. In order to save themselves, Walter's own guards forced him to hand over the public prosecutor, Guglielmo d'Asciesi and his son, Gabriele.

They shoved [the son] out of the gate of the palace into the hands of the enraged people and especially into the arms of the relatives and friends of those his father had executed . . . To increase the father's pain, the son was pushed out in front, and they cut him up and dismembered him. This done, they shoved out the [prosecutor himself] and did the same to him. Some carried a piece of him on a lance or sword throughout the city, and there were those so cruel, so bestial in their anger, and full of such hatred that they ate the raw flesh. Such was the end of the traitor and persecutor of the people of Florence. And note, he who is cruel, dies cruelly, so sayth the Lord.[10]

Another supposed eyewitness states that "they roasted [the father's] flesh and ate it."[11] The duke surrendered the palace and left town as quickly as he safely could.

A similarly ritualized rebellion took place in Naples more than 200 years later in May 1585. Rioting began there when the city council decided to reduce the legal size of a loaf of bread, in effect mandating a rise in food prices. The people from the poor neighborhoods of Naples blamed their representative on the town council, Giovan Vincenzo Storace, whom they forced to join a public debate at an Augustinian monastery, which served as a meeting hall for the common people. On his way to the debate the crowd subjected him to a ritualized lynching that borrowed from carnivalesque festivity and charivari degradations. Because of his gout, Storace was confined to a sedan chair, which the rebels seized and carried backwards in a kind of reverse triumph. They tore off his hat, his sign of office, and pelted him with garbage and bricks. He briefly found refuge in a chapel, but the throng ignored the sacred rights of sanctuary by storming in, capturing the hapless councilman, and entombing him alive. Certain elements in the crowd were not satisfied, however, with allowing him to suffocate quietly to death. Instead, they disinterred, tortured, stripped, castrated, mutilated,

[10] Giovanni Villani, *Cronica* (Florence: Magheri, 1823), vol. 7, p. 52.
[11] Francesco di Giovanni di Durante, "Memorie," manuscript in the Biblioteca Nazionale, Florence, MS Magliabecchiana, II, III, 280, fol. 22r–v.

and threw him over the walls of the monastery into the public street. For some time the corpse was dragged around town.

Then they cut out his intestines, his heart, and the other internal organs, which were cut up into little pieces that they avidly divided among themselves. They placed the pieces on top of cudgels and on the points of swords and whatever other sorts of weapons they had and carried them as trophies of a great deed even if it were a horrible cruelty. Many others marched with them displaying wherever they went those abominable relics. They said to the onlookers that they wanted to eat the pieces in proper fashion, but also some of them bit into the raw flesh, inhumanly sucking the blood.[12]

The gruesome triumphal procession wound up in front of the Royal Palace, where the crowd threw what remained of the corpse to the resident Spanish viceroy, chanting, "Here is bad government!'

Contemporaries perceived these two macabre rebellions with their systematic dismemberment and cannibalizing of government officials in light of vendetta rituals and public executions. Regarding the Florence outrages, Giovanni Villani concluded, "The success of this furious vendetta greatly quieted and placated the fury of the people."[13] Likewise the dismemberments resembled the punishments of public justice, particularly as administered to traitors and heretics, who were drawn and quartered and denied burial in consecrated ground. The fates of the men of Walter of Brienne in Florence and of Storace in Naples paralleled the vendetta massacres in Udine and the threats made to the patricians of Romans, with which this chapter began. By literally chopping up a civic official, the people cut up the civil order, ritually and symbolically severing the sinews binding authority and subject, an interpretation of dismemberment cogently expressed by the Neapolitan rioters themselves, who in throwing their councilman's body parts to the viceroy cried, "Here is bad government." By collectively breaking the taboo against cannibalism, the rioters cut themselves off from public authority, quite literally by eating it, and reincorporated themselves as a revitalized community. In Naples, at least, some were said to have wanted to cook Storace's flesh and to eat it properly, one assumes as a civilized sit-down meal, implying that some conceived of the cannibalism as a fraternal, and probably carnivalesque, communal feast, however repulsive such an idea may seem. By making their victim food,

---

[12] Tommaso Costo, *Giunta di tre libri al compendio dell'istoria del regno di Napoli. Ne' quali si contiene quanto di notabile, e ad esso regno appartenente è accaduto, dal principio dell'anno MDLXIII insino al fine dell'ottantasei. Con la tavola delle cose memorabili, che in essa si contengono* (Venice: B. Barezzi, 1588), fols. 139v–140r.

[13] Villani, *Cronica*, vol. 7, p. 52.

the rebels had turned him into prey, just as had the vendetta murderers of Antonio Savorgnan.

The great repertoire of rituals employed in carnivalesque festivities, charivari, and rites of violence presented the human body as an image of society itself, to be fed, reproduced, dismembered, and devoured. A pervasive ambiguity of meaning and incompleteness of function characterized these rituals, making them extremely fertile sources for creative protest.

BIBLIOGRAPHY

Entries marked with a * designate recommended readings for new students of the subject.

Ariès, Philippe and Margolin, Jean-Claude, eds. *Les jeux à la Renaissance.* Paris: Librairie Philosophique J. Vrin, 1982. A massive collective study of games and attitudes towards them.
*Bakhtin, Mikhail. *Rabelais and His World.* Cambridge, Mass.: MIT Press, 1968. Sometimes difficult and often obscure, this remarkable book written during the darkest hours of Stalin's Russia remains an immensely stimulating celebration of the cultural power of laughter.
Bristol, Michael D. *Carnival and Theater: Plebeian Culture and the Structure of Authority in Renaissance England.* New York: Methuen, 1985. Especially good on the Carnival elements in Shakespeare.
*Burke, Peter. "The Carnival of Venice." In *The Historical Anthropology of Early Modern Italy: Essays on Perception and Communication.* Cambridge: Cambridge University Press, 1987. Pp. 183–90. An excellent account of the transformation of Carnival from a civic festival to a commercial attraction.
  Popular Culture in Early Modern Europe. London: T. Smith, 1978. See chapters 7 and 8 for the World of Carnival and the Triumph of Lent. This highly readable book is still the starting point for any study of popular festivity.
Carroll, Linda L. *Angelo Beolco (Il Ruzante).* Boston: Twayne, 1990. The definitive study of Venice's leading Carnival playwright.
  "Carnival Themes in the Plays of Ruzante." *Italian Culture* 5 (1984): 55–66.
Cashmere, John. "The Social Uses of Violence in Ritual: *Charivari* or Religious Persecution?" *European History Quarterly* 21 (1991): 291–319.
Davis, Natalie Zemon. "Charivari, Honor, and Community in Seventeenth-Century Lyon and Geneva." In *Rite, Drama, Festival, Spectacle: Rehearsals Toward a Theory of Cultural Performance.* Edited by John J. MacAloon. Philadelphia: Institute for the Study of Human Issues, 1984. Pp. 42–57. The best single account of culture and sociology of charivari.
  *"The Reasons of Misrule" and "The Rites of Violence." In *Society and Culture in Early Modern France.* Stanford: Stanford University Press, 1975. Pp. 97–123 and 152–87 respectively. The first essay provides the classic

discussion of youth-abbeys and charivari, the second establishes the idea of rites of violence.

*Davis, Robert C. *The War of the Fists: Popular Culture and Public Violence in Late Renaissance Venice*. New York: Oxford University Press, 1994. A superbly researched, fascinating account of ritualized violence among Venetian artisans.

*Dundes, Alan and Falassi, Alessandro. *La Terra in Piazza: An Interpretation of the Palio of Siena*. Berkeley: University of California Press, 1975. The best study of the famous highly ritualized horse race, which has survived from the sixteenth century to the present.

Flandrin, Jean-Louis. *Families in Former Times: Kinship, Household, and Sexuality*. Cambridge: Cambridge University Press, 1979.

Foucault Michel. *Discipline and Punish: The Birth of the Prison*. Translated by Alan Sheridan. New York: Pantheon Books, 1977. The most influential theoretical work on the evolution of judicial punishment during the early modern period.

Gentilcore, David. *From Bishop to Witch: The System of the Sacred in Early Modern Terra d'Otranto*. Manchester: Manchester University Press, 1992. On charivari in southern Italy, see p. 59.

*Gilmore, David D. *Manhood in the Making: Cultural Concepts of Masculinity*. New Haven: Yale University Press, 1990. An excellent survey of the notion of "performative excellence," which contributed to ritualized violence among males.

Gluckman, Max. *Politics, Law and Ritual in Tribal Society*. Oxford: Oxford University Press, 1965. See chapter 6 on rituals of rebellion.

Gurevich, A. I. *Categories of Medieval Culture*. Translated by George Campbell. London: Routledge & Kegan Paul, 1985. Gurevich's work, including the books listed below, has been very influential in isolating the elements of traditional popular culture in Christian Europe.

Historical Anthropology of the Middle Ages. Edited by Jana Howlett. Cambridge: Polity Press, 1992.

Medieval Popular Culture: Problems of Perception and Belief. Translated by János M. Bak and Paul A. Hollingsworth. Cambridge: Cambridge University Press, 1988.

Kinser, Samuel. "Presentation and Representation: Carnival at Nuremberg, 1450–1550." *Representations* 13 (1986): 1–42. An important précis of Kinser's forthcoming study on Carnival.

Rabelais's Carnival: Text, Context, Metatext. Berkeley and Los Angeles: University of California Press, 1990. An excellent recent study of the relationship between Carnival practice and Rabelais's great carnivalesque book.

Klapisch-Zuber, Christiane. "The 'Mattinata' in Medieval Italy." In *Women, Family, and Ritual in Renaissance Italy*. Translated by Lydia G. Cochrane. Chicago: University of Chicago Press, 1985. Pp. 261–82. The best study of charivari rituals in Italy.

Kunze, Michael. *Highroad to the Stake: A Tale of Witchcraft*. Translated by William E. Yuill. Chicago: University of Chicago Press, 1982. For an account of the ritual execution of the Pappenheimer family for witchcraft, see pp. 402–15.

Le Goff, Jacques and Schmitt, Jean-Claude, eds. *Le charivari.* New York: La Haye, 1981. A collection of studies about charivari.

*Le Roy Ladurie, Emmanuel. *Carnival in Romans.* Translated by Mary Feeney. New York: George Braziller, 1979. A fascinating analysis of a Carnival festival that erupted in violence.

Meurant, René. *Géants processionnels et de cortège en Europe, en Belgique, en Wallonie.* Collection folkore et art populaire de Wallonie, vol. 6. Brussels: Ministère de la Culture Française, 1979. The most comprehensive study of the giant motif in European festivals.

Muir, Edward. "The Cannibals of Renaissance Italy." *Syracuse Scholar* 5 (Fall 1984): 5–14. For further information on the revolts against Walter of Brienne in Florence and Giovan Vincenzo Storace in Naples.

Civic Ritual in Renaissance Venice. Princeton: Princeton University Press, 1981. For Venetian Carnival see pp. 156–81.

Mad Blood Stirring: Vendetta and Factions in Friuli during the Renaissance. Baltimore: Johns Hopkins University Press, 1993. Discusses vendetta rituals and their connections with Carnival.

Perry, Mary Elizabeth. *Gender and Disorder in Early Modern Seville.* Princeton: Princeton University Press, 1990. An examination of the gendered nature of ritual disorders.

Rey-Flaud, Henri, *Le charivari: les rituels fondamentaux de la sexualité.* Paris: Payot, 1985.

*Scribner, R. W. "Reformation, Carnival and the World Turned Upside-Down." In *Popular Culture and Popular Movements in Reformation Germany.* London: Hambledon Press, 1987. Pp. 71–102. A fundamental work demonstrating the persistence of Carnival motifs in the Reformation.

Shahar, Shulamith. *Childhood in the Middle Ages.* New York: Routledge, 1990. Pp. 179–82 for discussion of the boy bishop during the Feast of Fools.

*Spierenburg, Pieter. *The Spectacle of Suffering: Executions and the Evolution of Repression: From a Preindustrial Metropolis to the European Experience.* Cambridge: Cambridge University Press, 1984. The basic work on the demonstrative character of judicial punishments.

*Turner, Victor W. *The Ritual Process: Structure and Anti-Structure.* Chicago: Aldine, 1969. Outlines Turner's highly influential theories about liminality.

*Underdown, David. *Revel, Riot, and Rebellion: Popular Politics and Culture in England 1603–1660.* Oxford: Clarendon Press, 1985.

Viguier, Marie-Claire. "Le 'Sermon des Juifs' à Carpentras: Carnaval ou Pourim?" *Annales du Midi* 101 (1989): 235–59. An exploration of the relationship between Christian Carnival and Jewish Purim.

4   Manners and the upper body

In the middle of the seventeenth century, a famous Polish writer of noble origins, Mikolaj Rej, wrote,

> You can tell the attitudes and inclinations of people from their comportment . . . Because when a rustic or cowardly person wants to say something seriously, what do you see? He squirms, picks his fingers, strokes his beard, pulls faces, makes eyes and splits every word in three. A noble man, on the contrary, has a clear mind and a gentle posture; he has nothing to be ashamed of. Therefore, in appearance, in his words, and in comportment he is like an eagle which without any fear looks straight at the sun, or like a commander-in-chief who by his noble posture and proud bearing inspires his soldiers and subordinates to courageous acts.[1]

To Rej manners made the man. They especially identified his class. The distinction between a peasant and a noble, so important to him, was manifest through behavior, primarily the gestures that accompanied speech, the comportment of the body, and facial expressions. Rej's ideal noble no longer imitated the rabid anger of a mad dog or wolf in avenging injuries but stood quietly at ready, perched above the fray of social life, espying everything like a great eagle.

The concern of Polish nobles to cut a fine figure was a direct product of what the pioneering Swiss sociologist, Norbert Elias, called the "civilizing process." In examining the history of manners he pointed to the sixteenth century as a critical moment in transforming human behavior through the spread of heavily ritualized social graces. Adopting "civilized" or "courtly" manners inculcated a high level of self-control over the behavior of the upper classes, who were the first to be influenced by the new ethic. The self-control implied by the new manners required the conscious, rational regulation of emotional expression and physical processes in what might be seen as an effort to subordinate the lower body to the upper.

---

[1] Quoted in Maria Bogucka, "Gesture, Ritual, and Social Order in Sixteenth- to Eighteenth-Century Poland," in Jan Bremmer and Herman Roodenburg, eds., *A Cultural History of Gesture* (Ithaca: Cornell University Press, 1991), 191.

A second aspect of the civilizing process in the sixteenth century came from the efforts of members of the educated classes to reform popular culture, especially all ritual behaviors associated with Carnival and the carnivalesque. Peter Burke has called this phenomenon the "triumph of Lent," and he has interpreted Brueghel's painting of the *Battle between Carnival and Lent* as an allegory in which the fat figure of Carnival on the tavern side of the painting represents traditional popular culture and the skinny figure of Lent on the church side signifies the clergy who were trying to obliterate or clean up popular festivals that, in their eyes, partook too much of the playful spirit of Carnival. The systematic attempt by the educated clergy, in particular, to "improve" social behavior might be understood as an effort to subordinate the lower classes to the upper.

Although the civilizing process began independently of the Protestant and Catholic Reformations, churchmen took a leading role in advocating a far-reaching moral reform that was greatly enhanced by the sixteenth-century changes in religious structures, beliefs, and rituals. Certain Calvinist regions such as Scotland, Holland, and Switzerland and the Quaker sects took the process to the most marked extremes. The civilizing process figuratively turned the walls of the monastery inside out, subjecting first the educated aristocracy and eventually even the peasantry to the systematic self-discipline once expected only of monks and nuns. For spiritual and social benefit, every civilized person adopted a repertoire of manners to surround and isolate their physical body, especially in the three areas characteristic of Carnival license: behavior relating to the consumption of food, the pursuit of sexual pleasure, and the acting out of violent impulses. Now instead of wolfing down hunks of meat, civilized people dined on delicate foods according to elaborate table manners; instead of making off to the woods on Midsummer Night's Eve, young women and men indirectly flirted and courted each other under watchful eyes; instead of feeding the corpses of enemies to dogs, men who had suffered an injury or insult dueled.

The new manners

A commonplace medieval image located Christ's divine nature in his upper body and his manhood below his belt, which suggested that pious Christians should follow Christ's example by seeking the divine in their hearts and heads and by suppressing the "animal" impulses that came from below the waist. Persons revealed how they valued these two halves of the body through their gestures, that is facial expressions, signs of greeting, shifts of the gaze, positions of the head, movements of the hips, and pace of the gait. The body through its postures produces a vast array of communications that can complement, contradict, or amplify the spoken word. These are what Paul Connerton calls "incorporating practices," because they reveal a memory that is a sediment in the body itself. The use of the hands in conversation and greeting is often quite unconscious, and you do not necessarily think before you shrug, grimace, or fold your legs, just as you do not have to recall the words of your childhood teacher to be able to ride a bicycle or swim. The body remembers how to do these things. Likewise, gestures are incorporated into practices that vary from time to time and place to place – men in northern Europe used to cry in public more often than they do now, and southern Italians employ their hands to communicate more readily than do the English.

Gestures seem natural only because everyone in the same society employs the same gestures, but they are in fact learned either through imitation of others or through conscious training. The ancient Roman Stoics established ideal models for gestures that deeply influenced educated persons, especially churchmen. The golden mean of moderation in all things supplied the governing principle of correct proportion: nothing should be done too quickly or too slowly, no action should be too jerky or too smooth, no gesture should be too calculated or too haphazard. The ancient ethic of moderation was revived in the twelfth century in the reformed monasteries, which in turn influenced aristocratic and bourgeois education. St. Bernard of Clairvaux, for example, thought that strange movements of the body revealed a diseased soul. Given the low levels of literacy, however, the medieval revival only touched a tiny percentage of the population.

A more lasting change that profoundly altered behavior commenced in the sixteenth century, largely due to the extraordinary influence of two books. The great Dutch humanist, Desiderius Erasmus, wrote *Manners for Children* (*De civilitate morum puerilium*), which was first published in 1530 but reprinted, translated, and plagiarized in hundreds of editions over the following three centuries. As Erasmus saw it, good manners are like a fine cloak, which becomes in a sense the body of the body, an outward sign that reveals the character of the soul. Other signs manifest in bearing, gestures, facial expressions, bodily movements, and speech also reveal a person's inner qualities. Such a view was a commonplace of Platonic thought, but the great achievement of Erasmus and his imitators was to transform the obscure abstractions of Neoplatonism into practical rules of behavior that subjected the inner person to an outer tyrant who in all expressions of feeling abhorred excess of any kind. The knowledge of these principles meant that proper manners could be taught and that they could be the same for everyone, no matter what the conditions of birth, or as Erasmus put it, although no one can choose his country or his father, everyone can acquire virtue and good manners.

The second book, also widely imitated and translated, was Baldesar Castiglione's *The Book of the Courtier*, published two years before *Manners for Children* in 1528. In contrast to Erasmus, Castiglione's book discussed the distinctive rules of a closed social class, the aristocracy of the princely courts. Whereas for Erasmus the function of good manners was to improve the inner life of the educated Christian, for Castiglione only appearances mattered, and all outward indications of inner feelings had to be repressed. Courtly manners demanded "honest dissimulation," to employ the famous oxymoron of the age. Honest dissimulation meant that whatever you felt or thought, you must behave according to the rules of politeness, and even more important you must appear to do so in an entirely natural way without any indication of strain or conflicting emotions. The gentleman or lady exhibits virtue by acting as if every motion and word required neither effort nor calculation. One of Castiglione's most powerful concepts was that the ideal courtier could be recognized by the grace of his or her gestures and movements. Grace was understood as practicing "in all things a certain *sprezzatura* [nonchalance], so as to conceal all art and make whatever is done or said appear to be without effort and almost without any thought about it."[2] Today we most commonly associate grace and nonchalance with sports heroes who succeed in making fantastic physical achievements appear effortless and natural even though they are the consequence of years of discipline and training. Castiglione insisted that the ideal courtier must be of noble blood, but his book and its many imitators came to be read as manuals of etiquette, which provided models for those who wished to look like an aristocrat no matter what their station at birth. As a result of the widespread desire to acquire some of the prestige of high society through imitation, Castiglione's ideas helped fashion standards of behavior for the modern world.

The extraordinary success of these two books in reforming manners and social rituals may have less to do with their intrinsic merits – neither is particularly original – than with the demands of their times. They appeared at the moment when the unity of Catholic Europe had collapsed and when the medieval chivalric ethic, which required a heavy dose of fantasy, no longer assisted social relations among people who faced massive social changes. As Norbert Elias pointed out, the books of

[2] Baldesar Castiglione, *The Book of the Courtier*, trans. Charles S. Singleton (Garden City, N.Y.: Anchor Books, 1959), 43.

manners created a new common ethic of behavior that made complex and discordant social relations seem less threatening. It gave educated men and women tools for social survival and provided very precise rules that anyone who exerted enough effort could emulate.

The first requirement of good manners involved the repression of emotions, especially the troublesome ones of fear, anger, and sexual desire. Persons denied or delayed all impulses, never admitted dread, controlled and channeled wrath, and sublimated lust through elaborate flirtations. Repression of emotions required a certain kind of lie, a socially useful lie perhaps, but a lie nevertheless. The courteous man lied to others about his feelings and if truly courteous probably lied to himself. This is what Castiglione called honest dissimulation or what might now be called a white lie.

At the same time the gentleman or lady received a contradictory message from the theorists of courtesy who were obsessed with making every deed and word appear natural, neither artificial nor false. A concern for telling the truth necessarily corrected courtesy's requirements of dissimulation, but the inconsistency between verbal honesty and emotional denial created by the new manners forced the courteous into fitful dilemmas and erratic behavior that are characteristic of what modern psychology calls the double bind, the attempt to live with opposing imperatives. The rituals of courteous manners assisted persons in living under such difficult social restrictions and incongruities.

Giovanni Della Casa's *Galateo*, which was the most successful popularization of Castiglione's ideas, best illustrates these conflicting imperatives. It was written between 1552 and 1555 while Della Casa was in retirement at his villa near Treviso, Italy. The book charmed so many because Della Casa chose as his narrator an ignorant old man who brought good manners down from the realm of the learned to the level of the simple gentleman who aspired to emulate those in the most fashionable circles. *Galateo* not only refashioned conduct but made unmentionable whole realms of human experience: a polite man never even alluded to another's wrath, gluttony, lust, avarice, or other unseemly desires, "in as much as these appetites are not evident in their manners of behaviour or in their speech, but elsewhere."[3] In other words those things not manifest through the accepted forms of gentle manners and refined speech should not even register themselves in the mind of the gentleman.

Della Casa also condemned a variety of things that had, in his

---

[3] Giovanni Della Casa, *Galateo*, trans. Konrad Eisenbichler and Kenneth R. Bartlett (Toronto: Centre for Reformation and Renaissance Studies, 1986), xi–xiii, xxi–xxii, 10–11, 19–24.

opinion, the attributes of deceit. Dreams in particular should not be openly discussed since they have no basis in reality and are nearly as bad as lies which purposefully violate reality. Della Casa seems to have inadvertently uncovered the very dilemma of his time, the forced distancing of polite behavior from emotions. The model of good manners, which rejected all extreme forms of behavior, denied even the existence of unpleasant emotions, a denial which in turn encouraged an artificiality of manners that he also found objectionable because it exemplified mendacity. In the post-Freudian world we can recognize that when unpleasant emotions are repressed, they will most likely manifest themselves in dreams and slips of the tongue, those little unconscious statements of the truth, the very things Della Casa insisted should be ignored. But having recognized the symptoms, Della Casa failed to see the pathology behind them and retreated from his own observations suggesting that the situation could not be changed and recommending that readers abide with the customs of the time ameliorated by the principles of moderation.

The proliferation of new formalities – the spread of the polite pronouns in the Romance languages, of ever more elaborate modes of address, of bowing, doffing hats, and moving with measured gravity – provoked considerable comment during the last half of the sixteenth century. There were those rough traditionalists who saw the whole trend as unmanly, even as the beginnings of a feminization of public life. Among the more thoughtful, such as Michel de Montaigne, the sense that the formalities promoted stability in social relationships and prevented violence co-existed with an understanding that the truth in all its unmannerly harshness had been sacrificed. Even those who were not the courtiers of a prince had to cultivate the virtue of honest dissimulation, the trait that required great discretion in expressing some thoughts and feelings. It became discourteous to be truthful. As a result the language of the princely court and of many other social settings avoided meaningful discourse. To be caught in a lie did not so much mean a loss of personal dignity or even credibility as a loss of honor in having failed to manage impressions properly. The best way to manage impressions was to perform the rituals of civilized manners with a certain air of nonchalance.

Most critical for the reformation of manners was the imposition of new standards of rectitude over gestures and the posture of the human body. Bad postures indicated faults: a slouch characterized an arrogant attitude, tilting the head signified hypocrisy, and leaning backwards indicated conceit. To counter flaws of temperament the geometric principles that so dramatically altered Renaissance architecture also came to be applied to body posture. The architecture of the upper body was especially subject to regulation, a trend that made the stoop-shouldered scholar or the congenital hunchback a repugnant image of deformity, even of social illness. Holding the upper body upright became the essential mark of the gracefulness demanded by Castiglione's book. The noble exercises of fencing, riding, and dancing assisted the acquisition and preservation of grace, and these "gentle" sports were integrated into the educational curriculum. At the same time the "rough" carnivalesque sports of football and bull baiting were soundly condemned. For the first time women began to wear tight corsets, thereby forcing their bodies to conform to geometric standards of bodily architecture, and every noble lady in Venice was miraculously, or perhaps we should say chemically, blessed with blond hair. By the seventeenth century what had started as an aspect of a noble demeanor became an aspect of religious righteousness. Moralists and educators encouraged children to be "upright," not just because good posture made them appear graceful but because "elegant bearing" was necessary to escape the moral trap of self-love: by walking with a straight back the virtuous elevate their eyes to God, whereas slouches only see and love things of this world. Uprightness became a synonym for religiosity, goodness, and morality.

The most compelling example of the influence of the new manners on pedagogy is the education program of the Jesuit Order as it evolved in the seventeenth century. Among the many innovations of Jesuit education, which included physical education as well as instruction in manners, was the emphasis on acting. By putting on plays and undergoing training in ballet, students learned the appropriate postures of the body, which was thereby reformed through the performance. As Georges Vigarello has put it, "playing a role involves putting it at a distance in order to dominate it better. Theater is here an exercise in control and vigilance where only noble positions and movements are chosen. It is an educational theory of vigilance."[4] Learning to "play a role" in Jesuit theater not only restructured the entire body and its repertoire of gestures, but the role also became the source of a new social identity. Ritual became theater. Social life became playing a part.

Although the reformation of manners entered the educational program of children throughout much of Europe, the exact forms it took varied according to region, class, and religion. Perhaps the most famous contrast was between the Spanish and French styles of walking, eating,

[4] Georges Vigarello, "The Upward Training of the Body from the Age of Chivalry to Courtly Civility," in Michel Feher, ed., *Fragments for a History of the Human Body* (New York: Zone Books), part II, p. 188.

and gesturing. The Spanish nobles were notably graver, more restrained in movement, less loquacious in speech than the French whose style was reputedly livelier and more exaggerated. Due to Spanish military and political influence on the peninsula, Italians tended to follow the Spanish model, although the conscious imitation of the French style could constitute a form of public protest against Spanish domination. Because of animosity to the Spanish after the prolonged war for independence, the Dutch avoided Spanish gravity in their manners and were seen by other Europeans as rough, blunt, and rude.

The Polish gentry, who in the sixteenth century constructed a "noble republic" that lasted until the partitions of Poland in the eighteenth century, developed an especially elaborate ritual code to distinguish themselves from the lower classes. A command of the ritual gestures of nobility became the essential mark of a class that felt itself particularly vulnerable to infiltration from below. Polish nobles, for example, were contemptuous of football or any sort of ball game, allowing only riding and hunting as suitable for the gentleman.

The extravagance of Polish nobles was notorious. As a late seventeenth-century writer put it, "human life is like a show with people the actors and God the creator and manager of the stage . . . in short, life is like a stage."[5] The elaborate rituals of welcome and departure at the country house of an aristocratic family illustrate the extremes these rituals could reach. A servant of the manor would sit atop a high tree or on the roof of the house to announce the arrival of visitors in time to permit the household to prepare its intricate welcome. After a series of deep bowings and embraces at the door, the guests were ceremoniously led into the house. A contemporary recounted the welcome ritual in his diary.

It was not without paying compliments, without ceremonies at the door or while taking seats. Next the host would rise asking the guest to give up his sword, which after long teasing would be done and the weapon would be placed carefully in a corner of the room. At this moment a servant would enter with several bottles and a glass on a tray; the glass . . . was emptied amidst more hugging and kissing.[6]

Banquets and hunts staged for the guests might last for weeks. Departure could become a considerable ordeal for the guest since the host's sense of exaggerated hospitality required him to delay the parting for as long as possible. He might even resort to taking the wheels off his guest's carriage or hiding the horses to make leaving impossible.

[5] Quoted in Bogucka, "Gesture, Ritual, and Social Order," in Bremmer and Roodenburg, *A Cultural History of Gesture*, 191.

[6] Ibid., 193.

Gestures of adulation and respect regulated relations between the various social ranks. Elaborate hat rituals were famous. To greet cordially a person of higher social standing a man had to bow just far enough to be able to sweep the floor lightly with his doffed hat. The hat also came off while reading a letter from a person of high rank or even when the name of the king or pope was mentioned in conversation. A subordinate would recognize his patron with a kiss of the hand, but this conventional gesture could be unctuously extended to kisses of the chest, stomach, knees, and feet. Custom regulated the nuances of the hand kiss, which was obligatory toward every older or higher-ranking person and toward every woman, even young girls. Politeness required that the person whose hand was being kissed remove his or her glove and extend the hand just high enough to allow the kisser to raise it slightly to his lips. Even slight variations in the performance of these rituals could convey powerful and disturbing social messages. When King Ladislaus IV Vasa was angered by the policies of the burghers of Cracow in 1644, he held out a gloved hand for the reception party to kiss. One of the city officials was so confused by the gesture that he thought the king had made a mistake and gravely bent his knee three times before the throne to buy time. He finally decided to attempt a kiss of the gloved hand, but at the last second the king removed his glove. The message of royal displeasure was clear.

At the opposite extreme from the exuberance of the Polish nobility were the Quakers, a puritanical Protestant sect that strived to eliminate all forms of ritual as an offense to the plain truth of God's Word. Found in England, Holland, and Pennsylvania, Quakers vehemently refused to conform to any of the conventions of deference or politeness. They would not employ courteous modes of address, used the insulting familiar form of "thee" and "thou" with social superiors, and disapproved of bowing, curtsying, and doffing hats. Quakers insisted that all forms of courtesy were merely "idle talk" and "empty ritual" and as such were affronts to God who was their only superior. They rejected what linguists call "phatic communication," which consists of greetings, phrases, and gestures employed to convey general sociability rather than to transmit specific meaning, and as a result non-Quakers considered Quakers extremely rude.

Quakers, nevertheless, could not entirely escape the rituals of social life. While rejecting gestures that showed respect, they practiced a decidedly egalitarian gesture of greeting and leave-taking, the shaking of hands. They did not invent the handshake, but they certainly made its use a potent symbol of equality that was an alternative to the dominant system of deferential gestures. Appearing first in sixteenth-century

Scotland and England, the handshake spread where and when the more elaborate rituals of hierarchy broke down, in the Dutch Republic in the eighteenth century, in France in the early nineteenth, even later in Imperial Russia, and finally in the Chinese imperial court in the early twentieth century. As the quintessentially modern form of greeting, the handshake indicated not so much a rejection of ritual, as the Quakers seemed to think, as an acceptance of an egalitarian system of ritualized gestures.

In a very broad way the reformation of gestures seems to have been more thoroughgoing and complete in the Protestant North of Europe than in the Catholic South. The different rates of change in these two regions created the modern stereotypes that Italians gesticulate more than northerners and the English are more reserved and cool than southerners. Peter Burke has identified these two different body languages as the flamboyant and the disciplined, and both are artificial creations of gestural cultures that began to be distinctive during the sixteenth century. The North–South division, however, has some important exceptions. Spanish gravity appears similar to English self-control. The Polish and general Slavic willingness to carry gestural display to extravagant ends creates yet another distinction that might be called the Eastern European style, but the phlegmatic Bohemians do not fit very well even into this category.

The most important point might be that gestures became after the sixteenth century one of the most important visible signs for establishing, sustaining, and recognizing differences. The critical differences can be those of class as in Spain and Poland, religion as among the Quakers and Irish, national or ethnic culture as in Bohemia and Hungary, and that of gender everywhere. Rather than supporting community as the rites of passage and calendrical rituals might do, the rituals of manners defined dissimilarity and operated through the actions of individuals rather than through large groups acting collectively. Manners refashioned people to conform to models of ideal behavior, recreating a new kind of tyranny, the tyranny of social fashion.

Dining rituals

No rituals are more widely practiced, more formative of social identity, or more differentiating of social groups than the daily habits of dining. The distinction between eating merely to consume food and dining as a form of sociability inhabits the very core of what we call culture. The anthropologist Claude Lévi-Strauss argued that distinguishing between food that is raw and food that is cooked provides one of the fundamental oppositions that help people classify their experience. From this point of view, nothing is more revealing of the basic assumptions of a culture than dining customs.

To mark civility the theorists insisted on masking as thoroughly as possible the fundamental fact that human beings are animals that survive by killing and eating other animals. Whereas carnivalesque rituals played with blurring the distinctions between animals and humans, as when Carnival masqueraders dressed up as bears or when vendetta killers represented themselves as rabid dogs, the rituals of manners radically reinforced animal–human oppositions. The distinction was typically made in two ways. One was to condemn animal-like habits in eating, and the other was to screen diners as much as possible from the reality that they consumed animal flesh when they ate.

A passage from *Galateo* illustrates well the first of these trends. Della Casa ridicules

those whom we sometimes see lying like swine with their snouts in the soup, not once lifting their heads and turning their eyes, still less their hands, from the food, puffing out both cheeks as if they were blowing a trumpet or trying to fan a fire, not eating but gorging themselves, dirtying their arms almost to the elbows and then reducing their napkins to a state that would make a kitchen rag look clean.

Nonetheless, these hogs are not ashamed to use the napkins thus sullied to wipe away their sweat (which, owing to their hasty and excessive feeding, often runs down their foreheads and faces to their necks), and even to blow their noses into them as often as they please.[7]

The slur that someone "eats like a pig" encapsulates the whole system of assumptions about civility – that humans must differentiate themselves from animals in every deed and act but most critically in the process of eating. One of the things most soundly blamed in Della Casa's humorous description is the mixing on the napkin of the juices from the food with human sweat and mucous, a disgusting merging of the animal and the human that threatened the whole system of distinctions made through manners.

In his *Book of Inns* (*Diversoria*), published in 1523, Erasmus provided a kind of ethnographic account of the kinds of eating habits he would later attempt to reform. He relates his experience of a German inn. In the dining room some eighty or ninety people of all sorts – men and women, adults and children, peasants and nobles – rubbed elbows with one another while performing whatever tasks they had to do during the respite from their travels. Some washed their clothes and hung them to

---

[7] Quoted in Norbert Elias, *The History of Manners*, vol. 1 of *The Civilizing Process*, trans. Edmund Jephcott (New York: Pantheon Books, 1978), 90.

dry on the stove, another washed his hands in a filthy bowl of water, a third cleaned his boots on the table. Evil smells permeated the dirty room, the floor of which was slick with spittle. When the communal meal was served, each guest dipped his or her bread into the common dish, bit off the bread, and then dipped it in again. The wine was sour, the guests sweaty and smelly, the stranger treated as if he were an exotic animal from Africa. Clearly one of the things Erasmus found so disturbing about the German inn was the undisciplined mixing of classes, functions, and bodily processes. He wanted the rituals of manners to build barriers that would assist the identification of differences and keep separate things separate.

In his *Manners for Children* he listed a series of such rules for the table:

If a napkin is provided, lay it on your left shoulder or arm.

Your goblet and knife, duly cleansed, should be on the right, your bread on the left.

Some people put their hands in the dishes the moment they have sat down. Wolves do that . . .

To dip the fingers in the sauce is rustic. You should take what you want with your knife and fork; you should not search through the whole dish as epicures are wont to do, but take what happens to be in front of you.

To lick greasy fingers or to wipe them on your coat is impolite. It is better to use the tablecloth or the napkin.[8]

Erasmus joined the recommendations of others to his own observations, a simple combination that helped the book become a remarkable publishing success and highly influential in reforming manners. The governing principles were those of moderation (do not fall upon the food like a famished wolf) and avoidance of pollution (clean the knife, do not spit on the table, wash your hands).

The ritual rules of dining focused particularly on the eating of meat. The ability to consume meat followed social distinctions: the poor ate very little because it was an extravagance, monks abstained from it altogether as a form of self-denial, but the aristocracy indulged themselves by devouring enormous quantities, especially in comparison to modern standards. It has been estimated that in a north German court in the seventeenth century meat consumption was at the extraordinary level of two pounds per head per day, which was *in addition* to the venison, fowl, and fish eaten at the same meals. Menus of gargantuan banquets exult in conspicuous consumption. At a banquet given by the Duke of Aumont in 1690, the guests were served 171 different dishes, including 16 different meats in the second course and 57 desserts. Although the treatises on manners emphasize the require-

[8] Quoted in ibid., 89–90.

ment of moderation in the consumption of meat, the reports of actual dinners among the upper classes leave little indication of self-restraint.

Nevertheless, during the sixteenth century well-mannered persons increasingly felt the need to disguise their meat and to distance themselves from it. In previous centuries at aristocratic banquets, the entire dead animal or large parts of it would be placed on the table. Whole rabbits, lambs, and pigs roasted on a spit appeared before the eyes of guests as might fowl complete with feathers. A quarter of veal or venison might be heaved onto the table, and an unbutchered roast beef, complete with head, was not unknown as a table decoration. The animal was then carved at the table in front of the guests, and skill at carving was one of the essential marks of a well-bred man. Gradually, however, the carcass of the animal came to be disguised – feathers came off fowl and heads were removed before the meat was brought to the table – and only a small portion of the animal actually appeared at the table to be carved. By the nineteenth century dining evolved to the "Russian system" supposedly introduced by the Russian ambassador to Paris. Serving from the table disappeared entirely, and all the carving was performed by a cook or butler out of the sight of diners who were served individual cut-up portions as happens today in fine restaurants.

This process of alienation from the eating of meat introduced "an invisible cage" of manners and implements around each diner. Napkins came into use, and each diner used a separate plate, cup, spoon, knife, and fork. Transferring food directly from the common serving plate to the mouth was prohibited. In giving advice to carvers a French treatise of 1672 warns that "the meat must never be touched . . . by hand, not even while eating."[9] Jean-Louis Flandrin has asked, "what was the reason for these precautions, two centuries before Pasteur's discovery of bacteria? Of what uncleanliness were people so afraid? Perhaps their greatest fear was of contact with others."[10] The ironic contrast between the widespread lack of hygiene and the near obsession with not touching food reveals a deep fear of pollution from bodies: the bodies of dead animals consumed at a meal, the bodies of companions, and even one's own body. Such fears exhibited in the rituals of manners contrasted with the gusto for flesh in carnivalesque festivities.

The rules for using utensils, especially the knife, divulge additional fears. The obvious danger of knives required that they be handled in a

[9] Quoted in ibid., 119.
[10] Jean-Louis Flandrin, "Distinction through Taste," in Philippe Ariès and Georges Duby, eds., *A History of Private Life*, vol. 3 of *Passions of the Renaissance*, ed. Roger Chartier, trans. Arthur Goldhammer (Cambridge, Mass.: The Belknap Press of Harvard University Press, 1989), 266–67.

special, formalized way to neutralize their image as weapons, an image activated at the table when they are employed to carve up a dead animal. Besides the functional rules never to point a knife at someone and always to pass it handle first, there was a more puzzling category of prohibitions that suggest symbolic or psychological meanings. It was strictly forbidden to eat a fish with a knife or to bring it into contact with egg-shaped objects such as potatoes or dumplings. The extremely fastidious avoided cutting an apple with a knife and peeled an orange with a spoon. In southern Italy a proverb enjoined leaving a knife in bread lest you stab Christ, and the French eventually abandoned cutting bread with a knife altogether, returning to the old use of the hands instead.

The most innovative contribution of the new manners in the sixteenth century was the introduction of the table fork. It first appeared in Venice and gradually spread among cultivated diners, arriving in France only in the late seventeenth century. What was its purpose? Certainly it is easier to pick up food with the fingers, and as anyone knows who has ever tried to teach a child table manners, forks are very hard to learn how to use. Although it might appear that forks are more hygienic than fingers, there are always certain foods – bread, cherries, chocolates – that are eaten with the hands no matter how refined the manners. It appears that cultivated people initially employed forks to spear pieces of meat from a serving tray and to pick up cut-up portions of meat to be placed in the mouth. Forks kept fingers away from meat less for reasons of cleanliness than for reasons of repugnance with the texture and juices (reminders of blood?) of cooked meats. Forks are distancing instruments: they keep our bodies away from the bodies of dead animals and are signs of a certain discomfort with food. It is telling that, more obviously than any other culinary habit, the styles of fork use distinguish the civilized from the boor and the European from the American. Forks create distance and represent cultural differences.

Among the middle and upper classes, table manners and banqueting etiquette became important markers of social distinction. The table became during the early modern period the most important locale for social interaction and cultivated conversation, replacing in some ways the council hall and town square, as social life became more centered in the home and more private. The fact that manners could be learned encouraged a certain individualism: a scholar or clerk from a poor background could distinguish himself at the table through refined dining habits and witty conversation, cutting a fine figure that belied his humble background, whereas the loutish country squire who did not know the rules might find himself desperately uncomfortable in the city or court no matter how large his estates or ancient his lineage.

One of the best indicators of how important the rituals of dining were can be seen in the fact that they often became the occasion for conflict, especially over seating arrangements. Among the upper classes guests sat at the table according to a strict hierarchy of precedence, a rule that could disrupt the most carefully planned banquet. In Poland anyone unsatisfied with his rank at the table or who thought his immediate neighbors beneath him cut the tablecloth in front of him or stomped out. In this way he severed the symbolic community of the table.

Different countries, of course, enjoyed different dining customs despite these general trends. The Poles and Russians seemed especially ebullient to outsiders. Polish banquets would be repeatedly and annoyingly interrupted by proposals for toasts, which obliged the guests to stand up, remove their hats, and wait for the common goblet to be passed around. For grand occasions the glass would be smashed after each toast, and an especially enthusiastic toaster might break the glass on his own head.

The Italians were noted for highly circumspect refinement. *Galateo* recounts a revealing story. A certain duke possessing very fine manners appeared one day at a banquet of the Bishop of Verona, who serves as the arbiter of taste in the book. The bishop noted one defect in his guest's manners but said nothing about it to him directly. Instead when the duke departed, the bishop ordered his courtier, Galateo, to accompany him out of town. When taking his leave, Galateo stated that the bishop wished to make the duke a gift and recounted that his master wished to compliment the duke on his manners, which were without parallel among other gentlemen, but that one slight fault had been detected: the duke smacked his lips too loudly when chewing, which made an unpleasant noise that offended others. The gift was a bit of advice on etiquette, indirectly and privately given under the assumption that that was the proper way to correct offenses of manners.

As Michel Jeanneret has pointed out, "manners are always potentially mannered. The code of politeness is an inherently unauthentic system which is bound to be duplicitous because it can never eradicate passion. Moralists of all eras have revealed its tricks: simulation and affectation have always been an intrinsic part of civilization."[11] The "mannerism" of manners conveys a sense of the inevitable artificiality of civility. The word "mannerism" is derived from *maniera*, which has been employed in Renaissance art criticism to describe the tendency toward stylistic elaboration for its own sake and the playful subversion of the rules of classicism that had been rigidly imitated in the early stages of the

[11] Michel Jeanneret, *A Feast of Words: Banquets and Table Talk in the Renaissance*, trans. Jeremy Whiteley and Emma Hughes (Chicago: University of Chicago Press, 1987), 45.

Renaissance. When applied to table manners the notion of mannerism implies a search for beauty and refinement through theatrical self-display, a creative playing with civility that transforms banqueting from an occasion for eating to a stage for the display of gracefulness.

The best example of this tendency can be found in Stefano Guazzo's *The Civil Conversation* of 1574 that purports to describe a small banquet held at Casale in honor of Duke Vespasiano Gonzaga. The food served at the banquet is not even mentioned, for recognizing such vulgar pleasures is deemed unworthy of such an august gathering. The meal is merely a pretext to show off elegance in manners and speech; banqueting becomes an exquisite exercise of finesse. The guests listen to music, recite poetry, act out theatrical declarations of love, and pose riddles. As Jeanneret notes, "conversation is the real food," and the rituals of dining completely displace eating. Word play and wit outshine substance; indeed, nothing of consequence is ever brought up. Nothing is allowed to interrupt the dreamlike mood, and real passions, such as love and devotion, are merely mimed, acted out for effect. They are not to be truly felt. Form has utterly replaced substance. The rituals are dead rituals that fail to constitute or represent actual social relationships, leading participants to pay minute attention to the details of the social performance because there is nothing else going on. Developments such as these led, of course, to the modern distrust of ritual as an empty shell, as performances without real meaning, the vain playthings of effete and superficial persons.

Courtship between the sexes

The high emotional and physical charge of sexual intimacy and the social consequences of pregnancy led traditional European society to swathe the contact between amorous young couples with layers of ritual. The rituals of courtship had long made it possible to approach marriage and sex discreetly and indirectly, but during the sixteenth century the aristocratic upper classes assumed the flirtatious dissimulations of the new manners for sexual and marriage proposals. A measure of the lasting influence of courtly manners can be found in the fact that in English when a man seeks to gain the affection of a woman, he is still said to be "courting" her. "See, how they kiss and court!" as Shakespeare put it.[12]

Traditional peasant courtship rites in France illustrate the role of ritual gestures in a couple's advance toward marriage. Robert Much-

---

[12] William Shakespeare, *The Taming of the Shrew*, IV, ii, 27, in *The Complete Works*, ed. G. B. Harrison (New York: Harcourt, Brace & World, 1968), 354.

embled has discussed how the spinning-bee (*veillée*), which was a winter gathering of village women and girls in a barn to spin and sew, provided the occasion for youthful courtship under the supervision of older women and the master of the house who prevented any violations of ritual forms. The women and girls would sit in a circle doing their work, while the boys hovered on the periphery trying to steal a kiss from the girls by tapping them on the shoulders or opening the upper part of their trousers to make an indecent gesture permitted only on these occasions. The girls responded with laughter and a gesture that half-hid their eyes with their hands. The supervising old women, the fascinated girls, and the taboo-testing boys each had a ritual role to play. After achieving eye contact at a spinning-bee, an interested boy might then start to hang around a girl's house for some months; if her parent's approved, they would let her slip out of the house some evening when the first conversation between the youths took place. As Muchembled puts it, "words are rare and chaste in evoking marriage or other questions of prime importance such as sex. In general, gestures suffice . . ."[13] These practices among the peasants reveal the need for innuendo regarding mating that made it possible to venture a tentative proposal without suffering the difficulties and potential misunderstandings of coming out in the open with words.

Mating rituals also demanded that men demonstrate restraint in wooing women, by delaying – often for years – sexual gratification and then only when the woman fully consented. In European culture there has long been a very clear distinction between rape and romance, a difference carefully demonstrated through the rituals of courtship. Fundamental to these rites was some kind of test of love, by which the woman verified the man's love by asking him to remain sexually abstinent while he professed words of great ardor. In the south of France well into the nineteenth century, a young man proved himself by clandestinely climbing into his fiancée's bedroom at night and sleeping with her but fully clothed and without any touching. A Catalan ditty evokes the concept exactly,

> Even the Holy Father of Rome
> Would not do what I have done:
> Sleep with you the whole night through
> And never touch your body[14]

[13] Robert Muchembled, "The Order of Gestures: A Social History of Sensibilities under the Ancien Régime in France," in Bremmer and Roodenburg, *A Cultural History of Gesture*, 135–36.

[14] Quoted in René Nelli, "Love's Rewards," in Feher, *Fragments for a History of the Human Body*, part II, p. 223.

Tests of love took many forms, including erotic games of petting and flirtation, and in societies that did not practice birth control the rituals had a practical function in that they gave women some opportunity to determine the reliability of a potential partner before risking pregnancy.

René Nelli has proposed that from the "really primitive and popular" tests of love such as these the rituals of chivalric love evolved, bequeathing to us the ideals of romantic love between men and women. In the medieval Provençal romances, the test of love took an elaborate ritual form called the *Asag* that involved the lover's gazing upon the body of the naked lady. The lady invited her lover to join her in a private place, often a garden or perhaps even her own bed chamber, where both undressed. Before she allowed him to lie beside her, she made him swear that he would not attempt anything that was not permitted by the Right of Love, which allowed touching, kissing, embracing, and holding, but no sexual acts. With the man deprived of all initiative, at least in theory, sex would be possible only at her request and on a later occasion if ever. There seems to have been no shame in the woman's daring unveiling of her body, which had an almost magical effect on men in the poems of the troubadours.

Chivalric tales always involved adulterous love because the lady at least was always married, and it is uncertain whether the *Asag* ritual was ever actually practiced or was merely a male fantasy in which men presented themselves as having survived the test of love rather than a test of arms, the usual stuff of the romances. The tremendous popularity of the troubadours' poems disseminated ideas of chivalric love, which were eventually transformed from a game among adulterous, idle aristocrats to become the most popular Western model for courtship leading to marriage. In the transition chivalric love itself underwent a civilizing process in which the frank openness about nudity was lost, and couples were expected to maintain a shy reserve about their bodies before marriage and to a certain degree even afterwards. The surviving courtship rituals retained the requirement that men must show sexual self-restraint to win their mates and that women must grant permission for intercourse to take place. Courtship rituals have had a persistent influence on ideas of love and marriage in the West, forming notions of proper conduct that have began to break down only in the late twentieth century with the spread of modern techniques of birth control.

The requirement that male suitors make an elaborate ritual display of their affection encouraged a certain extravagance in manners. The courting of a young woman from the Szamowska family who lived on a rural estate in eighteenth-century Poland provides a good example. When her gentleman suitor, Tollohub, was about to depart from the

Szamowska manor, she offered him a glass of wine as was customary. Tollohub, who was sitting on his horse, gulped down the wine, placed his empty glass between the ears of his mount, pulled out his pistol, and shattered the glass with one shot. He then jumped down, laid himself prostrate at her feet, and begged the young woman to marry him.

The diffusion of courtship rituals during the sixteenth century produced a sense of shame about the sexuality of the human body that can be compared to the ways dining rituals distanced people from the bodies of dead animals. In public, at least, the physical contact between members of the opposite sex was carefully regulated, and courting couples began to kiss mouth-to-mouth only in private. No longer were young newlyweds undressed by their friends and relatives who witnessed the first act of coitus. Married men and women ceased to sleep together naked and put on special night clothes creating, to paraphrase Erasmus, a body of the body.

By the seventeenth century in France, for example, courtship and marriage among the upper classes were rapidly becoming private family matters rather than the public celebrations demanded by traditional culture. As a by-product of this process, authorities attacked the carnivalesque aspects of sexuality. After 1640 in France all kinds of "indecent actions," such as charivari or obscene serenades, were prohibited by law. Nevertheless, many of the forms survived because they were popular, and the police had difficulties enforcing the prohibitions. In Toulouse in 1750 when a band of youths planned to serenade a widow who was about to remarry, the officer of the night watch arrested some of the merrymakers. However, when neighbors raised a ruckus about the arrests, the officer found himself reprimanded by his superiors, who declared that "according to the letter and spirit of the law the assembly of instruments used here did not constitute a charivari."[15] The traditional elements of charivari were gradually domesticated and made less offensive among the stable middle and upper classes who employed serenades and music making to liven up weddings. The aggressive charivaris of the male youth-abbeys, which the authorities wished to proscribe, survived clandestinely and only among the mobile artisans who had lost the protective social stability of rural villages. In both Protestant and Catholic countries after the Reformation where claims were made for the ministerial or clerical regulation of marital morality, vicars and parish priests were especially harsh in denouncing the libertine behavior of youth gangs. In addition, victims of charivaris no longer passively accepted abuse and refused to pay the

15 Fabre, "Families: Privacy versus Custom," in Ariès and Duby, *A History of Private Life*, 543.

extortion moneys demanded by the youth-abbey revelers. When property was damaged or stolen, authorities were increasingly quick to intervene with arrests and prosecutions.

By the eighteenth century, charivari became more a kind of theatrical performance than a form of ritual persecution. Dialect plays appeared in France and Italy, in particular, that held up the cuckolded husband and the lecherous widow as generalized objects of laughter and scorn. Instead of assaulting specific households or parading wayward indivi-duals backwards on an ass, stock characters enforced the values of society from the stage. The theatrical transformation of carnivalesque rituals took many forms: itinerant puppet theaters were enormously popular in the rural villages and among the urban poor, the masked characters in the *commedia dell'arte* provided a highly formalized bridge between ritual and theater, and the comedy of manners engaged some of the greatest dramatists of the Baroque.

In an odd gender reversal, groups of women began to replace the gangs of unmarried men to enforce local morality through female charivaris. They took over responsibility for punishing debauchery, defending the honor of a pregnant girl, ridiculing the wife of a man who took a young mistress, and harassing women of low repute. They sustained the moral standards of the community, which were now less obviously formulated through the misogyny of the young men than by the women's collective assertion of their own morality. The women employed practices derived from the old charivari without the violent overtones common in the masculine versions. They were so effective that a priest in the Vaud wrote to the local court in 1817 that even though he disapproved of popular sexual rituals in general, he thought charivaris performed by women assisted public virtue.

The shame of violence

The cooperation between the good form of civilized manners and the good government of disciplined rulership helped to constrain behavior, in particular behavior that led to violence. During the early modern period acts of violence that had once been considered normal and even pleasurable gradually became disgusting and shameful.

In his famous study, *The Autumn of the Middle Ages*, the influential Dutch historian, Johann Huizinga, described the violent tenor of daily life characteristic of late medieval society. In comparison to modern sensibilities both men and women seemed extraordinarily accustomed to witnessing and participating in cruel acts of violence, and many seemed to take a perverse pleasure in the pain of others. The songs of the troubadour Bertran de Born celebrated the gore of war: "I tell you that neither eating, drinking, nor sleep has as much savor for me as . . . to see the small and the great fall to the grass at the ditches and the dead pierced by the wood of the lances decked with banners."[16] Habits of mutilating captured prisoners and other unfortunates now seem to be a repugnant example of sadism, but during the Middle Ages the practice followed a perverse logic because it was costly to feed captives but dangerous to ransom them off. It seemed safest to disable them. The fear of enemies, real and imagined, sustained callous brutality. The reported cruelties of a renowned knight and his wife illustrate behavior that was hardly unusual.

He spends his life in plundering, destroying churches, falling upon pilgrims, oppressing widows and orphans. He takes particular pleasure in mutilating the innocent. In a single monastery, that of the black monks of Sarlat, there are 150 men and women whose hands he has cut off or whose eyes he has put out. And his wife is just as cruel. She helps him with his executions. It even gives her pleasure to torture the poor women. She had their breasts hacked off or their nails torn off so that they were incapable of work.[17]

As the previous chapter shows, violence infested ritual life, especially during carnivalesque festivals, in the judicial rituals surrounding executions, and in the stylized patterns of vendetta killing. What had once been a common form of amusement through inflicting pain in others became in the course of the early modern period the "abnormal" behavior of a demented person. The revulsion against enjoying cruelty for its own sake applied to the harming of animals as well as humans. As early as the 1520s in Venice, the annual Carnival slaughter of the pigs and bull became an embarrassment to the more cultivated patricians who sought to make the ritual illegal. For more than seventy years they only had intermittent success in convincing the populace of the shame of laughing at the pain of animals. In Paris a famous Midsummer Day ritual consisted of burning sacks of live cats. An imitation scaffold was erected over an enormous pyre of wood. The sack of cats was hung from the scaffold, and when the flames leaped up the crowd shrieked in pleasure at the cats' screams of agony as they were burned to death. During the sixteenth century the royal court often attended the burnings, and the king or dauphin was given the honor of lighting the pyre. By the eighteenth century, however, widespread repugnance at such behavior had limited sadistic amusements to semi-clandestine exploits among youthful artisans. When as an act of protest some Paris journeymen massacred the cat belonging to the wife of their master, the

---

[16] Quoted in Elias, *The History of Manners*, vol. 1, p. 193.   [17] Ibid., 194.

ritual language of violent derision was still sufficiently alive that the message of ridicule was understood, but the sense of shame had risen high enough that they found themselves in considerable difficulties with the law. Elias described this transformation in values as "an advance in the frontiers of shame," an advance that linked together the humane treatment of animals with a regard for the dignity of other human beings.

One substitute for rites of cruelty became spectator sports, which provided a socially permitted outlet for feelings of aggression. Boxing and football licensed violent combat within a carefully prescribed space and time and with established limits to the amount of mayhem the violence could legitimately produce. The amount of allowable violence declined or was at least regulated, and the objects of violence, that is the participants, supposedly submitted themselves voluntarily to pain and potential injury. Taking pleasure in the pain of animals and other humans did not disappear, but spectators distanced themselves from violence and its consequences by justifying it as sport. Carnivalesque rites of violence gave way to sports, which were framed with the carefully prescribed rules of the game and the rituals of support performed by fans who identified with the players and who acted with more emotional exuberance than they would permit themselves in daily life.

Criminal punishments and public executions reflected this transformation of sensibilities. In traditional Europe there had been a degree of crowd participation in the rites of judicial punishment. Persons locked in stocks were pelted with filth and abuse, and some might even be stoned to death. Exiles for crimes against the public order were denied "fire and water," that is the necessities of life, by all law-abiding citizens. The very severity of punishments came less from the statutory sentence inflicted upon a guilty party than from the intensity of participation by the crowd whose jeers and improvised malice reinforced official actions with notions of popular justice. Penal codes across Europe, in fact, borrowed extensively from traditional, popular rituals of censure. Sheriffs and magistrates relied on the ritual forms of charivaris to punish both men and women. In Hamburg in 1593 a woman who had beaten her spouse was sentenced, "in accordance with ancient custom," to ride backward on an ass led by her weakling husband. Courts in England ordered that "rough music," the English version of charivari cacophony, accompany penal processions of men and women riding backwards on a horse while dressed in the clothing of the opposite sex. Prostitutes and adulteresses were covered in honey, rolled in feathers, and paraded with baskets over their heads. Governments followed vendetta customs by ordering that the doors of the house of a violent family be removed or the house be torn down, the building stones removed, and the soil of the site salted.

During the seventeenth and eighteenth centuries, however, the surviving forms of ritual censure finally gave way to criminal prosecution and sentencing. The infliction of physical injury on the guilty became the exclusive right of the judicial authorities who displayed a growing restraint in mutilating criminals and who privatized punishment by making executions less public. The principle of ritual censure required that the punishment symbolically fit the crime: a thief was returned to the scene of the crime where the hand that stole was cut off, and a promiscuous woman might have her face mutilated so that she could no longer attract men. The new penal codes, however, removed punishments to restricted, special locations and introduced abstract sentences rather than symbolic penalties. Moreover, the judiciary gradually abandoned the practice of exemplary ritual torture, as was inflicted on the Pappenheimers, even when the law still called for it. When the statutes required a culprit to be burned alive, magistrates merely allowed the condemned to feel the heat briefly before being strangled. The opinion that convicts should suffer and their sufferings ought to be witnessed publicly gave way to imprisonment, which instead of displaying criminality and its consequences to the public removed criminals from view. In the early sixteenth century Thomas More first argued against capital punishment for thieves who stole to survive, noting how such extreme penalties gave them no incentive to spare the lives of their victims. By the eighteenth century judicial torture, exemplary punishments, and finally capital punishment itself began to disappear in the most enlightened states of Europe. The whole array of judicial rituals of punishment evaporated as a by-product of an expanding sensibility to the shame of violence even when violence was inflicted on the criminally culpable.

As authorities themselves abandoned ritual punishments, they became less tolerant of popular rites that led to disorder. Spaces and times that were once the privileged place for the illicit gradually came under public regulation. The esplanades outside of town walls had been the locale for the brawls of youthful gangs and the turf of unregulated prostitutes who entertained clients in the full light of day. At night the streets of towns and cities became the dangerous territory of the young who escaped the control of adults and public authorities. Implicit in the rituals of youth was the notion that the night belonged to them. They broke up merchants' booths, vandalized gardens and vineyards, stole or destroyed anything that was left unguarded. Throughout the early modern period governmental authorities strove to transform all open spaces into public property through the patrols of special night watches who recaptured the dark hours for respectable bourgeois citizens. The systematic official assault on the sources of disorder was launched through a public campaign against the traditional rituals of youth. Youth-abbeys, once moral watchdogs for the entire community, were delegitimated in town after town. In attempting the suppress the youth-abbeys, clergymen, teachers, and police officers imposed severe discipline on the exuberance of the young and invented substitute organizations such as sports clubs.

Carnivalesque play, which mixed the sacred and profane or inverted social superiors and inferiors, had once been the right of youth, but in both Protestant and Catholic countries after the Reformation, such play became sacrilegious. Even in the late eighteenth century, a French priest could still complain about the disorders of youth:

> They counterfeit the ceremonies and pay no heed to remonstrances. They run through the village in disguise, dancing, displaying carnival on Ash Wednesday. They enter the sanctuary during services, station themselves between the cross and the priest in processions as though they were clergy, turn their backs to the altar, laugh and talk during services, pound on the benches, fire pistols in church or in front of it on wedding days and holy days, dance in front of the church on the pedestal of the cross, even before catechism and during Advent, and sing obscene songs.[18]

To the pious, play itself was an offense to God. As Peter Burke has pointed out, reformers objected to Carnival and carnivalesque festivity both for the theological reason that they seemed to harbor survivals of paganism and for the moral reason that they encouraged sin. The whole ritual culture that celebrated the lower body, its drives and pleasures, came under systematic reforming assault. Drunkenness, gluttony, lechery, and violence, that is all forms of disorder, faced the hostility of clerics.

Catholic reformers sought to clean up and regulate the abuses of carnivalesque culture while Protestant ones usually tried to abolish them altogether. The clerical antagonism toward popular rituals and interest in ritual reform was not limited to western Europe. In the Orthodox world of Ukraine and Russia a similar assault on popular rituals flourished in the middle of the seventeenth century. In the case of Ukraine the influence of the Western reformers seems paramount, but in Russia the "zealot" priests, who received backing from Tsar Alexis, worked independently, striving to root out popular festivities from the church calendar.

The offensive against disorder, mounted by both secular and clerical

[18] Fabre, "Families: Privacy versus Custom," in Ariès and Duby, *A History of Private Life*, 565.

authorities, did not limit itself to youth gangs and popular festivity but implicated the ruling classes themselves, especially the aristocracy's habits of feuding. By the beginning of the sixteenth century, only a few cities and the kingdom of England had succeeded in significantly eradicating feuds, but by the end of the century the process was well underway throughout Europe. The example of the new manners succeeded where rigorous enforcement of the law had failed. Traditional values required that gentlemen respond to insults and injuries through retaliation, but by seeking to conform to the manners of the princely courts, an aristocrat had to accept certain restraints on his own conduct. He could hardly jump into deadly combat with a fellow courtier every time a dispute arose without hurting the interests of his patron and employer, the prince. Private vendettas were especially injurious to the authority of the prince. To resolve the injured courtier's dilemma of feeling the need for revenge but being unable to enact it freely, the princely courts developed compensatory measures that tied up revenge in the elaborate knots of the duel. The spread of dueling in the middle of the sixteenth century reduced the violence of traditional feuds among aristocrats and supplanted the collective family honor of the vendetta with the individualized concept of honor promulgated by the new manners.

The rituals of dueling had roots in medieval judicial and chivalric combats, but they were refashioned in the early sixteenth century in Italy as a private means for resolving conflicts among social equals. From the princely courts of Italy the dueling rituals spread to Spain, France, Germany, England, and eventually to the American South, where the duel persisted well into the nineteenth century. Military experts, aristocratic debating academies, and numerous writers devoted themselves to codifying the rules and propagating them both through exemplary conduct and in rule books. The best-known authority became Girolamo Muzio's *The Duel*, printed in at least nineteen editions in Italy alone during the sixteenth century. Muzio was copied, imitated, debated, and refuted in a vast literature on dueling that evolved after about 1550.

Dueling suddenly appeared, in part, as a by-product of changes in European weaponry and warfare that threatened the traditional position of the nobility as the warrior class. In the middle of the sixteenth century, the needlepoint rapier first appeared as a weapon. The rapier had little value on the battlefield but could be deadly in private combat since a single well-placed thrust could be fatal. At about the same time pistols became popular, and the danger of these two new weapons made it necessary to regulate private disputes. In addition, the famous success of the Swiss pike men in the Italian wars and the spread of field artillery in battle made the aristocratic cavalry highly vulnerable. Aristocrats who held too tenaciously to the old ways faced annihilation. The duel provided both a ritual frame to regulate private combat and an honorable compensation for the aristocracy's loss of military function.

The rules for the duel created the prescriptive guidelines for an extended ritual that consigned the expression of spontaneous anger to a series of formalities that kept opponents away from each other until they could meet on the dueling ground. The regulations that surrounded the combat itself – the formulas for insulting, challenging, answering a challenge, arranging a duel, and judging the outcome – created an elaborate ritual frame to regulate virtually every eventuality save for the outcome of the contest itself. In this respect dueling, deadly as it could often be, limited violence in much the same way as sports by designating a specific time and place for the contest and by limiting what can legitimately take place through the enforcement of complicated rules by neutral referees.

A precise succession of steps preceded a duel. When one party insulted or accused another of a dishonorable deed, the accused had to respond by "giving the lie," that is by stating loudly and clearly, "You lie in the throat." The original speaker then denied the lie by formally challenging the other to a duel, usually by throwing down a glove or some other pledge, such as a ring, dagger, or belt. Because the person challenged to the duel had the right to choose the weapons for combat, it was advantageous to be the first to give the lie, thereby forcing the other to make the challenge and to give up the opportunity to pick his best weapon. These preliminary stages could become quite complex with the exchange of challenges and counter challenges, the publishing of extended justifications printed on large sheets of paper suitable for posting, and minute disputes about honor and etiquette. The complexity of the rituals allowed the actual violence to be delayed indefinitely, even for years, and always gave someone who did not want to risk his hide an honorable way out, since it was virtually impossible to follow the ritual script perfectly, and any slip brought a gentleman's honor into question.

If the two disputants proceeded all the way to fighting, they found the forms for the actual combat relatively simple. The challenger met the challenged at a designated place at a designated time with designated weapons; each combatant was accompanied by a second who assisted him in his preparations and acted as a witness but who could not intervene in the fight; a neutral judge heard each duelist take an oath that his cause was just. After the duel another complicated set of rules determined how the outcome was to be judged. The seconds and the judge examined the wounds of each duelist, whether dead or alive, and toted up the score by evaluating the injuries according to a scale that ranked the various parts of the body: the loss of an eye was worth more than the loss of a tooth, a wound on the right hand more than one on the left, a mark on the front of the body more than one on the back. Whoever had inflicted the gravest wounds on the other was judged the victor in the fight, but confessions or statements made during the fight might alter the outcome about who had been correct in the quarrel.

Actual duels took many forms. Certainly the most celebrated French duel of the century was the one in 1547 between Jarnac, the brother-in-law of the young mistress of old King François I, and La Châtaigneraye, a familiar of the future King Henri II and his mistress, Diane de Poitiers. When Henri alleged that Jarnac had had an incestuous affair with the second wife of King François, Jarnac was obliged to give the lie, but the future king could hardly openly challenge a member of his father's court, so La Châtaigneraye took on the role as champion. The entire royal court took sides, and an enormous crowd of ladies and gentlemen witnessed the duel in which, contrary to all expectations, Jarnac killed La Châtaigneraye, the older, more experienced fighter. Jarnac quickly disabled his opponent with a thrust to the back of the knee, which came to be known as "Jarnac's stroke." Although Jarnac won the combat and theoretically received the favorable judgment of God, La Châtaigneraye's supporters did not give up, explaining away the loss so effectively that Jarnac failed to gain much prestige from his victory while La Châtaigneraye was not condemned. The duel succeeded in limiting the violence because unlike later in the century when the Wars of Religion opened an extremely bloody episode in French history, this dispute among royal courtiers did not evolve into a feud or civil war. Nevertheless, the moral and judicial value of the duel remained in dispute.

Elsewhere duels even ended feuds that had lasted for centuries. In 1568 two young champions from Friulan families that had been engaged in an intractable vendetta for more than 200 years fought a duel in a secluded field between Mantua and Cremona. When both duelists died from their wounds, the duel was declared a draw and the parity of deaths made it possible to end the vendetta. Although clerical moralists universally condemned the duel as an offense to the majesty of God, the duel vastly reduced what had been the endemic violence of the European aristocracy simply by transforming combat into a highly formalized ritual engagement.

With the rise of manners the upper body triumphed over the lower body. The reason and restraint represented by the upper body took precedence over the emotions associated with the lower body, both through the spread of self-control and through the attempts of church and state to obliterate carnivalesque rituals. This vast struggle, which has had such important implications for the creation of the modern, emotionally repressed but self-disciplined personality type, occurred primarily through a debate about ritual. The rituals associated with the human body and its physical capacities to eat, make love, and fight linked self-control with social control, creating a new world in which personal comportment of men and women internalized the external coercive authorities of reformed religion and absolutist states. Through the rules of decorum persons learned how to censor themselves, disciplining and even criminalizing their own emotions.

BIBLIOGRAPHY

Entries marked with a * designate recommended readings for new students of the subject.

*Ariès, Philippe and Duby, George, eds. *A History of Private Life*. Vol. 3: *Passions of the Renaissance*. Edited by Roger Chartier, translated by Arthur Gold-hammer. Cambridge, Mass.: The Belknap Press of Harvard University Press, 1989. A highly readable collection of articles on private life, several of which treat the civilizing process.
*Billacois, François. *The Duel: Its Rise and Fall in Early Modern France*. Edited and translated by Trista Selous. New Haven: Yale University Press, 1990. A stimulating anthropological and historical examination of duelling that concentrates on the sixteenth century.
Bogucka, Maria. "Gesture, Ritual, and Social Order in Sixteenth- to Eighteenth-Century Poland." In *A Cultural History of Gesture*. Edited by Bremmer and Roodenburg. Pp. 190–209.
*Bremmer, Jan and Roodenburg, Herman, eds. *A Cultural History of Gesture*. Ithaca: Cornell University Press, 1991. A stimulating collection of articles on various aspects of the history of gestures.
Bryson, Frederic Robertson. *The Point of Honor in Sixteenth-Century Italy: An Aspect of the Life of the Gentleman*. New York: Columbia University Press, 1935. Still useful as a guide to the prescriptive and literary texts on honor.
*Burke, Peter. *The Fortunes of the* Courtier: *The European Reception of Castiglione's Cortegiano*. University Park, Penn.: The Pennsylvania State University Press, 1995.
    The Historical Anthropology of Early Modern Italy: Essays on Perception and Communication (Cambridge: Cambridge University Press, 1987). On the new formalities in Italy see pp. 90–92. A collection of articles, all readable and stimulating.
    "The Language of Gesture in Early Modern Italy." In *A Cultural History of Gesture*. Edited by Bremmer and Roodenburg. Pp. 71–83.
    Popular Culture in Early Modern Europe. New York: Harper & Row, 1978. See

especially chapter 8, "The Triumph of Lent: the Reform of Popular Culture."

*Castiglione, Baldesar. *The Book of the Courtier*. Translated by Charles S. Singleton. Garden City: N.Y.: Anchor Books, 1959. The most influential text from the early sixteenth century that promoted the new manners.

Connerton, Paul. *How Societies Remember*. Cambridge: Cambridge University Press, 1989. A highly stimulating study of how human bodies remember through gestures and how the new manners of the sixteenth century reconfigured social states and memories.

*Darnton, Robert. *The Great Cat Massacre and Other Episodes in French Cultural History*. New York: Basic Books, 1984. The title essay traces the changing sensibilities about the symbolic language of employing violence against animals.

*Davis, Robert C. *The War of the Fists: Popular Culture and Public Violence in Late Renaissance Venice*. New York: Oxford University Press, 1994. A superbly researched, fascinating account of ritualized violence among Venetian artisans.

Della Casa, Giovanni. *Galateo*. Translated, with an introduction and notes, by Konrad Eisenbichler and Kenneth R. Bartlett. Toronto: Centre for Reformation and Renaissance Studies, 1986. A sixteenth-century treatise that popularized the new manners.

*Elias, Norbert. *The History of Manners*. Translated by Edmund Jephcott. Vol. 1: *The Civilizing Process*. New York: Pantheon Books, 1978. The classic, highly influential sociological study of manners in the sixteenth century.

Fabre, Daniel. "Families: Privacy versus Custom." In *A History of Private Life*. Edited by Ariès and Duby. Pp. 531–69.

Feher, Michel, ed. *Fragments for a History of the Human Body*. 3 vols. New York: Zone Books, 1989. An influential collection of essays of varying quality that expands the historical study of the body.

Flandrin, Jean-Louis. "Distinction through Taste." In *A History of Private Life*. Edited by Ariès and Duby. Pp. 265–307. A good historical survey of table manners in France.

Heal, Felicity. *Hospitality in Early Modern England*. Oxford: Oxford University Press, 1990. A fascinating study of the changes in the civilities afforded guests.

*Huizinga, Johan. *The Autumn of the Middle Ages*. Translated by Rodney J. Payton and Ulrich Mammitzsch. Chicago: University of Chicago Press, 1996. A new and much improved translation of Huizinga's masterpiece, previously known as *The Waning of the Middle Ages*. The book presents a fascinating portrait of fourteenth- and fifteenth-century social mores and cultural forms, especially courtly manners.

Jeanneret, Michel. *A Feast of Words: Banquets and Table Talk in the Renaissance*. Translated by Jeremy Whiteley and Emma Hughes. Chicago: University of Chicago Press, 1987. A study of humanist influence on manners and polite table conversation.

Kiernan, V. G. *The Duel in European History: Honour and the Reign of Aristocracy*. Oxford: Oxford University Press, 1988. The now standard study of the history of dueling across the centuries.

Mauss, Marcel. "Body Techniques." In *Sociology and Pschology: Essays*. Translated by Ben Brewster. London: Routledge & Kegan Paul, 1979. Pp. 97–123. The influential work that helped make gestures and body language an object of serious study.

McNeill, David. *Hand and Mind: What Gestures Reveal about Thought*. Chicago: University of Chicago Press, 1992.

*Muchembled, Robert. "The Order of Gestures: A Social History of Sensibilities under the Ancien Régime in France." In *A Cultural History of Gesture*. Edited by Bremmer and Roodenburg. Pp. 129–51.

Nelli, René. "Love's Rewards." In *Fragments for a History of the Human Body*. Edited by Feher. Part II, pp. 219–35. A quirky analysis of the *Asag* ritual.

*Ranum, Orest. "Courtesy, Absolutism, and the Rise of the French State, 1630–1660," *Journal of Modern History* 52 (1980): 426–51. An excellent short study of the spread of courtesies in France.

*Revel, Jacques. "The Uses of Civility." In *A History of Private Life*. Edited by Ariès and Duby. Pp. 167–205. Discusses the rise of manners in the sixteenth century.

Roodenburg, Herman. "The 'Hand of Friendship': Shaking Hands and Other Gestures in the Dutch Republic." In *A Cultural History of Gesture*. Edited by Bremmer and Roodenburg. Pp. 152–89. A fascinating account of the origins of the handshake.

Schmitt, Jean-Claude. "The Ethics of Gesture." In *Fragments for a History of the Human Body*. Edited by Feher. Part II, pp. 129–47.

*Thomas, Keith. *Man and the Natural World: A History of the Modern Sensibility*. New York: Pantheon Books, 1983. Traces the rising sensitivity toward the treatment of animals during the early modern period.

Vigarello, Georges. "The Upward Training of the Body from the Age of Chivalry to Courtly Civility." In *Fragments for a History of the Human Body*. Edited by Feher. Part II, pp. 149–99. A fascinating analysis of the history of posture.

Zagorin, Perez. *Ways of Lying: Dissimulation, Persecution, and Conformity in Early Modern Europe*. Cambridge, Mass.: Harvard University Press, 1990. A useful study, which concentrates on Protestant Europe, of the theme of honest dissimulation.

Part III

Ritual and representation

Bolsena is a quiet lake-side village dominated by an imposing castle, which looks today much as it did in the later Middle Ages. Built astride the ancient Via Cassia, Bolsena supplemented its hard-won income from olive trees and fishing by providing lodging for pilgrims on the road to the sacred shrines in Rome. There were hundreds, perhaps thousands, of towns in medieval Europe that profited from pilgrims who visited the locations of especially holy relics. They wanted to receive an indulgence that reduced the time to be spent in purgatory, to cure some malady, to rectify some wrong, or to experience a mystical illumination. Some traveled voluntarily for spiritual benefits, some to satisfy a penitential obligation imposed on them by their confessors, and some to fulfill a vow made at a moment of fear or distress. Pilgrims were the tourists of the Middle Ages, and from Canterbury and Santiago de Compostela to Jerusalem itself, they were a lucrative source of profit for the villages and towns along the pilgrimage route. The pilgrims suffered the travails of the journey, which left the traveler vulnerable to bad weather, disgusting inns, and vicious bandits, in order to participate in special rituals in the presence of especially powerful relics.

Many of the travelers to Rome briefly interrupted their journey at Bolsena to pray in the sanctuary of St. Christina, who in ancient times had reportedly walked across the waters of the lake to escape her pagan persecutors. In 1264 or thereabouts one of these pilgrims, a Bohemian priest named Peter of Prague, lingered long enough to celebrate mass at the altar in the martyr's subterranean shrine. The priest apparently had a troubled soul, which pestered him with doubts about the efficacy of the rite he performed.

He worried about the doctrine of the Real Presence, which held that when a duly ordained priest, such as himself, spoke the words of consecration the elements of the Eucharist were changed in substance, or "transubstantiated" in the technical jargon of scholastic theology, into the body and blood of Christ even though the bread and wine in their outward "accidents" still looked to the eyes and tasted to the tongue like bread and red wine. Peter supposedly wondered if he could possibly be worthy to perform such a miracle and even more perniciously worried that if the miracle really took place, why would God choose to hide his miracle by deceiving the senses? The priest's gnawing anxieties, however, were stilled in a convincing fashion. During the celebration of the mass, at the very moment he spoke the words of consecration, the host began to drip blood, staining the corporal in a pattern that seemed to reveal the face of Jesus. Such was the profusion of Christ's blood that drops also tinged the marble steps of the altar.

Overcome by the marvelous signification of the miracle, Peter, accompanied by witnesses of the prodigious event, set off along a winding dirt track to nearby Orvieto where Pope Urban IV was staying with the Papal Curia. After hearing the report of the miracle, the pope sent the Bishop of Orvieto, the Dominican Thomas Aquinas, and the Franciscan Bonaventura of Bagnoregio (the latter two both future saints) to Bolsena to verify the truth of the miracle and to retrieve any objects that might be considered relics. The investigating party returned with the stained cloth of the corporal, which became the singular treasure of the magnificent cathedral of Orvieto, while Bolsena was left with the bloodied marble steps to encourage future pilgrims to linger in veneration and perhaps to contribute a little something extra to the local economy.

Despite the profusion of details, the material relics that can still be viewed by visitors to Bolsena and Orvieto, and the reportedly official imprimatur of a papal and saintly investigation, little in this story may be true, at least true in the sense that a historian would accept. The first account of the miracle dates from the fourteenth century, and the story was one of many reports of bleeding hosts that appeared with the spread of the new feast of Corpus Christi, which the very same Pope Urban had established under the inspiration of the visions of Juliana of Liège. The example of the reputed miracle at Bolsena, however, illustrates the vitality of two phenomena especially characteristic of the later Middle Ages: the enormous ritual industry built around pilgrimage shrines and the widespread infatuation with the body of God. Given the popularity of the new feast of Corpus Christi, one can understand how the people of Bolsena and Orvieto might have been tempted to promote a little pious fiction to honor the local shrines and garnish their pocketbooks.

The cult of the body of God, celebrated every year in the Corpus Christi liturgy and everyday in the communion of the mass, fastened religious observance to a more general appreciation of sacred and profane bodies, making corporeal rituals integral to the religious vocabulary of Christians. The intense corporality of the doctrine of the

Real Presence always caused controversy in the church, especially in northern lands such as Bohemia, where in the early fifteenth century the Eucharistic heresies of Jan Hus challenged papal authority, and Germany, where in the early sixteenth Martin Luther's objections to transubstantiation and other papal doctrines ended forever the religious unity of much of northern Europe. Differing views about the corporeal aspects of ritual came to distinguish Catholic and Protestant Europe and eventually the medieval from the modern sensibility.

It may now be difficult for most educated, secularized Westerners who live in the aftermath of the great sexual repression and bodily oblivion of the modern age to appreciate fully how Christian Europeans once readily thought in bodily images and habitually juxtaposed sacred and profane bodies, but the old attitude persists, often in unexpected places and unanticipated ways. It can still be found, for example, even in contemporary Bolsena. I was once in a shop there waiting my turn to buy some eggs. Ahead of me were a group of aging women, one of whom seemed slightly demented. The day was the Saturday before the feast of Corpus Christi and the conversation turned to the famous local miracle of the bleeding host, a matter of considerable local pride and an event still commemorated in the town with an elaborate festival. The befuddled one talked in pious terms of the moment in the mass when the body of Christ was elevated, but the others could not resist a little joke at her expense, averring that the miraculous transformation she really wanted was the elevation of her husband's tired member. These grandmotherly, thoroughly Catholic ladies seemed to feel no contradiction in this bawdy little play with the language of the sacred, which in a naturalistic way connected human sexuality with Christian cosmology. Their joke shows how lay women and -men have always understood the sacred in their own way, in this case imagining the awesome transubstantiation of daily bread into the divine body through a simple analogy to the more common wonders of marital intimacy and conception. Eucharistic rituals have always derived much of their allure from associations with the mundane human processes of ingestion and procreation. These were rites that not only brought ordinary believers into contact with the divine but permitted them to see and even to ingest God, making his flesh their flesh in the most amazing moment ever offered to most believers.

In the early sixteenth century such familiar connections between body and spirit, between the profane and the sacred, came under attack from a group of tenacious reformers who were outraged by what they saw as dangerous mixing implied by Eucharistic rituals. Their theological assault, which attempted to place the Word of scripture above the mediating rite of the liturgy, paralleled the rise of manners, which as we have seen substituted the rational dominion of the upper body for the festive lower body of carnivalesque rites.

Unlike the believers in the miracle of Bolsena, who accepted the miraculous transubstantiation of the mass as a sign of God's mysterious involvement in the world, the reformers wanted rituals to pass a test of efficacy. They gauged the value of a religious ritual by examining the quality of the believers' spiritual response to it. The reformers wanted practical results. In their view rituals "worked" only when they improved the morals of the people. During the first third of the sixteenth century, the humanist writings of Desiderius Erasmus popularized this view. His great critique of outward ritualistic piety, which he depicted as folly unless it produced charitable behavior and self-knowledge, shifted the spiritual efforts of many pious lay persons and earnest clergymen from witnessing and feeling through ritual to hearing, reading, debating, and acting upon the scriptural Word. The question for them became less how the Word assumed flesh, as it did in the mass, than how the Word assumed meaning, as it did through preaching, prayer, and study.

The disciplined activity of interpreting the meaning of a text, what is called hermeneutics, might be contrasted with the experience of passively watching the celebration of the liturgy. The hermeneutical concerns of Renaissance humanism and Reformation theology, achieved through the rediscovery of pagan and Hebrew learning, dismembered the assumptions of ritual or at least brought them into contention for the educated classes of Europe, especially in the North. The Reformation neither began the hermeneutical debate, which stretched back to antiquity, nor entirely destroyed the ritual system, which persists to this day, especially among Catholics, Anglicans, and the Orthodox, but it did alter the institutional and ideological frame that had sustained many rituals, both Christian and secular, making ritual a highly problematic form of behavior in the modern world and intensifying the crusade against magical rituals and superstitious beliefs.

The process of gaining access to the sacred shifted from experiencing the divine body through sight, touch, and ingestion to interpreting the scriptural Word, a process that had wide-ranging implications for the status of ritual as well as for the mentality of lay believers. The hermeneutical assault on ritual has made it what might be called an "incommensurable discourse," which means that we now tend to interpret the rituals of the past through a radical process of translation. We insist on translating experience into words. The core question about a ritual has become "what does it mean?" rather than "what emotions does it evoke?" Such translations create misunderstandings of the bodies presented in traditional Christian rituals. As the post-modern philosopher of nihilism, Gianni Vattimo, has put it,

even in historical terms, it could be maintained that hermeneutic theory appears as a specific discipline in European culture precisely at the moment when, with the collapse of the unity of Catholic Europe, the problem of *Missverstehen* [misunderstanding] acquires a decisive importance at the level of society and culture.[1]

By moving from experiencing a ritual presence to interpreting a ritual *representation*, misunderstandings propagated themselves in that breakneck destructuring rush called the Protestant Reformation.

Before the Reformation the body of God in the mass and the bodies of the saints in their shrines were understood to be *present* in some quite literal sense. Communicants partook of the wafer because it presented Christ's actual human flesh to the tongue and mouth. Pilgrims made pilgrimages so that they might come into direct contact with a powerful spiritual being who still inhabited the physical space of his or her now dead body. Whereas Peter Venable had argued that relics were not just assistants to memory but the saints themselves who lived with God in incorrupt bodies, other theologians made declarations that implied all dead persons were, in fact, still coincident with their bodies and not just souls who had temporarily animated matter, which meant that the best access to the spiritual power of the saints might be through contact with their bodies. After the Reformation the nature of these divine or saintly presences became the subject of persistent and often contentious debates. The most radical critics began to insist that at best Jesus was merely *represented* in the bread and that saintly piety was better *represented* in the words of scripture and acts of charity than in disreputable bones or diverting images.

Although the Protestants were the most thorough in their skepticism about the efficacy of religious rituals, Catholics engaged in their own systematic reform of ritual practices after the meetings of the Council of Trent (1545–63). Whereas Protestants abolished or radically reinterpreted most religious rituals, Catholics sought to preserve them but also to eliminate abuses in ritual practice and to distinguish between those that conformed to canonical doctrine and those that exhibited magical or superstitious beliefs.

The Protestant and Catholic Reformations only partially succeeded in undermining many traditional religious practices and making the interpretation of the meaning of a ritual more important than experien-

---

[1] Gianni Vattimo, *The End of Modernity: Nihilism and Hermeneutics in Post-modern Culture*, trans. Jon R. Snyder (Cambridge: Cambridge University Press, 1988), 149.

cing it. Long after the Reformation much of traditional ritual practice persisted among the faithful and even the clergy. The Reformation produced many ironies and inconsistencies. Precisely because the Catholic reformers still retained a vital role for ritual in religious life, they may have been more successful in sustaining lay piety than the Protestant churches which in some ways attempted the impossible – the broad propagation of an intellectualized religion in a society where only a small minority could read at all, let alone read something as difficult as scripture. Even when literacy spread to near universal levels, an overly rational religion failed to sustain many souls, as is shown by the enthusiasm for Methodism and its variants in Britain and America in the nineteenth century and the spread of charismatic Protestantism and Catholicism in the twentieth.

Ritual did not disappear since it is impossible to imagine a society without collective rituals, but many persons, especially the educated, became skeptical about the efficacy of ritual and distrustful of the emotionally manipulative qualities of ritual behavior. Ritual became a problem that required constant adjustments and reforms, which is one of the reasons why Protestantism proliferated in so many churches and sects, each unable to agree with others on the proper level of ritual practice and the proper interpretation of the scriptural Word. The spiritual evocation of community that Christians had once widely experienced through participation in Eucharistic rites gave way to the fragmentation of Christian culture, the over valuing of minor distinctions in ritual practices, and the propagandistic misinterpretation of doctrinal differences among the various churches.

Both Protestants and Catholics shared an intolerance for what they saw as magic, an intolerance that was only magnified by Reformation controversies. In fact, the fifteenth through seventeenth centuries in Europe witnessed a dramatic expansion of fears about evil generated through magical means. Church authorities and public officials co-operated in rooting out what were thought to be the sources of dangerous magic. As a consequence they condoned or encouraged repeated pogroms against Jews who were accused of the ritual killings of Christian children, and they made a great effort to curb what they thought was witchcraft, bringing thousands of harmless men and especially old women under judicial investigation, torture, and horrific execution by burning.

Throughout the early modern period, in a way that often paralleled religious developments, governments at many different levels adapted, borrowed, and invented an extraordinarily rich repertoire of rituals devoted to creating what can be called "theater states" – city-states, principalities, and monarchies that enacted and represented power through ceremonial performances. As was the case with many religious rites, the human body – figured in theater states as the "body politic" – constituted the central image in these rites. In many places at the beginning of the sixteenth century, political rites were devoted to "presenting" the prince in some fashion, a tradition that made the reigns of many monarchs peripatetic as they rambled about the country from castle to castle and town to town to make themselves physically *present* to their subjects. The critical political rite, therefore, became the royal entry into a town, a liminal rite as the body of a prince entered the space of a city that also understood itself as a kind of legal body. The rites of passage of kings and queens, especially their coronations and funerals, also became highly significant for the entire political community because these rites of passage made possible the transition of rulership from the body of one monarch to the next. During the early modern period political rituals became sufficiently sophisticated for the physical presence of a king to be less essential to rulership than before, and the rites of presenting the monarch increasingly gave way to rites that *represented* his or her rulership.

5   The Reformation as a revolution in ritual theory

In the twelfth century Peter Lombard codified the seven sacraments and promulgated the doctrine that Christian ritual practice should be anchored to them, but that codification only became official church dogma in 1439. The sacraments, however, had deep roots in archaic Hebrew and early Christian rites, sharing with other ritual systems the typical functions of purification, initiation, sanctification, transition to death, and communion with the divine. Several of these sacraments, as we have seen, were rites of passage that marked out crucial moments in the lives of individuals. Two assisted the entry into Christian society: by washing away original sin *baptism* specified the network of kin around newborns and initiated babies as Christians, and through the ritual laying-on of hands *confirmation* admitted the Christian into the full responsibilities of church membership. Although rarely practiced as a sacrament, *marriage* provided a new couple with a recognized social identity as a wife and husband. The alternative to marriage as a passage of status was *ordination*, which after the eleventh century was incompatible with matrimony in the West (but remained possible among the Orthodox churches) and which set certain men apart as priests who could perform the other six sacraments for the laity. *Extreme unction* prepared the soul for the final passage of death. Each of these rites of passage would be experienced only once in a person's life.

Christians could repeat the other two sacraments, but the laity, at least, did so infrequently. For most people *penance* was an annual event when they confessed and received absolution from their parish priest or a mendicant friar. Laymen and -women might witness Eucharistic rites of *communion* quite often, but only the meticulously pious would actually receive the wafer more than once a year.

What made the rituals that constituted the official sacraments different from other rites? For most late medieval scholastic theologians a true sacrament had the following characteristics: first, it combined *matter*, which was understood as a material object such as the host, or a gesture such as the laying-on of hands, with *form*, which was a correctly repeated verbal statement in Greek or Latin; second, the participants must have the correct *intention*, that is their will must be in accord with the act and they must not create an obstacle to the sacrament's work by failing to repent a sin; and third, if all the above elements were in place, the sacrament conferred *grace* on the recipients. In practice the intention of the recipient of a sacrament came to matter more than the intention of the celebrant so that a true sacrament merely had to be performed by an ordained clergyman whose ritual actions worked automatically irrespective of his moral worth as long as he paid due attention to the matter and form of the rite. The inherent virtue in the ritual came from its proper performance (*ex opere operato*) rather than from any distinguishing spiritual traits of the individual celebrant (*ex opere operans*). Unlike a shaman or prophet, a Christian priest did not require any personal charisma because he worked his miracles solely through the powers of his office rather than through the powers of his soul.

As a supplement to the seven official sacraments, the "sacramentals" provided a repertoire of rituals that could be employed by lay persons rather than by priests alone but that worked because of some powerful association with the ritual of priest craft. Consisting of minor rites and benedictions, actions associated with protective processions and exorcisms, and numerous blessed objects, the sacramentals borrowed gestures or prayers from church rituals or provided objects taken away from church by the laity for their own use at home, on the farm, or in the shop. For example, to drive away bad storms candles that had been blessed on the feast of the Purification of the Virgin were lit or palms from Palm Sunday were placed on the hearth fire. The palms might also provide medicine for sick cattle or be placed under pillows to ward off witches. Holy water was especially efficacious for encouraging fertility in barren couples or repelling illness in animals and people. In the eyes of the church the sacramentals were a form of supplication, a way in which the laity might call upon God for assistance and blessings, but to many simple believers they seemed more like a form of apotropaic (protective) magic, a ritual that had broad effects against many sources of evil and misfortune. Although some historians have been tempted to see the magical elements in the sacramentals as survivals of paganism, this seems unlikely since the rationale for the power of these gestures and objects is clearly derived from the liturgy itself. It would be better to see them as lay forms of clerical Christianity, practices that may not have always been properly understood but were quasi-legitimate appropriations of official practices that served the needs of common people.

This lay attitude toward the sacraments and the sacramentals might be called "crypto-materialism," a belief that the sacred could be made manifest in ordinary objects when certain ritual words were spoken or ritual actions performed. Robert Scribner has suggested three ways in which "crypto-materialism" might be understood. First, many actions reveal that believers often thought they had established a kind of binding contract with the sacred being. During times of plague the Florentines frequently brought a panel painting of the Madonna of Impruneta from its suburban home to the heart of the city and offered her many gifts, but if the plague failed to abate, the painting would be reviled and spat upon as if she were a dishonest merchant who had failed to pay a debt. Throughout Europe vintners looked to St. Urban as a protector who revealed through the weather on his feast day how bountiful the harvest was going to be that year. If the weather turned bad, disappointed grape-growers might throw his image into the mud, humiliating a saint who had accepted their devotion but failed to keep his part of the bargain by safeguarding their interests properly.

Second, many lay believers approached sacred objects in a highly sensual way that cannot easily be distinguished from an aesthetic response. The sacraments and sacramentals provided a medium through which the spiritual came into contact with the profane by appealing to the human senses, and the senses appealed to most commonly were sight and sound. Not only did priests find visual representations useful as a means of instructing the illiterate in the Bible and lives of the saints, but the laity craved visualizations of miracles and protective patrons, which led to an enormous explosion of religious art, especially in the fifteenth century. At the same time musical elaborations of the mass and canonical hours provided employment for composers and stimulated a fashion for organs in churches, again especially in the fifteenth century.

Third, there was a widespread materialist conception of sacred powers, an idea sustained by the doctrines that emphasized the actual physical presence of Christ's flesh and blood in the Eucharistic wafer and wine. If God chose to reveal himself in this way in the mass would he not employ similar methods on more mundane occasions? Late medieval Christians *expected* to find the sacred manifest itself in material objects that could be seen, touched, smelled, tasted, and ingested. As the codification of a ritual system, the official sacraments and semi-official sacramentals depended upon the assumption that divine and saintly beings would make themselves present in material objects in response to the supplications of humans. These contractual, aesthetic, and sensual characteristics meant that Christian ritual demanded the presence of human and divine bodies to work its wonders.

"This is my body"

More than anything else Christian theologians base their claim to possess the single true faith on the doctrine of the incarnation. God came to earth by entering the womb of a virgin, and was, therefore, uncorrupted by Adam's transgression and the lust of procreation. Christ became through incarnation simultaneously God and a man, having all the attributes of both. God took on flesh, that is he became "incarnate," which meant that he felt pain, experienced thirst, shed tears, and died as all mortals die. By entering into the world in this physical way, God instituted an earthly organization among the apostles that became the church, and by allowing himself to suffer, bleed, and die on the cross he offered an all-sufficient sacrifice that made possible the salvation of corrupt humanity. Having inherited Christ's holiness, his merits, and his powers of sanctification, the church performed the work of mediating these benefits to humankind through the ministrations of the priesthood. This "work" constituted the sacraments. The incarnation made visible the invisible God, and by analogy the sacraments made visible the invisible efforts of the holy spirit. Of the seven sacraments, the Eucharist most obviously embodied the incarnation by offering the promise of salvation to each individual at a particular ritual moment in a way that the crucifixion did for all humanity at a particular historical moment.

Given the central importance of the incarnation, it became especially vital for Christians to demonstrate the dual nature of Christ as a god-man. He was not just another prophet, miracle worker, or mysterious spiritual being but the one true God who chose to become a man. During the fourteenth and fifteenth centuries, in particular, theologians, preachers, mystics, and artists concentrated more intensely than ever before or since on exploring the literal implications of Christ's carnality. Some of these explorations now seem quite strange, even irreverent. As Leo Steinberg has shown, in fifteenth-century Italy thoroughly Christian artists made visual allusions to Christ's phallus, showing that the god-man had *all* the attributes of other men. In many paintings the Virgin Mary pointed to the penis of the infant Jesus, and some scenes of the deposition from the cross obviously showed the outlines of Christ's adult member beneath the obligatory cloth that hid his sex from view. Allied to this concentration on the parts of Christ's body was the cult of the holy foreskin. Other than the consecrated host and perhaps some drops of blood shed on the cross, the fleshy residue from the infant Jesus's circumcision would have been the only bodily remnant of Christ on earth since the rest of his body was resurrected and ascended to heaven. The researches of Caroline Walker Bynum have shown that the cult of the holy foreskin seems to have had a certain charm for female mystics. When Catherine of Siena experienced her mystic marriage to the infant Jesus, she received from him a ring made not of gold but of his foreskin. A pious Viennese woman experienced a vision in which she received the holy foreskin in her mouth and discovered that it tasted as sweet as honey.

These images of the body, however, had less to do with sexuality than with fertility and resurrection, with the divine as the source of all life and with the death of the divine-man as promising a future paradise for all who believed in him. Controlling one's own body, especially through self-inflicted suffering and harsh self-discipline, did not so much indicate a rejection of the human body as its use to gain access to the sacred. Although both men and women devoted themselves to corporal religiosity, body-centered manifestations of piety seem to have been particularly intense among female mystics. Women experienced a whole range of psychosomatic phenomena: seizures, levitations, enlargements of parts of their bodies, catatonic states, and most notably "holy anorexia," the inability to eat anything other than the host. The ecstatically sensual female approach to God appears in mystic accounts of tasting the sweetness of Christ's flesh, kissing him deeply, entering his heart or even his entrails, and experiencing the sensation of being covered by his blood. The Counter Reformation visionary, St. Teresa of Avila, experienced the deeply sensual pain/pleasure of repeated penetrations by an arrow thrust into her body by a beautiful seraph.

Some late medieval writers even saw Christ's body itself as distinctly female because in the absence of a mortal father all his flesh came from Mary, making him the most completely "female" male to have ever lived. Christ was also the only male who shared with women the ability to nurture others through the body: Christ through his fleshy presence in the host, women through nursing at the breast. Women's milk itself was understood to have certain Christ-like qualities. Holy virgins were said to lactate without pregnancy and offered their miraculous breast milk to cure the afflicted. The fourteenth and fifteenth centuries saw a profusion of paintings depicting the Virgin nursing the Christ child, and the Dominican Order, in particular, promoted the cult of the Virgin nursing, which led John Calvin to remark in a rare moment of levity that there was a great deal of Virgin's milk around.

At the heart of incarnation theology was the Eucharistic rite of the mass. In each of the four gospels is an account of the last supper at which Christ instituted the mass:

Now as they were eating, Jesus took bread, and blessed, and broke it, and gave it to the disciples and said, "Take, eat; this is my body." And he took a cup, and when he had given thanks he gave it to them, saying, "Drink of it, all of you; for this is my blood of the covenant, which is poured out for many for the forgiveness of sins. I tell you I shall not drink again of this fruit of the vine until that day when I drink it anew with you in my Father's kingdom." (Matthew 26: 26–29)

The key phrase was "this is my body" or "Hoc est enim Corpus Meum" in the Latin of the Roman liturgy. Taken in a literal way the gospel account of the supper equated bread and Christ's sacrificed body, wine and his blood that was shed for the remission of sins.

The moment in the mass when the priest repeated the words of institution, often barely whispered in awe, was the most delicate and momentous in all Christian ritual: he had to repeat the verbal formulas in the ancient Latin tongue and perform the prescribed ceremonial gestures with exact precision. Only a consecrated priest could say the words, which were forbidden to laymen and all women who could not even touch the liturgical vessels of the mass with their bare hands. It was a moment of great mystery, of what one writer has called "the highest magico-liturgical tension," a moment for divine apparitions or demonic temptations, a moment full of magnificent possibilities and horrible dangers, a moment when anything could happen. The "disquieting space" of the altar made many priests remarkably anxious while others numbed themselves into a trance-like state because here they enacted the ultimate mystery of transforming a simple wafer of unleavened bread into the body of the living God, and each priest did this by speaking a few unadorned words while standing terribly alone.[1] A great deal of the power of the Eucharistic rites derived from the aesthetic simplicity of the ritual methods used to achieve such exalted results.

Ingesting the host put the Christian into contact with the ineffable through a mysterious food that brought both salvation and health, both signified by many late medieval writers with the same word, salus. Contemplating the host as food, however, could encourage unappetizing sensations since by eating the Eucharist the Christian cannibalized God, a distasteful expectation urged by reports of the bread turning into bloody flesh on the paten or in the mouth. Theologians discussed in detail the whole process: the fragmentation of Christ by chewing, slipping him down the throat to the stomach, and the awful prospect of his virtue mixing with the excrement of the bowels, a possibility that made the stomach and bowels the subject of considerable theological discussion. Some solved the problem by insisting that the divine food was entirely absorbed into the body in the stomach leaving no residue for the intestines, and the penitentials tried to eliminate any possibility of

[1] Piero Camporesi, "Consecrated Host: A Wondrous Excess," in Michel Feher, ed., *Fragments for a History of the Human Body* (New York: Zone Books, 1989), part I, p. 225.

contamination by transforming the Eucharist into a ritual of purification preceded by a rigorous fast that would leave the digestive tract empty.

The stomach, nevertheless, remained the crucial organ because it was here and only here that the absorption of the divine into the human could take place, translating the whole mystery of Christianity into a ritual of consuming God, and it was here in the stomach that the most profound considerations of Christian truth entered the dangerous realm of the King of Carnival who celebrated the gluttony of the lower body. The frank physicality of the late medieval infatuation with the Eucharist now seems at best quaint, at worst grotesque because the modern sensibility has placed a veil between believers and the bloody offering of the Eucharist, which has been "disincarnated" even in the post-Tridentine Catholic church.

So compelling was the miracle of Eucharistic sacrifice that every object associated with the ritual took on remarkable powers. As Eamon Duffy puts it, "power 'leaked' from the Host and the blood."[2] The altar cloth had healing powers, jaundiced persons could be cured by looking into the chalice after the mass, the consecrated host could extinguish dangerous fires, and the water and wine mixture used to wash out the chalice after the mass cured whooping cough. As a sacred object the host was especially effective against maladies understood to be caused by demonic agents, such as epilepsy, hysteria, madness, and possession. In Liège in 1374 authorities attempted to cure a group of flagellants considered to be possessed by demons by having the host shown to them and then placed on their heads.

Given the sublime ritual powers of the Eucharist, it is especially important to understand what the experience of communion might have been for the laity. Besides its significance for individual salvation, the mass became an important reinforcement of collective values because all Christian communities, whether the church, city, or state, were understood to be "bodies" or corporations (corpus = body). Celebrating the sacred body of the Eucharist abetted social cohesion, sometimes in a manipulative fashion to serve the interests of hegemonic elites, but for many simple believers there was certainly an authentic passion for the experience of unity with others as an antidote to the conflicts and turmoil of daily life, a desire manifest as the loss of the self in the group, imagined as the universal church, kingdom, town, village, or parish. A prayer found in many sixteenth-century English primers, used to prepare the lay believer for communion, expresses with simple beauty the craving for individual renewal within the body

[2] Eamon Duffy, *The Stripping of the Altars: Traditional Religion in England c.1400–c.1580* (New Haven: Yale University Press, 1992), 110.

of Christ, understood as the community of believers. In the prayer the communicant asks Christ that,

I may be worthy to be incorporated into Your body, which is the Church. May I be one of Your members, and may You be my head, that I may remain in You, and You in me, so that in the resurrection my lowly body may be conformed to Your glorious body.[3]

Since only a few exceptionally aristocratic or exceptionally pious believers received communion privately or more often than once a year, most people took the host along with a flock of neighbors and fellow parishioners and only on Easter Sunday when they heard a sermon that accentuated the obligations of social unity and the avoidance of the sins that disturbed the public peace, such as envy and wrath. In England taking communion was called "taking one's rights," which meant asserting one's membership in the community, and to suffer excommunication, that is the prohibition from receiving the sacraments, would have meant exclusion from both the universal community of believers and the local community of citizens. As is so often the case with social groups, insiders and outsiders were defined by what they ate or refused to eat: a community is what it eats, which is why the different food taboos of Christians and Jews – the abstinence from meat on Fridays or from pork in general – were so crucial to the identities of the respective communities. Although the ideal of social harmony conveyed in the communion rite may not have been achieved very often in the daily give and take of village life, the occasional ritual experience of utopia expressed a model for what society could be.

Taking communion implied a threat that God would retaliate against anyone who broke the peace of the community, a threat that magistrates and governors frequently employed in the rites of reconciliation between feuding families. In Italy when persons involved in a vendetta made peace, each received the Eucharist, celebrating their new collectivity as members of the body of Christ and publicly acknowledging that they put themselves in peril of the "vendetta of God" were they to break the peace, a vendetta that might deprive them of the protection of community in this life as well as of salvation in the next.

The experience of communion, however, did not require the actual ingestion of the host, which was taken far too infrequently to have a lasting effect on community feeling. For most people, most of the time, the experience of community came from seeing rather than eating the body of God. By the thirteenth century the celebrating priest would have been expected, immediately after speaking the Latin words of institution,

[3] Cited in Duffy, *The Stripping of the Altars*, 93.

"This is my body," to raise the host high above his head. The elevation became the most dramatic moment for the laymen and -women who witnessed the mass. Contributing to the mystery of the rite was its masterful staging on major feasts in the great churches. The priest, whose daily masses were a familiar, even homely event, became on those occasions an isolated, distant figure, obscured by a cloud of sweet incense and separated from the laity by the choir screen, a waist-high barrier that framed the liturgical drama, and during Lent he was hidden by a veil that entirely blocked the laity's view of the altar: he became a conjurer who performed his great miracle with his back turned to the viewers, muttering the words of institution while he bent over the altar. Hearing little or nothing of the words spoken, the congregation waited expectantly for the thrilling moment of elevation, which was announced by the ringing of bells and perhaps by the opening of the choir screen to assist viewing. On important feast days a blaze of expensive candles brought as gifts by the congregants lit up the altar, and sometimes a dark curtain behind it provided a backdrop to highlight the elevated host.

In English churches where the rood-screen might have blocked the view for the kneeling communicants, "elevation squints" or peep holes made it possible to spy at the elevation, and in large cathedrals where many masses were celebrated simultaneously, the timing of the sacring in each mass was staggered so that the laity could watch as many elevations as possible by moving about from altar to altar. In some Italian towns a cult of pious women emerged who would spend the day moving from church to church to watch elevations, which they witnessed with ecstatic shouts and screams. The visual and sensual character of lay devotion to the host is strikingly evoked in the criticism of the French Protestant reformer, Antoine Marcourt:

After that they had blown or spoken over the bread, which they hold between their fingers, and over the wine that they put in the chalice, that there remains neither bread nor wine, but by transformation, or as they say transubstantiation, the body of Jesus Christ is there under the accidents of the bread invisible hidden . . .
Instead of bread and wine (as they say) under the shapes or kinds visible, white or black, yellow or red, it is alone the body of Jesus Christ really and indeed entirely, corporally and personally in flesh and bone . . . They have provoked almost the universal world to manifest and public idolatry . . .
It is an overdulling and darkening of the spirit and understanding of the people to cause them to . . . stare at a little bread, at a visible and corruptible thing.[4]

Although both Protestant and Catholic reformers would later ridicule this intensely materialist sensitivity to the host as an example of the

---

[4] Antoine Marcourt, *A Declaration of the Masse, and the Fruyte Thereof* ([Wittenberg], 1547), no pagination. Spellings have been modernized.

gullibility of the masses, laymen and -women were, in fact, conforming to the pious behavior encouraged by the church itself. Virginia Reinburg has shown that late medieval prayer books, written in the French vernacular by clerics to guide the laity, represented the mass in a quite different fashion from how it appeared in the missals of the clergy. Whereas a priest was expected to have an intellectual understanding of the doctrine of transubstantiation and of the scriptural basis for the mass, nothing of the sort was expected of the laity who were instructed, rather, on how to assume their proper role in the ritual drama. The lay prayer books never explain the doctrine of transubstantiation and do not even mention the words of consecration spoken by the priest. One English treatise on the mass is quite explicit by instructing the laity to "worship" the gospel that even "when not understood, the power of God's word still avails."[5] These books did not encourage the laity to tax their wits in unraveling the difficulties of form, substance, and accidents in explaining how a wafer of bread could become the flesh of God, nor did prayer books introduce complex ideas about the incarnation, nor did they even present the words of scripture. The task of the laity was simply to envision Christ elevated on the cross whenever they saw the raised host. They were to adore, not think.

A vital part in the celebration of the mass, which barely appears at all in the priest's missal, was the ritual of the pax-board. After the priest prayed for peace and kissed the altar, he kissed the pax-board, and gave it to an acolyte who carried it through the congregation, for each member to kiss. Although kissing the board obviously reinforced the pledge of community harmony, some prayer books went further to compare it with partaking of the Eucharist. Kissing the pax-board shared with the host the same intense tactile materiality, the same sensuous contact with bodies, in this case indirect contact with the lips of all of one's fellow communicants. The mass for the laity incorporated a series of rites and practices that focused less on the sacrifice of Christ and the promise of salvation than on gestures derived from secular life, gestures that made the mass a communal rite of gift giving, sharing, and peace making.

Far from feeling alienated from the orchestrated ritual of the altar, which was the exclusive domain of the ordained clergy, the laity during the fourteenth and fifteenth centuries took up the Eucharistic cult with great enthusiasm, pushing for ever more elaborate Corpus Christi processions and plays; paying for more candles, more sumptuous altar cloths, more elaborate architectural frames for the mystic ritual; endowing chantries to finance the repetition of masses in perpetuity; and

---

[5] Quoted in ibid., 530.

building more altars along the side aisles of churches to create more spaces for more masses.

So popular became the cult of the host that it began to replace as the principal focus of lay piety the more traditional devotion to relics, that is the bones of holy martyrs and saints. The miracle at Bolsena represented only one of the numerous shrines that sprang up during the fourteenth and fifteenth centuries to revere a bleeding host. These shrines were particularly widespread in the German-speaking territories where pilgrims flocked to see hosts that had begun to bleed as proof against a skeptic, or because of mishandling by a clumsy priest or greedy layman, or because of an alleged ritual murder or profanation by Jews. When the village of Wilsnack was destroyed by arson in 1383, three bleeding hosts were miraculously preserved from the flames. So many pilgrims came to venerate the hosts of Wilsnack that the tiny village grew into a prosperous town. Questioning the authenticity of the Wilsnack hosts spurred a major theological controversy that drew in the Bohemian reforming theologian Jan Hus, Pope Urban VI, and the humanist churchman Nicholas of Cusa, revealing that even before the Reformation the excesses of the cult of the Eucharist created significant doubts among the more thoughtful. Hus and the Oxford don, John Wyclif, criticized the new Eucharistic practices on doctrinal grounds and stimulated the most important reformist movements before Luther. For the Hussites, in particular, the debate with the official church largely revolved around what they saw as abuses of priestly power in Eucharistic ritual.

On the eve of the Reformation, Eucharistic piety composed one of the great pillars of the Christian ritual system, a pillar that held up in a straightforward, material way a vast edifice of incarnation theology and spiritual mystery. There were, nevertheless, some cracks in that ritual structure, fissures revealed by the spreading feeling among many that the materiality of the sacramental system inhibited rather than assisted the true inward imitation of Christ. The goal of imitation might be better served, it was thought, by prayer and improved knowledge of the scriptures, the Word that assumed meaning through study rather than flesh through ritual.

From presence to representation

In 1569 in the midst of the bloody Wars of Religion in France, Michel de Montaigne looked back at the Eucharistic debates over the meaning of "Hoc est enim Corpus Meum" that had divided Catholic from Protestant and lamented, "how many quarrels, and what momentous ones, have been caused in the world by the uncertainty as to the meaning of the syllable *Hoc!*"[6] Although it is an exaggeration to explain all the Reformation as a dispute over theology, no other disagreement was as important for the transformations of the Christian ritual system as the Eucharistic debates. These debates brought the hermeneutical questions about the meaning of rites to the forefront: for the sacramental Protestants, at least, the phrase, "this is my body," now became a statement about how the divine was *represented* rather than *presented* in the sacraments, and the rejection of a divine presence in rites brought the efficacy of the entire ritual system into question.

Doubts about Christian ritual practice had surfaced long before Martin Luther and Ulrich Zwingli revised the sacramental system. There are even hints of sacramental disputes in the New Testament itself. In the thirteenth century, in place of the eternal return of the liturgical cycle, the followers of Joachim of Fiore sought to substitute a prophetic eschatology that promised the progressive transformation of history. If history moved in stages that advanced toward higher levels of spiritual understanding, as they thought, then the static repetitions of the liturgy might inhibit rather than assist a leap to the next stage. The Lollard followers of John Wyclif asserted in 1395 that the many material implements of liturgical ritual – the "wine, bread, and wax, water, salt and oil and incense"[7] – were the tools of wizards. In the fifteenth century the Hussites in Bohemia pursued a radical, anticlerical reform that reorganized worship around objections to Catholic Eucharistic practices: Hussite priests allowed the laity to sip from the chalice of consecrated wine, which had traditionally been prohibited to them. From this practice the Hussites came to be known as Utraquists, those who received communion "in both kinds" (*sub utraque specie*), a trait that reveals, however, a desire for even greater lay access to the Eucharist, whatever their animosities toward corrupt priests and clerical privilege.

Even in the Italian center of ecclesiastical Christianity, objections surfaced in the fifteenth century about the emptiness of ritual piety. The Dominican prophet, Fra Girolamo Savonarola, who was burned at the stake in 1498, had preached against "mere ceremonies," and Egidio da Viterbo, who was the Prior General of the Augustinians (Martin Luther's order), wrote that when the Eucharist was performed without the proper love and devotion, it was a "vain work."[8] Throughout the century some high ecclesiastics, monastic mystics, and lay followers of

---

[6] Michel de Montaigne, "Apology for Raimond Sebond," book 2, essay 12 in *The Essays*, trans. George B. Ives (Cambridge, Mass.: Harvard University Press, 1925), vol. 2, p. 301.

[7] Cited in Thomas M. Greene, "Ritual and Text in the Renaissance," *Canadian Review of Comparative Literature* (June–September 1991): 180.

[8] Ibid., 181.

the Modern Devotion (a fifteenth-century movement that emphasized individualist and inward spirituality) complained that the sacraments and especially the Eucharist had become empty formalities, practiced without humility or spiritual enlightenment. To these critics the sacraments had become worthless substitutes for true devotion.

Around the turn of the sixteenth century, as Thomas Greene has persuasively shown, "a kind of crisis confronted the communal, performative sign." This crisis in confidence in the efficacy of ritual can be seen in what Greene calls the "curious destiny" of the word "ceremony." Erasmus employed a Latin neologism *ceremoniolae*, which has been translated by one scholar as "trivial little ritual nonsenses." In English one of the sub-definitions of "ceremony" had become "a rite or observance regarded as merely formal or external; an empty form." The *Oxford English Dictionary*'s first recorded use of "ceremony" with a disparaging meaning is 1533, when it was contrasted to the true body of Christ: "Shal we become Jewes and go backe to the shadow and ceremonie, sith [even though] we have the body and signification whiche is Christ?" A social critic of the English aristocracy later complained that gentility is "a meer flash, a ceremony, a toy, a thing of nought." In fact, the word "ritual" as opposed to "rite" began as a pejorative word in English, first appearing according to the *OED* in 1570: "contayning no maner of doctrine . . . but only certayn ritual decrees to no purpose." The same pattern appears in the other vernacular languages of Europe during the sixteenth century. Giovanni Della Casa cited ceremonies, lies, and dreams as examples of illusions that should be ignored; these were things that consist "in appearances without substance and in words without meaning." In Italian *cerimonie* became a synonym for *vanità*. Struck by the degenerates who congregated around the pope, a French visitor reported in the middle of the century that "I only found ceremony there," and his compatriot, Michel de Montaigne, wrote "we are only ceremonies" to convey his disgust with the hypocrisy of social formalities. Rather than offering access to divine mysteries and hidden powers, "ceremonies" and by extension "rituals" came to be considered in the minds of some, at least, as synonymous with fraud.[9]

The intellectual resources for the most wide-ranging assault on ritual practices came from the Renaissance movement called humanism. The humanists devoted themselves to imitating the rhetorical eloquence of classical Latin and Greek as well as rediscovering the least corrupted

---

[9] For the above quotes and argument, see Greene, "Ritual and Text in the Renaissance," 181–82. Quote from Giovanni Della Casa's *Galateo* is cited in Edward Muir, *Mad Blood Stirring: Vendetta and Factions in Friuli during the Renaissance* (Baltimore: Johns Hopkins University Press, 1993), 254.

texts of ancient pagan and Christian writing. Humanism was a technique rather than a philosophy, a linguistic movement devoted to teaching how to write and speak persuasively and to understanding texts in the context of the time when they were composed, what we would now call a philological or historical approach. Although one can find humanists on opposite sides of most questions, and certainly there were both Catholic and Protestant humanists, there was a tendency among many of them to emphasize individual morality rather than collective ritual observances and a concern among all of them for hermeneutics, the process of discerning meaning. This new orientation came from their desire to imbue ethics in their students and readers but also from the very nature of the humanist enterprise itself. Reading and understanding ancient texts pushed the humanists toward valuing interpretation over experience, meaning over the presentation of mysteries.

Satire became one of the most popular polemical genres among the humanists, and no one was more savagely effective as a satirist than Desiderius Erasmus (c. 1466–1536), a lapsed monk whose writings mocked without mercy corrupt priests and credulous laity. Erasmus's critique of traditional ritual practices concentrated less on the rites themselves than on how priests and monks employed them to inflate their own pretentious authority and phoney piety: clerics "insist that they've properly performed their duty if they reel off perfunctorily their feeble prayers which I'd be greatly surprised if any god could hear or understand" and members of the many different religious orders "aren't interested in being like Christ but in being unlike each other."[10] Erasmus was especially savage about the "pharisaical ceremonies" of monks and friars who devoted themselves to absurd ritual regulations:

Many of them work so hard at protocol and at traditional fastidiousness that they think one heaven hardly a suitable reward for their labors; never recalling, however, that the time will come when Christ will demand a reckoning of that which he has prescribed, namely charity, and that he will hold their deeds of little account. One monk will then exhibit his belly filled with every kind of fish; another will profess a knowledge of over a hundred hymns. Still another will reveal a countless number of fasts he has made, and will account for his large belly by explaining that his fasts have always been broken by a single large meal. Another will show a list of church ceremonies over which he has officiated so large that it would fill seven ships.[11]

Erasmus and many other humanists were even more vehement in

[10] Quoted in Euan Cameron, *The European Reformation* (Oxford: Clarendon Press, 1991), 65.
[11] "The Praise of Folly," in *The Essential Erasmus*, selected and newly translated by John P. Dolan (New York: Mentor-Omega Books, 1964), 149.

criticizing what they saw as the superstitious nonsense and fetishism of lay piety. In the *Praise of Folly*, Erasmus lampooned the credulity of people who looked to images of the saints for miracles, who were taken in by the most preposterous relics, and who imagined that God was a lordly patron delivering favors in exchange for a few good works and prayerful solicitations. Erasmus was the quintessential intellectual snob, the kind of person who can still be found at the high tables of Cambridge or in the coffee houses of many American university towns, but he was also a masterful publicist feeding a huge market of intellectual parvenus who wanted to be able to chatter about the latest chic idea. The elitism of humanism made it attractive to half-educated aristocrats and social-climbing commoners alike but also limited its direct influence by orienting the reform of the church toward an arid intellectualism that was ill suited to most of the laity and many simple-hearted priests, monks, and nuns.

The problem of ritual for the humanist critics was not so much that the ceremonial practices of the church were inherently false but that they had been misused by those motivated by avarice and misunderstood by those naive enough to believe that merely performing ritual duties constituted righteousness. While condemning fake relics and super-stition, the pre-Reformation humanists, at least, did not oppose the truly pious forms of ritual behavior. Erasmus himself visited famous shrines. The wild poet, Ulrich von Hutten, both criticized craven priests and wished he could go himself on a pilgrimage to Jerusalem. What the humanists wanted to achieve was to reorient piety away from observing the liturgical forms of Christianity to understanding its substance. As Erasmus said, "You can only establish perfect piety when you turn away from visible things, which are for the most part either imperfect or of themselves indifferent, and you seek instead the invisible, which corresponds to the highest part of human nature."[12] In his best-selling handbook on Christian piety, the *Enchiridion*, Erasmus expounded a simple formula as the test for true righteousness: the proper imitation of Christ must be founded on prayer and knowledge. Deep and persistent prayer was to guide the Christian in his or her individual search for understanding, and the text to be understood was less the text of the liturgy than the text of scripture.

Perhaps the greatest achievement of the Christian humanists was the vast publishing enterprise that made available editions of the scriptures in the original languages rather than just in the Latin of the Vulgate edition. Erasmus himself produced a critical Greek edition of the New

---

[12] Quoted in Carlos M. N. Eire, *War Against the Idols: The Reformation of Worship from Erasmus to Calvin* (Cambridge: Cambridge University Press, 1986), 34.

Testament in 1516, and a consortium of humanist scholars at the University of Alcalà in Spain brought out by 1520 a "polyglot" Bible that allowed readers to compare original and translated versions of the sacred texts. Christian humanists learned ancient Greek to read the New Testament in the original, and after Johannes Reuchlin published a Hebrew grammar, they joined Jewish rabbis in puzzling over the meaning of the Word in the Hebrew scriptures.

As a consequence of this initiative in scriptural hermeneutics, by the 1520s many humanists, priests, and pious laymen and -women accepted a new criterion for what was proper ritual practice: did the rite appear in the Bible? That question is easier to ask than to answer since the rich complexity of the scriptural text allows different readers to interpret it differently. Traditional Christian rituals owed more to the long history of lay and clerical piety and to scholastic theology than to the Bible itself. The dilemma created by humanist learning was to reconcile ritual practices with the Biblical text. For their part the Protestant reformers found no justification in scripture for confirmation, ordination, marriage, extreme unction, and penance. The problematic evidence for the practice of penance in the Bible gave them considerable trouble, but they eventually dropped it as a sacrament because penance seemed a return to the purification of baptism and could not, therefore, be a separate sacrament.

Accepting the primacy of scripture, however, presented the reformers with a dilemma. On the one hand, they wanted to follow St. Paul's injunction that man is justified by faith alone by eliminating any claim that the sacraments could somehow constitute a pious work sufficient to achieve salvation. The central Protestant concept of justification meant that grace was an unmerited gift manifest in the faith of the elect Christian and understood through the preaching of the scriptural Word. On the other hand, scripture clearly authorized one sacrament, communion, and seemed to authorize a second, baptism, and accepting these two rites meant that the Protestant reformers had to develop a ritual theory to explain exactly what happened when communicants ate the Eucharistic bread and when infants or adults were baptized. Most Protestant churches kept both of these sacraments in some form, but once the radicals irrefutably demonstrated that *infant* baptism could not be found in the words of the Bible, mainstream Protestants had to abandon their own reliance on scripture alone and resort, as did Catholics, to historical authority based on the practices of the early church. As much as any issue, disagreements over the practice of baptism doomed the unity of the Protestant reform. As Euan Cameron has put it, "in short, the reformers were saddled with the sacraments;

the inner logic of their basic theme, which gave the rest of their teaching such tight logical coherence, on this topic gave them conflicting messages."[13] The assumed sacramental precedents in the Bible tested the intellectual ingenuity of the reformers, and their inability to agree on the proper interpretation of these rituals divided them into quarreling camps that eventually became separate sects and churches.

Most of the reformers could agree on simplifying the medieval conception of a sacrament by eliminating the scholastic jargon about the ritual components of matter, form, and intention. To them a sacrament consisted solely of a promise of God to which he attached a *sign*. As John Calvin put it, a sacrament is "an outward sign by which the Lord seals on our consciences the promise of his good will."[14] A sacrament "worked" because the recipient had faith. Moreover, since it was merely an alternative way of proclaiming the Word of God, a sacrament had to be openly and publicly delivered in the language of the congregation rather than hidden behind a chancel screen and mumbled in the strange Latin of the church.

The reformers had better success in finding a definition of a sacrament than in explaining how it functioned. Concerned as they were to insist that a sacrament was a sign of a sacred promise rather than a holy thing made present through ritual, the reformers stumbled in trying to agree on what a sacrament did. They struggled to resolve the tension between the meaning they thought they found in scripture and the experience they wanted to provide for believers by participating in a sacrament. The debate over the meaning of the two surviving sacraments, communion and baptism, brought out minute differences of interpretation that split the reform movement and destroyed the sense of social solidarity traditionally evoked in sacraments, especially in the Eucharistic communion.

The doctrine of transubstantiation promulgated by the Fourth Lateran Council in 1215 had compromised between literalist and spiritualist extremes by distinguishing, as we have seen, between the substance of the Eucharist, which was converted into the body and blood of Christ, and the accidents, the outer sensory appearances of bread and wine, which remained unchanged. This conception of a supernatural presence in a material object was worked out in the twelfth and thirteenth centuries by the scholastic theologians who employed the logical categories of Aristotle to make sense of the difficult problem presented by the scriptural text in which Christ distributes bread to his apostles and says, "This is my body."

[13] Cameron, *The European Reformation*, 156.   [14] Quoted in ibid., 157.

The sixteenth-century reformers thought this formula obscured the singularity of Christ's sacrifice of himself on the cross. As Luther put it, the holy ghost knows even more than Aristotle. In 1518 in a sermon about how to prepare for holy communion, Luther voiced his famous doctrine: "You will receive as much as you believe you receive."[15] This shift toward faith and the inner psycho-spiritual state of the believer did not, however, become for Luther what it meant for Ulrich Zwingli and most modern Protestants. Luther insisted on retaining the Real Presence in the Eucharist and refused either to abandon a ritual communion or to accept a symbolic interpretation of it. The ritual still *presented* God to the believer, who nevertheless could not gain access to God through any self-effort or without faith. Because humans are composed of more than mind and soul, they require God's presence in themselves as corporate beings: "The mouth, the throat, the body which eats Christ's body should also profit from it so it will live eternally and be resurrected on the Last Day . . . That is the heavenly power and the profit of Christ's body going into our body during the Lord's Supper."[16] The ritual generates power and produces profit. Ritual kept its efficacy for Luther, at least as long as the communicant is spiritually receptive, and ritual was still necessary for him, precisely because God must reach our bodies as well as our souls, and immaterial words are insufficient to the task. Luther retained belief in the Real Presence but rejected the scholastic idea that the "substances" of bread and wine changed during the consecration. Instead, he argued that *both* bread and body, wine and blood, coexist simultaneously in the same space, just as both God and man were present at the same time in the historical Jesus. Luther's idea of the coexistence of two substances within the communion wafer has often been called a doctrine of *con*substantiation to contrast his views with the Catholic theory of change called *tran*substantiation.

Most other reformers, however, could not abide Luther's persistent materialism. As early as the Second Zürich Disputation in 1523, the door to misunderstanding was opened forever. The very act of asking the question, "what does 'This is my body' mean?" tended to poison the living Eucharist among Protestants in a way that was symptomatic of a broad assault on the theory that rituals can make the divine *present* in the material.

Although most reformers could agree in criticizing the Catholic and Lutheran solution to the ritual problem, they could not find a mutually satisfactory alternative understanding of the meaning of "This is my

---

[15] Quoted in Heiko A. Oberman, *Luther: Man between God and the Devil*, trans. Eileen Walliser-Schwarzbart (New York: Doubleday, 1989), 240.
[16] Quoted in ibid., 243.

body." Andreas Karlstadt, Johannes Oecolampadius, Martin Bucer, and Ulrich Zwingli each pounced on different words as most significant, conjured up different inferences, and pulled out different explanatory passages from various places in scripture. In one of the stranger moves, Karlstadt focused on the word "This" (*Hoc*), asserting that when Christ said, "This is my body," he was pointing to himself rather than the bread, a claim that removed all sacrificial significance from the bread and radically devalued the ritual commemoration of the last supper. Once Luther's colleague at the University of Wittenberg, Karlstadt was an early radical whose uncompromising biblicism led him to attack all externals in religious practice, opposing the use of holy water, sacred salt, and images in churches. What other reformers saw as indifferent or useless objects, Karlstadt saw as deeply evil, which pushed him to attack all forms of Eucharistic adoration as idolatry and to eliminate many ritual practices.

In contrast to Karlstadt whose influence was limited by his own prickly personality, Zwingli developed an original and a highly influential, rationalist position by 1524: all previous theorists, he asserted, had misunderstood the function of the word "is." When Jesus says "is" (*est*), he actually meant "signifies" (*significat*): thus when he said, "This is my body," he meant, "This [bread] *signifies* my body." The function of *est* in the sentence moved from equating body and bread to dissociating them in a radical way, to detaching definitively Christ's human and divine natures. The bread now entered the semantic realm of representations rather than serving as a vehicle for the presentation of God to humanity. In accord with the other reformers, Zwingli reached this position by privileging the spiritual qualities of faith over the work of the sacraments, but he also betrayed humanist influences derived from the study of classical rhetoric: for him the phrase, "This is my body," was an example of biblical metonymy, a figure of speech that means a "change of name." A metonymy typically substitutes the "name" or "sign" of one thing for the name of another thing. In this case Zwingli argued that the Catholic reading of the passage misunderstood the metonymy of scripture by taking literally the substitution of the word "body" for the word "bread." The Catholics assumed that the substance, "bread," was changed into the substance, "body," whereas Zwingli insisted that the only change was in the names. Zwingli and his heirs understood the trope of metonymy as the key to biblical mysteries, which were often misunderstood precisely because of the characteristics of metonymy. Unlike a metaphor which compares the likenesses in things, as in "a wine-dark sea," the comparisons in metonymy seem arbitrary as in the use of the color red in a traffic light to indicate "stop" or on a flag to signify communism. Body and bread do not appear to be alike at all, and the very absence of any sensory resemblance between the two makes the metonymy especially powerful as a form of figurative language. The Zwinglians emphasized this verbal phenomenon of substituting one word for another, instead of depicting the sacrament as an action that changed one substance into another.

Zwingli became so concerned about metonymical confusions on the part of the laity that he sought to eliminate them entirely by stripping down church rituals to their essentials and removing any confusing images or distracting decorations from church altars. Zwingli's insight into the metonymy of the Bible powerfully influenced the reformed as distinct from the Lutheran strain of Protestantism, especially the more radical sects and movements that sought a completely purified Christianity, and he opened the on-going Eucharistic debates to a wide range of new interpretations, translations, reductions, and mystifications.

In response to all this Luther fumed: instead of accepting the lord's invitation to his supper, the "sacramental fanatics," as Luther called Zwingli and his defenders, presumed to invite the lord to their little commemorative meal. Why should God Almighty bother to answer such presumption? Luther insisted on the presence of God's actual body, arguing that we ingest flesh, not its meaning: "I would eat dung if God demanded it."[17] To Luther a mystery can be experienced but never understood, whereas for the Zwinglians the mystery of the bodily presence of Christ in the bread and the wine could never produce spiritual benefits, only harmful misunderstandings. Luther held fast to the emotional appeal of ritual while Zwingli wanted to intellectualize the faith. Martin Luther recognized the potential costs of Zwingli's abolition of presence in ritual, probably because Luther was a better psychologist than logician. As Heiko Oberman has pointed out, Luther was a man as concerned with the devil as with God, and Luther knew that Satan loves individualism: "He can penetrate the psyche and control it. He can twist and cripple even the believing Christian so that, lost in introspection, he despairs of God and the world. But there is one thing the Devil cannot do: he cannot become really present flesh."[18] To Luther the presence of God in the rite freed Christians from the problem of distinguishing the temptations of the wily demonic enemy from the inner workings of the holy spirit, it freed Christians from wrenching introspection and self-doubt, it freed Christians from the cage of their own bodies.

For the Zwinglian rationalists after the 1520s, the Word of God no longer assumed flesh; it assumed meaning. Meanings were disputed,

[17] Quoted in ibid., 244.   [18] Ibid., 243.

and meanings were misunderstood. Rituals henceforth demanded words of explanation, whether from theologians or modern scholars, who play the same game, and the disputation of meaning fed doubt and a distrust of the sensory evidence that came from seeing and feeling, even a distrust of the emotions summoned by ritual performances. The Zwinglian endeavor suggested a whole theory about the relationship between communication and behavior, a theory that had significant consequences for notions of identity formation, alienation, and individualism.

After the Marburg Colloquy of 1529 failed to bring agreement between the two sides, the reform movement split between allegiances to Zwingli's Zürich and Luther's Wittenberg. Reconciliation between these two opposing tendencies in Eucharistic interpretation had to await a later generation when John Calvin succeeded in combining the positive elements of Luther's and Zwingli's ideas into a coherent logical synthesis. Calvin accepted Zwingli's insight that sacramental speech tended to be expressed in metonymy, but insisted that there was a "spiritual presence" of Christ in the material, visible sign of the bread: "the body of Christ today is called bread, inasmuch as it is the symbol by which the Lord offers us the true eating of his body."[19] Calvin reoriented interpretation toward the material, visible bread, because without it there would be no sacrament, no mystical presence of Christ. Regina Schwartz has explained Calvin's understanding of the operations of metonymy: by substituting the name "body" for the name "bread," the metonymy drew attention to the "visible sign," thereby locating the invisible, spiritual presence of Christ in the material world. The bread was necessary for the mystery of the divine presence but not sufficient for it and not substituted by it. Bread remained bread even while Christ's spiritual presence was made evident through consecration.

As Ann Kibbey has pointed out, Calvin understood the bread as a *figure* of Christ while it remained at the same time true bread even after consecration. The failure to see this, according to Calvin, was precisely what was wrong with transubstantiation, which turned the bread into a "mask" or mere appearance, and therefore destroyed its sacramental power: "The nature of the Sacrament is therefore canceled, unless, in the mode of signifying, the earthly sign corresponds to the heavenly thing. And the truth of this mystery accordingly perishes for us unless true bread represents the true body of Christ."[20] However, Calvin was concerned that the sacrament be understood as something more than just a symbol, a fiction that assisted piety. The sacrament was still a mystery because in

---

[19] Quoted in Ann Kibbey, *The Interpretation of Material Shapes in Puritanism: A Study of Rhetoric, Prejudice, and Violence* (Cambridge: Cambridge University Press, 1986), 54.

[20] Quoted in ibid., 48.

the very act of renaming a piece of bread the body of Christ, the material shapes of bread and wine "have the reality" of the spiritual Christ "joined with them."[21] This is apparently what Calvin meant when he states the bread is a figure of Christ: it was as if the sacrament reshaped the dough into the figure of Christ with a spiritual bread mold.

Even while rejecting transubstantiation Calvin reasserted the religious value of material objects in sacramental rites: common bread, true wine, believing communicants, and perhaps most powerfully the clearly proclaimed *words* of consecration must be present for Christ to be present. Regina Schwartz shows how in Calvinism the "words" of scripture now took on an almost material significance; words had a tactile, sensual appeal that led Calvinists to "touch" the truth, to "digest" the scriptures, to "taste" the Word of God, and to "drink" the blood of the covenant.

Puritan followers of Calvin adopted his sacramental views to create a whole new kind of anti-liturgical ritual that emphasized the spiritual significance of mundane materiality within a religious world-view that had supposedly disenchanted material objects. This paradox can be illustrated by the design and practices of Emmanuel College, Cambridge. Founded in 1584 on the site of a Dominican Priory that had been suppressed by King Henry VIII, Emmanuel was from the beginning an intensely Protestant institution with strong Puritan leanings that trained generations of ardent young preachers. In transforming the old Dominican buildings, the Puritan dons turned what had been the friars' chapel into the dining hall of the new college so that the fellows now broke their common bread in the exact location where the Eucharistic host had once been raised for idolatrous adoration. The first fellows of Emmanuel celebrated the lord's supper while seated around their dining table, integrating the communion rite into daily life and transforming routine meals into a kind of continuous religious ritual. Suffering persecution during the 1630s, many of the Puritan graduates of Emmanuel sought refuge in the new American colonies where they could practice their religion freely. Some thirty of the first 100 university graduates who settled in New England were Emmanuel men, including John Harvard who endowed a new college in his name on the Emmanuel model in a Massachusetts village renamed Cambridge.

The only other sacrament of the Catholic seven to survive the scrutiny of the mainstream Protestant reformers was baptism, which seemed to be at least indirectly authorized by scripture. As was the case with the Eucharist, retaining baptism created problems of interpretation because

---

[21] Ibid., 55.

the Protestants' reliance on faith as all sufficient did not leave much logical room for sacramental rites, and yet most reformers were unwilling to abandon them altogether.

For Catholics baptism cleansed infants of the inheritance of original sin and was akin to the sacrament of penance, which was necessary to absolve the believer of sins committed later in life. In rejecting the sacrament of penance, the reformers invested baptism with even greater significance than Catholics, but they could not quite agree on what that significance was. All of them junked the notion of baptism as a quasi-magical exorcism that eliminated the physical residues of original sin; most concentrated on baptism as a promise that sin need not control the lives of the faithful; and all except for Zwingli thought baptism stimulated faith because of the influence of the holy spirit.

The baptism debates, even more than the Eucharistic debates, divided the Protestant movement into moderate reformist and radical camps. Division sprang from two issues: specifying the role of faith in the baptismal rite and interpreting its scriptural foundations. If faith were to be understood as necessary to make a sacrament efficacious, then, some radicals logically argued, there was no reason to baptize infants who were as yet incapable of discerning the workings of faith. As Karlstadt put it, "inarticulate children" had no need of baptism because they were not capable of even knowing what sin was, let alone of committing one. Moreover, the Bible offered no warrant for infant baptism since Christ was clearly a mature adult when baptized and provided little justification for baptizing anyone since Jesus had not instituted the rite among his disciples. These radicals advocated baptizing only adults who exhibited the fullness of ripened faith. From the practice of "rebaptizing" those who had already been baptized as infants, the radicals came to be called Anabaptists (*ana* = *re*-baptists). For them the soul had to be transformed before baptism by listening to preaching, studying scripture, and praying intently, and the willingness to undergo baptism meant that the believer entered into a binding covenant with God that led to a lasting personal testimony, which in the view of some would result in martyrdom. Baptism itself became a highly charged ritual for these faithful adults, a moment of great spiritual and psychological significance that produced a dramatic release of tension and a state of deep inner calm.

No matter how consistent with scripture, the Anabaptist case presented a severe challenge to the mainstream of "magisterial" reformers, such as Luther, Zwingli, and Calvin, because adult baptism implied there must be a test of faith, which only some would pass. The consequence of such an exclusive baptismal rite was that it created sects, that is separate groups of the elect, rather than churches, which incorporated all members of the community, both saved and damned. Insisting that their goal was to bring about a reform of the entire church, the magisterial reformers fought adult baptism with a range of convoluted arguments that have little merit in either logic or scripture.

The Protestant debate about baptism is significant largely because it reveals the implications of ritual practices for the constitution of the community. Without the comprehensive rite of passage of infant baptism, the magisterial reformers recognized that Christianity's total-izing claims to provide a single universal truth were hollow, and therefore they pushed the Anabaptists to the margins of the reform movement. In the worst cases they helped to legitimate a vicious persecution of Anabaptists that included murdering tens of thousands of them, leaving only a tiny remnant in Europe. In North America, however, sects surviving from the European persecutions and later reinventions of baptist theology constitute the backbone of evangelical Christianity.

The most radical attempts to abolish all ritual from religious worship were isolated and largely ephemeral, illustrating how impossible it is to conceive of any kind of collectivity without the binding force of shared ritual activities. Caspar Schwenckfeld, a brilliant exiled nobleman from Silesia, has usually been labelled a Spiritualist for his advocacy of an entirely inward, "spiritual" piety. Refusing to organize his own reformed church or even to lead a movement, Schwenckfeld advocated what he called the "inward Eucharist," by which he meant that the "eating" of God's body was to be understood purely metaphorically as achieving spiritual understanding of God's Word. Schwenckfeld abandoned all outward rites, both baptism and communion, and to the degree that he imagined any kind of collective religious activity at all, it seems to have involved occasional group discussions of scripture. The disdainful arrogance of Schwenckfeld's intelligence and the isolating individuality of his piety limited its appeal. By its very nature Spiritualism failed to lead to any sort of lasting organization, but as an orientation it has reappeared among exceptional individuals across the centuries, periodi-cally revitalizing Lutheranism in particular.

Although the humanist critique of ritual abuses began within the embrace of Catholicism and many of the critics of the older generation including Erasmus himself not only refused to join the Reformation but actively criticized it, an official Catholic reassessment of the role of ritual in the church was long delayed until the waning days of the Council of Trent, which met with several long interruptions between 1545 and 1563. The political implications of the Protestant reform, especially in the Holy Roman Empire, and the unwieldy size of the vast bureaucracy of the church made it difficult to move, and besides most Catholic prelates thought radical change neither possible nor desirable. It was one thing to acknowledge the consequences of lay ignorance and the cupidity of those who benefited financially from celebrating the sacraments, but it was quite another to go along with the reformers' rejection of the sacramental edifice of the church and the elimination of the special status of priests as ritual specialists. When the Council finally issued its decrees it reaffirmed traditional Catholic dogma regarding the mass, retaining transubstantiation and the mass as a sacrifice, and refused to allow any consideration of the Eucharist as merely a sign that promised salvation or even less as a simple commemorative meal that served as a reminder of Christ on the cross. Even as they were brought under stricter regulation, commemorative masses, relics, sacramentals, saints' days, and all the seven sacraments were not only reaffirmed as efficacious but reasserted as essential guides for the road to salvation. Instead of rejecting the role of liturgical rites, the Council of Trent reinvigorated their celebration.

Most of the Tridentine reforms concentrated on technical matters of ritual practice, especially in promoting uniformity throughout the church. In 1562 in its twenty-second session, the Council passed a decree on the correct observation of the mass that attempted to limit abuses arising from avarice, superstition, and irreverence. For example, stipends for the saying of masses were to be regulated by the bishops. Most of the pronouncements concerned matters external to the mass itself, such as guaranteeing that masses be celebrated only in consecrated places, rowdy conduct be banished, unsuitable music be prohibited, the celebration of many simultaneous masses be curtailed, and the observance of fixed numbers of memorial masses be eliminated.

The most contentious issues arose from attempts to bring consistency to the bewildering variety of mass rites celebrated across Catholic Europe. To create order out of the ritual chaos, the church needed a uniform missal, but the Council relegated the completion of this task to the pope. A papal commission under Pius IV (1559–65) and Pius V (1566–72) eventually solved the problem by issuing a new universal missal based on a revised version of the old Roman missal. In effect, the entire church with its enormous variety of local saints' days, special practices, variant prayers, and adaptations to historical change had to conform to the liturgy as it had supposedly been practiced in the city of Rome in the eleventh century. As a consequence many of the additions and perceived abuses of the later Middle Ages were eliminated. Votive masses, which had supplied the vast industry of masses for the dead, were greatly reduced. Numerous feast days were dropped from the liturgical calendar, especially the profusion of local saints' days, but special provisions were made for those churches that could prove a feast day had been in practice for at least 200 years. Under these provisions, most of the early medieval orders, such as the Benedictines, were allowed to retain their distinctive ritual observances, and the dioceses of Milan, Trier, Cologne, Liège, Braga, and Lyons kept their own rite, as did a few individual churches, such as the basilica of St. Mark in Venice.

The governing principle of the commission seems to have been to create clarity by stripping away distorting additions to the basic forms of the mass and liturgy. Nevertheless, much of what the more radical Protestants considered to be distractions and unjustified additions were retained, such as polyphonic music, sumptuous clerical vestments, saints' images, holy water, and multiple altars. The Catholic reform impulse was consistently clerical and elitist. The authority of the hierarchy, the bishops in particular, was enhanced rather than reduced as the Protestants had demanded with their concept of the priesthood of all believers. Few concessions were made toward creating a stronger ritual bond between the priest and laity: the chalice continued to be reserved for the priesthood, and the mass text was still in Latin. Rather than making the priesthood bend down to the level of the simple laity, the reforms required the laity to raise themselves in obedience to clerical directions and in rigid observance of liturgical rites. There was certainly a concern, especially among the Jesuits, that the laity be better instructed in the meaning of the mass and liturgy, but it took generations, even centuries, for this concern to have any measurable effect at the lowest social levels and in the provincial corners of the Catholic world. Perhaps the most innovative provision was the recommendation that the laity should receive the Eucharist every time they came to mass rather than the yearly communion that was normal before Trent. To enforce uniformity Pope Sixtus V established in 1588 the Congregation of Rites, which was charged with enforcing the celebration of the mass and liturgy in the prescribed forms.

The Catholic reform avoided the austere intellectualism of the Protestants despite the erudition of the prelates at Trent, but they hardened practice into an obsessive ritual rigidity that fettered the marvelous liturgical creativity of the later Middle Ages. Both Reformations produced unintended ironies. While the Protestants found it difficult if not impossible to escape the hold of collective rituals on religious practice, the Catholics promoted ritual observances in which the ritual experiences of the laity could be carefully controlled and correctly interpreted by properly trained clergy.

The sixteenth-century crisis in the "communal, performative sign," which had led a learned few to see ritual observances as a diversion from true spiritual concerns or worse as a manipulative fraud, stimulated a vast debate about what a rite is and what it does. The orientation of the Protestant reformers can be summarized in the motto, "Finitum non est capax infiniti" ("the finite cannot contain the infinite"), and their attempts to work out the implications of this insight led them to eliminate or dilute the cult of the saints, to abhor or destroy religious images, and to revise or drop sacramental rituals. In so doing they created a new theological metaphysics by drawing precise boundaries between the spiritual and material worlds, breaking the deeply mysterious connections between the two made evident in traditional rituals. In the course of the Eucharistic controversy, ritual theory moved from Luther's vision of a mysterious corporeal presence in the rite to Zwingli's terse representation of a divine promise in it and finally to Calvin's powerful, albeit exclusively spiritual, return to an idea of presence in the sacrament. Zwingli's introduction of the rhetorical trope of metonymy created a new theoretical paradigm for understanding ritual, just as it disenchanted ritual practice so thoroughly that the Protestant laity and later reformers retreated from its most astringent implications.

The Protestants thereafter faced a tenacious dilemma: even though the theological reformers doubted the efficacy of many rites, all communities require them. What seemed perfectly logical and necessary in theory, floundered in the actual implementation of reform. Perhaps most ironic was the fact that as the message worked its way into the churches and onto the streets the method of reform was often to substitute one ritual for another. Even as it promoted scriptural reading, lucid preaching, and spiritual understanding, the Protestant Reformation was itself a ritual movement that employed traditional ceremonies in new ways and introduced new ceremonies to demarcate differences among various religious groups. Whatever the theologians thought, unsophisticated Protestants and untutored Catholics identified themselves more by the rituals they observed than by the dogmas they asserted.

BIBLIOGRAPHY

Entries marked with a * designate recommended readings for new students of the subject.

*Bell, Rudolph. *Holy Anorexia*. Chicago: University of Chicago Press, 1985. A fascinating if controversial argument that connects the fasting of late medieval female mystics to modern anorexia.

Bornstein, Daniel and Rusconi, Roberto. *Women and Religion in Medieval and Renaissance Italy.* Translated by Margery J. Schneider. Chicago: University of Chicago Press, 1996. A useful collection of articles by Italian scholars that argue women's distinctive religious experiences derived from their social lives rather than from biology.

Brown, Peter. *The Cult of the Saints: Its Rise and Function in Latin Christianity.* Chicago: University of Chicago Press, 1981. Although he treats the period of the early church, Brown's work has been highly influential in understanding the cult of the saints during the late Middle Ages.

Bynum, Caroline Walker. *Fragmentation and Redemption: Essays on Gender and the Human Body in Medieval Religion.* New York: Zone Books, 1991. This collection and Bynum's works cited below constitute the most substantial and innovative contribution to late medieval religious history of the past generation. These highly influential studies point out the ways in which the religious behavior characteristic of women can be best understood through reference to their attitudes toward food, nurturing, and the human body.

   *Holy Feast and Holy Fast: The Religious Significance of Food to Medieval Women. Berkeley: University of California Press, 1987.

   *Jesus as Mother: Studies in the Spirituality of the High Middle Ages. Berkeley: University of California Press, 1982.

   The Resurrection of the Body in Western Christianity, 200–1336. New York: Columbia University Press, 1995.

*Cameron, Euan. *The European Reformation.* Oxford: Clarendon Press, 1991. A good general survey of the Reformation with an especially lucid discussion of the reformation of the sacraments in chapter 11.

Camporesi, Piero. *Bread of Dreams: Food and Fantasy in Early Modern Europe.* Translated by David Gentilcore. Cambridge: Polity Press, 1989.

   *"The Consecrated Host: A Wondrous Excess." In Fragments for a History of the Human Body. Edited by Michel Feher. New York: Zone Books, 1989. Part III, pp. 220–37. A stimulating if sometimes fanciful introduction to the allure of the cult of the host in early modern times.

   The Incorruptible Flesh: Bodily Mutation and Mortification in Religion and Folklore. Translated by Tania Croft-Murray; Latin texts translated by Helen Elsom. Cambridge: Cambridge University Press, 1988.

Clark, Francis, S. J. *Eucharistic Sacrifice and the Reformation.* Devon: Augustine, 1981. A learned discussion of the theological issues surrounding the Eucharist.

*Duffy, Eamon. *The Stripping of the Altars: Traditional Religion in England c.1400–c.1580.* New Haven: Yale University Press, 1992. A massively documented argument in favor of the vitality of late medieval religion, the unity between clerical and lay beliefs, and the absence of conflict between ritual practice and reading the Word.

Geremek, Bronislaw. *The Margins of Society in Late Medieval Paris.* Translated by Jean Birrell. Cambridge: Cambridge University Press, 1987. Contains many examples of semi-pagan practices in Christian rituals.

*Greene, Thomas M. "Ritual and Text in the Renaissance." *Canadian Review of Comparative Literature* (June–September 1991): 177–97. A concise and brilliantly suggestive examination of the issues ritual presented for the text-centered Reformation. This is the best starting point for thinking about the decline of ritual understanding in the sixteenth century.

Jungmann, Joseph A. *The Mass of the Roman Rite: Its Origins and Development.* Westminster, Md.: Christian Classics, 1986. A heavily theological and often highly technical study from a Catholic point of view.

Karant-Nunn, Susan C. *The Reformation of Ritual: An Interpretation of Early Modern Germany.* Forthcoming. A reinterpretation of the Protestant Reformation centering on ritual, available too late for consideration in this book.

Kibbey, Ann. *The Interpretation of Material Shapes in Puritanism: A Study of Rhetoric, Prejudice, and Violence.* Cambridge: Cambridge University Press, 1986. See especially chapter 3, "Iconoclastic Materialism," for an insightful reinterpretation of the sacramental and iconoclastic views of the Puritans that gives much greater weight to their appreciation of the material world than traditional historiography admits.

Kilgour, Maggie. *From Communion to Cannibalism: An Anatomy of Metaphors of Incorporation.* Princeton: Princeton University Press, 1990. A literary scholar looks at how Eucharistic debates structured thinking during the early modern period.

Kinser, Samuel. "Presentation and Representation: Carnival at Nuremberg, 1450–1550." *Representations* 13 (Winter 1986): 1–42. This perceptive article introduced the distinction between presentation and representation as an issue in the study of rituals.

Lansing, Carol. *Purity and Power: Cathar Heresy in Medieval Italy.* Oxford: Oxford University Press, forthcoming. See chapter 8 for a discussion of the miracle of Bolsena.

Le Goff, Jacques. *The Birth of Purgatory.* Translated by Arthur Goldhammer. Chicago: University of Chicago Press, 1984. Traces the evolution of the idea of purgatory, which provided the theological foundation for much of the late medieval penitential system and expansion of rituals.

Luther, Martin. "The Pagan Servitude of the Church." In *Martin Luther: Selections from His Writings.* Edited and translated by John Dillenberger. Garden City, N.Y.: Doubleday, 1961.

*Oberman, Heiko A. *Luther: Man between God and the Devil.* Translated by Eileen Walliser-Schwarzbart. New York: Doubleday, 1989. Among the enormous number of Luther studies and Luther biographies, this brilliant portrait presents Luther more as a medieval monk than the great originator of modern sensibilities.

Pater, Calvin. *Karlstadt as the Father of the Baptist Movement: The Emergence of Lay Protestantism.* Toronto: University of Toronto Press, 1984. The best study of the elusive radical reformer.

Reinburg, Virginia. "Liturgy and the Laity in Late Medieval and Reformation France." *Sixteenth Century Journal* 23 (1992): 526–47. A lucid examination of how lay people before the Reformation assigned very different meanings to liturgical rituals than did the clergy, especially by associating them with tribute gestures and charity.

Rothkrug, Lionel. "German Holiness and Western Sanctity in Medieval and

Modern History." *Historical Reflections* 15 (1988): 161–249. A rather idiosyncratic and controversial view of the character of German ideas about the holy, which is developed in this and the articles below.

"Holy Shrines, Religious Dissonance and Satan in the Origins of the German Reformation." *Historical Reflections* 14 (1987): 143–286.

"Popular Religion and Holy Shrines." In *Religion and the People.* Edited by James Obelkevitch. Chapel Hill: University of North Carolina Press, 1979. Pp. 20–86.

"Religious Practices and Collective Perceptions: Hidden Homologies in the Renaissance and Reformation." *Historical Reflections* 7 (1980), entire issue.

*Rubin, Miri. *Corpus Christi: The Eucharist in Late Medieval Culture.* Cambridge: Cambridge University Press, 1991. The best general discussion of the spread of Eucharistic rites and observances in the centuries before the Reformation.

Scribner, R. W. "Cosmic Order and Daily Life: Sacred and Secular in Pre-industrial German Society." In *Religion and Society in Early Modern Europe, 1500–1800.* Edited by Kaspar von Greyerz. London: German Historical Institute, 1984. Pp. 17–31. Demonstrates that the borders between the sacred and secular in daily life were quite permeable. Scribner's work is crucial for understanding the ritual aspects of the Reformation. Reprinted in *Popular Culture and Popular Movements in Reformation Germany.* London: Hambledon Press, 1987.

The German Reformation. Houndsmills: Macmillan, 1986. An excellent introduction that synthesizes the current research on the Reformation and is especially strong on social history.

Steinberg, Leo. *The Sexuality of Christ in Renaissance Art and in Modern Oblivion.* London: Faber and Faber, 1984. A brilliant examination of the theological implications of the doctrine of incarnation, which required Renaissance artists to depict Christ having all the attributes of a man, including sexual ones.

Turner, Victor and Turner, Edith. *Image and Pilgrimage in Christian Culture: Anthropological Perspectives.* New York: Columbia University Press, 1978. Based on anthropological fieldwork in Mexico, this study also examines the historical tradition of pilgrimage.

Whiting, Robert. *The Blind Devotion of the People: Popular Religion and the English Reformation.* Cambridge: Cambridge University Press, 1989. Concentrating on Devon and Cornwall, Whiting argues that the English Reformation appealed to many simple lay believers. Should be compared to the contrasting views of Duffy cited above.

Zika, Charles. "Hosts, Processions and Pilgrimages: Controlling the Sacred in Fifteenth-Century Germany." *Past and Present* 118 (1988): 25–64. An examination of how veneration of the host displaced the relics of the saints as the centerpiece of liturgical practice and popular religious veneration on the eve of the Reformation.

6   The Reformation as a ritual process

In a private ceremony on September 29, 1521, Luther's colleague and disciple at Wittenberg, Philipp Melanchthon, and his students received communion in both kinds for the first time. With this act of ritual defiance, Luther's Eucharistic theories began to have practical consequences for worship. All that autumn and early winter, steps toward reforming the mass quickened in Wittenberg. In October the university students pelted the hermits of St. Anthony with dung and stones as they attempted to collect alms in the streets and heckled their sermons, even preventing the consecration of holy water. Demonstrations against the mass forced the Augustinians out of town, and by December celebrations of the mass had largely ceased.

On Christmas Eve a crowd broke into the parish church, blew out the candles lit for the midnight mass, sang lewd songs to squelch the priest's recitation, and threatened him with bodily harm if he did not quit the ceremony. When the police arrived, the crowd moved outside where it continued to harass the celebrant with singing and shouts and then, emboldened by success, moved on the Duke-Elector's castle church to disrupt the service there. On Christmas day Luther's associate and fellow priest, Andreas Karlstadt, invited the congregation to take communion without confessing or fasting, and in a massive popular response over the next few days more than 2,000 Wittenbergers took the mass in both kinds. Always pushing the limits, Karlstadt then announced his engagement to a sixteen-year-old girl and invited the outraged prince and the bishop to the wedding. By altering the ritual experiences of the laity, the Protestant Reformation was transformed from a narrow theological debate among professors to a mass movement that has had lasting effects.

Protestant

In the classic theory of the relationship between religion and society in the development of modern Europe, Max Weber argued that the ritual

185

reforms and austere rationality of Protestantism "disenchanted the world." In place of traditional Catholic rituals that granted sacral qualities to many kinds of material objects and spaces, the Protestants removed the holy from the created world to a transcendental one. By reducing the number and significance of the sacraments, by divesting church rituals of their quasi-magical powers, and by stripping away the miracle-working authority of the clergy, the Protestants abolished the traditional props of community identity. The body of God was no longer the model for the body of society.

In recent years, however, historians of early modern European religion have considerably revised Weber's formula, especially by taking seriously the ritual behavior of Protestants. As can be seen in the above example, Melanchthon and Karlstadt did not eliminate ritual so much as change it in a dramatic, expansive way. The Protestant "disenchantment" certainly curtailed the intensely material presentation of God and the saints, but rather than simply replacing immanence with transcendence, the Protestants of the sixteenth century sought to redefine the place of the sacred in the world. Natalie Zemon Davis has succinctly summarized the difference between Catholic and Protestant notions of collective rituals: "If for the Catholics urban space had its hot points and cold points, for the Calvinists the environment was – well, not lukewarm, for that would have to be spewed forth – but held together by a middling tension, by listening and by watchfulness."[1] The contrast Davis makes here is between a Catholic appreciation of the variability of spiritual presences in the created world and a Protestant caution about measuring and therefore containing the spiritual, but the difference between the two was more one of degree than of kind.

As a consequence of the Reformation, the traditional ritual system of Christianity diverged into separate Protestant and Catholic ritual "languages," to borrow Davis's term. Despite their emphasis on the Bible and interpretation, Protestants still experienced the sacred through rituals, and the Reformation itself was largely achieved through a "ritual process." Robert Scribner notes how most people of the sixteenth century were poorly tutored in theology but extremely adept at ritual ways of behaving. While the clerical reformers, themselves, may have hoped that true reform would come from a better popular understanding of doctrine, the actual Reformation was accomplished through a ritual process that worked in several ways: there were protests that occurred within the frame of the liturgical calendar, such as the singing of "scurrilous songs" during mass on a solemn feast day; there were

---

[1] Natalie Zemon Davis, "The Sacred and the Body Social in Sixteenth-Century Lyon," *Past and Present* 90 (1981): 59.

disruptions of Catholic rites by an apparently anti-ritual action, such as throwing the baptismal font from the roof of the church to prevent infant baptisms; there were parodies of Catholic rites that created a carnival-esque counter-liturgy, such as the mock administration of last rites to a man who play-acted sickness; and there were iconoclastic acts that took place within a ritual context, such as the damaging of an image of a saint on his or her feast day.

These rituals of reform ranged from simple desecrations by indivi-duals to complex, collective counter-rituals and battles over ritual that divided whole communities over the appropriateness of some ceremony. In Germany there were reports of an innkeeper who pissed into a sacred water vessel and placed it on the altar during mass and of a man who defecated into the mouth of a crucifix. In Magdeburg for the celebration of the feast of the Assumption of the Virgin, it was customary to bless various flowers and herbs, which were then taken away by the laity to protect animals and humans from disease and accident. After an evangelical preacher spoke against the practice in 1524, some of his congregants went from church to church, removing the flowers and herbs which they scattered about and danced over in the market-place. In one church a stone- and egg-throwing fight broke out, which led to image breaking and the closing of all churches.

Among the nearly eighty examples that Scribner has collected of reform rituals in Germany, one of most revealing occurred in Augsburg in 1533, at a time when the city was divided into Catholic, Lutheran, and Zwinglian camps. The great banking family of the Fuggers, who had served both popes and emperors, were fervent Catholics and patrons of St. Mortiz's church. In opposition to them stood the churchwarden, Marx Ehem, whose evangelical leanings had troubled the atmosphere in the church when he locked up the sacristy to prevent the celebration of the mass and sealed the "Holy Sepulcher" to prevent the popular rite of "laying Christ in the grave" on Good Friday. To halt the Ascension Day ceremony he absconded with all the dramatic paraphernalia of the liturgy, including an image of Christ seated on a rainbow and surrounded by angels and the dove of the holy spirit, a statue that had traditionally been pulled up through a hole in the roof of the church to demonstrate Christ's ascension into heaven. When Antonius Fugger heard of the latest of Ehem's outrages, he commissioned the making of a new, even more sumptuous figure than the old one in an attempt to block Ehem's subversion of the traditional liturgical rites. When Ehem got wind of Fugger's planned intervention, he boarded up the hole in the ceiling used for the rite. On Ascension Day, the Fuggers managed to stage the rite anyway, forcing Ehem to go to the mayor to stop the celebration, and when this failed he invaded the church with a gang of supporters who stood in a circle holding their knives in a threatening way. After breaking up the service, Ehem's men lowered the new images from the roof and "accidentally" let the rope slip so that the new Christ was smashed. This "debate" over the implementation of the Reformation in Augsburg took the form of a dispute over the control of church rituals, a dispute carried out not by a rowdy mob but by important patrician families who considered the control of rites of the church part of their rights of patronage. Ehem's vehemence in attempting to abolish the Ascension Day drama testifies to how important these rites were understood to be: they were not just something that could be allowed to fade away as the understanding of the guileless believers improved but were deemed dangerously powerful practices that had to be stopped immediately and completely for the reform to have any meaning at all.

A great deal of the Reformation took place through little local disputes such as this one in Augsburg. These often involved acts of iconoclasm. Iconoclasm refers to the removing, breaking, or defacing of religious statues, paintings, and symbols, such as crucifixes, a common feature of the Reformation even when the theological reformers themselves discouraged or denounced it. One of the most intriguing questions of the Reformation is why did people feel so impelled to commit acts of symbolic and ritual violence against supposedly inanimate objects, which ranged from the crude props of ecclesiastical dramas, such as the Ascension figures in Augsburg, to magnificent works of art.

The recollections of Guillaume Farel, the evangelical reformer of Geneva before the arrival of John Calvin, provides us with a beginning point to answer this question. As a boy his parents took him to visit the modest shrine of the Holy Cross at Tallard, which was supposedly fabricated out of fragments of the true cross of Calvary. Prostrated before the crucifix, the pilgrims listened to a priest who reported that when the devil sent hail and thunderstorms, the cross shook violently, even sending off sparks to quell the storm. The supplicants then heard a plea for donations. What Farel remembered most of all about the shrine was his own fear, reinforced by the apprehension of his parents and the other pilgrims. The implication here was that enshrined images conveyed an awesome power, a power that could protect but also destroy. There were good reasons for anxiety because an image capable of quelling dangerous storms might also be able to create them were the offerings made to it insufficient.

A deep sense of fear helps explain the often systematic eradication of images and the ritual forms that eradication took. In Germany during the Reformation crucifixes were smashed, decapitated, dismembered, mocked, defiled, and destroyed. Crucifixes were smeared with cow's blood, paraded through the streets in a mock Carnival procession, carried over the shoulder like a weapon of war, and sold for lumber. Many of the attacks on crucifixes were certainly part of a general hostility toward images, but also assaulting such objects could demonstrate contempt for the doctrine of the Real Presence since the crucifix paralleled the host as a medium for presenting Christ's sacrifice. The irony here was that to eliminate the vestiges of the theology of sacrifice in the liturgy, the images of sacrifice had themselves to be sacrificed.

Most iconoclastic acts took place in an elaborate ritual context that often displayed the characteristics of a rite of passage with its three stages of disaggregation, transition, and reintegration. An example took place in Ulm in 1530. Two women stole from the churchyard the image of Christ that was used for the Holy Week re-enactments of the entombment and resurrection and took it to a series of spinning-bees, which as we have seen were occasions for bawdy humor and youthful courting. At one of the spinning-bees three men spoke to the image, and when it failed to answer, one of them cut off its hand with his sword. In another house, the Christ image was shoved from a table when it refused to help itself and was then thrown from a window. After this series of humiliations, the statue was finally returned to its place in the churchyard.

Scribner has shown how this example of iconoclasm can be understood as a form of desecration that took on the structural forms of a rite of passage. First, the image was disaggregated from its sacred location by its removal to the profane locale of the spinning-bee where sexual liaisons were contemplated and proposed. Taking Christ to a spinning-bee was not far removed from taking him to a whorehouse. The expulsion of sacred images from churches to locales such as the marketplace or a tavern was a common form of disaggregating the image from its sacred space. In a village in Saxony in the 1530s, iconoclasts took an image of St. John to a bathhouse where it was hung upside down.

Second, during the transitional phase, the Ulm image was tested with taunting questions and the severing of a hand. In the test the iconoclasts asked the image to prove its authenticity. Elsewhere images were dragged through the mud or drowned in a stream. In one case after a statue of a saint failed to return a toast in a tavern, beer was flung in its face.

Third, the Ulm image was reintegrated into its former society of the churchyard, but it had now been desacralized through the humiliating rite of passage. Just as the usual human rites of passage discussed in the first chapter typically assisted the elevation of a youth or official to a higher status, the rite of degradation described here brought about a lowering of status and proved the image to be nothing more than its component materials: a piece of wood, a block of stone, a concoction of paint and human artifice. After this three-stage rite, the material of the image could safely be put to some useful purpose, such as firewood or building materials. Scribner recounts a marvelous example of a combined rite of passage that deconsecrated images at the same time that it consecrated a marriage among two people who had been committed to celibacy in the old order: in Esslingen in 1532 when a evangelical preacher married a former nun, all the food for the wedding feast was cooked over a fire fueled by the images from his church.

Other images went through the usual judicial rituals of judgment and punishment. Images hauled out of the churches of St. Gallen were put into the stocks, a statue in Ulm was "interrogated under torture," an image of St. Francis from Nebra in Saxony was hung from the gallows, and a St. Peter from an abbey near Kaufbeuren was hung upside down, then "disembowelled." Sixteenth-century Germany produces an enormous variety of quasi-judicial mutilations of images: eye gougings, hands cut off, ears and noses slit, and decapitations. In England one of the most stunning examples can be seen in the Lady Chapel of the cathedral at Ely. Iconoclasts broke nearly all of the stained glass and removed the free-standing images for an unknown fate, but they could not easily eradicate the hundreds of limestone reliefs of the saints and angels that decorated the walls. Instead, each was systematically decapitated, and oddly once the heads were chipped off little other damage was done to them. They were now all as "dead" as if they had faced the executioner's axe.

In other examples, less obviously judicial forms of degradation were employed. One common form of degradation was to allude to prostitution or to employ gender role reversals. In Memmingen after an image of the Virgin was sold for ten gulden, a common saying arose that the Memmingers "had sold our blessed Lady," inferring they had prostituted her. Elsewhere monks or clergy were compelled to pull a plow through the streets in imitation of the rite of degradation usually reserved for sexually promiscuous females. Notorious as sexual predators, priests were hunted like game by the women of Zwickau and forcefully expelled by the women of Hildesheim.

One of the most prominent features of the rituals of reform was the frequent interchangeability between inanimate images and living representatives of the old order, such as unreformed priests and monks. Both could suffer ritual humiliations, judgment, and degradation. In fact, both served as *figures* of a powerful system that had engendered fear.

There may have been a certain safety in mutilating an image rather than a person, but given the remarkable violence against images, it is important to point out how little actual violence there was, at least in the early phases of the German Reformation, against the priests of the old order. Except during the excesses of the German Peasants' War (1524–25) and the French Wars of Religion (1562–98), the worst fate most of them suffered was the deprivation of a living and the scorn of the neighborhood. The rituals of reform actually seem to have channeled hostility toward ecclesiastical property, implying that the issue was more often about the signifying and charitable role of the church in the world than a social rebellion against corrupt clergy.

There were, however, important respects in which ritual iconoclasm must be distinguished from the rites of degradation to which living persons were subjected. Images themselves raised problems, not so much because the reformers took literally the injunction in the Decalogue against all graven images but because of the role they had in religious rituals. None of the reformers argued that *all* images of the human form should be eliminated as have some adherents of Islam, and the waves of iconoclasm spared images that had no liturgical function, even when they appeared in churches. In fact, several of the reformers were quite fond of having their portraits painted. As a rule tomb sculptures that represented the deceased were saved even in churches where every graven or painted image of a saint or Christ was blotted out. Iconoclasm raised issues about spiritual presences in material forms and, perhaps even more powerfully, about sight itself as a source of information about the world. Since one of the characteristic traits of rituals is that they are publicly witnessed and work to create dramatic visual impressions as a way of stimulating certain psycho-spiritual states or of aiding memory, it is not surprising that theories of sight should affect the understanding of how both rituals and images work, but for the Protestant reformers the real problem came from the presence of certain kinds of images in a ritual context, a context that gave the images a saintly or divine identity and a pious function. It is no accident that the destruction of images was so often accomplished through a profaning rite of passage because images, like the Eucharist, were the foundations of the traditional ritual system, the sites at which rites made the numinous present in the material world.

As we have seen in the fascination for watching the elevation of the host, traditional Christianity honored sight as the most important sense for acquiring knowledge of the divine. Because the physical world was the medium through which God made himself known in the world, religious images best assisted this process. According to John of

Damascus, Christians directed their prayers toward an image or reliquary because God or the saint might be present there, not in the sense that the spiritual being was *in* the image itself but that she acted *through* it. The "truth" of the image was not that it was an accurate representation of the actual Virgin Mary, for example, but that her presence was made evident through it when she responded to supplications, typically by answering prayers or performing miracles. Some images, therefore, worked better than others. John of Damascus developed a very sophisticated theory of images that was later adopted by St. Thomas Aquinas and other scholastic apologists for Christianity. In that theory John distinguished between *latria*, the adoration reserved only for God himself, and *dulia*, the reverence offered to the world God created: thus, the Christian could legitimately express *dulia* for the image itself, as a medium through which the saint became present in the world. Aquinas added further distinctions, such as *hyperdulia*, which should be reserved for the Virgin Mary, but these very sophisticated theological distinctions would certainly have been lost on the unlettered laity. As was the case with the doctrine of transubstantiation, the theologians may have had a clear idea of what was "present" in images, but others, including many priests themselves, certainly did not.

Whatever the theologians asserted, many believers testified to dramatic emotional and spiritual experiences deriving from their reverence toward images. Approaching images involved a precise ritual vocabulary of gestures of respect and postures of submission, such as those employed by Giovanni Morelli in his private attempt to expiate his fatherly sorrow. As Zwingli complained, devotees would "kneel and bow, remove hats, burn incense and candles [before images], kiss them, decorate them with gold and jewels, call them merciful and gracious, touch them as if they could really heal or forgive sins."[2] The problem does not seem to be that all this activity was useless for most Christians, that is images failed to work for them, but exactly the opposite: they thought images worked very well; sacred images constituted the most potent medium for gaining access to supernatural powers.

The question is why did some images seem to work so well? The answer to that question might lie in the extromission theory of vision as it was understood in the era before Kepler. The extromission theory assumed that the process of vision involved the object acting upon the eye. According to the most common version of the theory, every object produced "species" or "rays," which emanated out from the object through space and were projected into the eye, producing a sensation of

[2] Quoted in Carlos M. N. Eire, *War Against the Idols: The Reformation of Worship from Erasmus to Calvin* (Cambridge: Cambridge University Press, 1986), 21.

the object in the viewer. The object was active and powerful, the eye passive and receptive. Leonardo da Vinci explained the theory concisely: "Just as a stone flung into the water becomes the centre and cause of many circles, and as sound diffuses itself in circles in the air: so any object placed in the luminous atmosphere diffuses itself in circles, and fills the surrounding air with infinite images of itself."[3]

The extromission theory persisted, especially outside of learned circles, in large part because it identified the physics of human sight with spiritual insight, connecting mortal viewers to spiritual forces through the power of the gaze. Lee Wandel has described the process precisely:

Each visual image was not only active, it generated "infinite images of itself." Religious images, images of the sacred, of the supernatural, were even more powerful; their reflective powers were multiplied. These images not only moved toward the human eye in a process of emanation. They also reflected that which was invisible, the unseen: the sanctity of the saints, the holiness of Christ. Like the surface of water, religious images made visible patterns of light, the hidden world of the divine; their material substance provided the glazing which caught and reflected the invisible world. Religious images both in the process of being seen through "the luminous atmosphere" to the eye, and as the mirror of the invisible world, made manifest that which the eye could not see.[4]

It was exactly this power of the gaze that troubled the Protestant reformers who wanted to redirect attention to the Word, thereby replacing sight as the privileged sense with hearing. In so doing, they hoped better to control the meaning imputed to religious experiences: they could become *the* interpreters of scripture through preaching, but the profusion of statues, paintings, and reliquaries in the churches where they spoke distracted the congregation through compelling emanations. The problem with images was not that they were impotent idols but that they were too authoritative, too irresistible, too diverting in luring the laity back into a world of traditional ritual behaviors that fostered what the reformers thought were illusions about the nature of sacred presences in the material world. Much of the violence of iconoclasm should be understood less as an unmasking of images as false idols than as a reaction to their religious potency.

Reformers attacked images and the rituals that surrounded their veneration because of what images were reputed to do. As usual Zwingli was especially clear in his critique. To him idolatry was not false religion or pseudo-paganism: even the pagans, he said following St. Augustine,

---

[3] Quoted in David D. Lindberg, *Theories of Vision from Al-Kindi to Kepler* (Chicago: University of Chicago Press, 1976), 161.
[4] Lee Palmer Wandel, "The Reform of the Images: New Visualizations of the Christian Community at Zürich," *Archiv für Reformationsgeschichte* 80 (1989): 108.

knew that their gods were not *in* images. Idolatry was the natural by-product of human perception whereby viewers passively received active emanations from images. Because viewers perceived the similarity between the body of the image and their own body, they assumed that the image had the same faculties and powers they have. The emanations from an idol fabricated in the image of man, "compels the mind dwelling in a body," to quote Augustine, "to suppose that the idol's body too has feeling, because it looks very like its own body."[5] Zwingli noted the logical consequence of Augustine's insight:

Thus God forbid the source of it all. Whoever honors the idols, before and after holds them in his heart as gods, that is, as fathers or helpers. For this reason they are idols. For who honors the stone ass in the fish market or the golden hen on the small tower? For what reason? For the reason that man perceives divine help in no ass or hen.[6]

Because of the very nature of sight, Zwingli thought, any human image that represented a divine being would inevitably lead to idolatry. The only solution was to remove all such images.

Images, moreover, ate up pious resources that could better be spent in assisting the poor, whom Zwingli described as the true "image" of God. The hope of reformers such as Zwingli was that the assets devoted to paying for religious images, endowing perpetual masses, and supplying the ritual props of the liturgy could be transformed into "food of the poor." The true pious work of the Christian shifted from fulfilling certain ritual duties to fulfilling charitable obligations. Iconoclastic reformers destroyed oil lamps that required continual feeding, forbade expensive candles, and removed crucifixes to sell the wood as lumber, the proceeds from which became alms for the poor. Rather than the consequence of an irrational destructive urge, iconoclasm can be seen as part of a vast social project that reoriented Christian work toward solving the practical problems of the community. Charity became the pious alternative for image veneration.

John Calvin's position on religious images took the argument a step further by concentrating on the "image" of God, defined as humanity in the Hebrew scriptures. Calvin attributed special religious significance to the human shape, which was itself the true "figure" of God, the living images that contrasted to the false images of the Catholic church, and he borrowed the term, *iconic* ("exact image"), which had been used to

---

[5] Quoted in Ann Kibbey, *The Interpretation of Material Shapes in Puritanism: A Study of Rhetoric, Prejudice, and Violence* (Cambridge: Cambridge University Press, 1986), 47.

[6] Quoted in Lee Palmer Wandel, *Always Among Us: Images of the Poor in Zwingli's Zurich* (Cambridge: Cambridge University Press, 1990), 73.

identify artistic representations of religious figures, to describe the elect
Christian celebrating the sacraments:

When I ponder the intended use of churches, somehow or other it seems to me
unworthy of their holiness for them to take on images other than those that are
living and iconic, which the Lord has consecrated by his Word. I mean Baptism
and the Lord's Supper, together with other ceremonies by which our eyes must
be too intensely gripped and too sharply affected to seek other images forged by
human ingenuity.[7]

To Calvin's eyes figures of the saints and Christ in churches detracted
from the living icons of the congregation, the believers performing ritual
duties. He wanted Christians to look at one another during church
services rather than at alluring images. In order to create the clear visual
space for the rituals of the reformed church, Calvinists had to rid
churches of statues and paintings, making whitewashed walls and bare
altars as necessary for Calvinist ritual as a profusion of statues and
paintings were for Catholic ones.

  Beyond the reformers' polemical pamphlets and the preachers'
learned sermons, which established the theoretical groundwork, the
Reformation was in practice a battle over the right forms of sacramental
rituals. How did the laity react to the dramatic changes in ritual practice
that came with the Reformation? There cannot be a single answer to this
question because the Reformation movement took many different
forms, served many different interests, and adapted to a wide variety of
regional and national differences. In some locales lay protests forced
reluctant clergymen to adopt reforms to the mass; elsewhere, clerical
alterations of the old ways led to popular resistance. It is also important
to remember that the Reformation was an arena of conflicts, and
conflicts always involve at least two sides. Even in the areas of Switzerland and Germany where Protestantism seemed to harmonize with
popular sentiment, there were disaffected minorities, refugees, secret
adherents to the old ways, and open disagreements about what the
reform should do. Many of the reforms were more theoretical than
actual, barely touching the surface of the traditional ritual system, which
persisted in lay practice or reasserted itself in reformed religion in ways
that continued to plague the consciences of the rigorous-minded.

  The variety of lay responses to reform is especially revealing in
England where the official commitment to Protestantism varied
according to the inclinations of different monarchs who had the full
power of the law to force their will on the entire kingdom. What was
legal and religious one year might be a gross impiety the next. England

---

[7] Quoted in Kibbey, *The Interpretation of Material Shapes in Puritanism*, 45.

moved toward a moderate reform under King Henry VIII (1509–47), who severed ties with the papacy, dissolved the monasteries, and confiscated their land, but who refused to move the reform very far theologically. The Henrician Reformation has been aptly called "Catholicism without the pope," and at its most extreme adopted positions that were at best luke-warm Lutheranism. Under his son, Edward VI (1547–53), the reform swerved in a radical direction toward Zwinglian ideas, complete with systematic acts of iconoclasm, dramatic alterations of the rite of the mass, and a purging of Catholics in high places. Edward's half sister Queen Mary (1553–58), however, returned England to full compliance with the old Catholic faith while persecuting the evangelicals of the previous reign. Finally, Queen Elizabeth I (1558–1603) compromised to establish a theologically broad-minded, national Protestant church that did not recognize papal authority but tolerated some variety in liturgical practice.

Historians have not been able to agree about why most of the English laity responded so passively to this history of religious gyrations, and to a certain extent the various opinions of historians have anachronistically continued the Reformation debates into the present: those inclining to Catholicism emphasize such things as the religious vitality of traditional rites and lay resistance to liturgical changes while those of Protestant or Marxist leanings accentuate popular enthusiasm for reform. Evidence can be cited to support both positions.

The English counties of Devon and Cornwall witnessed in the Prayerbook Rebellion one of the most famous reactions against the liturgical reforms of the Edwardine Reformation, and yet Robert Whiting has argued that there was also significant popular enthusiasm in the area for the reform movement. Much of the antagonism of the reform-minded was directed against the mass itself. While under interrogation after the return of Catholicism under Queen Mary, one Agnes Priest declared, "I would rather die than I will do any worship to that foul idol which, with your mass, you make a god." This seemingly humble woman had a homely way of illustrating her rejection of transubstantiation, denying "that a piece of bread should be turned by a man into the natural body of Christ . . . and mice oftentimes do eat it, and it doth mould and is burned."[8]

Whiting observed in Devon and Cornwall a "drastic and comparatively rapid reduction of commitment to the traditional rites in the Reformation decades."[9] While major parts of the liturgical calendar

---

[8] Quoted in Robert Whiting, *The Blind Devotion of the People: Popular Religion and the English Reformation* (Cambridge: Cambridge University Press, 1989), 24–25.
[9] Ibid., 33.

persisted, certain rites, especially those associated with the mass and the sacraments questioned by the reforming preachers diminished. Even when under King Edward there was an official attack on a variety of ritual practices associated with the old religion, there was little local opposition until the Prayerbook Rebellion broke out in 1549, and Whiting thinks that the motives of the insurgents were not entirely or even predominantly religious. Perhaps most remarkable was the fact that the parishes themselves fully cooperated with stripping the altars bare of relics, images, and the rich furnishings of the mass so that when Queen Mary reasserted Catholicism, the cost of restoring the altars was extremely high. According to Whiting, most of the peasants and artisans only expressed opposition to the reduction of the number of feast days, which eliminated holiday occasions when they could rest from labor.

Nothing could be more different from this sanguine view of the Reformation than Eamon Duffy's reading of much the same evidence. To him the elimination during Henry's and Edward's reigns of saints' relics, chantries, intercessory masses, rosary beads, fastings, indulgences, images, stained-glass windows, vestments, and especially the sacramentals of bells, holy water, and blessed candles – in short the whole vast enterprise of traditional liturgical practice – was a "disaster for lay religious life." By stripping the altars all across England of their sacred inventories and the chantries of their financial endowments, the Reformation confiscated enormously valuable resources, some stolen by local hands, some reverting to the Crown. Duffy argues that given the intensity of official scrutiny, especially in the implementation of the reforms of 1547–48, the cooperation of the parishes and most of the laity is less evidence of enthusiasm for the new creed or hostility to the old ways than fear of royal authority. If nothing else, the success of the English Reformation is an indication of the strength of Tudor government, and although there were areas of sincere Protestant commitment, especially in London, in most places the destruction of the old order was a "grudging fulfillment of the will of the Crown, and sometimes an attempt to anticipate the actions of the Crown in order to save something from the wreckage."[10]

Although Duffy is certainly correct in emphasizing the persistent vigor of traditional ritual practices, his defense of Catholicism misses the degree to which English communities were deeply divided on religious issues and had already begun to express themselves in diverging ritual languages before Henry VIII ever thought of divorcing Catherine of Aragon. Rather than applying some form of retrospective polling to

[10] Eamon Duffy, *The Stripping of the Altars: Traditional Religion in England c.1400–c.1580* (New Haven: Yale University Press, 1992), 480.

discover what the majority might have wanted had they been given the choice, it seems most important to understand what was at stake in both forms of ritual life. Duffy argues that,

At the heart of the Edwardine reform was the necessity of destroying, of cutting, hammering, scraping, or melting into a deserved oblivion the monuments of popery, so that the doctrines they embodied might be forgotten. Iconoclasm was the central sacrament of the reform, and as the programme of the leaders became more radical in the years between 1547 and 1553, they sought with greater urgency the celebration of that sacrament of forgetfulness in every parish in the land.[11]

Deplorable as it now seems since so many artistic treasures were lost, iconoclasm certainly became for a time a necessary sacrament in the eyes of the reformers who sought to replace the dead figures of the saints with the living figures of Christian believers, but the reformers themselves would never have seen their destructions, so often carried out in the dead of night, as a "sacrament of forgetfulness" but rather as a rite of purification that made possible a true rite of remembrance, a rite that prompted the Christian to remember God's words rather than some artist's idea of his image.

The two ritual languages, Catholic and Protestant, reached the point where they could not be expressed in the same place without violent results: they became persistent antagonists that structured "right action" in different ways, each having their own strengths and weaknesses as rituals. The strength of Catholic ritual remained the psycho-spiritual power of its visualizations and its chronic weakness the ambiguity of meaning conveyed by those visualizations. Protestant ritual, especially as it evolved in the more thoroughly reformed locales such as England under Edward VI or Scotland, Switzerland, and Holland, provided clarity of meaning through the declaration of seemingly unambiguous words at the cost of visual impoverishment. The quintessential sacrament of iconoclasm was repeated throughout England in 1547 and 1548: chapels were denuded of their idols, the images hidden away, smashed, or sold; niches once rich with statues were plastered shut; stained-glass windows emitting a gaudily colored light were broken and replaced with clear glass; and the now bare walls, once polluted with images, were whitewashed pure and lettered with edifying inscriptions condemning idolatry. From the walls of the churches now radiated God's Word, which entered the mind of the viewer just as alluring idols had once projected infinite images of themselves into the viewer's soul.

[11] Ibid.

Orthodox

During the sixteenth century the lands of the Orthodox faith were separated from the areas of western and northern Europe embroiled in the Reformation controversies by the Ottoman Empire, which extended into Europe to grasp most of the Balkan peninsula and Hungary. The principal breaches in this wall of Islamic authority were the German-speaking communities in Hungary, many of which converted to Lutheranism, and Protestant Transylvania, which was a client state of the Ottomans. Transylvania had a significant minority of Orthodox believers and bordered Orthodox Moldavia, a situation that provided limited contacts between the vast Orthodox population of the lower Danube basin and some of the most radical Calvinist and anti-Trinitarian followers of the Reformation who found refuge in Transylvania and brought with them ambitions to outflank their Catholic enemies by introducing reform measures among the Greek Orthodox churches.

When Protestantism came into contact with Orthodoxy, the issue of reform took on a different orientation than it had in the confrontation with the Catholics. Lutherans, in particular, sought contacts with the Orthodox because on many dogmatic issues, such as the Trinity and the lord's supper, they were in substantial agreement, but when it came to the practical ritual problems about the appropriate forms of worship and iconoclasm, the two had substantial differences with the Orthodox closer to the Catholic attitude. The Protestant message arrived among the Greek Orthodox at a particularly inopportune moment because during the early sixteenth century the Ottoman oppression of Orthodox Christians was at its peak with the confiscation of ecclesiastical property and closure of many churches. Under these conditions the sacrality of church buildings diminished in favor of the transportable icons, which were rescued from expropriated church buildings. Striving to survive in this hostile environment, the Orthodox forged their religious identity ever more fervently around reverence for icons. As a consequence the Orthodox saw all Protestant attacks on ritual practices as a form of iconoclasm that threatened what they cherished most dearly.

The strange case of the attempted Reformation of Orthodox Moldavia during the brief rule of Jacob Heraclides revealed the problems of imposing a Protestant conception of ritual on an Orthodox populace. In 1561 this Greek soldier-of-fortune obtained the title of Duke of Moldavia and proceeded to impose a strict, Calvinist conception of ritual in a land where native sentiments in favor of reform were completely absent. Surrounded by German Lutheran and Polish

Calvinist advisers who were foreigners in a heavily Slavic Orthodox land, Heraclides attempted to force ritual reforms more rapidly and thoroughly than had been tried even in England. He at first pressured the local Moldavian nobility to convert by staging "public debates" that were actually propaganda displays portraying Orthodox rites as "superstition," "stupid ceremonies," "inane sacred rites," and "idolatry."[12] Like Henry VIII in England, Heraclides suppressed the monasteries in order to confiscate their wealth for his own use, but he challenged traditions more directly than Henry ever did by melting down silver and gold crosses taken from the most revered monasteries and using the precious metals to mint new coins with his own image on them. The blasphemy of this expropriation was so scandalous that the people refused to use the coins, and Heraclides played into the hands of his Orthodox critics who gleefully pointed out the central contradiction in his iconoclasm: the supposed reformer had substituted his own personal portrait for the image of God in an astounding act of idolatry. Although Heraclides stopped short of actually removing icons from Orthodox churches, his plundering of gold and silver icon covers, reliquaries, and crucifixes enraged the Orthodox enough to provoke an armed rebellion against him. Not two years into his reign, Heraclides was defeated and executed. Many of his Protestant bully boys were either lynched or exiled in reaction to the religious desecrations they had perpetrated.

Despite the potential advantages to be gained by greater cooperation with the Greek Orthodox churches, the Protestants seemed to have learned little from the Moldavian disaster and refused to back away from advocating iconoclasm among the icon-sensitive Orthodox. Formal negotiations in 1574–81 and again in 1716–25 between different Protestant groups and the Patriarch of Constantinople foundered on the issue of the place of icons in Christian worship: even when the two sides agreed that a certain variety in ceremonies was tolerable, the Protestants could not resist attacking images.

The most remarkable attempt at a Protestant-style reform of Orthodoxy came during the fascinating career of the philo-Protestant Patriarch of Constantinople, Cyril Lucaris (1620–38), who with the backing of the English and Dutch embassies advocated reforming rites and image veneration in the very heart of Orthodoxy. Attracted to the logical rigor of Calvinism, Lucaris at first proceeded with caution by publishing a tract on the fundamental principles of reform. He never actually tried to abolish the veneration of images, but his views, however abstractly

---

[12] Sergiusz Michalski, *The Reformation and the Visual Arts: The Protestant Image Question in Western and Eastern Europe* (London: Routledge, 1993), 107.

stated, created a great furor among most of the clergy and laity. He was twice stripped of his office and finally assassinated by the Ottomans.

In the far north beyond the reach of the Ottoman empire, the Polish–Lithuanian commonwealth separated the German Protestants from the Russian Orthodox. For the most part this barrier limited the influence of the Reformation among the Russians except during the last decades of sixteenth century when Catholic and Protestant strife in eastern Poland spilled over into Russia. The more direct avenue for the influence of Protestant ideas on Russian Orthodoxy was through the Baltic states of Livonia and Estonia, which were dominated by German burghers who had enthusiastically adopted Lutheranism and who provided Russia's principal point of contact with Western European culture.

The Russian church had accepted Greek Orthodox theology when the Rus' were originally converted to Christianity, but 500 years of isolation from Constantinople and the intensely defensive patriotism that evolved in response to the Mongol invasions had led to many differences in religious practice between Greek and Russian Orthodoxy. In particular Russian ritual focused even more than the Greeks on the cult of icons, and the Russian Orthodox were especially noted for celebrating miracles associated with certain images. This sturdy strain of iconolatry, deeply embedded in Russian consciousness, can be seen in the *Tale of Past Years*, a legendary account of how Christianity arrived in Russia. In the story when Grand Duke Vladimir decided to lead his people into the Christian fold, he chose the Eastern over the Western rite because he was so impressed with the greater liturgical splendor of the Greeks.

Icon veneration was so strong in Russia that heretical movements invariably differentiated themselves from the mainstream by advocating iconoclasm. In the fourteenth and fifteenth centuries, there were a series of these movements that in many ways anticipated Reformation arguments against the alleged idolatry of image worship. The adherents of the most important of these heresies were called "Judaizers" by their persecutors. Supporters of the heresy probably had nothing to do with actual Judaism and were even unlikely to have come under any direct Jewish influences, but their strict adherence to the law of scripture and their attempts to re-establish Old Testament ceremonies, including the observation of the sabbath and the rejection of religious images as idols, confused their enemies. No matter how unsuitable it was as a label for these Christian heretics, the term "Judaizer" contributed to the sadly grotesque tradition of Russian anti-Semitism by associating actual Jews with active opponents to the Orthodox hierarchy and Tsar.

In the late fifteenth century several different movements were lumped together under the label Judaizers, but all they seemed to have had in common was the rejection of image worship. By 1500 they had been driven underground or into extinction by vicious persecutions. Once the Reformation was established in the Baltic communities, however, Livonia and Estonia provided a refuge and ideological support for the remaining Russian Judaizers. By the middle of the century, a certain fusion had taken place among at least some of the Protestant and Judaizing groups. Tsar Ivan the Terrible, whose expansionist aims led him to invade Livonia in 1558, sought to root out these heretics wherever he could find them. When his forces took Polotsk in 1563, Ivan ordered that a former Judaizer turned pastor of a small Protestant community, along with all the Calvinists and Jews of the place, be drowned through holes cut in the ice of a local river. To Ivan their distaste for icons bound them all together and made them traitors to a Russian identity created through icon rituals. Ivan himself even conducted a formal debate with a Protestant diplomat posted to Moscow on the subject of the veneration of icons. The Protestant argument was the standard complaint about the sacralization of material objects, but Ivan's response, which he plagiarized from a theological defender of Orthodoxy, provides an insight into the role of icon rituals in Russia. To Ivan the central problem with the Protestants was that they had never proven the validity of their faith through miracles, but the icons of Russia provided evidence of numerous miracles. Even worse, Ivan complained, the Protestants had reviled the saints by destroying their altars and images.

Consequently you not only fail to worship holy images, but you throw them out of your churches and homes, though all of the nooks and crannies of your homes ought to be filled with images of the saints. Which ought to be regarded as an even greater sin, since in this way you show contempt for God himself and oppose him. Who as punishment for your godlessness afflicted you with irreconcilable sects and divisions.[13]

Despite the famous persecutions of Ivan the Terrible, advocates of reforming ceremonies and icon worship did not entirely disappear in Russia. In the mid-seventeenth century, Patriarch Nikon provoked an internal conflict within Russian Orthodoxy by advocating a variety of liturgical reforms, including the elimination of icons that did not follow the correct iconography. Although Nikon's reforms were an attempt to clarify and reinvigorate the liturgy, he was opposed by the Old Believers who thought he was about to inaugurate official iconoclasm. Many people took back their small private icons that they kept in churches for fear they would be destroyed. The controversy over liturgical reform

[13] Quoted in ibid., 139.

arose again at the end of the seventeenth century when Tsar Peter the Great (1682–1725) initiated his "improvements" of Russian customs after his visit to England and the Netherlands, but in this case the disputes seem to have come more from the paranoia of conservatives than from any changes Peter actually attempted to enforce.

In the Polish–Lithuanian commonwealth, the picture became quite complex during the last half of the century. The vast peasant majority were resolutely Orthodox, but influential portions of the nobility and gentry were attracted to various forms of Protestantism. Calvinism captivated the elites in Lithuania while Anabaptism and Arianism spread in the Ukraine. These elites sponsored a vast crusade of propaganda, especially against the Orthodox liturgy and the cult of the saints. For example in eastern Poland, Orthodox churches were closed, but unlike in the West where formerly Catholic churches were typically transformed into Protestant ones so that religious rites of some sort were still available to the masses, the Orthodox churches were usually destroyed or adapted for profane uses as taverns or barns. The Arian noble Strzemeski appropriated one of the Orthodox churches in Zydaczow for a pigsty, for which he was later condemned as a blasphemer. Official declarations against images were often accompanied by acts of iconoclasm. Polish Protestant nobles seemed to develop their own rite of iconoclasm that consisted of running icons through with a saber. In the struggle among the various confessions, the Roman Catholics were finally victorious during the period from 1595 to 1599 and began to transform Poland into one of the most thoroughly Catholic countries in Europe. Although support from the Polish crown was crucial in this victory, the Catholics had an advantage over the Protestants in their willingness to be flexible about retaining certain Orthodox elements in the liturgy, especially those relating to icon veneration.

Despite the recurring attraction to Protestantism among some sectors of the nobility of eastern Europe and the occasional Orthodox intellectual, significant reforms of ritual life failed to take hold among the peasant masses. The absence of strong civic culture in eastern Europe, except in the Baltics, and the cultural seclusion of much of the vast region limited the possibilities for a reform that was both too theoretical and too threatening to traditional religious sensibilities. Religious piety and cultural identity remained deeply attached to icons, those paintings that provided such a reassuring visual presence and continuity with a miraculous past when God had intervened for the comfort of believers. The Turkish menace to the cultural survival of the Greek Orthodox, the paranoia and isolation of the Russians, and the persistent political weakness of the governments in between, especially

Poland–Lithuania, meant that the ritual bonds of community, as tenuous as they were, could not be subjected to even the slightest revision without deeply threatening the very survival of the community itself.

Catholic

The ritual processes of the Reformation in the Catholic world followed two distinct tendencies: one, regulations imposed from above and the other, pietistic practices expressing lay enthusiasm for Christian renewal. The regulatory path was set out by the decrees of the Council of Trent, which attempted to standardize liturgical practices in order to eliminate abuses and the confusing variety of rites. The Council charged bishops with putting into action what had been determined at Trent, but the effective implementation of the Tridentine decrees varied enormously across Europe and the Americas. They were perhaps most thoroughly enforced in the papal state itself and northern Italy where the interests of the landed elites and the church hierarchy often coincided, but even there implementation was controversial and uneven. In southern Italy it took 200 years or more for the decrees to be realized in a systematic way. The emperors in Germany, the kings of France, and the kings of Spain all resisted the reforms to some extent because they either seemed prejudicial to royal prerogatives or failed to answer Protestant objections to Catholic practices. Ireland missed out almost entirely on the Catholic Reformation, largely because of hostility toward the overt practice of Catholicism from the dominant English. Outside of Italy the decrees were welcomed without significant official resistance only in Portugal and Poland, but even there actual compliance lagged behind stated goals for many years.

The pietistic strain of the Catholic Reformation appeared independently of the Council of Trent and evolved from the extraordinarily abundant repertoire of late medieval ritual practices that the laity and clergy reinvigorated and redeployed, in part as a Catholic response to the Protestant threat and in part as a general revival of Catholic piety that coincided with the Reformation but was not entirely dependent on it. At every point where Protestant reformers had criticized traditional ritual practices – the non-biblical sacraments, proliferation of sacramentals, use of images, cult of the saints, liturgical processions, masses for the dead – Catholics responded by reasserting the spiritual value of such rites, producing more processions, more elaborate decorations for churches, more side altars, more images, more magnificent music, more bejeweled chalices, richer liturgical vestments, even more saints. The pietistic trend consisted not just in the enforcement of liturgical uniformity but in the elaboration of a distinctively Catholic ritual vocabulary that contrasted with Protestant rituals, especially in the emphasis placed on the miracles of the saints and the Eucharist.

The principal Catholic strategy was to employ liturgical processions to demonstrate community cohesion and conformity. As early as 1528 in Paris King François I personally joined a procession designed to compensate the Virgin for a sacrilegious act committed against a statue of her in a public street. After hearing mass in the local church, the party proceeded to the location of the desecration where the king replaced the defaced statue with a new, silver-plated one. When the substitute statue was itself defiled it had to be replaced anew, and the repeated defacement of these images of the Virgin gave them miraculous qualities in the eyes of local Catholic women who considered them especially efficacious for difficulties in pregnancies. One woman reported that after praying before the original broken statue, she felt the dead baby in her womb come back to life. Catholics had answered Protestant iconoclasm by reasserting the miraculous potential of image veneration.

Protestant polemics against the Eucharist made defending the sacrality of the communion wafer a goal of many Catholic processions. In 1535, also in Paris, the king joined as a bare-headed, humble penitent a vast procession devoted to combating Protestants who had tacked up posters that "blasphemed God of the blessed Sacrament of the altar."[14] Along the processional route residents were obliged to stand in front of their houses holding a lighted torch while they watched pass the procession in which priests and acolytes carried an impressive array of precious relics including, besides the host, which was given pride of place, the remains of six saints, the crown of thorns, a piece of the cross, a drop of Christ's blood, and a drop of the Virgin's milk. Ending with a high mass at Notre-Dame, the procession was followed by the public execution of six Protestants convicted of heresy.

By the last decades of the sixteenth century, newly founded or revived confraternities composed of lay brothers institutionalized the rejuvenation of Catholic ritual through regular processions. In the pietistic atmosphere after Trent the most favored of these was the Confraternity of the Holy Sacrament, most chapters of which had been established in towns long before the Reformation era. In periodic processions these brothers displayed the host for public veneration in an elaborately decorated pyx carried beneath a canopy as the relics of saints would have

---

[14] Cited in Barbara B. Diefendorf, *Beneath the Cross: Catholics and Huguenots in Sixteenth-Century Paris* (Oxford: Oxford University Press, 1991), 46. For a full account of these processions, see 45–47.

been in earlier times. The cult of the Eucharist became so vital that witnessing the miracle of the mass as often as possible began to displace other forms of pious activity. For example, by the middle of the sixteenth century in Cuenca, Spain, the numbers of persons who requested in their wills that special masses be said in their memory rose dramatically among all social classes, but as Sara Nalle has shown, the practice was more popular among women than men.

More disturbing than reassuring for many viewers were the penitential companies whose members wore hoods over their faces as they whipped themselves bloody while processing through the streets several times a year. Although flagellant companies had spread widely as a menacing phenomenon during the fourteenth century, the practice had died out except in a few pockets in northern Italy and southern France until the Wars of Religion, and the Catholic Reformation encouraged a widespread revival in the late sixteenth century, especially in France and Spain. By disguising identities and reminding viewers of convicts facing execution, hoods made the flagellants anonymous. The bloodied bodies of unrecognizable friends and neighbors stumbling down the street could cause widespread terror. In 1575 the Blue Penitents so frightened the children of Toulouse that they fled the approaching procession. In fact, such flagellants purposely tried to alienate their neighbors. As a French apologist from the early seventeenth century put it, such severe self-discipline became a form of self-martyrdom: "In the eyes of the world made effeminate by its pleasures, [the penitent] will appear to be possessed by a hatred for himself and seem to act as an executioner of his own life, but though it be said that he is lost for the earth and damned in the opinion of men, he will grow in God's esteem."[15]

In their missions to southern Italy, which lacked an effective parish structure to regulate reform, the Jesuits encouraged penitential devotions adapted to the region's peculiar religious traditions of radically segregating the sexes from one another. At the culmination of a mission, all the men of a community would gather in a church, while the women remained outside, "and while the men beat themselves, these women scream with tears and loud groans for mercy from God." The practice of flagellation during these revivalist missions took on an almost apocalyptic character: a description of a rural mission in 1630 reported that "those who beat themselves with iron chains, far from turning red with a lot of blood, actually turned white as their bones were revealed through

---

[15] These are the words of Etienne Molinier, a Black Penitent from Toulouse, cited and translated by Robert A. Schneider, "Mortification on Parade: Penitential Processions in Sixteenth- and Seventeenth-Century France," *Renaissance and Reformation* 10 (1986): 133.

lacerated flesh."[16] Jesuit missionaries attempted to substitute doctrinally acceptable practices for the pious practices that had evolved in the absence of ecclesiastical supervision, such as instituting the "Slaves of the Virgin Mary," which consisted of seven local men laden with chains who processed to a church where they flung themselves down before the altar pleading for mercy on behalf of the entire community.

Perhaps the most powerful accomplishment of Catholic Reformation rituals was their ability to go beyond representing abstract truths such as Eucharistic doctrines, to evoke deeply disturbing emotions, especially fear and grief. The ritualized summoning of painful experiences was especially marked in Spain with the Holy Thursday rites, which Maureen Flynn has called a "spectacle of suffering." From sunset to midnight young and old, men and women, flooded the streets of Spanish towns to bemoan the impending death of Christ. According to the Gospels of Matthew and Luke, as Christ contemplated his crucifixion while praying in the garden of Gethsemane his apostles asked to share in his suffering. Emulating these first Christians, Spanish companies of female and male *disciplinantes* re-enacted the gospel scenes more emotionally than literally by sharing a simple meal together, then walking barefoot through the streets as they flagellated themselves. The rite created a memory of the last supper and the agony in the garden by leading penitents to discover God through the extreme limits of physical suffering, concentrating all the mundane miseries of the participants on their own self-tortured bodies, which through flagellation became akin to the tortured body of Christ. Pain became a medium of exchange with God, a means of making a sacrificial offering to him. The Spanish Holy Thursday rite exemplified the critical difference between Catholic and Protestant ritual vocabularies. For the Catholic evoking an emotional response and discovering God through intense physical sensations garnered spiritual merit. For the Protestant concerned to understand the biblical text correctly, the imitation of Christ came less through the body than the mind.

The most dramatic of Catholic rituals extended penance, the sacrament so disputed by the Protestants. The elaborate ritual of penance, the Spanish *auto de fe*, which literally meant a theater of faith, was performed during the height of the Catholic enthusiasms of the seventeenth century. The *auto* symbolically pre-enacted, in effect, the last judgment, stimulating deep anxiety among viewers over how they would fare when they stood before God on the last day. Everything

[16] Both quotations translated in David Gentilcore, *From Bishop to Witch: The System of the Sacred in Early Modern Terra d'Otranto* (Manchester: Manchester University Press, 1992), 69.

about the *auto* seemed designed to promote fear and to offer the possibility of relief from fear by asserting that suffering bodily pain in this life would relieve the soul from worse punishments in the next. Organized through the cooperation of ecclesiastical and secular authorities, *autos de fe* brought together an assortment of sinners and criminals for a vast public rite of penance that displayed in a dramatic fashion the essential elements of the sacrament: contrition, confession, and satisfaction or punishment. The prisoners usually consisted of persons alleged to have been blasphemers, bigamists, witches, Judaizers (in the Spanish sense of the word, former Jews who had reverted to the old faith), or Protestants who were forced to march in a procession of sinners that usually went through the streets of the city from the cathedral to the town hall or place of punishment. These processions would typically include some thirty or forty convicted souls, but in moments of intense crisis they could be far larger. In Toledo in 1486 alone there were three *autos*, one parading 750 sinners and two displaying some 900 each.

A 1655 *auto* in Córdoba illustrates the abundant symbolic character of the rites. Soldiers bearing torches that would light the flames for those to be burnt led the procession, which included three bigamists who wore on their heads conical miters or hats painted with representations of their sin, four witches whose miters depicted devils, three criminals with harnesses around their necks to demonstrate their status as captives, and a group of barefoot, bare-headed repentant sinners dressed in yellow tunics that were marked with bands the width of which indicated the seriousness of their transgressions and carrying unlit candles to represent their lack of faith. Criminals who had escaped justice were represented in the procession by effigies made in their likeness, and those who had died before punishment were carried in their coffins. Each of these sinners appeared before their neighbors and fellow citizens stripped of the normal indicators of their status, dressed only in the emblems of their sins. Among them walked a few who wore the infamous *sanbenitos*, a kind of tunic or vest with a yellow strip down the back, and a conical hat painted with flames. These were the *relajados*, the unrepentant or relapsed sinners who were going to be "relaxed," that is strangled and burned at the culminating moment of the *auto*. The procession ended in the town square at a platform from which the prisoners would perform their penances before the public as if on the stage of a theater: forced to their knees the sinners were asked to confess and to plead for re-admission into the bosom of the church. For those who did confess, a sentence was announced that would rescue them from the pains of purgatory and the flames of the *auto*. The penalties depended upon the crime and displayed a great variety that included joining a penitential procession for a number of Fridays, requiring self-flagellation in public, or demanding that the penitent continue to wear the badges of shame for a prescribed period of time.

The most horrendous scenes of suffering awaited those who refused to repent or who had relapsed into sin or heresy, which meant that even if they chose to confess, they would not be considered sincere. If holdouts repented prior to the reading of the sentence, then the *auto* was a success, a triumph of the Christian faith over its enemies, and everything that could possibly elicit a confession was attempted, including haranguing, humiliating, and torturing the accused until their stubborn will broke. If the accused finally repented after the sentence was read then they would be strangled before burning, but if they held out to the very end, they would be burned alive. From the ecclesiastics' point of view, the refusal to repent was a disaster for the entire church because the flames opened a window into hell, and they would certainly prefer to see the church's authority acknowledged through confession than to see the power of Satan manifest in such a public fashion. It is reported that crowds witnessed the violence of the *autos de fe* with silent attention in a mood of deep dread not so much of the inquisitors, it seems, as for the inevitability of the final day of divine judgment that would arrive for them all. The core assumption of the *auto* ritual was that the infliction of bodily pain could save a soul from damnation. As one contemporary witness put it, the inquisitors removed "through external ritual [the sinners'] internal crimes, as was done by the early church."[17] It was assumed that the public ritual framework for the sacrament of penance would have a salutary effect on those who witnessed the *auto*, encouraging them to repent before they too faced the divine scourge.

The two paths we have identified of Catholic ritual reform, the regulatory and the pietistic, separated ecclesiastical authority and lay spirituality in a way that was clearer in theory than in practice. The distinction between the two courses of reform masks what was in many respects a common "system of the sacred," as David Gentilcore calls it, a luxuriant garden of rites that cannot be consistently classified into official and popular, clerical and lay varieties. Everyone shared a common ritual vocabulary for defining collective identities. Moreover, what has often been called popular religion actually lumps together a wide diversity of religious cultures that shared common assumptions about the nature of supernatural power, access to which was by no means monopolized by priests. Nowhere was this more obvious than in the attempts by Counter-Reformation bishops to reinvigorate the parish

---

[17] Quoted in Maureen Flynn, "Mimesis of the Last Judgment: The Spanish *Auto de fe*," *Sixteenth Century Journal* 22 (1991): 292.

as the approved location for the celebration of reformed rituals. Before the Council of Trent parishes were notoriously weak, especially in the face of other institutions that more closely matched the social structures of the villages: youth-abbeys, all-male confraternities and flagellant companies, community associations, and the private altars and chapels of kin groups. The goal of what Angelo Torre has called "parish formation" was to transform the parish church into the most important place for all ritual observances within a certain territory and to make it the only local institution that possessed legitimate ecclesiastical authority. Through frequent visitations of the parishes the bishop would then be better able to oversee ritual practices.

This was easier said than done. Making parishes undisputed religious and social centers required considerable cooperation and negotiation between church authorities and the laity. Those bishops who were most successful were those who found the means to link their obligations to regulate ritual practice with the pious inclinations of the congregations. Especially in rural areas religious worship took place in many different locales, and even the parish church itself was a highly segmented space, with different social and kinship groups using the space in different ways. First of all, there was a profusion of side altars, scattered haphazardly throughout the church, some placed against columns in the middle of the church, some backed up against the main altar, crowding it with an abundance of ex-votos (mementos of miracles granted) hanging from the ceiling. Within any one church there was a multiplicity of cults, each devoted to a saintly protector, but each also had a human patron or patrons who jealously guarded any threats to their favorite cult. Second, much of what appeared and went on in the church did not conform to accepted church practice; 250 parishes have been studied in three dioceses in southern Piedmont in the late sixteenth century; in only two of these was the baptismal font correctly placed in the prescribed location. Parish priests also lacked the will or ability to perform their liturgical duties outside of the narrow confines of the church: again in Piedmont in the seventeenth century some 65 percent of the parishes lacked the special liturgical box – the pyx – for carrying the host outside the church to the sick and dying, and a quarter of the priests admitted they never ventured to isolated farms. Many persons had to rely on other ways of gaining access to sacramental power than through the parish priest, adding to the widespread segmentation of ritual practices. Third, it was often unclear exactly what or where the parish church was. In some places the ancient parish had been abandoned, in others there were disputes between churches for the title, and in yet more cases the parish had disappeared entirely. In its capacity to exercise ritual jurisdiction over a defined territory, the parish was a highly dubious institution, and yet to enforce the regulations of Trent bishops had to rely on it.

The visits of bishops to the parishes, as required by Trent, resulted in endless disputes as the ecclesiastical authorities attempted to define who in the community, whether an individual or family or political institution or corporate organization such as a confraternity, had legal responsibility for each ritual object and church furnishing. These often highly contentious disputes sometimes concerned seemingly trivial issues, such as who owned the ropes for pulling church bells. A priest in the diocese of Alba complained in 1653 that since the town owned the bell ropes the community council would not let him ring bells to announce decrees of the bishop, thereby undermining the authority of the church. In addition the dividing line between who could perform church rituals and who could not, that is the distinction between priest and layman, was vaguer than one might expect. A priest was a priest because he performed sacraments. If this were true, then anyone who acted in a sacramental fashion attained a quasi-priestly status. As a result, in their visitations to parishes, bishops showed great sensitivity to the exact details of ritual practice, especially the rites of confraternities and families at their private altars, because the ritual act itself conferred status on individuals, groups, and even buildings. In the diocese of Asti in 1626, for example, the episcopal visitor was furious when he discovered that the local confraternity of flagellants had presented their crucifix for the people to kiss in exchange for alms. He was angry not because of the implications of idolatry but because the flagellants had taken money for a ritual service, which was the exclusive prerogative of priests. The problem was, as Angelo Torre has put it, that "ritual acts lay down lines of classification between social groups, and who has prerogatives over what."[18] Any attempt to change any ritual had implications for the distribution of power within the community and the prestige of individuals and groups. It should not be surprising that attempts to reform rituals provoked enormous controversies.

Although bishops might be censorious about the crudest abuses of ecclesiastical property, such as using parish churches as stables or taverns, they had to avoid head-on confrontations with parishioners sensitive to their ritual rights. The most successful reforms came when bishops co-opted the laity by redefining or restructuring established lay practices. The conciliatory bishops often succeeded when they limited themselves to three areas. First, exercising control over the multiplicity

[18] Angelo Torre, "Politics Cloaked in Worship: State, Church and Local Power in Piedmont 1570–1770," *Past and Present* 134 (1992): 57.

of side altars eliminated some of the most obvious distractions from the centrality of the high altar in the parish church. Side altars tended to segment the public church into the private spaces of aristocratic landlords, kin groups, or confraternities, and bishops had to make these groups responsible for maintaining a part of the church without allowing them to destroy the public character of the parish and its forms of worship in what was often a delicate balancing of private and collective interests. Second, bishops had to redeploy existing forms of collective worship into the parish organization, eliminating semi-private cults and the display of ex-votos, which distracted worship from the high altar. The cult of the Virgin of the Rosary, preached by the Dominicans, assisted this effort by redirecting prayer away from private altars to the collective repetition of the rosary at the high altar under the direction of the parish priest. Third, bishops enhanced rituals that assisted in developing a community identity. By promoting the cult of the host at the high altar, the thaumaturgical appeal of many of the saintly cults on side altars diminished, and the host itself served as a metaphor for the unified body of the community, whose competitive and envious members joined together for worship at a single altar. Confraternities devoted to the body of God assisted in translating private interests into communal ones. The elaboration of the cult of the Eucharist achieved far more than a response to the Protestants. It became a synecdoche – the part that stood for the whole – of the community, strengthened by a reinvigorated, bishop-controlled, parish-based reformation of worship.

Rites of malevolence

The traditional ritual system had always embraced a wide variety of practices that offered multiple ways for gaining access to supernatural powers. If the problem were illness, various ritual cures could be tried ranging from the incantations of the local wise woman to a pilgrimage to the shrine of a miracle-working icon. The Protestant Reformation had, of course, reoriented ritual theory, raising new questions about what rituals do and what they mean, and even though Orthodox and Catholic Christians did not accept Protestant answers to these questions, they too became sensitized to the implications of ritual actions. The hermeneutics of ritual had occupied Christian theologians since the time of the early church, but the controversies of the sixteenth century raised these issues to a higher level of consciousness among the laity than ever before, making the intentions behind the performance of a rite, the details of the performance itself, and the reputed results of the performance the subject of great concern for both religious and secular authorities.

Stimulated perhaps by an elevated awareness of the power and dangers of ritual, some Christians imagined that if church rites could do good then it seemed reasonable that demonic rites could work evil. Fears of malevolent ritual fixated on different groups at different periods of history – lepers, Moslems, and heretics, for example – but during the early modern period two groups, who were often at the margins of their communities, were the most common objects of dreadful allegations: Jews, whose own rites were misunderstood or imagined to harm Christians, and witches, who were persons (most often old women) thought to kill babies, create pains in others, spread disease among livestock, and cause other mischief through ritual means. Neither group seems to have been guilty of anything other than nonconformity to Christianity and in the case of most alleged witches not even that, but the logic of Christian ritual powerfully stimulated the imagination, resulting in some of the most horrendous episodes of scapegoating in history and leaving Western culture with a nasty heritage of bigotry.

The Christian persecutions of Jews and alleged witches were not interchangeable, that is the rationales and social conditions of the persecutions were often quite different, but in both cases Christians imagined that Jews and witches accepted the inherent power of Christian rituals and perverted them to serve their own sinister purposes. With a long medieval history, Christian mistreatment of Jews began to intensify during the late fifteenth century, decades before the Reformation. The intellectual justification for the discovery and interrogation of alleged witches also crystallized in the fifteenth century, inaugurating the great witch-hunt, which lasted from about 1450 to 1750 but was most intense from about 1550 to 1650.

The core fantasy about Jewish ritual was the blood libel, the belief that certain Jewish rites, especially those of Passover, required Christian blood for their efficacy. There are numerous tragic examples of blood libel allegations, which reveal far more about the concerns of Christians with the body and blood of their God than they do about actual Jewish rites. Perhaps the most famous case was the 1475 trial in Trent in northern Italy for the ritual murder of a two-year-old boy, named Simon, who was later beatified and whose story led to an anti-Semitic propaganda campaign that resulted in allegations of ritual murder by Jews in many other places. Easter and Passover coincided in 1475, and the local preachers in Trent spent much of Holy Week sermonizing against the Jews. In a climate of rising religious tensions, an accident precipitated a horrible persecution. The Christian boy Simon went missing on Holy Thursday, which led to a city-wide search for the child, but then on Easter Sunday the child's dead body was found in a ditch that ran through the cellar of a Jewish family's house. The boy had apparently fallen into the ditch, and his lifeless body had been carried away by the current, only to become lodged in the Jews' cellar. The coincidence of the location of the discovery of the body with the ritually charged season of the year produced a disaster for the Jews of Trent. Eighteen Jewish men and one woman were arrested and eventually confessed under torture to a scenario of ritual murder that clearly issued from the imaginations of the Christian magistrates rather than anything the Jews had actually done.

In the torture sessions of the various defendants, the pieces of a fantastic story appeared. On the eve of Passover, the Jew Samuel announced to his fellows that they needed a Christian child to sacrifice for the Seder rituals, and the obligation fell on Tobias, head of another Jewish family. Tobias lured Simon to the synagogue where on the day of Passover, the rabbis tore at the boy's flesh to collect the blood for mixing with Seder wine and matza. Later the lifeless body was thrown in the ditch. While none of this had actually taken place, once the accused Jews realized that they were themselves becoming the hapless victims of a Christian fantasy with no hope of avoiding death, they began to confess to additional details to escape from further tortures. The magistrates were particularly interested in how several men stretched the boy crosswise with a rope to imitate the crucifixion of Christ while a rabbi called Old Moses cut the child's penis in a perverse parody of circumcision. The final sentences against one of the Jews described him "as Bloodeater and drinker, and blasphemer of the holiest passion of Jesus Christ His Godly Majesty and the Most Praised Virgin Mary."[19] R. Po-Chia Hsia, the principal student of the Trent trial, has noted how common were allegations of blood drinking and cannibalism against Jews and witches, allegations that reveal how the Christian obsession with the Eucharist as the body of God nourished the idea that anti-Christian rituals, had they existed, would also require a supply of bodies, especially the bodies of Christian children.

The Trent trial echoed other stories of Jewish men crucifying Christian boys who then became martyrs to the faith. It is clear that the blood libel of ritual murder was a Christian fiction, but it is a fiction that like many paranoid inventions about evil conspiracies may have derived in part from a misunderstanding of real practices. Noting how the myth of ritual murder posits that the blood of the sacrificed child was to be used for the unleavened bread of the Passover rite, the matza, Yisrael Yaakov Yuval has argued that the blood libel derived from Christian

---

[19] Quoted in R. Po-Chia Hsia, *Trent 1475: Stories of a Ritual Murder Trial* (New Haven: Yale University Press, 1992), 89.

misunderstandings of Jewish ritual.[20] Christians rather preposterously assumed the Jews accepted that the host was the body of God. In the fantasy world of the blood libel, Christians thought Jews were jealous of the power of Christian rituals that produced the blood of God and imitated or perverted or subverted those rituals by employing the blood of an innocent Christian male-child.

This misunderstanding was made possible by the common ritual repertoire of the two religious traditions. In early Christianity the host, which was presented as the redeeming body of Christ, derived from the Passover bread, which rabbinical Judaism interpreted as symbolizing the redemption from Egypt. In both religions the most important rituals employed unleavened bread, which carried an enormous symbolic burden. A famous passage in the Haggada, "This is the bread of affliction that our forefathers ate in the land of Egypt," contrasted with Christ's prayer over the bread at the last supper, "This is my body, given up for you."

Three Passover rituals involve handling unleavened bread in a way that Yuval thinks Christians could have easily misinterpreted. The first was the burning of the hametz bread on the eve of Passover. To the Hebrews the burning of the hametz symbolized the removal of impediments to redemption, but for Christians the burning, which coincided with the timing of the crucifixion of Jesus, was a form of host desecration, a way of showing contempt for the Christian God. In 1399 an inquisition trial over the burning of the hametz resulted in the execution of eighty Jews. The second example was the tradition for the proper treatment of the 'eruv matza. In Germany the 'eruv matza was commonly affixed to a wall in the synagogue, where it was kept on display so that its redemptive significance would not be forgotten by the faithful, but in Christian eyes, this was another form of host desecration, the nailing of the Eucharistic body of Christ to the wall of the synagogue, just as they thought Jews had nailed his historical body to the cross. In several incidents in Germany in the early sixteenth century when accusations of host desecration were made, authorities found confirming evidence when they went to the synagogue only to find what they took to be a host nailed to the wall. The third example comes from the eating of the *afikoman*. At the beginning of the Seder, the head of the household who presides over the rite picked up three matzot and broke the middle one into two pieces. He then wrapped the broken matza in a cloth, which concealed the broken pieces until the end of the meal when after opening a door for Elijah the *afikoman* was eaten as a dessert, serving as

[20] 'Christian Perceptions of Jews: Hametz, Matza, and the Host," a lecture delivered at Northwestern University, 1994. Cited here with permission of the author.

a symbolic reminder of the redemption of Exodus. Christians imagined that the three matzot denoted the Christian concept of the Trinity, with the middle matza standing for Jesus. Thus, the breaking of the *afikoman* re-enacted the murder of Christ.

Christian and Jewish rituals certainly cross-pollinated each other, and it is even possible that the *afikoman* ceremony, which spread among Jews during the Middle Ages, borrowed some elements from the Christian handling of the host. The disastrous Christian misunderstandings of Jews derived, to a considerable degree, from the similarities between the two ritual systems, especially the ceremonial eating of unleavened bread. Christian hermeneutics caused the problem, even before the Reformation, and once the central issue in Christian disputes became the meaning of the host, then the Jewish matza was vulnerable to further misinterpretation by Christians sensitized to seeing enormous significance in minute ritual distinctions.

Christian hostility toward what was deemed to be magical rituals intensified during the later Middle Ages and the Reformation era. The hostility, in many respects, derived from attempts to differentiate magical practices from properly religious rituals, no easy task since the distinction was seldom apparent simply from observing the forms of the rite. At the most general level, people loosely used the term "magic" simply to describe the practices of those they feared or found alien and threatening: "What I do is miracle; what you do is magic."[21] During the controversies of the period, the word "magic" was often applied as a term of opprobrium, a marker of contempt, to Jews, Moslems, pagans, heretics, the theologically ignorant, and Christians who celebrated a different form of the liturgy. At the same time, however, magic was more than a term of polemical rhetoric because both learned clerics and simple lay persons accepted the reality of magical rites as rational operations that had great potential for harm. The problem with magic was not just that it represented false practices or delusions but that it identified powerfully dangerous ones. The problem with magic was not that it failed to work but that it worked all too well.

Before the seventeenth century, nearly everyone accepted the reality of magic as a form of collaboration with the demonic enemy. Specifically, most understood magic as a means of invoking the power of demons or the working of harm by ritual means. The fear of harmful magic stimulated the great witch-hunt of early modern Europe.

---

[21] Jacob Neusner, "Science and Magic, Miracle and Magic in Formative Judaism: The System and the Difference," in Jacob Neusner, Ernest S. Frerichs, and Paul V. McCracken Flesher, eds., *Religion, Science, and Magic: In Concert and in Conflict* (Oxford: Oxford University Press, 1989), 63.

Although belief in the reality of harmful magic and of witches had been widespread for centuries and there had been occasional witch trials throughout the Middle Ages, systematic witch-hunts only began when ecclesiastical and secular authorities showed a willingness to employ the law to discover and punish alleged witches. The climate of Reformation controversies certainly exacerbated what was a growing trend. During that period thousands of persons, most of them women and especially old women, were accused of and tried for practicing witchcraft. Brian Levack estimates that about half of these alleged witches were executed, most often by burning, and notes that the persecutions were extremely uneven both in space and time. Rather than a steady flow of cases, as one would find for other crimes, witchcraft trials characteristically took place during localized crazes when there was an upsurge of paranoia that multiplied allegations against vulnerable members of the community.

People in many different social situations from shepherds in the mountains of Switzerland to the Calvinist ministers in lowlands of Scotland thought they perceived the workings of witches. The idea of witchcraft tended to refer to two kinds of ritual practices. The first kind were called in Latin, *maleficia*, or doing harm. These rituals might involve a simple sign or a complex incantation, but what bound them together as *maleficia* was the belief that the person who performed such acts intended to harm someone or something by drawing upon some supernatural and mysterious power. The range of possible *maleficia* was broad. They included binding an unwilling lover by sprinkling dried menstrual blood in his food, bringing disease to a pig by cursing it, burning a barn by marking it with a hex sign, bringing wasting diarrhea to a child by reciting a spell, and killing an enemy by stabbing a wax statue of him. Although some of these ritual acts might employ religious objects (such as stolen pieces of the host) or religious gestures (such as the sign of the cross) thereby simulating the sacramentals if not the sacraments, what distinguished witchcraft from priestcraft was less the form of the ritual act than the intention behind it. *Maleficia* were deeds designed to be harmful rather than beneficial. Intentions, however, are often obscure, making it difficult to distinguish between white magic designed to bring beneficial results, such as the cure of a child or the recovery of a lost object, and black magic designed to bring malevolent ones.

Most forms of *maleficium* derived from what Guido Ruggiero calls the "poetics of the everyday," those innumerable rites – whether simple or complex – devoted to solving the practical problems of everyday life, problems of health, love, reproduction. Women who specialized in healing, for example, were especially vulnerable to accusations of witchcraft. Healing women might employ gestures derived from the priest's rites, as did a woman called La Draga in late sixteenth-century Friuli, who attempted to cure babies by making the sign of the cross, anointing them with oil, and repeating several Our Fathers and Hail Marys, actions she combined with elaborate concoctions that included wormwood and garlic. With the high infant mortality rates of the sixteenth century, however, signing a sick baby could be very risky. If the baby recovered, a woman like La Draga would be considered a powerful healer; if it died, she might be denounced as a dangerous witch who had caused the death, even if she considered herself someone whose magic counteracted the evil ways of witches. Ritual power worked for good or ill, and the intention of an action could usually only be discovered by the result. The logic of witchcraft beliefs implied that a bad ending must have been caused by bad intentions.

In the give and take of everyday social tensions, however, the widespread acceptance of the reality of witchcraft also meant that it could be used as a form of intimidation, in which a declaration of intent defined a rite as magical rather than anything intrinsic to the action itself. When a young man in the south of Italy tried to break off his courtship with Maria Mosella, the girl's mother threatened him, declaring: "If you don't come to my house any more, I'll make you come by wicked means, and that 'by means of this cross of Christ, if I do like so, you won't live two hours.' "[22] What distinguished the mother's signing of the cross on this occasion from the pious use of the gesture on other ones was simply her declared purpose of harming the reluctant lover. As this example suggests, there were certainly some people who did intend to do harm through ritual means.

While the practice of *maleficium* was certainly sometimes real, the second kind of ritual practice associated with witchcraft, *diabolism* or *sorcery*, was exceedingly rare if it existed at all. The diabolism theory of witchcraft asserted that the witch had declared allegiance to the devil, and besides practicing harmful magic she worshipped Lucifer as her god in a kind of devilish liturgy that inverted the values and practices of Christianity. The essential characteristics of diabolism involved four types of imagined activity: a pact with the devil, celebrating the witches' sabbath, practicing nocturnal flight, and sometimes the metamorphosis of a witch into an animal. Two of these crucial elements presumed the celebration of demonic rites, the pact with the devil and the witches' sabbath.

The devil's pact gave the witch the ability to accomplish *maleficia* in

---

[22] Quoted in Gentilcore, *From Bishop to Witch*, 221.

Figure 7   Witch kisses the devil's ass, from Francesco Maria Guazzo, *Compendium Maleficarum*.

exchange for which she became obliged to serve and worship Lucifer. The most influential witchcraft treatise, the *Malleus Maleficarum* or *Hammer of Witches*, had an extensive discussion of the ceremony of the pact. After the prospective witch had declared her intention to enter his service, Satan appeared to her, often in the alluring form of a handsome young man who offered her a demonic lover, called an *incubus*, and other rewards, although Satan was always cheap with his gifts. To obtain these inducements she had to renounce her allegiance to Christ, usually signified by stomping on the cross. In some versions of the pact, the devil rebaptized her, guaranteeing that her soul belonged to him. She then had to pay homage to him in an act that revealed the perverted character of the new bond: she bowed down to him backwards in the "bridge" position by raising her belly upward while she supported her arched body with her arms and legs, offering her uncovered genitals to him; other versions had her kiss his ass (see figure 7). To signify that she was one of his own, the devil marked her body in a hidden place, what was called the "witch's tit," the sign of her allegiance that inquisitors and judges searched for on accused witches. Before he let her go, she received explicit instructions about the evil deeds she was to perform, and the devil gave his new witch whatever potions or amulets she might need.

In this type of pact, the witch, who was nearly always a woman, came under the devil's spell. He now used her to serve his purposes. There was, however, an alternative kind of pact called necromancy, usually performed by learned men who, under the guidance of books of conjuration translated from Arabic and Greek treatises on magic, summoned demons in order to obtain esoteric knowledge. These sorcerers usually followed some written formula to trap the demon or genie, possibly in a bottle, and force him to follow the magician's commands. Although there was some taint of a demonic pact to the practice, the sorcerer, unlike the witch, had powers over the devil who worked the magician's will rather than vice versa. The magician's spells required the devil's cooperation to work, but the relationship was more akin to a business bargain than a perverted subjugation, and none of the theological commentators imagined male magicians indulging in orgies in a way that was *de rigueur* for female witches. As a consequence of the Renaissance rediscovery of certain ancient alchemical texts, the practice of necromancy and conjuration to achieve benevolent ends became quite fashionable among intellectuals between the late fifteenth and early seventeenth centuries. The great artist, Benvenuto Cellini, tells in his *Autobiography* about a midnight excursion to the Colosseum in Rome where he and some companions attempted to conjure demons with the aid of a necromancer's book of formulas. Although necromancy was always theologically suspect since it implied a rapport with the devil, it seldom led to serious allegations requiring legal investigation and punishment. The more respectable branches of alchemy and astrology were practiced in the courts of kings and popes, and even the more suspect forms of conjuration found a place within the walls of the Vatican itself.

The second presumed demonic rite of witchcraft was the sabbath, which when combined with belief in the devil's pact created the intellectual and legal conditions for the great witch-hunt of the sixteenth and seventeenth centuries. Calling the witches' collective worship of Satan a "sabbath" after the Jewish and Christian uses of the word to designate their weekly holy day indicates that the fully developed rite derived more from the imaginations of Christians than from some vestige of pagan practice, but there were certain practices associated with the sabbath that are less obviously depraved inversions of contemporary social values than simply strange. The ancillary stories of nocturnal flight

Figure 8   Witches sacrifice babies, from Francesco Maria Guazzo, *Compendium Maleficarum.*

and metamorphoses into animals may be evidence, as Carlo Ginzburg had argued, not so much of the imaginative resources of inquisitors and witch-hunters as of a hidden shamanistic culture that had survived in Europe since pre-Christian times.

The deviant values of the witches' sabbath certainly had psychological as well as historical origins. The usual sufferings of human beings produced nightmares and delusions that seemed to find an explanation in the demonic conspiracy of witches. As Brian Levack has pointed out, human psychology contributed two elements found in the sabbath: the practice of cannibalistic infanticide, perhaps the most depraved iniquity that was conceivable (see figure 8), and naked dancing, an engrossingly scandalous practice, not just because of the shamefulness of nudity but also because it obliterated all social distinctions represented by distinctive clothing. In addition to these two fantasies, the hostile attitude of the Christian church toward sex stimulated a belief that the sabbath must involve ritualized copulation and perverse sex acts. In Catholic lands it was also assumed that the sabbath must parody the mass by repeating the Nicene Creed backwards and consecrating a disgusting host made of garbage, manure, or rotten vegetables.

The sabbath appeared in many variations, tailored to local beliefs and expectations. One of the fullest accounts comes from the tragic trial of the Pappenheimer family in Bavaria in 1600. In her confession under torture, the mother, Anna Pappenheimer, gave a full account of her participation in a witches' sabbath that supposedly took place at night on a hill south-west of the village of Tettenwang.[23] Witches arrived from near and far flying in on broomsticks and pitchforks. The assembled company largely consisted of women, young and old and most of them naked, but there were a few male warlocks and even some children. Devils arranged the witches in two circles around a fire, each placed in a hierarchy according to her rank as a witch. With a clap of thunder and a profusion of smoke, Satan himself suddenly appeared with his eyes glowing, dressed in black and in a regal purple robe and so disgusting in his demeanor that he often farted loudly emitting a horrible stench. The assembled witches and warlocks bowed low before him, praying in a travesty of the Lord's Prayer, "Our Satan which art in Hell . . ." Still on their knees, a number of witches approached their master with sacrificial offerings of the corpses of unbaptized infants. Then demons brought forward the newly recruited witches who made a pact with the devil.

There followed an infernal banquet of disgusting foods, including horse meat, ravens, crows, toads, frogs, and "boiled and roasted infants, without hands and feet, like sucking-pigs." The feast lacked any salt, since the devil hates all good things, and any witch who hid salt to use at the feast was severely beaten. The peculiar logic of thinking up the sabbath rituals led to imagining how the liturgical implements of the church might be perverted by the devil. Anna Pappenheimer recounted that during the banquet she had been forced to bend over with her buttocks raised to become a naked human candleholder. "They thought very little of me . . . I was always having to hold a candle, for they stood me on my head and – begging your pardon – stuck a candle in my backside." After the feast an orchestra of demons played tuneless, screeching, dance music that aroused a mad lust in the witches and their demon lovers who began a wild spinning dance that finally broke down into an indiscriminate orgy. The witches engaged in every conceivable sex act with any demon or warlock who grabbed them, committing "sodomy as well as ordinary fornication, between the breasts, under the

[23] The account that follows and the quotes come from Michael Kunze, *Highroad to the Stake: A Tale of Witchcraft*, trans. William E. Yuill (Chicago: University of Chicago Press, 1987), 274–80.

armpits, from the back, and from the front." Finally, after general exhaustion the orgy subsided, and Satan demanded a final homage in the somber culmination of the demonic rite. Transforming himself into a black billy goat, Satan rose from his black throne to receive his worshipers. Crawling of all fours, "like dogs," the witches approached their master, then twisted into the "bridge" position, their "private parts turned toward the heavens," and kissed the goat's genitals from behind. Satan selected a favored few for his private pleasure.

Before flying off each witch had to give an account of the evil she had committed since the last sabbath, and if she had failed or been laggard in her duties she was beaten on the soles of her feet or severely whipped. The witches were then given new assignments to cause harm, which in the Pappenheimers' case was limited by the impoverishment of their own imaginations. All they could envision was killing cattle, ruining a harvest, or making a pastor sick. In cases from more elevated social levels, the imagined havoc could be far more spectacular. In the famous case in Bergen in 1590 against Anna Pedersdotter Absalon, the wife of a Lutheran minister who was Norway's most noted humanist scholar, a servant testified that Anna had turned her into a horse to ride to the sabbaths where on one occasion the witches were ordered to wreck all the ships that came into the Bergen harbor and at others they planned to burn the town and cause a flood.

By the middle of the seventeenth century the very excessiveness of these reputed demonic ceremonies led the legal authorities across Europe to decriminalize what seemed to them acts that were certainly unprovable and probably imaginary. The blood libel against Jews and the great witch-hunt against women arose from the dark side of the Christian imagination, a dark side that had a long history but that intensified during the sixteenth century. Although there were many causes both social and political for this horrible amplification of persecutions, the Protestant and Catholic controversies about the meaning of divine rituals certainly played a role by stimulating horrible fantasies about presumed demonic rituals.

BIBLIOGRAPHY

Entries marked with a * designate recommended readings for new students of the subject.

Accati, Luisa. "The Spirit of Fornication: Virtue of the Soul and Virtue of the Body in Friuli, 1600–1800." In *Sex and Gender in Historical Perspective*. Edited by Edward Muir and Guido Ruggiero, translated by Margaret A. Gallucci with Mary M. Gallucci and Carole C. Gallucci. Baltimore: Johns

Hopkins University Press, 1990. Pp. 110–40. A marvelous account of official attempts to eliminate assumed diabolic elements in Carnival revelry.

Ankarloo, Bengt and Henningsen, Gustav, eds. *Early Modern European Witchcraft: Centres and Peripheries.* Oxford: Clarendon Press, 1990. An important and influential collection of specialized studies of witchcraft.

Aston, Margaret. *England's Iconoclasts.* Oxford: Clarendon Press, 1988. Strong on legal aspects of iconoclasm.

  Faith and Fire: Popular and Unpopular Religion, 1350–1600. London: Hambledon Press, 1993.

*Bossy, John. "The Counter-Reformation and the People of Catholic Europe." *Past and Present* 47 (1970): 51–70. The fundamental article in establishing that the great success of the Counter Reformation was to make the parish the center of collective worship.

  *"Holiness and Society." *Past and Present* 75 (1977): 119–37.

  *"The Social History of Confession in the Age of Reformation." *Transactions of the Royal Historical Society.* 5th series, 25 (1975): 21–38.

Bushkovitch, Paul. *Religion and Society in Russia: The Sixteenth and Seventeenth Centuries.* New York: Oxford University Press, 1992. The best study of religion in Orthodox Russia.

*Carroll, Michael P. *Madonnas That Maim: Popular Catholicism in Italy Since the Fifteenth Century.* Baltimore: Johns Hopkins University Press, 1992. An analysis by a sociologist of the doubleness of sacred power that can either heal or harm.

Christian, William, Jr. *Local Religion in Sixteenth-Century Spain.* Princeton: Princeton University Press, 1981. An elegant analysis of village cults, especially sensitive to the ways in which clerical and lay sensibilities coincided rather than contrasted.

Cohn, Norman. *Europe's Inner Demons: An Enquiry Inspired by the Great Witch-Hunt.* New York: Basic Books, 1975. Connects the witch-hunt of the sixteenth and seventeenth centuries with a long tradition of persecution going back to the early Christians, medieval heretics, and the Knights Templar.

Couliano, Ioan P. *Eros and Magic in the Renaissance.* Translated by Margaret Cook. Chicago: University of Chicago Press, 1987. Arguing that magical practices were precursors for modern psychology and sociology, Couliano sees the key to the power of magic as being its appeal to sexual desire and the manipulation of memory.

Crew, Phyllis Mack. *Calvinist Preaching and Iconoclasm in the Netherlands 1544–1569.* Cambridge: Cambridge University Press, 1978. An examination of the relationship between theology and iconoclasm.

Crouzet, Denis. *Les guerriers de Dieu: la violence au temps de troubles de religion vers 1525– vers 1610.* 2 vols. Seyssel: Champ Vallon, 1990. The most comprehensive study of the French Wars of Religion, emphasizing especially the ritualized nature of interconfessional violence.

*Davis, Natalie Zemon. "The Sacred and the Body Social in Sixteenth-Century Lyon." *Past and Present* 90 (1981): 40–70. A very influential re-evaluation of the role of ritual by both Protestants and Catholics in the urban life of a city that had significant representations of both faiths.

*Delumeau, Jean. *Catholicism between Luther and Voltaire: A New View of the Counter-Reformation.* London: Burns & Oates, 1977. A highly influential and provocative interpretation of Catholic Europe which emphasizes the cultural and religious dichotomies between the ecclesiastical hierarchy and the laity. It argues that from the sixteenth to eighteenth centuries both Protestant and Catholic reformers were attempting to Christianize a population that was in many ways still pagan in its sensibilities and ritual practices.

Diefendorf, Barbara B. *Beneath the Cross: Catholics and Huguenots in Sixteenth-Century Paris.* New York: Oxford University Press, 1991. Building upon the insights of Natalie Zemon Davis and others, this book is the most thorough study in English of the relationship between Catholic and Protestant in a highly contested situation. It is replete with examples of ritual demonstrations on both sides.

Eire, Carlos M. N. *War Against the Idols: The Reformation of Worship from Erasmus to Calvin.* Cambridge: Cambridge University Press, 1986. An examination of the views of the leading reformers on icons.

Flynn, Maureen. "Mimesis of the Last Judgment: The Spanish *Auto de fe.*" *Sixteenth Century Journal* 22 (1991): 281–97. A brilliantly evocative article that employs semiotic analysis to understand the meaning of the rituals of the *autos.* Flynn argues that the experience of witnessing an *auto* filled spectators with dread about their own final day of judgment.

——— "The Spectacle of Suffering in Spanish Streets." In *City and Spectacle in Medieval Europe.* Edited by Barbara A. Hanawalt and Kathryn L. Reyerson. Minneapolis: University of Minnesota Press, 1994. Pp. 153–68. An account of Holy Week re-enactments of Christ's suffering and an examination of the belief in the spiritual value of physical pain.

Forster, Marc R. *The Counter-Reformation in the Villages: Religion and Reform in the Bishopric of Speyer, 1560–1720.* Ithaca: Cornell University Press, 1992. A fine nuanced study of the implementation of the decrees of the Council of Trent in Germany.

Freedberg, David. *The Power of Images: Studies in the History and Theory of Response.* Chicago: University of Chicago Press, 1989. A useful beginning point for the study of the social power of images.

*Gentilcore, David. *From Bishop to Witch: The System of the Sacred in Early Modern Terra d'Otranto.* Manchester: Manchester University Press, 1992. Perhaps the best study of the post-Reformation era in a backwater of the Catholic world. It is especially adept in showing how a common "system of the sacred" cut across clerical/lay and literate/illiterate cleavages, a system that provided the people of southern Italy with a variety of ritual means for gaining access to sacred powers and that broke down the distinction between magic and ritual.

Ginzburg, Carlo. *Ecstasies: Deciphering the Witches' Sabbath.* Translated by Raymond Rosenthal. New York: Penguin, 1991. Argues that the stories of nocturnal flight and animal metamorphoses associated with the witches' sabbath are evidence of the survival from pre-Christian times of Eurasian shamanistic practices.

*——— *The Night Battles: Witchcraft and Agrarian Cults in the Sixteenth and Seventeenth Centuries.* Translated by John and Anne Tedeschi. Baltimore: Johns

Hopkins University Press, 1983. An account of agrarian cult in Friuli, called the *benandanti*, who practiced white magic, which was interpreted as witchcraft by the Inquisition.

Hoffman, Philip T. *Church and Community in the Diocese of Lyon, 1500–1789*. New Haven: Yale University Press, 1984. A study of the interrelations between the ecclesiastical hierarchy and the laity in a Catholic community with a substantial Huguenot population.

*Hsia, R. Po-chia. *The Myth of Ritual Murder: Jews and Magic in Reformation Germany*. New Haven: Yale University Press, 1988. The most important recent study of the blood libel mythology.

Social Discipline in the Reformation: Central Europe 1550–1750. London and New York: Routledge, 1989. Argues that both the Protestant and Catholic Reformations were part of a common movement to enforce social discipline on the laity.

Trent 1475: Stories of a Ritual Murder Trial. New Haven: Yale University Press, 1992. An account and analysis of the famous trial of the Jews of Trent for the ritual murder of the Blessed Simon.

*Kieckhefer, Richard. *Magic in the Middle Ages*. Cambridge: Cambridge University Press, 1989. The best general survey of the problem and practice of magic during the medieval period.

"The Specific Rationality of Medieval Magic." *American Historical Review* 99 (1994): 813–36. In this piece Kieckhefer argues that there was near universal acceptance during the Middle Ages of the reality and rationality of magical practices, which gained their power from the invocation of demons.

*Klaits, Joseph. *Servants of Satan: The Age of the Witch Hunts*. Bloomington: Indiana University Press, 1985. A useful survey.

Klaniczay, Gabor. *The Uses of the Supernatural Power: The Transformation of Popular Religion in Medieval and Early Modern Europe*. Edited by Karen Margolis, translated by Susan Singerman. Cambridge: Polity Press in association with Basil Blackwell, 1990. A collection of studies about various aspects of ritual practices, especially interesting in connecting the decline of witchcraft accusations with the rise of cases involving were-wolves.

*Kunze, Michael. *Highroad to the Stake: A Tale of Witchcraft*. Translated by William E. Yuill. Chicago: University of Chicago Press, 1987. The disturbing account of the trial and execution of the Pappenheimer family in Bavaria in 1600 for witchcraft.

*Levack, Brian P. *The Witch-Hunt in Early Modern Europe*. 2nd. ed. London: Longman, 1995. The best general account of the much studied and discussed subject.

Levi, Giovanni. *Inheriting Power: The Story of an Exorcist*. Translated by Lydia G. Cochrane. Chicago: University of Chicago Press, 1988. An examination of the ways in which a priest-exorcist enhanced his social influence.

Lindberg, David D. *Theories of Vision from Al-Kindi to Kepler*. Chicago: University of Chicago Press, 1976. Useful for understanding the extro-mission theory of sight.

MacKay, Angus. "Popular Movements and Pogroms in Fifteenth-Century Castile." *Past and Present* 55 (1972): 33–67. An examination of the connection between popular religious enthusiasms and the increase of pogroms on the eve of the expulsion of the Jews from Spain in 1492.

Martin, John. *Venice's Hidden Enemies: Italian Heretics in a Renaissance City*. Berkeley and Los Angeles: University of California Press, 1993. One of the very best studies of Protestants in Italy.

Michalski, Sergiusz. *The Reformation and the Visual Arts: The Protestant Image Question in Western and Eastern Europe*. London: Routledge, 1993. Broad in scope and vision, Michalski connects the Protestant debate about religious images to the iconoclasm of Eastern Orthodoxy.

Monter, William, ed. *European Witchcraft*. New York: John Wiley & Sons, 1969. A useful collection of documents and studies.

Ritual, Myth and Magic in Early Modern Europe. Brighton: The Harvester Press, 1983. Despite its somewhat misleading title, this fine book is a useful study of the origins of toleration.

Nalle, Sara T. *God in La Mancha: Religious Reform and the People of Cuenca, 1500–1650*. Baltimore: Johns Hopkins University Press, 1992.

O'Neil, Mary. "Sacerdote ovvero Strione: Ecclesiastical and Superstitious Remedies in Sixteenth-Century Italy." In *Understanding Popular Culture*. Edited by Steven Kaplan. New York: Mouton, 1989. A good example of the ways in which clerical and popular curing existed in the same ritual system.

*Ranum, Orest. "The French Ritual of Tyrannicide in the Late Sixteenth Century." *Sixteenth Century Journal* 11 (1980): 63–81. Examines the ritualized character of assassination during the Wars of Religion.

Roper, Lyndal. *Oedipus and the Devil: Witchcraft, Sexuality and Religion in Early Modern Europe*. London and New York: Routledge, 1994. Provides the theoretical framework for understanding how the sexual differences between the bodies of men and women played a role in the psychic framework of magic and witchcraft.

Rose, Elliot. *A Razor for a Goat: A Discussion of Certain Problems in the History of Witchcraft and Diabolism*. Toronto: University of Toronto Press, 1989.

Ruggiero, Guido. *Binding Passions: Tales of Magic, Marriage, and Power at the End of the Renaissance*. New York: Oxford University Press, 1993. A fascinating examination of the ways in which binding magic permeated what Ruggiero calls the "poetics of the everyday."

Sabean, David W. *Power in the Blood: Popular Culture and Village Discourse in Early Modern Germany*. Cambridge: Cambridge University Press, 1984. An important study of the ritual aspects of popular life after the Reformation.

Schneider, Robert A. "Mortification on Parade: Penitential Processions in Sixteenth- and Seventeenth-Century France." *Renaissance and Reformation* 10 (1986): 123–45.

*Scribner, R. W. *Popular Culture and Popular Movements in Reformation Germany*. London: Hambledon Press, 1987. See especially chapter 5 on "Ritual and Reformation" for an analysis of the Protestant use of ritual behavior to enact and represent reform.

"The Reformation as a Social Movement." In *The Urban Classes, the Nobility and the Reformation: Studies on the Social History of the Reformation in England and Germany*. Edited by Wolfgang J. Mommsen with Peter Alter and Robert W. Scribner. Stuttgart: Klett-Cotta, 1979. Pp. 49–79.

*"The Reformation Movements in Germany." In *The New Cambridge Modern History*, vol. 2, 2nd ed., *The Reformation 1520–1559*. Edited by G. R. Elton. Cambridge: Cambridge University Press, 1990. The best short introduction to the subject reflecting current research.

*"Ritual and Popular Religion in Catholic Germany in the Time of the Reformation." *Journal of Ecclesiastical History* 1 (1984): 47–77.

Steinberg, Leo. *The Sexuality of Christ in Renaissance Art and in Modern Oblivion*. London: Faber and Faber, 1984. An intriguing examination of the implications of Christ's carnality for artistic representations.

Summers, David. *The Judgment of Sense: Renaissance Naturalism and the Rise of Aesthetics*. Cambridge: Cambridge University Press, 1987.

*Thomas, Keith. *Religion and the Decline of Magic*. New York: Charles Scribner's Sons, 1971. The magisterial study of the ubiquity of magical practices in early modern England.

Torre, Angelo. "Politics Cloaked in Worship: State, Church and Local Power in Piedmont 1570–1770." *Past and Present* 134 (1992): 42–92. This is a superb, detailed study of the implementation of the Tridentine decrees in three dioceses in the southern Piedmont, a study which demonstrates how the performance of religious rites constituted the social hierarchy and how bishops had to accommodate the social interests of the community to reform ritual practices and make parishes the principal locus of worship. The full argument can be found in his *Il consumo di devozioni: religione e comunità nelle campagne dell'Ancien Régime*. Venice: Marsilio, 1995.

Trevor-Roper, H. R. *The European Witch-Craze of the Sixteenth and Seventeenth Centuries and Other Essays*. New York and Evanston: Harper & Row, 1969. Although outdated in many respects, the witch-craze essay still serves as a useful introduction to the subject.

Walker, D. P. *The Decline of Hell*. Chicago: University of Chicago Press, 1964. Discusses the waning of rituals of purification.

Wandel, Lee Palmer. *Always Among Us: Images of the Poor in Zwingli's Zurich*. Cambridge: Cambridge University Press, 1990.

"The Reform of the Images: New Visualizations of the Christian Community at Zürich." *Archiv für Reformationsgeschichte* 80 (1989): 105–24.

Voracious Idols and Violent Hands: Iconoclasm in Reformation Zurich, Strasbourg, and Basel. Cambridge: Cambridge University Press, 1995. An especially useful and original study of the sociology of iconoclasm.

Weber, Max. *The Protestant Ethic and the Spirit of Capitalism*. Translated by Talcott Parsons. London: Unwin, 1985. The classic theoretical statement on the materialist and pyschological implications of Protestant theology.

7   Government as a ritual process

In the mid-sixteenth century a group of English merchants witnessed the Palm Sunday ceremonies at the Kremlin during the reign of Ivan the Terrible. They saw a grand procession that featured a float of a huge fruit tree bearing five singing boys dressed in white robes. The leading cleric of Russia, the metropolitan of Moscow, rode a horse disguised as a donkey and carried a gold-covered Gospel. Then came Ivan:

One of the Emperours noble men leadeth the horse by the head, but the Emperour himselfe goyng on foote, leadeth the horse by the ends of the reine of his bridle with one of his hands, and in the other of his handes he had a braunch of a Palme tree: after this followed the rest of the Emperours Noble men and Gentlemen, with a great number of other people.[1]

Although these Englishmen were well-traveled men of the world, they were deeply impressed by the splendor of Ivan's procession, which exemplified the majesty of his reign and which seemed quintessentially Russian to them. Little did they know that what appeared to be a venerable Russian tradition was rather new and had foreign origins. The Palm Sunday procession had been imported from the West to Moscow earlier in the century. Although the procession simply re-enacted an episode from the Bible, the story of Christ-the-king's entrance into Jerusalem provided a useful model for demonstrating the divine sanction of royal authority. Despite the tsar's apparently humble position of walking after the seated metropolitan, Ivan turned the procession to his advantage, enhancing his own majesty through a display of public piety that contrasted with his famous penchant for personal cruelty. In all parts of Europe – Catholic, Protestant, and Orthodox – liturgical rites

---

[1] Richard Hakluyt, *The Principall Navigations Voiages and Discoveries of the English Nation* [1589] (reprint ed., Cambridge: Cambridge University Press, 1965), 341f., quoted and discussed in Michael S. Flier, "The Iconography of Royal Procession: Ivan the Terrible and the Muscovite Palm Sunday Ritual," in Heinz Duchhardt, Richard A. Jackson, and David Sturdy, eds., *European Monarchy: Its Evolution and Practice from Roman Antiquity to Modern Times* (Stuttgart: Franz Steiner, 1992), 109–10.

provided a vast repository of representational images that city officials and princes adapted to the needs of government.

Political ritual or ritualized politics tends to camouflage tensions, especially by representing more political *harmony* than may actually exist. The principle of harmony is necessary for any state, which by definition transforms differences into singularity: Protestants and Catholics, Lyonnais and Parisians, nobles and peasants, all became one as the subjects of the King of France. Observing the harmony expressed in state rituals, many scholars of European ceremonies have been influenced by the analysis of the Balinese "theater state" by the anthropologist Clifford Geertz. As he summarized, "the dramas of the theatre state, mimetic of themselves, were, in the end, neither illusions nor lies, neither sleight of hand nor make-believe. They were what there was."[2] Geertz's concept of the theater state derives from his insight that these rites do not imitate social reality as much as they imitate themselves in the recurrent repetitions of rituals. Through their repeated enactment they create the idea of the state as something that transcends the particular individuals who inhabit and govern it. The repetition of gestures and formulaic statements is, of course, one of the attributes that distinguishes ritual from more spontaneous behavior. From this point of view the repetitions of rituals actually formulated a kind of constitution of the state. As Geertz remarked in another context, ceremonies served both as a "model of" society, that is a representation of existing arrangements, and a "model for" society, a kind of instruction booklet for how the state ought to be put together, creating a ceremonial constitution. Rituals set apart the rulers of the state from others and defined the relationships among its constituent subjects or citizens. Such rites "constitute" in the sense that their performance created a ritual structure for the state in an era before written constitutions: "The state is invisible; it must be personified before it can be seen, symbolized before it can be loved, imagined before it can be conceived."[3]

Despite the representations of harmony in political rituals, they always take place within a social context of *disharmony*. States exist precisely because people do not seem to be able to get along among themselves without them. All states are formed around the hegemonic power of some group or person who attempts to manage conflict through force and the law. As Georges Balandier argues, "the supreme ruse of power is to allow itself to be contested *ritually* in order to consolidate itself

---

[2] Clifford Geertz, *Negara: The Theatre State in Nineteenth-Century Bali* (Princeton: Princeton University Press), 136.

[3] Michael Walzer, "On the Role of Symbolism in Political Thought," *Political Science Quarterly* 82 (1967): 194.

more effectively."[4] From this point of view state rituals achieve exactly the opposite from what Geertz claimed: they perform a sleight-of-hand trick that makes coercion less evident, submission more palatable, and the banality of power more glorious. States require rites in order to mask or legitimate hegemony, thereby creating the necessary fictions of government.

Whether political rituals function to exemplify harmony or mask disharmonies, the core question is how do they constitute political ideas? David Kertzer suggests that the essential characteristic of political rituals is that they promote *schematic thinking*. Ritual performances produce schemata or abstract formulas that organize the perceptions of the persons who have repeatedly witnessed them. Because they lack qualifications and discourage critical thinking, the images of political rituals are ambiguous in their meaning but direct in their emotional appeal. They present simple absolute truths. They encourage a single course of action. And they achieve these things by framing some images more prominently than others, focusing attention on certain objects, and enhancing some characteristics of a person and suppressing others. Rituals stimulate the senses in multiple ways through musical performances, artistic splendor, and sumptuous pomp. The brilliance of the ritual display will not only garner more attention but will be better remembered. Beauty, like pain, aids memory. Kertzer points out that it is the combination of instruction in simplified ideas and an appeal to the emotions that gives rituals their power to influence. But "our symbol system . . . is not a cage which locks us into a single view of the political world, but a melange of symbolic understandings by which we struggle, through a continuous series of negotiations, to assign meaning to events."[5] Political rituals become part of the struggle of governing and of living under a government.

During the Middle Ages among the kingdoms and city-states of Christian Europe a symbolic system developed that created a vocabulary for the rites of state. These rites were mostly borrowed and elaborated from other ritual vocabularies, such as the biological and social rites of passage; the liturgical calendar; the stylized combats of the joust and duel; the cultivated gestures of greeting, hospitality, and dining; and the forms of submission and humility found in the sacraments. The most important borrowing, however, derived from the mystic body of Jesus.

---

[4] Quoted in Peter Stallybrass and Allon White, *The Politics and Poetics of Transgression* (Ithaca: Cornell University Press, 1986), 14.

[5] David I. Kertzer, *Ritual, Politics, and Power* (New Haven: Yale University Press, 1988), 175.

Two passages in scripture suggested body metaphors for the relationship between Christ and the church.

For as in one body we have many members, and not all the members have the same function, so we, who are many, are one body in Christ, and individually we are members one of another. (Romans 12: 4–5)

Wives, be subject to your husbands as you are to the Lord. For the husband is the head of the wife just as Christ is the head of the church, the body of which he is the Savior. Just as the church is subject to Christ, so also wives ought to be, in everything, to their husbands. (Ephesians 5: 22–24)

These corporeal images were commonly interpreted in two ways: (1) the church was a single body composed of many members with Christ as the head, or (2) Christ married the church just as a husband marries a wife, making two bodies into one as happens in sexual union, but Christ-the-husband remained ever dominant over wife-the-church.

The idea of Christ as the head of the body-church or as the husband of the wife-church became a model for the relationship between a bishop and his flock, the pope and the church, and eventually through a series of ideological and ritual borrowings for the relationship between the king and his kingdom. In a separate but parallel evolution, cities also came to represent themselves as a body or corporation. Long before the state became the abstract legal entity it is today, it was a *body politic*. The chronic problem of political rituals in Christian countries was to establish and represent the relationships between these various kinds of political bodies and their parts. What began during the Middle Ages as an intimate pattern of borrowings, largely of secular governments from the church, evolved by the eighteenth century into distinctive ritual spheres with the ceremonies of the triumphant absolutist monarchs competing with the devotions of the church.

Civic rituals

Between the twelfth and eighteenth centuries all across western Europe the inhabitants of countless towns schooled themselves to a high level of civic consciousness that has been remarkably persistent, often competing with and outlasting loyalty to religion, king, political ideology, faction, and even family. The resilience of civic identities, that identification of individuals with their home town, has been one of the distinguishing characteristics of modern European civilization. A "citizen," which literally means a city-dweller, now implies a sensibility as well as a whole range of legal rights and obligations that are necessary for the success of modern states. How did this happen?

The search for an answer might begin by pondering a comment made by Geertz with regard to political charisma, "A world wholly demystified is a world wholly depoliticized."[6] Communities such as early modern cities, very few of which had more than a hundred-thousand inhabitants and most only a few thousand, can be understood to have existed on several levels. A city was a defined physical space, usually marked out by city walls, that in its aggregation of structures contrasted with the surrounding countryside devoted to farming. It was also a legal space, a place in which certain statutes applied, certain legal privileges pertained, certain jurisdictional rights were exercised. It was furthermore a social space, a location for persistent and frequent interactions – some friendly, others antagonistic; some egalitarian, others hierarchic; some voluntary, others coerced – interactions that created a sensibility toward who was a member of the community and who was an outsider. And it was perhaps most of all an idea, a place identified by a name and symbols that elicited a certain sensibility, which at its best was manifest as civic virtue or patriotism, at its worst as nativism or jingoism. The task for late medieval and early modern cities was to transubstantiate these disparate characteristics of a community into a mystic body, a mystified city – to paraphrase Geertz again – that made possible a politicized city.

The rites of the church assisted this process. Among the enormous range of ritual practices available to the citizens who created the identities of cities, two were especially useful: the cult of the saints and the civic procession. Each city had its own patron saint or sometimes several patron saints who, it was thought, especially favored this city above all others and who could be trusted to watch over it and to intercede with God on its behalf. One of the chief ritual tasks of citizens was to guarantee the good favor of the patron saint through propitiations and supplications. Although the tradition of patron saints existed all across Christian Europe, the cults of patron saints were most fully elaborated in Italy where the independent city-states faced the vital necessity of strengthening civic identities to diminish obstinate internal strife and to withstand external threats.

These Italian cults became the seedbeds for civic virtue and loyalty. In Milan citizens looked to St. Ambrose, the church father who had resided there and had written the liturgy celebrated in its churches. In Florence the patron was St. John the Baptist, a cult that revolved around the magnificent Romanesque baptistery where every Florentine child was baptized. In Venice protection was found in the Evangelist St. Mark

---

[6] Clifford Geertz, "Centers, Kings, and Charisma: Reflections on the Symbolics of Power," in Joseph Ben-David and Terry Nichols Clark, eds., *Culture and Its Creators: Essays in Honor of Edward Shils* (Chicago: University of Chicago Press, 1977), 168.

whose body had been brought to the city in the ninth century and was housed in the radiant mosaic-covered basilica, one of the artistic masterpieces of the world, which served as a kind of visual chronicle of the Venetians' long, loving association with their patron. As a fifteenth-century canon of the basilica put it, "I was born a Venetian and live in this happy homeland, protected by the prayers and guardianship of St. Mark, from whom that Most Serene Republic acknowledges its greatness, its victories, and all its good fortune."[7] Hans Conrad Peyer argued that the "state miracle" of these cults sanctioned the established political order of the Italian city-states, especially the republics which lacked a charismatic prince or figure-head.

Essential for gaining the special protection of a patron saint was to possess the body or part of the body of the saint. Some cities, such as Milan with St. Ambrose or Rome with St. Peter, could plausibly assert that the saint's bones had been there all along. In other places they had to be "discovered," as Charlemagne supposedly did when his horse stumbled over the burial site of the martyrs Felix and Regula who became the patrons of Zürich, or "translated" as happened when the remains of St. Nicholas were brought to Bari or St. Mark to Venice. Especially during the Crusades the theft of relics from the Holy Land and Near East stimulated a lucrative trade in old bones so highly prized by the growing cities of western Europe, which needed supernatural patrons to bolster their newly found but shaky and sometimes illegitimate worldly power. Even the most obscure town strove to obtain the head or finger or toe of some heavenly protector.

Once relics were in place, the saint had to be honored on a regular basis, usually with an annual procession in which the relics would be displayed and sometimes carried through the streets of the city by priests accompanied by town officials. In Siena icons of the Virgin were carried in processions on her feast days, but in 1308 the city government commissioned Duccio to paint a more elaborate panel, the famous *Maestà*, which would become the central altarpiece in the cathedral, making more flamboyant representations possible. Henceforth, instead of carrying an image of the Madonna through the city, a procession of all the citizens filed past the dazzling painting on her feast days, especially the Assumption. Legislation made participation in the processions compulsory for all citizens of Siena and its subject towns, and everyone except for criminals and other malefactors had to make offerings of candles. Beginning in 1310 the town also sponsored on the feast of the Assumption a horse race, the *palio*. In Siena devotion to the Madonna

---

[7] Quoted in Edward Muir, *Civic Ritual in Renaissance Venice* (Princeton: Princeton University Press, 1981), 91.

and participation in the rituals of her cult became the centerpiece of civic life, providing succor during times of war and plague. Even after Siena lost its independence in 1555 to the Grand Dukes of Tuscany, the cult of the Virgin persisted, and the *palio* survived, not so much as an expression of the unity of the city, which no longer mattered, as as a source of pride and identity for the constituent neighborhoods or *contrade*. To this day the *contrade* still run the *palio* twice a year and consider it the most vital part of their collective lives. Now each neighborhood sponsors processions through the streets in anticipation of the race, and the prize is a banner with an image of the Virgin painted on it.

In Venice, which survived as an independent city-republic until 1797, the annual processions of the doge served as a living representation of the supposedly unchanging constitution of the regime. A dozen times a year or more, the leading office holders participated in lengthy processions, which could last as long as five hours, through the streets of the city, always winding their way back to the great basilica of St. Mark where these hard-headed politicians humbled themselves before their protector saint (see figure 9). The symbols carried in the processions, including a sword, umbrella, candle, stool, and foot cushion, represented grants of authority reputedly given to the Venetian doge by Pope Alexander III in 1177. In Venetian political lore these gifts made the doge the equal of the pope and the emperor. The order of procession defined the legal relationship between the various political and bureaucratic offices within the Venetian hierarchy. Although these processions took place on feast days of the church, the basilica and its rituals were entirely controlled by the civil authorities. The grand basilica of St. Mark was, in fact, merely the private chapel of the doge, while the bishop's cathedral was located in an obscure corner of the city. If the bishop participated at all in these processions, it was as an invited guest.

The civic rituals of Venice represented the complete appropriation of liturgical forms and rites to sanctify the ruling regime, an appropriation best exemplified by the famous marriage of the sea ceremony. Each year on Ascension Day at the beginning of the sailing season (good sailing weather was to Venetian prosperity what sufficient rain was to farming communities), the doge was rowed in a sumptuously decorated, gold-painted ceremonial barge to the mouth of the sea where he dropped a gold ring overboard as he declared, "We marry thee, Oh sea, as a sign of true and perpetual dominion."[8] Borrowing from the notion that Christ was the bridegroom of the church and therefore its undisputed master, the rite of the Venetian marriage of the sea, which established the doge

[8] Ibid., 122.

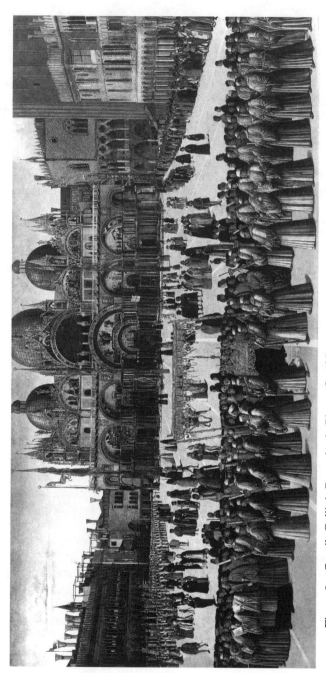

Figure 9 Gentile Bellini, *Procession in Piazza San Marco.*

as the bridegroom of the sea, was interpreted as establishing Venetian power over its subject colonies abroad and as guaranteeing safe sailing through propitiation. The government constructed and represented its colonial dominion through ritual and forced subject cities to celebrate the feast days of St. Mark and to organize processions in his honor just as happened in Venice itself.

In Italy the civic procession and its accompanying ritual practices became the principal mechanism for representing governmental authority. The procession had such deep resonances with the symbols of authority that, as Loren Partridge and Randolph Starn have noted, even the painted walls in the council chambers where the men in the inner circles of power gathered created the illusion that the viewer was walking in a procession. The image projected in these frescoes equated participation in a procession with being a high official. As the examples of Siena and Venice indicate, Italian cities united the villages of the surrounding countryside and more distant territories to them by requiring subjects to join civic processions in the capital city or to emulate them at home. As a result, one of the forms of rural resistance to urban domination was to reject these ceremonial obligations. In the late thirteenth century the mountain peoples of the Garfagnana region cut off the right hand of a notary from a local village who had taken a candle to the festival of Santa Croce in Lucca, an act of symbolic subjugation that offended his neighbors.

Although only in Italy were there powerful city-states that exercised sovereign authority over the countryside, wherever cities flourished processions became integral to urban government. In Germany, the Low Countries, France, England, and Spain, the organizers of civic processions struggled with the contradictory impulses of representing, on the one hand, as much local autonomy as possible from the emperor, king, or prince and demonstrating, on the other, the town's loyalty to the sovereign. By strictly adhering to the order in which officials marched and the routes followed, both often described as an ancient custom even when they had been formulated not long before, officials sustained the appearance of conforming to precedents. The political force of processions derived from the fiction of unchangeability, but, in fact, political pressures frequently altered them. After King Charles VIII's first entry into Paris in 1484, the king's bench put the entire Parlement of Paris on trial for having altered the processional order of the delegation that welcomed the king to the city. Although the king's judges argued that the established processional order had been in place since time immemorial, it actually dated from the previous century.

Most innovations took place on the fringes of rigidly structured processions, especially in the three types of pageants: (1) allegorical tableaux vivants in which actors maintained static poses, (2) pantomimes in which actors moved but did not speak, and (3) set pieces in which actors delivered lines to an audience. These pageants were either carried along on floats or appeared on fixed stages that the procession passed along the way. The embellishments of pageants show that although elementary processions created a structure for dramatic representations, they failed to make meaning clear enough simply by marching officials and citizens through the streets in a strictly hierarchic order. Unadorned processions were subject to many possible interpretations, and pageants attempted to resolve ambiguity by fixing meaning.

Some pageants attempted to dramatize the stories of hagiography and the Bible. The guild procession of St. George in Norwich, for example, staged a mock battle between a member dressed as the dragon, "Snap," so-called from the sound made by its metal-lined jaws, and another dressed as the warrior saint. In many cities, such as York and Coventry, Corpus Christi processions became the occasion for elaborate pageants often adapted to a peculiarly local view of Christian theology and history. As civic rituals, these pageants represented the local social order by displaying local guild members and officials, who gained reputation among their fellows by creating elaborate and novel presentations. Especially when pageants were mounted for visitors, as in the case of a diplomatic reception or a royal entrance, Latin epigrams and mythological allegories referred to esoteric ideas that benefited the position of the sponsors or flattered the visitors.

Besides honoring patron saints and regularly parading in processions, which nurtured citizenship, civic ritual also reproduced power relationships. Civic ritual both represented the utopian ideal of a harmonious community and reminded citizens of the possibility of coercion if they failed to accommodate themselves to those in power. The most obvious expressions of force were marching militiamen or soldiers who frequently appeared in civic processions. In the communes of medieval Italy, the parade of military might be fixed on a *carroccio*, a cart or wagon pulled in battle and in many civic processions especially during wartime. Siena's thirteenth-century version was a brightly painted wagon with a flag waving atop a tall mast. The *carroccio* was a venerated object: a lamp had to burn day and night next to it in imitation of the lamp that always burned in the presence of the consecrated host, the people of Siena and defeated enemies swore oaths of obedience in its presence, and its loss in battle was a great catastrophe. The exhibition of the *carroccio* served multiple purposes, discouraging Siena's enemies, providing a symbolic object for patriotic loyalties, and averting rebellion by demonstrating the commune's strength.

In some places the military parade not only represented force but applied it. In London before the reign of Henry VIII, the Midsummer Watch combined a ceremonial demonstration of the power of the city's oligarchs with the practical task of deploying guards to stand night watches throughout the city to protect the houses of the rich. The members of the watch staged an elaborate procession on Midsummer Night's Eve, taking charge of the night by marching through the city ranks of armed men dressed in the livery of the Lord Mayor and sheriff and by miming fights with the great "Soldan," the king of the Turks, who hardly presented a threat to London. One of the most extreme cases of militarized civic ritual was Turin, which during the late sixteenth and seventeenth centuries was completely reoriented and rebuilt to create vast open spaces for the ceremonial deployment of the military capacities of the duke. The architecture of this planned city created a theatrical backdrop that aestheticized the crude facts of military domination. Theorists of Turin's urban renewal explicitly recognized that the entire city was a theater for these ceremonial presentations of armed might.

Civic rituals attempted to establish a symbolic center of harmony through the veneration of patron saints and the frequent parades of authoritative officials, in so doing creating the idea of the unified city. The realities of urban life, however, always required at least an implied threat, an implicit recognition that the nature of society is inherently unharmonious and that power is unequally distributed. These often contradictory tasks meant that considerable organizational ingenuity and artistic energy was required in the planning of civic rituals, making them one of the most notable occasions for creative invention during the Renaissance.

Entries

Cities were physically and symbolically vulnerable at their gates. The need to construct a ceremonial entry for important persons, such as foreign diplomats, visiting princes, or the sovereign of the land, divulged the fragility of the city's power, the precariousness of welcoming a mighty outsider into the defenseless heart of the city.

Entries into cities might be classified into three types: receptions, in which the person entering the city was treated with honor but as a formal equal, a person with no claims to govern the place visited; advents, in which Christ's entry into Jerusalem on Palm Sunday provided a model for expressing the spiritual authority of the pope or monarch over the city; and triumphs, in which the imitation of the victorious entry of an ancient Roman general insinuated that the visitor had conquered the city. The very different messages communicated by each of these reveals how crucial it was to execute ceremonial entries with great care.

To regulate the perilous variables of the entry, many towns and princes appointed a special ceremonial official, called the herald, whose original function of managing tournaments evolved into that of ritual handyman, a specialist in the formalities necessary when one sovereign or his representative met another. To keep track of the conventions of such meetings, heralds began to keep "ceremony books," a record of the precedents established when ambassadors and princes arrived at cities or courts. Among the many details recorded in these books several items predominated: descriptions of the visitors' and receivers' movements, gestures, and dress; who met whom and where; processional routes; and listings of the gifts given and their value.

A typical entry in the *Ceremonial Book* of Florence described the visit of the Duke of Milan in 1450.

There was a very great number of our most distinguished citizens with many youths in rich and highly ornamented clothing along with all our rectors and the trumpeters and fifers of our city who went to the meeting place which was more than eight miles [away from the city]. The entry was made through the Prato gate with all the usual ceremonies of the entry that have been narrated for other times. Such was the triumph of his entourage in travelling to another place that it needs mention: the quantity of his baggage, his retainers so nobly and richly dressed, and all the other retainers of his princes and barons, the least well dressed of whom were in very rich brocades. From what I saw our people had to strive hard to match his company, because it seemed to me they excelled all the other splendors of our city. And [the duke] came into the square where our excellent Lords awaited him and dismounted his horse at some distance from the door [of the Palace of the Government], and our Lords came to meet him where he had dismounted and greeted him. And in similar fashion his most generous wife dismounted at the same place and with the same ceremonies as her most glorious duke. Then they went to the Servi church, which they had come to visit on account of a vow. Then they moved on to the Medici palace . . .[9]

Other entries produced only laconic lists of the value of gifts given visitors. Among the items recorded for 1470 we can read that

An orator from Venice visited our Signoria on October 12. He was presented with gifts and honored at the cost of L. 280.0.0

[9] Published in Richard C. Trexler, *The Libro Cerimoniale of the Florentine Republic*, Travaux d'Humanisme et Renaissance, no. 165 (Geneva: Droz, 1978), 85. The translation is mine.

An orator of the King of England visited our Signoria with letters dated . . . from
. . . We covered his expenses at the cost of L. 111.13.7

The Lord Tadeo da Imola visited our Signoria on December 3. He was
presented with gifts at the value of L. 136.11.0

Mr. Antonio da Verzelli, orator of the Duke of Milan, visited our Signoria. He
was presented with gifts at the value of L. 162.1.0 on December 8.

An orator of King Ferdinand [of Naples] visited our Signoria on January 15. He
was presented with gifts that amounted to L. 163.1.0[10]

The ceremony books are replete with what we would now call
protocols, descriptions of movements, locations, dress, and gifts that
become prescriptive by virtue of having been noted down for future
reference. Richard Trexler has pointed out how these diplomatic
protocols were forms of what might be called "systematic actions."
"The systematic mode of ceremonial perception presumed that the title
or dignity of each visitor determined a fixed behavior by the
receptionists and a fixed gift. The quality of each *persona* and not his
intentional or internal attitude, was what mattered: the visitor could
not demand more nor the commune give less."[11] What the protocols
achieved was to eliminate the need to evaluate the sincerity of the
parties to a reception. Whatever the actors thought of one another or
imagined about the motives of the other, they committed themselves to
recognizing their mutual positions merely by going through the forms
of the ceremony –by meeting the duke at a certain spot or by giving an
ambassador a token of a certain value. Exactly where the two parties
met each other, that is how far beyond the city gates the reception party
traveled, and the value of the gift were calculated according to what
became during the fifteenth and sixteenth centuries a precise index of
honors, what Patricia Fortini Brown has called "measured friendship,
calculated pomp."

The dangers inherent in opening the city to a powerful outsider were
met with ceremony. The rigidity of the reception provided a ritual
defense of the city just as the circumference of walls provided a
military one. Like baptism or a knighting ceremony, the formalities of
the entry constituted a rite of passage marking the spatial separation of
the foreign visitor from the outside world, the dangerously liminal
stage of the visitor's passing across the threshold of the town gate, and
the reaggregation of the visitor with the outside world when he or she
left.

Since the visit of any influential foreigner, no matter how ritualized,

[10] Ibid., 110. The translation is mine.   [11] Ibid., 62.

reverberated with the discordant undertones of local power and prestige, entries were often fraught with tensions. The scrupulous observance of mutually accepted gestures and procedures pledged a certain level of security, but the rigidity of the forms meant that the slightest deviation could be interpreted as a deliberate insult. The consequences could be quite absurd. The Duke of Burgundy, Charles the Bold, famous for his nasty temper, confounded smooth relations because of his literal adherence to the forms of etiquette. In 1473 at Trèves the Emperor Frederick III met Charles at some distance from the town, an apparent surprise that led to a long discussion about exactly how the entry should take place. Although the emperor wanted to honor Charles by riding side-by-side with him into the city, the duke refused, preferring to observe protocol by riding respectfully behind his superior. As the wrangling wore on, it began to rain, drenching everyone including the emperor who put on a cloak for protection, but Charles refused to cover himself because pride would not allow the obscuring of his jewels. Since their master remained uncovered none of the members of the Burgundian party could put on their cloaks either. The frictions of personality and power, on the one hand, and protocol and etiquette, on the other, frequently threatened disorder at ceremonial entrances.

Although the formal equality of the reception characterized many entries, especially those of diplomats, other kinds of entries represented inequality, especially the sovereignty of the prince over a city. In places where the prince resided permanently in the city and the city benefited from the relationship, receptions might be relatively untroubled. Such was the case in many of the small principalities, such as the Duchy of Ferrara in Italy or the Duchy of Guelders in the East Netherlands, where familiarity with the prince and a balance of interests made ceremonial harmony possible. In Rome or Paris, however, where relations between the prince and the city were always fraught with legal and political tensions, the entry ceremonies became highly constructed, ideologically driven events that occasioned a struggle to interpret the relationship between the two legal bodies of the prince and the city.

By the Renaissance two models were available for representing this relationship. One was the *advent*, a form of entry based on the biblical account of Christ's entry into Jerusalem on Palm Sunday:

When they had come near Jerusalem and had reached Bethphage, at the Mount of Olives, Jesus sent two disciples, saying to them, "Go into the village ahead of you, and immediately you will find a donkey tied, and a colt with her; untie them and bring them to me. If anyone says anything to you, just say this, 'The Lord needs them,' and he will send them immediately."

. . .

The disciples went and did as Jesus had directed them; they brought the donkey and the colt, and put their cloaks on them, and he sat on them. A very large crowd spread their cloaks on the road, and others cut branches from the trees and spread them on the road. The crowds that went ahead of him and that followed were shouting,

> "Hosanna to the Son of David!
> Blessed is the one who comes in the name of the Lord!
> Hosanna in the highest heaven!"

When he entered Jerusalem, the whole city was in turmoil, asking "Who is this?" The crowds were saying, "This is the prophet Jesus from Nazareth in Galilee." (Matthew 21: 1–11)

When the entry of the pope or king was constructed in imitation of this scene, it had a theological purpose of announcing that the visitor was the expected one and the city was another Jerusalem. This imagery compared the human prince with the divine Christ and the mundane city with Zion, bringing the eternal into the temporal and defining the relationship between the ruler and the city in spiritual rather than just in legal terms.

The advent form of the entry ceremony provided sturdy assistance to the cult of divine kingship, which evolved most fully in France and England but was imitated by princes elsewhere. As Larry Bryant has put it, the French king's entry into Paris ignored the reciprocal rights and legal obligations between the king and city in order to create "a transcendent moment and an expression of a universal truth," defining the monarch's "messianic–eschatological mission" rather than a particular theory of government.[12] The success of the French monarchy in developing a cult of divine kingship became the envy of European royalty, but faced with often recalcitrant cities which were not about to see their jealously guarded privileges obscured by a fog of ceremonial sanctity, other princes could make only limited use of the advent image. The Counts of Burgundy, renowned for their dedication to courtly pomp, attempted to imitate the French cult of divine kingship. For his entrance into Ghent in 1458, Philip the Good consulted biblical experts for advice on the decorations, but the hostility of the town to the count's assertion of authority over them resulted in an impoverished festival. Although the court ceremonies of these Burgundian princes became fantastically convoluted and elaborate, their subject cities in Flanders

---

[12] Lawrence M. Bryant, "The Medieval Entry Ceremony in Paris," in János M. Bak, ed., *Coronations: Medieval and Early Modern Monarchic Ritual* (Berkeley: University of California Press, 1990), 113.

countered with a palpably Spartan attitude toward festivity, rejecting it as serving the interests of an unpopular "foreign" prince.

The other model for a ceremonial entry was the *triumph*, which derived from the ancient victory parade of a Roman general who arrived in Rome aboard a chariot with a grand entourage exhibiting booty and captives. Both Scipio Africanus and Julius Caesar received such a welcome, and triumphal arches were often built to memorialize victorious generals. During the imperial period of Rome the triumph became the exclusive privilege of the emperor and his relatives, which created an association between the triumphal form and the representation of legitimate rulership. Perhaps the Emperor Frederick II's entry into Capua in 1237 was an attempt to revive the ancient triumph, but the full reappearance of the form came during the fourteenth century with Petrarch's poem, "I Trionfi," which sets forth a Christianized version of the Roman triumph, made up of a procession in which personifications of love, chastity, death, fame, time, and eternity ride past the viewer on chariots. The enormously influential poem created an archetype for imagery and ceremonies that were made to order for the ambitious Renaissance popes, princes, and kings who could simultaneously associate themselves with the power of Caesar and the virtues of Christianity by mounting a triumphal entry into a city. During the fifteenth and sixteenth centuries the triumph deeply influenced the visual arts. The sculptured frieze at the Castelnuovo in Naples, showing King Alfonso in a triumphal chariot, remains a prominent example. Loren Partridge and Randolph Starn have called the triumph the "master myth" of Renaissance politics, a myth which could be recycled with many embellishments and refinements to create a distinctive language of rulership.

One of the most famous, or perhaps one should say infamous, Renaissance triumphs was Pope Julius II's entry in 1506 into Bologna, which he had recently conquered with a mercenary army. After receiving the keys to the city, Julius was carried on a throne-chair beneath a canopy through thirteen triumphal arches erected in his honor. The triumph allowed him to perform a dual role of beneficent pope who bestowed blessings from his papal throne and of conquering Caesar who passed through the arched monuments that celebrated his victories. Pope Julius, who had scandalized even his jaded contemporaries by appearing in armor before his assembled troops, became exceedingly fond of the triumph, and the following year tried to transform into a triumph the advent procession of his Palm Sunday entry into Rome. He commissioned the building of nine triumphal arches, each inscribed with lavish praise of his military successes. Julius's overweening ambition scandalized his own master of ceremonies, that specialist in precedent and protocols, who planned a counter-demonstration more appropriate to a Palm Sunday advent. As Samuel Kinser has shown, the master of ceremonies arranged to have every church in Rome erect flower-bedecked altars along the processional path and then flanked them with waving clerics, recreating Jesus's entry into Jerusalem to obscure the triumphal arches in a forest of palm fronds and cheering religious.[13] Ever sensitive about its tenuous privileges and lacking the deep tradition of civic rituals found in the north Italian city-states, the city of Rome and its many communities of transient religious always found excessive papal grandiosity difficult to swallow. Although Rome was the ancient home of the triumph, a triumphal entry in Renaissance or Baroque Rome was a tangled affair.

As was the case with so many ceremonial forms, the triumph could be adapted to a range of meanings. At one extreme a triumph confirmed a military conquest. In 1507 after the suppression of a rebellion against the French occupying Genoa, King Louis XII made a triumphal entry into the city. As he passed the city gate he struck it with his sword, thereby signifying his conquest and Genoa's loss of liberty. Lining the streets of his parade route were rows of young girls, the virgins of Genoa, who knelt before him and begged for mercy. After delivering a harsh verbal rebuke to the assembled citizens, Louis watched as officials standing on a stage ripped up and burned the Genoese book of statutes and customary privileges. In this case the triumph signified defeat.

The triumphal entries of French kings into their own loyal cities, however, revealed a more gentle royal hand. Paris boasted its own prestigious corporate bodies including the guilds, cathedral chapter, city council, university, Parlement, and Estates General, from which the king needed both political and symbolic support. In his entry the king recognized the customary and legal privileges of these bodies while he accepted their acknowledgment of his sacred charisma. Through speeches and tableaux vivants, the various corporations of Paris reminded the king that although he possessed the perfect body of Kingship, his own fallible person was subject to correction from them. At least until the Wars of Religion of the late sixteenth century when this easy concord of mutual recognition broke down, royal entrances into Paris managed to represent a harmonious body politic that submerged the persistent tensions so evident elsewhere. Even London lacked until the eighteenth century a similar ceremonial affinity with its sovereigns.

Closely tied to the ceremonial entry was the idea of a *progress*. In a

---

[13] The description here closely follows an unpublished paper by Samuel Kinser, cited with permission of the author.

progress the pope or monarch proceeded from place to place in a continuous journey that linked the various parts of the domain through the physical presence of the sovereign. The progress evolved from medieval customs of kingship in which kings and queens enjoyed the hospitality of their subjects, moving from castle to castle and making their power known across the land. By the sixteenth century royal progresses became a series of carefully orchestrated ceremonial displays. The greatest genius of the progress was Queen Elizabeth I of England, who starred in a long-running, moving spectacle of her own fashioning, transforming herself into the adored object of her subjects. Her successor James I, who avoided progresses for more private ceremonies that asserted the divine right of kings, undermined in practice the sacrality he so ardently advocated in his long-winded treatises on kingship because he failed to display his sacred body to his waiting subjects.

Showing the sacred body of the prince could best be accomplished through entries and progresses. The most successful of these demanded the talents of artists, architects, musicians, Latinists, dramatists, and ceremonial specialists, who created a form of outdoor public theater, which was witnessed by far more people than any other artistic production of the age. Pope Clement VIII, for example, organized a grand progress in 1598 from Rome to Ferrara, a formerly independent city that had recently reverted to the papal state. In the progress from town to town, the host was carried in a crystal container affixed to the back of a pony, which arrived with great pomp the day before the pontiff did. Tableaux vivants along the way illustrated principles of sacred rulership. Eventually the magnificent procession arrived in Ferrara, which was now symbolically attached to Rome through the papal progress. The body of God and the body of the prince-pope proceeded in tandem to unify the body politic.

Regal ceremonies

The courts of the royal houses created the most spectacular displays of ceremonial pomp in European history. The sixteenth to eighteenth centuries was the great age of European monarchy, an era distinguished by the widespread erosion of the traditional privileges of towns and nobles, the assertion of the divine right and absolute authority of kings, and the expansion of the cult of monarchy in the arts, drama, and ritual. Many kings, courtiers, and observers of princes were fully aware of the theatrical dimension of governmental ceremonies and of the need of monarchs to act their part convincingly and with dignity. A study of rituals published in 1719–20 by J. C. Lünig echoed the idea of a ceremonial theater state in the title, *Theatrum Ceremoniale*. Although none of the European monarchs could afford to ignore their public image, none surpassed the calculated, theatrical "presentation of the self," to borrow the famous formula of Erving Goffman, of the "Sun King," Louis XIV (1643–1715).

Regal ceremonies can be understood in two distinctive ways. The first type of rites *enacted* kingship. An example of rites of enactment would be the coronation, the performance necessary to make someone a king. In the strictest cases, such as in Poland, before the rite of coronation, a king was not a king at all, just a king-in-waiting. The Holy Roman Emperor was termed the Emperor-Elect until he found the time and means to go to Rome for an official coronation. Some never made it. In theory at least, only through a coronation could a mere man become a sacred king. These rites were similar to what J. L. Austin calls a "performative utterance," a statement that makes something happen, as when a bride and groom say, "I do," to become a married couple. In many kingdoms, some combination of gestures and verbal statements was the necessary constitutive act of kingship.

A second type of regal ceremony *represented* kingship. The term "representation" covers many different kinds of performances, and some theorists would argue that even rites that purported to enact were merely a kind of representation, a way of signifying rather than acting. What does "representation" mean in the context of a regal ceremony? There are several possible answers. As we have seen in the case of diplomatic entries, one simple meaning of "to represent" was "to stand in place of." An ambassador stood in place of his sovereign. When an envoy representing a king arrived in a city or another court, he had to be treated – at least in a ceremonial sense – as if he were the king. Objects could also stand in place of the king as would be the case with a royal emblem, a coin, or a portrait. As we saw with the theory of the advent, the king could take the place of Christ, a kind of representation necessary for the divine right of kings, and during the Renaissance and Baroque periods some kings were represented as ancient heroes, such as Hercules or Caesar, or pagan deities, such as Apollo. In an even more abstract sense the king could represent the state, an idea Louis XIV supposedly encapsulated with his famous line, "the state is me" ("l'état c'est moi"), but since the modern idea of the state was slow to develop, most people in early modern Europe would have seen themselves as living in a kingdom rather than a state. Perhaps most universally, however, kings represented kingship. The individual, mortal, fallible man who was named king represented – or "embodied" to employ the term used by contemporaries – the universal, eternal, perfect King, that is the idea of kingship.

All of these forms of representation came together in the meaning of representation as a theatrical performance because the idea that the king was an actor permitted him to play many possible roles and to follow many possible scripts. The most famous example of regal representation as theater can be found in the court of France where Louis XIV occasionally played the part of himself in court dramas: Louis, the actor, represented himself both as a man and as the King of France, and to mix the representations even more he sometimes did this while dressed in the costume of Apollo. It was this mutually reinforcing effect of multiple representations that constructed the regality of early modern princes.

Enacting rites as opposed to theatrical representations tended to cluster around the most critical moment in monarchical regimes, especially the period of interregnum between one king and his or her successor, the period during which the questions *who* was in power and *when* did he or she take power came to the fore. The interregnum ceremonies attempted to isolate the exact moment of the transfer of power, but a ceremonial performance always took time to arrange, especially if it was supposed to take place in a special place such as Rome or Rheims or Westminster. The problem of timing the transfer of power became the crucial ceremonial problem of enacted rites, and the liminal period of the interregnum could be as fraught with dangers for the institution of monarchy as entries were for cities.

A cluster of enacting rites of passage framed interregna and made royal successions possible. The most important of these rites of passage were coronations and funerals. The English word, "coronation," usually designates a variety of ceremonies associated with the ascension to authority of a new monarch in which the actual crowning may not necessarily be the most important action. The ritual complex of the interregnum could include the predecessor's funeral, the new king's visit to the shrine of a patron saint, dressing the new monarch in regal attire, his anointment, blessing, crowning, oath taking, enthronement, entrance into the capital city, and first formal act of government, such as the *Lit de justice* in France or addressing Parliament in England.

A variety of traditions contributed to the hybrid ceremonies of European coronations. The Vikings, for example, emphasized the enthronement. The candidate for kingship sat upon the throne of power and obtained the shouted acclamation of the people. Once the king was enthroned a lawman carried a brand of fire around the borders of the court to delineate a sacred place in which such profane activities as fighting were banned. The most powerful models, however, came from the Carolingian and Ottonian monarchs who in turn had borrowed from Vizigothic and Byzantine ceremonies to create a rite of sacred kingship in which the crucial moment was unction, the anointment with holy oil. Anointment was widely imitated in Christian kingdoms, although in practice and interpretation the action varied considerably. In Germany the unction of kings was on the head like priests, but a different kind of oil was used. In Denmark both the king and queen were anointed on the lower right arm and on the shoulders. In Poland, where the rite was likened to the setting apart of a bishop, the king received the holy oil on his head, chest, shoulders, and arms.

The most successful monarchies in late medieval and early modern Europe were certainly those of England and France. The coronation ceremonies of these two monarchies influenced each other and were widely imitated elsewhere. The English coronation tended to emphasize legal and constitutional issues, such as the relationship between the king and other privileged bodies. The French rites focused on the consecrated character of the king and his relationship with ecclesiastical authorities. Perhaps the most crucial development in the history of coronations was the combination of the consecration and crowning in one ceremony, which took place at the coronation of the Carolingian monarch, Louis the Pious, in 816. This basic ceremony was inherited by the Capetian dynasty established in France in 987 and lasted through dynastic changes and revolution until 1830. During the first two centuries of the Capetian dynasty, every king crowned his own successor in pre-succession rites, but the new kings also underwent a later formal consecration and crowning at Rheims. After 1223 the Archbishop of Rheims performed the anointment at the same time as the crowning, but the requirement of going to Rheims, although it bolstered the sacred nature of kingship, lessened the legal significance of the consecration and coronation for enacting kingship. Since it could take some time for a new king to get to Rheims and practical considerations required that the actual accession to power be understood to take place at the moment of the old king's death, the coronation gradually became a mere affirmation of a succession that had already occurred. The French coronation ceremonies evolved into a celebration of sacred kingship performed in front of the vast crowds that assembled in Rheims. Besides the propensity for ever more costly decorations, the few additions to the ceremony over the centuries were largely manifestations of *la religion royale*, including the display of the Holy Ampulla and the exercise of the king's touch, which was his ability to cure the disease of scrofula through the thaumaturgic power of kingship.

The interregnum ceremonies in England and France attempted to solve the difficulties of royal succession through the remarkable concept of the king's two bodies, a legal fiction whose history has been explored by Ernst Kantorowicz. Although the idea evolved among canon lawyers and royal bureaucrats during the Middle Ages, it was most fully developed during the sixteenth century as a theory of kingship that explained royal ceremonies. The theory posited that the king had two bodies, one of which was his physical, defective, mortal body, that is the body he possessed as a human being; the other body was that of the King (with a capital "K"), the insubstantial, perfect, immortal embodiment of kingship, which was immune to the frailties, illnesses, and decay of the human body. For the English the King was what the lawyers called a "corporation sole," a legal body that could be represented at any one time by only one person, the legitimate king of England, but that legal body did not die with him. In the jurist's formula, "the king, as king, never dies."[14] The king's two bodies were even identified by different names, the body natural and the body politic. When in 1603 the kingdoms of Scotland and England were united in the person of James I, Francis Bacon recommended that the new crown be named Great Britain to express the "perfect union of bodies, politic as well as natural."[15]

Rooted in the theological doctrine of the dual nature of Christ as both a man and God, the Anglo-French theory of the king's two bodies became remarkably influential. The conception spread in both hereditary monarchies, such as those of England and France, and elected ones, such as Poland's. In the sixteenth century, Joachim Bielski enunciated the principle for the Polish crown, "the royal person dies, the crown dies not".[16] Even in republican Venice with its elected doge, a figurehead who lacked any dynastic claims to authority, interregnum ceremonies represented two kinds of doges. At the death of a doge two silver emblems were made, one a large one with the name of the deceased on it and a smaller one, which was similar save for the absence of the name. In a simple ceremony, the large emblem was smashed and the smaller one retained to be given to the new doge after his election. "In this alone are [the two kinds of doges] different: that the one is temporary and governs a single part. Both are equally called the Prince: for being the first, and grandly revered and honored by all, he represents a truly absolute Prince to those who see him in his majesty, with so many

[14] Richard A. Jackson, *Vive le Roi! A History of the French Coronation from Charles V to Charles X* (Chapel Hill: University of North Carolina Press, 1984), 7.

[15] Quoted in Ernst H. Kantorowicz, *The King's Two Bodies: A Study in Medieval Political Theology* (Princeton: Princeton University Press, 1957), 24.

[16] Aleksander Gieysztor, "Gesture in the Coronation Ceremonies of Medieval Poland," in Bak, *Coronations*, 153.

ornaments acquired by means of his valor; but in fact he is tied by the laws in a way that his position is not at all different from the other positions of any magistracy."[17]

In many regimes the concept of the king's two bodies was depicted as a literal fact. Tomb monuments sculpted two figures, the one on top showed the king or queen dressed in all the finery of office, complete with royal robes, crown, and scepter, but the lower one represented a very different body, the naked, decaying, worm-eaten corpse actually present within the sepulcher. The best examples can be found in the French royal necropolis at Saint-Denis in the suburbs of Paris.

Ralph Giesey has examined the funeral traditions of the French kings, demonstrating how the representation of the king's two bodies in these ceremonies solved the interregnum problem of instantaneous succession and made the coronation ceremonies legally unnecessary even though they survived as an expression of royal sacrality. After 1422 when a French king died it became customary to place a wax effigy of the deceased on the top of his coffin. Dressed in royal attire and adorned with the royal insignia, the effigy represented the king alive. Gradually what began quite incidentally as a way of representing a dead king whose body was too decomposed for showing, became the focus of an elaborate ceremonial performance devoted to sustaining the fiction that the King never died. Between death and burial government officials and members of the royal courts behaved as if the king were still alive. The Parlementaires continued to wear their red robes of office, the entry of the corpse into Paris was a triumph rather than a funeral cortege, and the household officers continued to conduct their daily round of duties just as they did when the king was still among them. This performance of the King-is-still-alive drama focused on the effigy, which was dressed in the king's coronation robes and rested on a bed of state. Perhaps most remarkable was the daily routine of setting the table and serving meals to the effigy. The account from the funeral of François I is quite fantastic:

And in this state the effigy remained for eleven days. And it is to be understood and known that during the time the body was in the chamber next to the great hall, as well as while the effigy was in that hall, the forms and fashions of service were observed and kept just as was customary during the lifetime of the king: the table being set by the officers of the commissary; the service carried by the gentlemen servants, the bread-carrier, the cup bearer and the carver, with the usher marching before them and followed by the officers of the cupboard, who spread the table with the reverences and samplings that were customarily made. After the bread was broken and prepared, the meat and other courses were brought in by an usher, steward, bread-carrier, pages of the chamber, squire of

---

[17] Quoted in Muir, *Civic Ritual in Renaissance Venice*, 272.

the cuisine and . . . The napkin was presented by said steward to the most dignified person present, to wipe the hands of the [king]. The table was blessed by a Cardinal; the basins of water for washing the hands presented at the chair of the [king], as if he had been living, and seated in it. The three courses of the meal were carried out with the same forms, ceremonies and samplings as they were wont to be during the life of the [king], without forgetting those of the wine, with the presentation of the cup at the places and hours that the [king] had been accustomed to drink, two times at each of his meals.[18]

The new king had to remain aloof from all of this, watching the ceremonies while hidden at a discreet distance, because the fiction that the old king was still alive required the temporary invisibility of the new king. Finally, after a fixed number of days, a funeral service was performed in the cathedral of Notre-Dame in Paris, after which the funeral procession made its slow way to the suburban abbey of Saint-Denis. As the king's coffin was lowered into the grave, the stewards of the royal household cast their batons of office into the grave to mark the moment when their official responsibilities ended. Finally, the critical moment of transition arrived. The Admiral of France slowly dipped the banner of France over the grave until it touched the coffin. Three times the words, "Le roi est mort," "the king is dead," were intoned to the weeping and wailing of the assembled crowd. Then immediately, the cry went up, "Vive le roy," "long live the king," followed by the name of the new incumbent. In the split second between "the king is dead" and "long live the king" the transition took place between one mortal king and the other. Usually within a few weeks the new king underwent his coronation at Rheims at which the cry was heard, "Vivat rex in aeternum," "may the king live for eternity."

At least until the assassination of Henri IV in 1610, the French solved the interregnum problem with the ceremonial fiction that after the death of the king the King was still alive, a fiction made possible by the theory that he had two bodies, one mortal piece of flesh in the coffin and one immortal idea represented in the effigy. The instantaneous transition acclaimed at the dead king's funeral theoretically made the coronation redundant, because the *k*ing was by then already the *K*ing. In the crisis following Henri IV's assassination, his heir, the boy who became Louis XIII, had to succeed instantly and his childish hold on power be strengthened. The idea of the king's two bodies was replaced by the dynastic idea that little Louis inherited the *image* of his father Henri. The legal right of succession and biological heredity guaranteed the automatic passage of kingship from father to son and eliminated the

---

[18] Quoted and translated in Ralph E. Giesey, *The Royal Funeral Ceremony in Renaissance France* (Geneva: Droz, 1960), 5.

need for the prolonged fiction of the living effigy. The murder of Henri IV had created a dangerous political crisis because Henri had acceded to the throne only after a long and bloody civil war in which he had led the Huguenot faction. Only through his conversion to Catholicism in 1593 had Paris come to accept his rule, and his assassin Ravaillac claimed to be acting on intelligence that Henri planned to turn France over to the Protestants. It was not immediately known whether the assassination was part of a deeper conspiracy and what the reaction of the Paris crowd might be. International tensions were also high because at the time of his death Henri was preparing for a war in Germany. To make matters worse, Henri's heir was only eight years old and needed all the legitimacy that could be mustered. It was just too perilous a situation to sustain for weeks the fiction that Henri was still alive through the display of his effigy.

The most immediate problem was to designate Louis's mother, Marie de Médicis, regent, but her widespread unpopularity made many powerful aristocrats search for an alternative. To alleviate the crisis, young Louis's protectors invented a new ceremony of transition, hastily performed within hours of Henri's death. Louis appeared in a formal *Lit de justice* (bed of justice) in which he inaugurated his reign and confirmed his mother as regent. In a *Lit de justice* the king sat enthroned (at one time he had reclined on a cushion, hence the term "bed of justice") before the assembled Parlement of Paris, which as the superior court of the realm had to ratify royal decrees to make them legal. On the morning of his inaugural *lit*, Louis and his mother burst in on a chaotic scene as a group of bishops argued with the presidents of the Parlement over seating arrangements. The command of the little king solved the dispute. He was then enthroned beside his mother who asked those present to advise the new king in the conduct of his affairs. A rather disorderly session ended with the legal confirmation of the regency.

The 1610 crisis destroyed the traditional ceremonies for inaugurating a new king in France. The king's first *lit* had previously occurred sometime *after* his predecessor's funeral and his own coronation. Just as the performance of the royal touch served as a fulfillment of the consecration portion of the coronation ceremonies, the *Lit de justice* ceremony fulfilled the promise of justice symbolized by the crowning. In the hasty arrangements made for Louis XIII, however, the *lit* served to authorize his mother's regency before Henri's effigy had even been made let alone the funeral mass celebrated. Louis's presence at the *lit* also obliterated the core fiction of the traditional royal funeral whereby the new king was to remain out of public view while the display of his father's effigy made it evident that the King's perfect body lived even though the king's physical one was dead. Although Henri IV's funeral followed the usual ceremonies, the fiction was fatally compromised and never resurrected.

Louis's precipitous *lit* also raised havoc with the coronation rites. Although coronations had not actually inaugurated a reign in France for a long time, the officials in charge of the arrangements for Louis XIII had to rethink how to structure the coronation in light of the *lit*. To solve the problem created by the demise of the idea that the effigy lived on after Henri's death, they invented a new fiction, that of the "sleeping king." On the morning of the coronation, two archbishops came to the door of chamber where young Louis waited and knocked three times, each time calling out Louis's name. Louis's delayed response implied he had to be aroused from sleep. After he was "awakened" the young king was taken to his coronation. The idea that the new king had been asleep preserved the notion that the King never dies. The king just awakens to Kingship. The 1610 arrangements established a new ceremony by opening the reign with a *Lit de justice*, diminishing the significance of the royal funeral, and culminating with the coronation of the newly awakened king. When it happened that the next two Bourbon kings were also minors when they acceded to the throne, the procedure became an established tradition.

The coronation ceremonies themselves remained important not because they made the *k*ing a *K*ing but because they limited his authority and made a powerful impression on the people. The importance of the consecration in the coronation can hardly be exaggerated even though it had no constitutional significance. For example, during the seven years between the death of his father and Charles VII's coronation in 1429, Joan of Arc always called the king "the Dauphin," the official title of the heir apparent. Only after his crowning did she begin to call him "gentil roy." As an untutored if exceptionally devout subject, Joan did not grasp the legal technicalities about the king's two bodies but understood quite well that the coronation consecrated the king as a sacred person.

The young Louis XIV was not crowned until eleven years after the death of his father in 1643, the ceremony delayed by the nobles' revolt of the Fronde. Louis later asserted with complete legal justification that he had been king since the death of his father and that the coronation had nothing to do with it. The ceremony simply announced his kingship, and, he added, it made his reign "more august, more inviolable, and more holy."[19] Nevertheless, his coronation was a grand affair that gained considerable popular attention.

[19] Quoted in Peter Burke, *The Fabrication of Louis XIV* (New Haven: Yale University Press, 1992), 43.

After a magnificent progress to Rheims, Louis stood before the officiating priest (on this occasion the Bishop of Soissons filled in for the Archbishop of Rheims) to swear his oath of office and promise to respect the rights of his subjects. The assembled multitudes in the congregation were then asked if they accepted Louis as their king, in a vestige of the public acclamation that had empowered early kings. The ecclesiastic then blessed the royal insignia that included the scepter, spurs, and sword of Charlemagne, and the ring with which Louis married the kingdom, a symbol interpreted in light of the scriptural references that Christ had married the church. The archbishop anointed the king's body with oil drawn from the Holy Ampulla, a bottle that legend reputed to have been delivered from heaven by a dove when the first Christian king of France, Clovis, was baptized. Finally, the bishop placed the scepter in Louis's right hand, the "hand of justice" in his left, and the crown on his head. These bare outlines do not do justice to what was, in fact, a lengthy and complex ceremony that included interminable hours of prayers and litanies as well as a solemn mass at the conclusion. Although only a few thousand notables could fit into the cathedral to witness the coronation ceremony, published descriptions and illustrations of it found a vast market all across France.

Within days of the consecration the king began to perform the royal touch, the curing of the skin disease of scrofula by touching the afflicted and saying "the king touches you, God cures you." Whereas his father had touched some 800 or 900 after his coronation Louis XIV touched more than 3,000 two days after his, an indication that popular enthusiasm for the rite was still strong. The anointment from the Holy Ampulla made possible the most impressive royal trait, the reputed ability acquired through a ritual to perform miraculous healings. The healing force passed through the direct touch of the royal hands, revealing in this, the most exalted of ceremonies, the same simple belief in the power of the touch that animated so many other rituals. The contact between one body and another, from the healings of a simple country cunning woman to the rites of vassalage, provided the tactile basis for a ritual performance.

Besides the *Lit de justice*, funeral, and coronation, a fourth ceremony completed the French interregnum rituals. From the point of view of the Parisians nothing much counted until the new king made a triumphal entry in Paris. There was no requirement that this take place, and sometimes it occurred before the coronation in Rheims, but given the importance of the capital city, the acceptance of the new king in Paris signified the acceptance of all France. The route was fixed. The king entered at the Saint-Denis gate and traced in the opposite direction the same route as the funeral cortege of his predecessor: the transition between one king and another was figured as an exiting and entering of the great city. During the fourteenth and fifteenth centuries, the kings received the keys to the city and confirmed the rights of its citizens, but these legalistic ceremonies gradually diminished in significance to be replaced by magnificent pageantry, especially tableaux vivants performed at various stops along the route. These tended to depict the glories of previous French kings, Charlemagne and St. Louis in particular, reminding the new monarch of his illustrious progenitors and his responsibility to emulate them. The pageants represented the continuity of the dynasty. Other cities presented the king with triumphal entries, and for most of his subjects the official life of a French king consisted of a series of magnificent entries.

Although all royal courts became theaters for the performance of princely ceremonies and a fountainhead for the new courtly manners, none matched the ceremonial intensity of the court of Louis XIV at Versailles. Here the king's everyday life became completely ritualized. Arising with the sun, the Sun King, performed a daily "kingrise" called the *lever*. The king's every action, from putting on his shirt to urinating, was undertaken in a ceremonial way and involved the participation of an honored member of the court down to the gentleman responsible for handling the chamber pot. Going to bed consisted of the *coucher* ceremony. Every meal became a ritual performance, even on the least formal occasions. Courtiers vied for the honor of being allowed to watch the king eat or, even more, to be allowed to serve his food to him. To be spoken to while the king ate or to be invited to dine with him was the highest accolade imaginable. In the court there were complex rules about who could wear a hat and when they could wear it, who could sit down (only women and only in the evening), how to knock at a door (scratch with a fingernail kept long for the purpose), and how to express emotions such as laughing (don't unless the king does first). The king's activities, such as attending mass, presiding over council meetings, walking in the garden, hunting, playing cards or billiards, and spending evenings with his mistresses followed an exquisitely planned and timed regime, one that so ritualized daily life that every act in Louis's routine, even performing his excretory functions, looked like a ritual. The king was always an actor on the stage of his own kingship, obliged to turn in an exemplary performance day in, day out, without any relief from his role as a sacred person.

Even when Louis himself was absent, the rituals of kingship still had to be observed in the presence of the objects that represented him. To wear a hat in the room where the table was set for his dinner or to enter his bedroom without genuflecting were grave offenses. Subjects could never turn their backs on his portrait. As Norbert Elias has argued, the elaborate rituals of court society, especially their clockwork precision and their symbolic character, made the regimentation and centralizing power of the modern state possible. The microcosm of Versailles became the model of the well-run state.

One of the effects of this routine was to create the appearance that the rituals embodied timeless truths and continued ancient traditions. That appearance, however, was deceiving. As Peter Burke has shown, the royal rituals of Louis XIV had a history, many of them invented during his own reign. His court was noticeably more formal in its ritual behavior than that of his father or grandfather. Louis XIV's taste for theater and elaborate allegories revived the Renaissance magnificences of the previous century, especially those of the court of King François I. The amplification of court ritual, including the *lever/coucher* and the appointment of a Grand Master of Ceremonies, derived from the time of King Henri III. Louis also attempted to imitate the gravity of Spanish court rituals, which were designed to insulate the king from court factions. The paragon of Spanish decorum was Louis's uncle and father-in-law, Philip IV (1621–65), whom the Sun King ardently desired to surpass. Philip rarely made public appearances, but when he did his gravity of bearing exemplified the calm dignity of the Spanish ideal of *sosiego*. The French ambassador to Philip's court was deeply impressed by the king's ability during his appearances to create an image of serene harmony by remaining "like a marble statue" when he spoke, moving only his lips. In building Versailles, in fact, Louis XIV endeavored to surpass Philip's grand new palace, the Buen Retiro, both of which served as spectacular stages for the performance of royal rituals.

The most common pattern in early modern kingdoms was for ceremonial practices to circulate among the prestigious courts of Rome, Spain, France, England, and the Holy Roman Empire. These ceremonies, in turn, were imitated and adapted by the lesser courts, especially the minor courts of Germany and the kingdoms of eastern Europe. Polish royal ceremonies, for example, presented a curious blend of archaic traditions and fashionable importations from France and elsewhere. Faced with the problem of representing the dual nature of kingship at the death of a monarch, the Poles devised an elaborate pantomime that survived from 1370 until the end of the monarchy. Instead of displaying an effigy representing the eternal King, a knight interrupted the royal funeral in the Cracow cathedral when he rode in on a horse. The visor of his helmet was closed, making him anonymous so that he could impersonate the dead king. With considerable noise and commotion, the knight collapsed onto the cathedral pavement, breaking the shaft of his lance. At the same moment officials smashed the royal seal, symbolically ending the reign. Although the new king was allowed to carry out his political duties immediately after his election, he was barred from acting as a judge until after the consecration of the coronation, creating an inextricable bond between the sacrality of his persona and royal justice. During the coronation ceremony allusions were made that he had been sleeping until this day, and the judicial insignia were displayed in a way to emphasize that the king had not yet come to his full authority: the grand marshal carried the staff pointing downwards and the standard-bearer kept the royal banner furled. Only the climactic anointment transformed him into a sacred being, a King in the fullest sense.

In Russia Peter the Great (1689–1725) reformed his kingdom along Western lines, no more thoroughly than in his transformation of imperial rituals. In 1696, to celebrate his victory over the Crimean Tartars at Azov, he staged a Roman triumph, complete with classical arch decorated with huge reliefs of Hercules and Mars. The new imagery contrasted with the traditional iconography of the Tsar that represented him as a humble, if saintly, servant of God. Unsatisfied with merely importing Western models, Peter tried to destroy the old. One of the most solemn traditional religious ceremonies was the Palm Sunday procession that, as we have seen, Ivan the Terrible had promoted to sacralize the cult of the Tsar. Peter, in contrast, treated the occasion with contempt by making a travesty of holy rituals. In 1692 he organized his "Most Comical and Most Drunken Council," which staged a blasphemous parody of the Palm Sunday procession. In time the Russian court was utterly transformed. French became the preferred language; Italian artists received the most patronage; and the pageantry of the Renaissance replaced Byzantine solemnity.

Although Protestant monarchs could not help but be fascinated with the pomp and splendor of the great Catholic courts in France and Spain, the Protestant princes had to make delicate calculations in adapting royal ceremonies to accord with Protestant criteria for proper ritual behavior. Much of royal ritual had been borrowed from the Catholic liturgy, and monarchical political theory owed a great deal to canon law. One of the central changes of the Reformation had been to eliminate the ordination of priests and the consecration of bishops, that setting apart of a certain class of persons with the holy oil of chrism. Once priests were no longer sacred, could kings continue to be? Once holy oils were thrown away, what could be used to anoint a king? The first Protestant coronation in Denmark, that of King Christian III and Queen Dorothea in 1537, fused old practices and new ideas. In place of the mass, Lutheran preachers delivered sermons and prayed for the new monarchs, but the anointing, crowning, and presenting of regalia continued as before. Strangely enough, even the Latin phrases derived from the Roman mass were still kept.

During the Tudor period the English coronation ceremonies followed the vicissitudes of the Reformation. Henry VIII (1509–47) attempted to rewrite the coronation oath to emphasize his autocratic powers; the Protestant caretakers of Edward VI (1547–53) pushed for a more thoroughly Protestant and simple coronation; Mary (1553–58) brought back the sacramental elements of the rite; and Elizabeth (1558–1603) followed what would become her pattern of compromise and avoidance of open conflict. On the eve of Elizabeth's coronation the Protestants seemed ascendant: prayers were said in English, and the queen's chaplain failed to raise the host during the mass in recognition of Protestant antipathy to the elevation. Although she excluded nearly all high-ranking Catholic bishops from the coronation, Elizabeth insisted that one of them perform the anointing. It is not clear from the record exactly what happened, but during the mass she may have actually left the throne for a curtained closet so that she would not have to watch the elevation of the host or take communion herself. Whatever she did during the actual coronation, the main emphasis shifted from the perilous ritual forms that symbolized Catholicism or Protestantism – forms that were bound to offend somebody – to the pageantry of her coronation procession. These displays "enacted a drama of stylized reciprocity and affection" between Elizabeth and her subjects, a much safer theme than the theology of the liturgy.[20]

In all of these princely ceremonies, the commoner subjects of the prince had, at best, a passive role. They crowded outside the coronation cathedral while the great paraded and prayed. They lined the streets to mourn the dead and cheer the newly ascended. There were, however, medieval traditions of more active popular involvement in the cardinal moments of the lives of princes that endured into early modern times. The most notorious examples of commoner participation were *ritual pillages*, which Italians called *allegrezze* ("celebrations"). Pillages occurred in Bologna at news of the election of a number of popes who had palaces there, in Venice after the announcement of the election of a new doge, in Florence when Cosimo de' Medici was enthroned duke in 1537, and in Mantua when a member of the ruling Gonzaga family was married or had a child. During the reign of the Duke of Ferrara, Ercole

---

[20] Richard C. McCoy, "'The Wonderfull Spectacle': The Civic Progress of Elizabeth I and the Troublesome Coronation," in Bak, *Coronations*, 223.

I, certain events – his election in 1471, his marriage in 1472, the birth of his first child in 1476, and his death in 1505 – incited ritual pillages in the subject city of Modena. To celebrate these events there were the usual pageants, bonfires, and fireworks displays, but also a large crowd gathered at the town hall, forcibly freed the prisoners awaiting trial, and looted the building. In particular, the crowd sought the records of criminal investigations and trials, which they wanted to burn, and on one occasion when an official was slow to produce them, the crowd threatened to kill him. Although ritual pillages sometimes appear to be anarchy or mere criminality, the disorders were always limited to specific objects, usually the property of the prince or the town hall, and expressed the sense of reciprocal expectations between the ruler and the ruled. They followed what one historian has called a "flexible plot," a recurrent repertoire of patterns of behavior that were improvised on the spot. A prince could either suffer from his subjects' joy or attempt to control their reaction. In 1505, for example, Ercole's successor, Alfonso I d'Este, ordered officials in Modena to free prisoners immediately in order to prevent the burning of criminal records and the storming of the prison.

In Rome the interregnum period between the death of one pope and the election of his successor was called the Vacant See, a special time when papal government was completely suspended and general freedoms, impossible during normal times, prevailed. The peculiar character of the rituals of the Vacant See derived from the fact that unlike French kings the pope did not have two bodies but what Paolo Prodi calls, "two souls." He was both the Bishop of Rome, that is the head of the universal Catholic church, and the prince of the Papal State, a wide band of territory that divided the Italian peninsula across the middle. As a territorial prince he faced the same representational issues as a king, but "unlike contemporary kings," as Laurie Nussdorfer notes, "the popes of the early modern period could die. No ceremonial fiction maintained a papal reign in the way that funeral rituals prolonged the rule of the Renaissance kings of France. Indeed, at the time when such performances reached their apex in sixteenth-century France, papal legislation aimed in precisely the opposite direction. The pontiffs strove to ensure that no individual or body in Rome automatically inherited the papal authority at their death."[21]

Usually lasting about two months, or until the cardinals could agree on a successor, the Vacant See began when the cardinal chamberlain removed the "ring of the fisherman" from the deceased pope's finger

---

[21] Laurie Nussdorfer, "The Vacant See: Ritual and Protest in Early Modern Rome," *Sixteenth Century Journal*, 18 (1987): 173.

and broke it. With the tolling of the "Patara" bell, which only rang at Carnival and when a pope died, prisoners were released, lay officials of the city of Rome called out the police to guard against the ecclesiastical potentates of the Papal Curia who might try to exceed their authority, and popular "disorders" often began. The usual objects of ritual pillage were the statues of the deceased pontiff, especially if he had been an unpopular pope. When Pope Julius II died, his recently conquered subjects in Bologna destroyed a bronze statue of him by the great Michelangelo. In Rome the traditional object of attack was the pope's statue on the Capitol. In 1559, disgusted by the tyranny of the Pope Paul IV's nephews, the Romans sacked the offices of the Inquisition and defaced the pope's image. The crowd later returned to the Capitol and brought along a stone cutter who decapitated the statue. The severed head was then dragged around the city in ridicule for four days. In 1590 the Romans tried to do something similar to the statue of Sixtus V on the Capitol. Some of the most dramatic ritual pillages of a Vacant See occurred when the despised Urban VIII died in 1644. When the Patara bell rang out news of the death, a furious crowd stormed up the Capitoline hill with the intention of destroying Bernini's great marble bust of Pope Urban, which was in the chamber where the city council met. Anticipating the attack, the Barberini relatives of the pope arranged for a guard to protect the statue, but the crowd only retreated to pulverize a stucco image of the pope at the Jesuit college.

Lurking behind these disorders were several deeply ingrained traditions that came to the fore during those liminal moments such as an interregnum. These traditions included the vicarious punishment of an effigy, the idea that justice derives from the people, and the principle that the people consent to the be ruled. Even if the artisans and citizens of Rome had no direct say over the deliberations of the cardinals, even if the people of Modena were not in the position to reject the rule of the Este family, and even if the people of Brussels who lined the streets for the entry of the Duke of Burgundy were unable to avoid the dominion of a foreign prince, all of these crowds were sensitive to their rights and privileges, especially to the notion that the normal rules of law and order broke down during princely rites of passage. Ritual pillages expressed the betwixt and between character of an interregnum. The forms these pillages took remained relatively fixed: the crowd attacked the physical objects that represented the prince's rule – his palace, the records of his criminal judgments, his statue. The emotional impulse behind the pillages could be celebratory or angry or shift from one intense emotion to another. They could be ritual *allegrezze* or ritual punishments. The ritual pillage allowed urban crowds to assert that the authority of a prince died with him while they lived on.

The constructed regality of early modern kings and queens relied, to a considerable degree, on the standard ceremonial forms of the rites of passage, triumphal advents and entries, progresses, pageants, and enthronings. The most influential models, such as the court etiquette of Philip IV who placidly ruled his far-flung dominions that stretched from the Philippines to Sicily with near immobility or the daily kingrise and kingset of Louis XIV whose rulership moved with the regularity of the heavens, projected an image of a perfectly harmonious government under a sacred prince. At the same time, however, the actual performance of many royal rituals expressed the disharmonies of the political world, whether manifest as a shoving match to determine who would sit next to King Charles VI at his coronation banquet at Rheims in 1380 or a Roman mob's smashing of the bust of Pope Urban VIII before his body was even cold. The ritual processes of government represented a hierarchic and orderly world, but they also reproduced the tensions of domination and subordination. Regal ceremonies both imagined what might be and displayed what really was.

BIBLIOGRAPHY

Entries marked with a * designate recommended readings for new students of the subject.

Austin, J. L. *How To Do Things with Words*. Cambridge, Mass.: Harvard University Press, 1962. The theoretical basis for understanding a ritual as a "performative utterance." For criticisms see citations of Derrida and Schwartz below.
Bak, János M., ed. *Coronations: Medieval and Early Modern Monarchic Ritual*. Berkeley: University of California Press, 1990. An important collection of studies of coronation ritual.
Baldwin, Robert. "A Bibliography of the Literature on Triumph." In *"All the World's a Stage . . .": Art and Pageantry in the Renaissance and Baroque*. Edited by Barbara Wisch and Susan Scott Munshower. University Park, Penn.: Department of Art History, The Pennsylvania State University, 1990. Pp. 358–85. The best starting point for further research on triumphs.
Bergeron, David M. *English Civic Pageantry 1558–1642*. London: Edward Arnold, 1971.
*Bertelli, Sergio; Cardini, Franco; and Zorzi, Elvira Garbero. *Italian Renaissance Courts*. London: Sidgwick and Jackson, 1986. A beautifully illustrated collective study reflecting the new interest in court culture.
*Bloch, Marc. *The Royal Touch: Sacred Monarchy and Scrofula in England and France*. Translated by J. E. Anderson. London: Routledge & Kegan Paul, 1973. The masterpiece on sacred monarchy.

Brown, Elizabeth A. R. "The Ceremonial of Royal Succession in Capetian France: The Funeral of Philip V." *Speculum* 55 (1980): 266–93.

Brown, Patricia Fortini. "Measured Friendship, Calculated Pomp: The Ceremonial Welcomes of the Venetian Republic." In *"All the World's a Stage . . ."*. Edited by Wisch and Munshower. Pp. 136–87.

Bryant, Lawrence M. "Configurations of the Community in Late Medieval Spectacles: Paris and London during the Dual Monarchy." In *City and Spectacle in Medieval Europe*. Edited by Hanawalt and Reyerson. Pp. 3–33.

The King and the City in the Parisian Royal Entry Ceremony: Politics, Ritual, and Art in the Renaissance. Geneva: Droz, 1986. The now standard study of royal entrances by a member of the American school of French royal ritual, a group that also includes Giesey, Hanley, and Jackson, all cited below.

"The Medieval Entry Ceremony in Paris." In *Coronations*. Edited by Bak. Pp. 88–118.

Burchard, Johann. *At the Court of Borgia, Being an Account of the Reign of Pope Alexander III Written by his Master of Ceremonies Johann Burchard*. Translated and edited by Geoffry Parker. London: The Folio Society, 1963. A highly useful diary by the papal master of ceremonies.

*Burke, Peter. *The Fabrication of Louis XIV*. New Haven: Yale University Press, 1992. The best recent study of the court of Louis XIV and an excellent example of the cultural history of monarchical representations.

*Cannadine, David and Price, Simon, eds. *Rituals of Royalty: Power and Ceremonial in Traditional Societies*. Cambridge: Cambridge University Press, 1987. A significant collection of studies on royal rituals.

Cartellieri, Otto. *The Court of Burgundy*. Translated by Malcolm Letts. New York: Barnes & Noble, 1972. The standard study of the most ceremonial of late medieval courts.

Casini, Matteo. *I gesti del principe: la festa politica a Firenze e Venezia in età rinascimentale*. Venice: Marsilio, 1996. An important revisionist study of political festivity in the Renaissance. The article cited below offers a good introduction in English to Casini's ideas.

"*Triumphi* in Venice in the Long Renaissance." *Italian History and Culture* 25 (1995): 23–41.

Chittolini, Giorgio. "Civic Religion and the Countryside in Late Medieval Italy." In *City and Countryside in Late Medieval and Renaissance Italy: Essays Presented to Philip Jones*. Edited by Trevor Dean and Chris Wickham. London: Hambledon Press, 1990. Pp. 69–80. Chittolini is the leading figure in the movement to recast Italian history as a history of regions rather than of city-states or a proto-nation.

Crouzet-Pavan, Elisabeth. *"Sopra le acque salse": espaces, pouvoir et société à Venise à la fin du Moyen Age*. 2 vols. Rome: Ecole Française de Rome, 1992. An elegant and heavily documented work that erects a discussion of ritual life on an appreciation for the struggle to control the difficult ecology of the Venetian lagoon.

Derrida, Jacques. "Signature, Event, Context." *Glyph* 1 (1977): 172–97. An important critique of Austin's idea of "performative utterance."

*Duchhardt, Heinz; Jackson, Richard A.; and Sturdy, David, eds. *European Monarchy: Its Evolution and Practice from Roman Antiquity to Modern Times*.

Stuttgart: Franz Steiner, 1992. A fine compilation of articles, several of which analyze monarchical rituals.

*Dundes, Alan and Falassi, Alessandro. *La Terra in Piazza: An Interpretation of the Palio of Siena*. Berkeley: University of California Press, 1975. A pioneering anthropological study of the rituals surrounding the famous annual horseraces in Siena.

*Elias, Norbert. *Court Society*. Translated by Edmund Jephcott. New York: Pantheon Books, 1983. Provides a sociological grounding for understanding the highly ritualized behavior of princely courts.

*Elliott, J. H. "Philip IV of Spain: Prisoner of Ceremony." In *The Courts of Europe: Politics, Patronage and Royalty*. Edited by A. G. Dickens. London: Thames & Hudson, 1977. Pp. 169–90. As always with the work of J. H. Elliott, this article lucidly lays out many of the core issues suggested by monarchic ceremony.

Enright, Michael J. *Iona, Tara, and Soissons: The Origins of the Royal Anointing Ritual*. New York: Walter de Gruyter, 1985.

Fügedi, Erik. "Coronation in Medieval Hungary." *Studies in Medieval and Renaissance History*. New series 2 (1980): 159–89.

*Geertz, Clifford. *The Interpretation of Cultures: Selected Essays*. New York: Basic Books, 1973. An extraordinary collection of studies that opened the way for the contemporary study of ritual, especially as applied to religion and the state.

Negara: The Theatre State in Nineteenth-Century Bali. Princeton: Princeton University Press, 1980. The brilliantly influential study of the Balinese "theater state," a concept that has been widely adapted for the study of European state ceremonies.

Giesey, Ralph E. *Cérémonial et puissance souveraine: France, XVe–XVIIe siècles*. Translated by Jeannie Carlier. Paris: Armand Colin, 1987.

"Inaugural Aspects of French Royal Ceremonials." In *Coronations*. Edited by Bak. Pp. 35–45.

"Models of Rulership in French Royal Ceremonial." In *Rites of Power: Symbolism, Ritual, and Politics since the Middle Ages*. Edited by Sean Wilentz. Philadelphia: University of Pennsylvania Press, 1985. Pp. 41–64.

The Royal Funeral Ceremony in Renaissance France. Geneva: Droz, 1960. The most important work in the body of American scholarship on French monarchic ritual.

Gieysztor, Aleksander. "Gesture in the Coronation Ceremonies of Medieval Poland." In *Coronations*. Edited by Bak. Pp. 152–64.

Ginzburg, Carlo, coordinator of the Bologna Seminar. "Ritual Pillages: A Preface to Research in Progress." In *Microhistory and the Lost Peoples of Europe*. Edited by Edward Muir and Guido Ruggiero. Baltimore: Johns Hopkins University Press, 1991. Pp. 20–41. The source for information on ritual pillages of the property of popes. Compare with the Nussdorfer article cited below.

*Goodin, Robert. "Rites of Rulers." *British Journal of Sociology* 29 (1978): 281–99. A useful examination of the problem in defining rituals.

Gorse, George L. "Between Empire and Republic: Triumphal Entries into Genoa During the Sixteenth Century." In *"All the World's a Stage . . ."*. Edited by Wisch and Munshower. Pp. 188–257.

Graham, Victor E. and Johnson, W. McAllister. *The Royal Tour of France by Charles IX and Catherine de' Medici: Festivals and Entries 1564–6*. Toronto: University of Toronto Press, 1979.

*Gundersheimer, Werner L. *Ferrara: The Style of a Renaissance Despotism*. Princeton: Princeton University Press, 1983. Still the best study of a single court in Renaissance Italy.

Hanawalt, Barbara A. and Reyerson, Kathryn L., eds. *City and Spectacle in Medieval Europe*. Minneapolis: University of Minnesota Press, 1994. A fine collection of articles dealing with various aspects of urban spectacles.

Hanley, Sarah. *The Lit de Justice of the Kings of France: Constitutional Ideology in Legend, Ritual, and Discourse*. Princeton: Princeton University Press, 1983.

Heers, Jacques. *Fêtes, jeux et joutes dan les sociétés d'Occident à la fin du Moyen Age*. Montreal: Institut d'Etudes Médiévales, 1971. An excellent general study of festivals and games that unfortunately is still unavailable in English.

Hoffmann, E. "Coronations and Coronation Ordines in Medieval Scandinavia." In *Coronations*. Edited by Bak. Pp. 125–51.

Jackson, Richard A. *Vive le Roi! A History of the French Coronation from Charles V to Charles X*. Chapel Hill: University of North Carolina Press, 1984.

Jacquot, Jean, ed. *Les fêtes de la Renaissance*. 3 vols. Paris: Editions du Centre National de la Recherche Scientifique, 1956–75.

James, Mervyn. "Ritual, Drama, and Social Body in the Late Medieval English Town." *Past and Present* 98 (1983): 3–29. An excellent study of English civic drama and pageantry.

Kantorowicz, Ernst H. "The 'King's Advent' and the Enigmatic Panels in the Doors of Santa Sabina." *The Art Bulletin* 26 (1944): 207–31.

The King's Two Bodies: A Study in Medieval Political Theology. Princeton: Princeton University Press, 1957. Sometimes difficult but well worth the effort, this book lays out the theoretical history of the all important concept of the king's two bodies.

Kempers, Bram. "Icons, Altarpieces, and Civic Ritual in Siena Cathedral, 1100–1530." In *City and Spectacle in Medieval Europe*. Edited by Hanawalt and Reyerson. Pp. 89–136.

*Kertzer, David I. *Ritual, Politics, and Power*. New Haven: Yale University Press, 1988. Highly readable and always completely lucid, this is the best introduction to the study of political ritual.

Lindenbaum, Sheila. "Ceremony and Oligarchy: The London Midsummer Watch." In *City and Spectacle in Medieval Europe*. Edited by Hanawalt and Reyerson. Pp. 171–88.

Lünig, Johann Christian. *Theatrum ceremoniale historico-politicum* [. . .] Leipzig, 1719–20; reprinted, Vienna: Bors & Müller, 1953. The remarkable general survey of rituals that exemplifies the eighteenth century's encyclopedic and comparative approach. Lünig should be compared with the *Bibliotheca ritualis* by Francisco Antonio Zaccaria, discussed in the epilogue.

MacKay, Angus. "Ritual and Propaganda in Fifteenth-Century Castile." *Past and Present* 107 (1985): 3–43.

McCoy, Richard C. *The Rites of Knighthood: The Literature and Politics of Elizabethan Chivalry*. Berkeley: University of California Press, 1989.

" 'The Wonderfull Spectacle': The Civic Progress of Elizabeth I and the Troublesome Coronation." In *Coronations*. Edited by Bak. Pp. 217–27.

McRee, Ben R. "Social Separateness and Gild Ceremony: The Gild of St. George." In *City and Spectacle in Medieval Europe*. Edited by Hanawalt and Reyerson. Pp. 189–207.

Mitchell, Bonner. *1598, A Year of Pageantry in Late Renaissance Ferrara*. Binghamton: Medieval & Renaissance Texts & Studies, 1990.

Italian Civic Pageantry in the High Renaissance: A Descriptive Bibliography for Triumphal Entries and Selected Other Festivals for State Occasions. Florence: L. S. Olschki, 1979. The beginning point for the study of Italian civic rituals.

The Majesty of State: Triumphal Progresses of Foreign Sovereigns in Renaissance Italy, 1494–1600. Florence: L. S. Olschki, 1986.

"A Papal Progress in 1598." In *"All the World's a Stage . . ."*. Edited by Wisch and Munshower. Pp. 118–35.

Muir, Edward. *Civic Ritual in Renaissance Venice*. Princeton: Princeton University Press, 1981. A comprehensive study of the rituals of the Venetian doges.

Nader, Helen. "Hapsburg Ceremonies in Spain: The Reality of the Myth." *Historical Reflections* 15 (1988): 293–309.

Nicholas, David. "In the Pit of the Burgundian Theater State: Urban Traditions and Princely Ambitions in Ghent, 1360–1420." In *City and Spectacle in Medieval Europe*. Edited by Hanawalt and Reyerson. Pp. 271–95.

Nijsten, Gerard. "The Duke and His Towns: The Power of Ceremonies, Feasts, and Public Amusement in the Duchy of Guelders (East Netherlands) in the Fourteenth and Fifteenth Centuries." In *City and Spectacle in Medieval Europe*. Edited by Hanawalt and Reyerson. Pp. 235–70.

Nussdorfer, Laurie. "The Vacant See: Ritual and Protest in Early Modern Rome." *Sixteenth Century Journal* 18 (1987): 173–89. An important companion piece to the Ginzburg article cited above.

*Partridge, Loren and Starn, Randolph. *Arts of Power: Three Halls of State in Italy, 1300–1600*. Berkeley: University of California Press, 1992. Important both for its theoretical sophistication and for the comprehensive character of the research, this book examines the forms of political representation in Italian town halls.

"Triumphalism and the Sala Regia in the Vatican." In *"All the World's a Stage . . ."*. Edited by Wisch and Munshower. Pp. 22–81.

Peyer, Hans Conrad. *Stadt und Stadtpatron im mittelalterlichen Italien*. Zürich: Europa, 1955. An examination of the relationship between the cults of patron saints and civic institutions, a book which has unfortunately never been translated.

Phythian-Adams, Charles. "Ceremony and the Citizen: The Communal Year at Coventry, 1450–1550." In *The Early Modern Town*. Edited by Peter Clark. London: Longman, 1976. Pp. 106–28. An influential article, one of the first examples of the social history of civic rituals.

Pollack, Martha D. *Turin, 1564–1680: Urban Design, Military Culture, and the Creation of the Absolutist Capital*. Chicago: University of Chicago Press, 1991. A fine study of the relationship between military necessities and representations of monarchy.

Prevenier, Walter and Blockmans, Wim. *The Burgundian Netherlands.* Cambridge: Cambridge University Press, 1986. Includes a discussion of Burgundian court ritual.

Rosenberg, Charles M. "The Use of Celebrations in Public and Semi-Public Affairs in Fifteenth-Century Ferrara." In *Il teatro italiano del Rinascimento.* Edited by Maristella de Panizza Lorch. Milan: Edizioni di Comunità, 1980. Pp. 521–36.

Ruiz, Teofilo F. "Elite and Popular Culture in Late Fifteenth-Century Castilian Festivals: The Case of Jaén." In *City and Spectacle in Medieval Europe.* Edited by Hanawalt and Reyerson. Pp. 296–318.

*Sacks, David Harris. "Celebrating Authority in Bristol, 1475–1640." In *Urban Life in the Renaissance.* Edited by Susan Zimmerman and Ronald F. E. Weissman. Newark, Del.: University of Delaware Press, 1989. Pp. 187–223.

Schneider, Robert A. *The Ceremonial City: Toulouse Observed, 1738–1780.* Princeton: Princeton University Press, 1995.

Public Life in Toulouse, 1463–1789: From Municipal Republic to Cosmopolitan City. Ithaca: Cornell University Press, 1989.

Schramm, Percy Ernst. *Herschaftszeichen und Staatssymbolik: Beitrage zu ihrer Geschichte vom Dritten bis zum Sechzehnten Jahrhundert.* 3 vols. Stuttgart: Hiersemann, 1954–56. The most important single work on the history of imperial and royal symbolism. On Schramm's work, see J. M. Bak, "Medieval Symbology of the State: Percy E. Schramm's Contribution." *Viator* 4 (1973): 33–64.

A History of the English Coronation. Translated by L. G. Wickham Legg. Oxford: Clarendon Press, 1937. The only significant work by Schramm available in English.

Schwartz, Regina M. *Remembering and Repeating: On Milton's Theology and Poetics* (Chicago: University of Chicago Press, 1993).

Silver, Larry. "Paper Pageants: The Triumphs of Emperor Maximilian I." In *"All the World's a Stage . . ."*. Edited by Wisch and Munshower. Pp. 292–331. Demonstrating the prestige of pageantry, this article discusses the artistic representations of pageants that never actually occurred.

*Silverman, Sydel. "The Palio of Siena: Game, Ritual, or Politics." In *Urban Life in the Renaissance.* Edited by Susan Zimmerman and Ronald F. E. Weissman. Newark, Del.: University of Delaware Press, 1989. Pp. 224–39.

Stinger, Charles. "Roma Triumphans: Triumphs in the Thought and Ceremonies of Renaissance Rome." *Medievalia et Humanistica.* New series 10 (1981): 189–201.

Strong, Roy. *Art and Power: Renaissance Festivals, 1450–1650.* Berkeley: University of California Press, 1984.

Trexler, Richard C. *The Libro Cerimoniale of the Florentine Republic.* Travaux d'Humanisme et Renaissance, no. 165. Geneva: Droz, 1978. One of the earliest ceremonial books that has been published.

Public Life in Renaissance Florence. New York: Academic Press, 1980. A brilliant, evocative portrait of the city from the point of view of its public rituals.

Vestergaard, E. "A Note on Viking Age Coronations." In *Coronations.* Edited by Bak. Pp. 119–24.

Waley, Daniel. *Siena and the Sienese in the Thirteenth Century*. Cambridge: Cambridge University Press, 1991. A summary of the research on this important late-medieval city-state.

*Walzer, Michael. "On the Role of Symbolism in Political Thought." *Political Science Quarterly* 82 (1967): 191–205.

*Wilentz, Sean, ed. *Rites of Power: Symbolism, Ritual, and Politics Since the Middle Ages*. Philadelphia: University of Pennsylvania Press, 1985. Contains several important articles on political ritual.

Wisch, Barbara. "The Roman Church Triumphant: Pilgrimage, Penance and Processions Celebrating the Holy Year of 1575." In *"All the World's a Stage . . ."*. Edited by Wisch and Munshower. Pp. 82–117.

Wortman, Richard S. *Scenarios of Power: Myth and Ceremony in Russian Monarchy*. Vol. 1: *From Peter the Great to the Death of Nicholas I*. Princeton: Princeton University Press, 1995. The most important application to Russia of the techniques of ritual study and political representation developed for the study of western European monarchies.

Zapalac, Kristin. *In His Image and Likeness: Political Iconography and Religious Change in Regensburg, 1500–1600*. Ithaca: Cornell University Press, 1990. Traces the relationship between civic imagery and the Reformation.

Epilogue: mere ritual

By the eighteenth century "ritual" had become a dirty word. Like rhetoric, that other great interest of the Renaissance, ritual came to imply insincerity and empty formality, the very antithesis of the Enlightenment values that prized individual spontaneity and authenticity. How did it happen that what had been the path to God in the medieval period had for many people become a pernicious form of deception by the early modern period?

The great social thinkers of modernism, such as Herbert Spencer, Max Weber, and Edward Shils, hypothesized that ritual behavior was incompatible with modern values and that the numbers of rituals performed declined as European society evolved into modernity. This once widely accepted proposition now seems inadequate if not just plain wrong. All societies sustain themselves and represent their most cherished ideals through rituals. The quantity of rituals in Western culture has not declined so much as the nature of ritual practices has changed, and it changed largely because of the ritual revolution of the early modern period. The once widespread Christian rites of passage, the liturgical calendar, carnivalesque inversions of Christian mores, formality of courtly manners, Eucharistic presentation of God to humanity, and the theatrical representation of royal authority have largely given way to other kinds of ritualized public events – celebrations of birthdays and anniversaries, music festivals, mass spectator sports, televised religious services and evangelists, patriotic holidays, and political party conventions, all managed by professional promoters and image consultants. Commercialization and professionalization have replaced the liturgy and priestcraft, but anyone who has ever acquiesced to the thrill of collective involvement at a concert or football game has participated in something akin to the ritual experience but without the rich theological tradition to explain it. Even the new forms of religious expression associated with the evangelical and charismatic movements are pervaded with reinvented forms of ritual worship that are often on far shakier theological ground than anything rejected by the Reformation, and as the periodic resurrections of Elvis Presley indicate, Protestants also have a craving for saints.

Although the number of rituals has not declined, their status in society and their ability to present the sacred have been radically demoted as a consequence of the ritual disputes of the early modern period. The origins of those disputes can be found in Antiquity. The prophets of the Hebrew scriptures railed against ritualistic sacrifices that substituted for true obedience to the commandments of God, and Christ condemned the Pharisees for their blind adherence to the forms over the substance of religion. In the Greek and Roman worlds the Stoics criticized vain rituals that inhibited acquiring true inner knowledge. The reassertion of the values of Stoicism during the Renaissance and the recovery of Hebrew hermeneutics during the Reformation prompted a revolution in ritual theory. The ritual dispute in the sixteenth century took the form of a debate about whether rituals presented something, such as the body of Christ or the king, or merely represented the eternal God or the perfect King, a debate that sets off the "long Reformation" as the most crucial epoch in Western history for transforming the understanding of ritual.

The theoretical debate of the reformers in answer to the question, "what do rites do?," raised the issue of the efficacy of ritual and the sincerity of the participants. Doubts about efficacy especially inhibited Protestants. In England Archbishop Thomas Cranmer, in rejecting the sacramental quality of the coronation rites of Edward VI, was particularly hostile to the anointment of the king with holy oil. King James I wondered whether he should perform the king's touch, and King William III refused to touch scrofula victims at all. The question of the sincerity behind a ritual performance afflicted both Protestants and Catholics. Many sixteenth-century writers, such as Giovanni Della Casa, who criticized the insubstantiality of showy manners, and Etienne de La Boétie, who considered royal ceremonies drugs that tranquilized the people into submission, thought that rituals corroded morals by encouraging the celebration of form over substance, vanity over sincerity. During the seventeenth century a rationalist critique of empty ceremonies cut across confessional divisions, including thinkers as diverse as the Jesuit-trained Blaise Pascal, the Protestant William Shakespeare, the Jew Baruch Spinoza, the disaffected courtiers of Philip IV of Spain, and reform-minded French Catholic priests, including Jean-Baptiste Thiers and Pierre Lebrun, who wrote during the reign of Louis XIV.

The process that unraveled the traditional ritual system was most startling in France. In the course of the eighteenth century France moved from what was officially, at least, a thoroughly Catholic country to one in which there was, in Alexis de Tocqueville's words, "the total rejection of any religious belief," and from the most completely sacralized monarchy to one in which the king had become the persistent object of crude tavern jokes.[1] Roger Chartier has labelled these two transformations, the "dechristianization" of France and the "desacralization" of the monarchy. These processes culminated in the Revolution that propounded the cult of Reason to replace Christianity and cut off the king's head along with many other heads to establish a revolutionary republic.

During the seventeenth century the Catholic Reformation in France, despite many geographical variations, had been quite successful in imposing regular Sunday church attendance and the annual reception of holy communion at Easter. There had also been a proliferation of lay confraternities, especially those devoted to the Eucharist. Beginning around 1730, however, although Sunday and Easter observances persisted, the near-universal acceptance of other Catholic ritual obligations began to drop off dramatically. The first signs appeared in the service of the cult of the dead. Moneys to fund masses for the dead dried up, and testators became indifferent about where their bodies were to be buried. After about 1750 the number of persons declaring a religious vocation collapsed, reaching a low point in the 1770s and creating a serious shortage of priests. What new priests there were tended to come from the rural classes, especially the peasantry, rather than from among the children of learned professionals and the prosperous bourgeoisie as in earlier centuries, indicating a loss of prestige for the clergy as a social group. The same trend can be found among both male and female religious orders. Laymen began to desert the penitential confraternities in favor of the Masonic lodges, which practiced explicitly non-Christian collective rituals.

The causes of this momentous decline in the position of Catholicism in France may have been less the consequence of the famous rationalist criticisms by the *philosophes* than of conditions within the church itself. During the early eighteenth century many Catholic priests were attracted to Jansenism, which like Protestantism was hostile to the external show of mechanical liturgical observances. Jansenist priests refused to grant the solace of the sacraments to members of their congregation unless they demonstrated a rigorous preparation that included deeply felt contrition and thorough knowledge of church doctrines. Unable to meet the strict new standards, many communicants were turned away from mass and alienated from the church. The attempts by the Jansenists to infuse ritual with greater spirituality backfired, undermining the very

[1] De Tocqueville quoted in Roger Chartier, *The Cultural Origins of the French Revolution*, trans. Lydia G. Cochrane (Durham: Duke University Press, 1991), 92.

faith they hoped to promote and exacerbating the gap between the religion of the clergy and the spiritual needs of the laity. When the episcopal hierarchy and the Jesuits attacked the Jansenists, the ensuing controversies within the church further undermined public confidence. The fury over the Jansenists peaked at mid-century coinciding with a rapid increase of migrations from the countryside to the cities, movements of population that further undermined the ties of dependency and collective observance that had traditionally disciplined the peasantry. In the cities the church failed to create new parishes to keep up with population shifts, which meant that the parish-centered structure of the Catholic Reformation was undermined.

This process of dechristianization during the eighteenth century may have been peculiarly French, but similar social trends appeared elsewhere during the late eighteenth and early nineteenth centuries, destroying piece by piece much of what remained of the traditional ritual system. The lower classes were attracted to the religious revivalism of the *convulsionnaires* in France and the Methodists in England. The literate classes leaned toward deism. By the time the Romantics of the nineteenth century began to lament what had happened, the old order was gone, except in isolated backwaters in the Mediterranean, eastern Europe, and the Americas.

The desacralization of the king appears to have been much more sudden and catastrophic in France than in England or the German principalities where official Protestantism gradually diluted royal sacrality, replacing it with the idealized domesticity epitomized by George III (1760–1820), the benevolent head of the country's royal family. In France Louis XIV's successor, Louis XV (1715–74), could not quite stomach the daily round of royal ceremonies established by his father and was known to fake his nightly *coucher*, climbing out of bed after the ceremony to spend the evening in his private apartments. When Robert Damiens attempted to assassinate him in 1757, the exemplary ritual punishment of this isolated zealot failed to reconstitute the inviolate monarchy. Rather than accept the conclusions of the official investigation, the Jansenists and Jesuits accused each other of conspiring in the attempted regicide. When a minor judicial official blabbed rather too loudly in an inn about the Damiens affair and was executed for speaking against the king, the punishment made matters worse for the royal reputation because many thought it outrageous to put a man to death just for speaking his mind. Instead of preventing future assassination attempts and anti-royal talk, these events only encouraged imitators.

The disenchantment of the French with their king, in fact, may have originated in large part from the transformations in royal rituals during the seventeenth and eighteenth centuries. The innovation of 1610 when Louis XIII began his reign with an inaugural *Lit de justice* rather than the traditional interregnum ceremonies provoked the collapse of the royal ritual system that had displayed the sacred body of the King to the people. The genealogical fictions of the new king appearing in the "image" of his predecessor and of the "sleeping king" awakening to his kingship failed to compensate for the loss of the king's two bodies. Louis XIV's substitution of an exacting round of court ceremonies for grand public rituals, especially the triumphal entry, made the king less present to his subjects, and the numerous visual representations of him proved insufficiently magnetic as substitutes. By the eighteenth century the waning of Catholic observances undercut the evocative power of the Eucharist, which had been the most powerful model for sacralizing the body of the king. The Jansenists, moreover, found the notion of sacred kingship blasphemous. To them the Holy Ampulla was a fraud, the king's touch indecent, and the coronation ceremony at Rheims a farce. They argued that the coronation should represent the election of the king by the people. Rather than making the king a consecrated person, the ceremony should merely ask God to ratify the people's decision. To all these undermining influences must be added the expansion of the literate public. Schooled in rational criticism, subjected to burgeoning slander against the king, and titillated by pornography that featured members of the royal family, "public opinion" no longer found kingship mysterious, admirable, or intimidating. By the last half of the eighteenth century, the remaining royal rituals had literally become an empty show.

Dechristianization and the desacralization of the monarchy certainly contributed to the cultural origins of the French Revolution, but these processes also created a problem for the revolutionaries. As Mona Ozouf has argued, one of the tasks of the revolution was "the transfer of sacrality" from the Old Regime of kings to the new republic of citizens. The planners of revolutionary festivals systematically dismantled the traditional rituals of Christianity and monarchy, replacing them with new revolutionary ones. The revolutionaries created a new calendar to substitute for the liturgical calendar, replaced saints' cults and coronations with liberty trees and female personifications of liberty, and substituted holy days with election day festivals. Political clubs and Masonic lodges took over from penitential confraternities. Processional routes were reconfigured to celebrate the revolution, and the traditional processional order based on rank and precedence yielded to the new principles based on political function and age. Unlike some Protestant visionaries who quixotically believed that all ritual should be abolished, the French revolutionaries understood that all societies required collective observances to create unity and consensus. But unlike the Protestant innovations, little of what they created has lasted, probably because the new festivals, while strong on symbolic meaning, failed to stimulate deep emotions.

In many respects the French Revolution foretold the modern condition of condemning traditional rituals while struggling to find lasting substitutes. Later revolutions, such as the Russian, Chinese, and Cuban, have attempted to build a revolutionary society around a new ritual calendar. Even if these totalizing examples of revolution could not obliterate old ritual presences, they all exhibited a poisonous contempt for what traditional ritual represented, a contempt that betrayed, perhaps, a fear of the persistent power of ritual.

The modern intolerance toward "mere ritual" originated in the ritual revolution of the sixteenth century and the deritualizations of the eighteenth. Modern rationalists have often imagined themselves to be above the delusions and obscurantism of religious rituals, even as they are oblivious to the secular rituals in which they participate. The rituals of modern mass culture have created a shifting and transient sense of the sacred, now invested in the political ideology of the moment, romantic love of nature, charismatic leaders, jingoistic nationalism, idealized domesticity, or endless cults, fads, ephemera. If societies demand rituals, then changing societies will produce changing rituals.

The modern muddle about ritual is a legacy of the ritual revolution of the sixteenth century, which shifted attention from the emotive power of rituals to questions about their meaning. The modern attitude perpetuates a misunderstanding that ritual must be interpreted, its hidden meanings ferreted out, when what rituals do is not so much mean as emote.

BIBLIOGRAPHY

Entries marked with a * designate recommended readings for new students of the subject.

*Burke, Peter. "The Repudiation of Ritual in Early Modern Europe." In *The Historical Anthropology of Early Modern Italy: Essays on Perception and Communication*. Cambridge: Cambridge University Press, 1987. Pp. 223–38. Sets out the issue of the decline of ritual.

Chartier, Roger. *The Cultural Origins of the French Revolution*. Translated by Lydia G. Cochrane. Durham: Duke University Press, 1991. An effective synthetic reinterpretation of the eighteenth century.

*Colley, Linda. *Britons: Forging the Nation, 1707–1837*. New Haven: Yale University Press, 1992. Discusses the transformation of British public life around Protestantism and the evolution of kingship from a cult of sacred royalty to exemplary domesticity.

Goodman, Dena. "Public Sphere and Private Life: Toward a Synthesis of Current Historiographical Approaches to the Old Regime." *History and Theory* 31 (1992): 1–20. A useful guide to the recent historiography of the eighteenth century.

Habermas, Jürgen. *The Structural Transformation of the Public Sphere: An Inquiry into a Category of Bourgeois Society.* Translated by Thomas Burger with the assistance of Frederick Lawrence. Cambridge, Mass.: MIT Press, 1989. Habermas provides the philosophical foundations for explaining the secular character of public institutions since the eighteenth century and the parallel decline of faith in public rituals.

Hunt, Lynn. *Politics, Culture, and Class in the French Revolution.* Berkeley: University of California Press, 1984.

*Merrick, Jeffrey W. *The Desacralization of the French Monarchy in the Eighteenth Century.* Baton Rouge: Louisiana State University Press, 1990. Lays out the case for desacralization as contributing to the French Revoltion.

*Ozouf, Mona. *Festivals and the French Revolution.* Translated by Alan Sheridan. Cambridge, Mass.: Harvard University Press, 1988. Demonstrates how much the Revolution depended upon a newly invented non-Christian ritual system.

Picart, Bernard. *The Ceremonies and Religious Customs of the Various Nations of the Known World: Together with Historical Annotations and Several Curious Discourses Equally Instructive and Entertaining.* 7 vols. London: William Jackson, 1733–39. Along with Zaccaria, cited below, a good example of the encyclopedic interest in religious rituals during the eighteenth century.

Van Kley, Dale K. *The Damiens Affair and the Unraveling of the Ancien Régime, 1750–1770.* Princeton: Princeton University Press, 1984. Along with Merrick's and Woodbridge's work, this study shows the consequences for the monarchy of the loss of faith in Christianity during the eighteenth century.

Woodbridge, John D. *Revolt in Prerevolutionary France: The Prince de Conti's Conspiracy against Louis XV, 1755–1757.* Baltimore: Johns Hopkins University Press, 1995.

Zaccaria, Francisco Antonio. *Bibliotheca ritualis.* 3 vols. Rome: symptibus Venantii Monaldini ex typographio Octavii Puccinelli, 1776–81; reprinted, New York: Burt Franklin, n.d. A good example of the encyclopedic approach of comparative rituals, typical of the Enlightenment

Glossary

Advent. The liturgical season of preparation before Christmas that begins on the Sunday closest to November 30.

Anabaptism. Literally, "re-baptism." A term to describe a radical trend in the Reformation that first appears in the 1520s. Anabaptists insisted on adult baptism, rejecting infant baptism as contrary to scripture, and on the rigorous simplification of religious rituals. They tended to establish sects that existed outside of the official Protestant churches, and some of these groups practiced primitive communism, polygamy, and rigid moral discipline. Anabaptists suffered from persecution and extermination at the hands of Catholics and other Protestants alike.

Annunciation, feast of the (March 25). Commemorates the announcement by the angel Gabriel to the Virgin Mary that she would bear the Christ child.

Anointment or unction. The application of holy oil at baptism, the ordination of a priest, or the coronation of a monarch.

Apotropaic magic. Rites designed to avoid evil influences or *maleficia*.

Ars moriendi. The art of dying. An extended ritual of penance that spread during the fourteenth and fifteenth centuries to assist the dying and their relatives and that preceded extreme unction.

Ascension, feast of the. The fortieth day after Easter, commemorating Christ's ascension to heaven. In some churches before the Reformation an image of Christ was raised through a hole in the roof of the church building.

Avignonese papacy. See **Babylonian Captivity** and **Great Schism**.

Babylonian Captivity (1305–78). Seven successive pontificates when popes resided in Avignon to escape the turmoil of Rome.

Baptism. A rite of purification in which the person baptized is either immersed or sprinkled with water. In Christianity it also signals admission into the church and is usually accompanied by name-giving. One of the seven sacraments of the Catholic church, baptism was retained as a sacrament by Protestants.

Body politic. A term derived from the political theory of the king's two bodies, which posited that a king by virtue of being a man had a mortal and fallible body, called the body natural, and by virtue of being a king also had an eternal and perfect body, called the body politic.

Calvin John (1509–64). French reformer who established a theocratic regime in Geneva and whose *Institutes of the Christian Religion* influenced reformers all over Europe. The Calvinist Reformation was more rigorous than

Lutheranism or Anglicanism in both simplifying religious rituals and eliminating rites not found in scripture. Besides Switzerland Calvinism dominated the Reformation in Scotland, Holland, and parts of Germany and guided the theocracy established in New England. Significant Calvinist minorities could be found during the sixteenth and seventeenth centuries in France (called Huguenots), England (called Puritans), and Hungary.

Candlemas (February 2). Commemorates the presentation of Christ in the temple and the purification of the Virgin Mary. In the East the presentation was emphasized, but in the West the purification was more important, making it a Marian festival characterized by the blessing and distribution of candles.

Carnival. Literally, "goodbye to meat." A period of festive license lasting from a day to several weeks immediately preceding Lent. Carnival festivity characteristically celebrated indulgence in food and the joys of sexuality but could also be a dangerous time of aggression.

Carnivalesque. Carnival-like festivals of license that could occur at any time of the year but were most frequent in May and June or after Autumn harvests.

Caul. The inner membrane enclosing the fetus, a portion of which is sometimes found on the infant's head at birth. In these situations, the person born with the caul is assumed to possess special powers, in some cases to have been born with a second soul.

Chalice. A goblet for the consecrated wine of the Eucharist.

Charivari. A form of ritual judgment typically administered by young men against alleged violations of community standards for proper sexual or marital behavior. Usually involving mocking songs and making noise, those subjected to a *charivari* would sometimes be dragged from their homes and subjected to ritual humiliations and even assault.

Civilizing process. A term used by historians and sociologists to describe the spread of polite manners and social mechanisms that promoted self-control.

Corporal. The cloth upon which the priest places the consecrated elements of the Eucharist during the celebration of the mass.

Corpus Christi (or Domini), feast of. A Catholic festival observed on the Thursday after Trinity Sunday in celebration of the Real Presence of Christ. Established in 1264, the feast became during the fourteenth and fifteenth centuries the most prominent festival of the church, marked by pageants, miracle and mystery plays, and vast processions that included city officials, princes, and bishops, all demonstrating their devotion to the Eucharist.

Dance of death. Often performed as a masque on All Souls' Day and frequently represented in paintings and engravings, the dance encouraged repentance by warning Christians that death could take them at any time.

Diabolism or sorcery. Worship of the devil or calling upon demonic powers to achieve some desired end. A diabolist or sorcerer attempts to control demonic beings whereas a witch or warlock is controlled by them.

Doge. The elected prince of the republic of Venice, whose principal duties were ceremonial.

Duel. A highly ritualized form of private combat that became especially widespread among European aristocrats after the middle of the sixteenth century.

Easter. The commemoration of Christ's resurrection, celebrated in the Western church on the first Sunday after the first full moon after the vernal equinox. The Easter season in the liturgical calendar extends from Ash Wednesday at the beginning of Lent to Pentecost. Before the middle of the sixteenth century, observant Catholics typically partook of the Eucharist only once a year on Easter Sunday.

Epiphany, feast of (January 6). Commemorated in the East: the baptism of Christ, and in the West: the adoration of the Magi.

Eucharist. A Christian sacrament in which bread and wine are consecrated and consumed. Interpreting how to understand the relationship between this ritual and the biblical account of the last supper in which Christ enjoined his apostles to eat bread and drink wine in remembrance of him became one of the most contentious issues of the Reformation.

Fools, feast of; Day of the Boy Bishop. An ecclesiastical counterpart of the revelries of carnivalesque festivals. Although several different feast days betrayed elements of the Feast of Fools, the Feast of the Holy Innocents (January 6) most commonly became the Day of the Boy Bishop, who was chosen from among the choir-boys in a cathedral to satirize clerical rules in a day of misrule.

French Wars of Religion (1562–98). A series of wars between French Protestants, known as Huguenots, and Catholics. The most famous episode was the Massacre of St. Bartholomew (1572) when King Charles IX acquiesced to the assassination of the Protestant leaders who had gathered in Paris for the wedding of his sister to the Protestant King of Navarre, Henri of Bourbon. The killings spread to become a general slaughter of Protestants. The wars ended when Henri succeeded to the French throne and converted to Catholicism.

German Peasants' War (1524–25). Occasioned by Martin Luther's attacks on papal authority and defiance of the Holy Roman Emperor, the peasants of Swabia, Franconia, and Thuringia revolted against the economic and social abuses associated with German feudalism. Luther himself repudiated the revolt. The most radical elements adopted Anabaptism.

Godparents. The persons who sponsor an infant at baptism and become the child's spiritual guides. The obligations of artificial kinship implied in godparentage could be quite extensive and could include incest prohibitions.

Grace. The unmerited favor of God that produces spiritual regeneration and promises eternal salvation. One of the major disputes of the Reformation involved the role of sacraments in conferring grace.

Great Schism (1378–1417). The division of the Western church into rival camps led by Roman and Avignonese (French) claimants to the papacy. The schism followed the period (1305–78) when all popes resided in Avignon. The schism seriously undermined papal authority and led to the rise of conciliarism, the doctrine that a general council of the church held final authority.

Hermeneutics. The activity of interpreting texts, especially scripture. Although hermeneutics had always been one of the principal activities of Christian thinkers, a revival of Greek and Hebrew hermeneutics in the fifteenth and early sixteenth centuries opened an extensive debate about the correct interpretation of the Bible and of the meaning of church rituals.

Honest dissimulation. The attempt to be honorable and truthful in a situation where social conventions require the concealment of true beliefs and feelings behind a facade of polite manners and circumspect speech.

Host. The bread or wafer consecrated in the Eucharist.

Huguenot. A French Protestant, usually a Calvinist.

Humanism. A term derived from the *studia humanitatis* or humanities curriculum that has come to designate a philological and historical approach to the study of ancient texts in Latin, Greek, and Hebrew. Humanists tried to find the least corrupted versions of a text and to interpret its meaning in the context in which it was written. Humanists also tried to imitate the style of ancient writers. Humanism does not imply any consistent philosophical or ideological position but does point to a method of interpretation.

Hus, Jan (1369–1415). A professor at the University of Prague and popular preacher who challenged the primacy of the pope by asserting the superiority of scriptural authority. His liturgical reforms included granting to the laity the wine of the Eucharist as well as the bread. He was burned at the stake at the Council of Constance, leaving a legacy of religious nationalism in Bohemia.

Iconoclasm. Literally, "the breaking of images." During the Reformation iconoclasts opposed the use of images in religious worship and defaced or destroyed ritual objects in churches.

Iconolatry. The worship of images, especially the intense devotion to images found among the Orthodox, the Russian Orthodox in particular.

Incarnation. The doctrine that God became a man by entering the womb of a virgin. Uncorrupted by original sin and the lust of procreation, Christ was simultaneously God and a man, partaking of the attributes of both.

Incubus. A male demon or familiar who provides a witch with her powers but also controls her. A *succubus* is a female demon who serves the same function for warlocks.

Interregnum. The period between the death of one king or pope and the ascension to the throne of a successor. Fraught with many potential dangers, interregna were typically periods of extensive and unusual ritual activity.

Jansenism. The doctrine prevalent among some Catholic priests in eighteenth-century France, which emphasized the impossibility of depraved humankind willfully doing good. By emphasizing rigorous spiritual preparation for the sacraments, Jansenists alienated many lay believers from the liturgical functions of the church.

King's touch. The practice of the Kings of France and England of touching to cure scrofula, a symptom of which was skin lesions.

Lent. Period from Ash Wednesday to Easter Eve during which the forty weekdays are devoted to penitence and fasting in commemoration of Christ's forty-day fast in the wilderness. Lent is preceded by the public indulgences of Carnival and followed by the holy celebrations of Christ's resurrection at Easter.

Liminality. A concept derived from the second or transitional phase of a rite of passage during which a participant crosses a threshold (*limen*, hence liminal) into a temporary state outside of his or her normal social status. Liminal states characteristically involve the inversion or abandonment of normal social rules. See **Rites of passage**.

Lit de justice. Literally, "bed of justice." The ceremony in which the King of France sat enthroned before the Parlement of Paris, which as the superior court of the realm ratified royal decrees.

Liturgy. In the technical language of the Christian churches, the order for the celebration and administration of the Eucharist. The liturgical calendar refers to the form of celebration designated for each day of the year. In a more general sense liturgy refers to all the various prescribed forms of public worship.

Luther, Martin (1483–1546). A German priest and professor who began the Protestant Reformation by nailing his ninety-five theses against indulgences on the door of the Wittenberg church in 1517. Luther's Reformation not only questioned papal authority but initiated the reformation of ritual through limiting the number of sacraments to three and later two, eradicating sacramentals and other additions to biblical rituals, emphasizing the spoken Word in the vernacular over the ritual in the mass, and opening a debate on the doctrine of the Real Presence. Luther's Reformation spread throughout much of Germany and Scandinavia and influenced the early Reformation in England.

Maleficium. Working evil through curses or magical acts. The magic associated with witchcraft and sorcery.

Mass. In the Roman Catholic tradition, a ritual celebration of the Eucharist in which bread and wine are consecrated. High masses for special occasions include extra prayers, incense, music, and the assistance of a deacon and subdeacon. Low masses consisted of simplified ceremonies and no music.

May Day (May 1). A major carnivalesque holiday, especially in England, that included Morris-dances, decorations of flowers and ribbons, and the erection of a maypole.

Midsummer (June 24). A carnivalesque festival held near the summer solstice, which was often the occasion for sexual promiscuity.

Missal. The book containing the service of the mass for the entire liturgical year.

Modern Devotion (*devotio moderna*). A program of study and prayer developed during the fourteenth century by the sisterhoods and brotherhoods of the Common Life and made popular among lay Christians during the fifteenth century by the treatise, *The Imitation of Christ* by Thomas à Kempis. The modern devotion emphasized private worship and moral introspection rather than collective sacramental observances, creating the ethical foundations for the devaluation of ritual practices.

Morris-dance. An English dance, possibly derived from the Spanish *morisco*, which became an essential part of village festivals at least by the sixteenth century. Consisting of five men and a boy, who was dressed as a girl and called Maid Marian, the dance came to be associated with the license of May Day and was prohibited by the Puritans.

Orthodoxy. To be understood in two senses: (1) following correct theological doctrines and practices as established by the church, that is not adopting heretical, original, or independent-minded opinions; and (2) the Eastern or Greek church, which separated from the Western Catholic church in the ninth century. The Orthodox recognize the Patriarch of Constantinople as their head or, as was the case with the churches of Russia and Rumania, established a doctrinal communion with him. Although there are many minor liturgical differences between the Eastern Orthodox and the Western Catholic churches, the most divisive issues have involved the dating of Easter, clerical celibacy, and the role of icons in religious worship.

Pageant. The addition to a procession or entrance of floats, tableaux, allegorical or symbolic devices and arches, dramatic presentations, speeches, music, and sumptuous decorations that make the ceremony more spectacular. Pageants typically attempt to establish the religious, political, or ideological meaning of the ceremony.

Penance. A sacrament of the Catholic church abandoned by most Protestants. As a sacrament, penance involved several stages, including the recognition of sin, inner contrition, confession to a priest, paying a penalty, and absolution by a priest.

Pentecost. Among Jews a harvest festival celebrated on the fiftieth day after Passover. Among Christians a feast, also called **Whitsunday**, celebrated on the fiftieth day after Easter to commemorate the descent of the holy spirit to the disciples of Christ, which was often symbolized in late medieval churches by the release of a dove or by dropping balls of fire from the roof.

Prophylactic magic. Ritual acts designed to ward off misfortune or disease.

Purgatory. A doctrine that posited an intermediary place that was neither heaven nor hell to which most of the dead would go after death to receive punishment for the sins they had committed in life. Much of the late medieval expansion of religious rituals derived from an attempt to reduce the amount of time souls spent in purgatory.

Purim. A Jewish festival to commemorate the deliverance of the Hebrews from Haman. Held in the spring, Purim betrayed many carnivalesque features, including the mock coronation of a clown-king who was symbolically put to death.

Puritanism. A broad and inexact term to describe those who wished to push for further reform than had been achieved by the established Anglican church, especially in the simplification of rites to eliminate all vestiges of Catholic practice. Puritans were deeply influenced by the Calvinist Reformation in Switzerland.

Pyx. A vessel or box to contain the consecrated host during processions or when a priest went to administer the last rites to a dying person.

Real Presence, doctrine of the. The belief that the body and blood of Christ are really present in some way in the consecrated wafer and wine of the Eucharist. Defining the exact nature of the Real Presence became one of the most contentious issues in the Reformation.

Relic. A physical remnant of the body of a saint or some object associated with him or her.

Rites of passage. Rituals that demarcate the passage from one biological or social condition to another. According to Arnold Van Gennep, these rites characteristically follow three distinct phases: (1) separation, which displaces the individual from his or her previous station, (2) transition (or liminal), which temporarily suspends the subject between the old and new position, and (3) aggregation, which brings the subject into a new status.

Rites of violence. A form of public disturbance or protest that employs – often in derision or inversion – the gestures, symbols, or processional routes of public rituals.

Rogation Days. The three days before Ascension Day. Before the Reformation they were characterized by collective prayers that often asked for divine protection of crops and in some places by the "beating of the bounds," a procession to mark out the boundaries of the parish community.

Sabbat or witches' sabbath. The collective ritual worship of Satan in a ceremony defined in several different ways but usually involving the sacrifice of Christian babies, the profanation of Christian symbols, orgies, homage to the devil, and sometimes nocturnal flight. There is no evidence that anyone in the late medieval or early modern periods actually celebrated the sabbat, which was undoubtedly invented by learned clerics who may have misinterpreted certain kinds of peasant magic and folklore.

Sacrament. According to the late medieval scholastic theologians, a sacrament was a ritual distinguished by the following criteria: (1) it combined *matter*, such as the bread of the host, with *form*, which was a correctly repeated verbal statement in Latin; (2) recipients of the sacrament must have the correct *intention*, generally understood to mean that they must willingly receive the sacrament and must have repented their sins; and (3) it conferred *grace* on the recipients. The seven sacraments, made official in 1439, were baptism, confirmation, marriage, penance, communion, ordination, and extreme unction. The Protestant reformers generally reduced these to two – baptism and communion – but they disagreed to a considerable degree on exactly what took place during a sacrament.

Sacramentals. Minor rites and benedictions employed by lay persons for spiritual benefit. These included lay processions that imitated clerical processions, exorcisms of people and animals, and the use of blessed objects. Although the sacramentals lacked the theological justification of the official seven sacraments, the Catholic church actively promoted them as a lay form of clerical Christianity. Protestants, on the other hand, were especially critical of the sacramentals and tried to eliminate them entirely.

Sacring. The act of consecrating the Eucharistic elements.

Scholastic theology. The strain of medieval theology taught in the universities that attempted to reconcile classical philosophy with Christianity. The principal figure was Thomas Aquinas (1227–74), whose *Summa theologiae* became the basis of Catholic theology.

Tableau vivant. Literally, a "living picture." During the Renaissance period a tableau vivant consisted of a group of actors in costume who stood silent and motionless on a fixed stage or moving float to represent a scene. Tableaux vivants were frequently a feature of liturgical processions, especially Corpus Christi, and of princely entrances.

Thaumaturgic. Of or pertaining to the working of miracles.

Transubstantiation. After 1215 the official Catholic doctrine explaining the Real Presence of Christ in the Eucharistic elements of bread and wine.

According to Thomas Aquinas's exposition of the doctrine, at the moment of consecration the bread and wine change substance, becoming the whole body and blood of Christ in every particle, while the outward appearances, or "accidents," retain the aspect but not the substance of bread and wine.

Trinity Sunday. The Sunday following Pentecost. Trinity Sunday begins the longest liturgical season of the year, called "after Pentecost," which lasts until Advent.

Whitsunday. See **Pentecost**.

Witchcraft. The action of performing *maleficium* while under the influence of demonic powers. A female witch or male warlock might also be understood to participate in a witches' sabbat, although this would not be an essential characteristic. A witch can be distinguished from a sorcerer in that a demon controls the witch whereas the sorcerer controls the demon.

Youth-abbeys. Urban gangs composed of young unmarried men who were led by an "abbot" and who assumed authority over the streets of a town by organizing carnivalesque festivities, conducting gang fights, performing charivari against married couples, and participating in gang rapes of vulnerable young women.

Zwingli, Ulrich (1484–1531). A Swiss reformer who began the Reformation in Zürich in the early 1520s. Like Luther he denounced indulgences and abuses of ecclesiastical authority, but he differed from Luther on several doctrinal issues, especially on the interpretation of the Real Presence.

Index

Absalon, Anna Pedersdotter, 223
adolescence, 27. *See also* youth-abbeys
Advent: liturgical season of, 58, 60–61; ceremonial entry form of, 239, 242–44
Agatha's day, St., 63
Agnes, St., 72
Aiguillette, 40–41
Alba, 211
Albania, 97, 106
Albertus Magnus, 40
Alcalà, University of, 170
Alenquer, 96
Alexander III, Pope, 235
Alexis, Tsar, 140
Alfonso, King of Naples, 244
All Fool's day. *See* Feast of Fools
All Saints' day, 71
All Souls' day, 46, 51, 71
Ambrose, St., 233; day, 75
Amsterdam, 109
Anabaptists, 20, 21, 177–78, 203
Angelico, Fra, 101
animals in rituals, 87–88, 107–8, 110, 127, 137–38
anointment, 248–49, 270
Anthony, St., hermit, 185
Aquinas, Thomas, St., 148, 192
Arianism, 203
Ariès, Philippe, 44, 45
Aristotle, 172–73
Arles, 28
art of dying (*ars moriendi*), 14, 45–48
Asag, 134
Ascension day, 58, 66–67, 187–88, 235–37
Asciesi, Gabriele d', 112
Asciesi, Guglielemo d', 112
Ash Wednesday, 63
Assumption of the Virgin, feast of the, 187
Asti, 211
Augsburg: marriage ceremonies in, 33, 35–38; Reformation in, 187–88

Augustine, St., 23, 193–94
Augustinian Order, 166, 185
Aumont, Duke of, 128
Austin, J. L., 247
auto de fe, 207–9
Avignon, 6, 49

Bacon, Francis, 250
Bakhtin, Mikhail, 91–92, 107
Balandier, Georges, 230
Balkans, 22, 199
Bamberg, 65
banquets, wedding, 34–38
baptism, 20–27, 155, 170; sacramental debates about, 176–78
Barcelona, 87
Bari, 234
Bartholomew's day, St., 95
Bavaria, 110–11, 222
Becker, Carl, 1, 9
Behn, Aphra, 39
Benandanti, 26
Benedict of Nursia, St., 78; order of, 57; rule of, 78–79
Bergen, 223
Bernard of Clairvaux, St., 119
Bernardino of Siena, St., 26, 74–75
Bertran de Born, 137
Bible and sacraments, 169–71
Bielski, Joachim, 250
birth, rituals associated with, 25–27
bishops: authority of, over ritual practice, 179–80; during Catholic Reformation, 210–12
Black Death, 44, 69
Blasius's day, St., 63
bleeding hosts, 165
blood libel, 213–16
Bodin, Jean, 40
body: in rituals, 8; lower, 81–114, 161; politic, 8, 153, 232, 246; of God, 158–76; of saints, 151; upper, 117–44

Bohemia, heresies in, 6. *See also* Hus, Jan;
    Utraquists
Bologna, 95, 244, 259
Bolsena, 147–50, 165
Bonaventura of Bagnoregio, St., 148
Boniface VIII, Pope, 57
Borgia, Cesare, 110
Borgia, Lucrezia, 99
Bossy, John, 21, 67
Bourdieu, Pierre, 6
Braga, 180
Brazil, 22
Brown, Patricia Fortini, 241
Brueghel, Pieter (the Elder), 81–84, 89,
    118
Bryant, Larry, 243
Bucer, Martin, 173
Buchholz, 98
Burgundy, 110, 242–43
burial, places of, 50
Burke, Peter, 89, 118, 126, 140, 257
Bynam, Caroline Walker, 86, 158

calendars, 16, 55–79; reform of, 79;
    revolutionary, 273–74
Calvin, John, 159, 171; on baptism, 177;
    on images, 194–95; on the Eucharist,
    175–76
Calvinism: and manners, 118; in Lithuania,
    203; in Orthodox lands, 199–201
Cambridge, 77
Cameron, Euan, 170
Candlemas, 58, 61–63, 156
cannibalism, ritual, 81–82, 85–86, 112–13,
    214, 221
Canterbury, 32
Cantilene, 101–2
Capua, 244
Carnival, 63, 81–93, 118, 189; violence in,
    85–86, 106–8
carnivalesque festivity, 93–98, 146
Carolingians, 249
Carpentras, 90
Carroll, Linda, 88
Caesar, Julius, 244
Cassirer, Ernst, 2
Castiglione, Baldesar, 120–21, 123
castration magic, 40–41
Catherine of Siena, St., 159
Catholic church, attitudes toward marriage,
    31, 35. *See also* Reformation, Catholic
caul, powers of the, 25–26
Cellini, Benvenuto, 220
ceremony: books, 240; sixteenth-century
    definitions of, 167. *See also* rite, ritual
Cervantes, Miguel de, 93

Cesena, 110
charivari, 27, 98–104, 135–36, 138
Charles VII, King of France, 254
Charles VIII, King of France, 237
Charles the Bold, Duke of Burgundy, 242
Chartier, Roger, 271
Chaumont, 95
Chester, 70
children, imagined ritual sacrifice of,
    213–15, 221–23. *See also* infants,
    baptism of
Christ: dual nature of, 118; life of, in the
    liturgy, 60–72. *See also* Advent,
    Ascension day, Christmas, Corpus
    Christi, Easter, Epiphany, Eucharist,
    Holy Week, host, incarnation
Christian III, King of Denmark, 25
Christina, St., 147
Christmas, 58, 60–61, 66
circumcision, 20–21, 214
civic rituals, 232–39
civilizing process, 117
class, manners define, 117
Clement VIII, Pope, 246
Clendinnen, Inga, 6
Cockaigne, land of, 89. *See also* Carnival,
    carnivalesque
Cologne, 180
Commedia dell'arte, 136
communion, 65, 148, 155, 176. *See also*
    Eucharist, host, mass
confirmation, 155, 170
confraternities, 69, 210–12, 271; of the
    Holy Sacrament, 205
Congregation of Rites, 180
Connerton, Paul, 119
Constantine, Roman Emperor, 60, 73
Córdoba, 208
Cornwall, 196
coronations, 247–50, 254–55, 270
Corpus Christi, feast of, 67–70, 148–49,
    164, 238
Corsica, 106
Council of Trent. *See* Trent, Council of
courtly manners, 120–22. *See also* manners
courtship between the sexes, 132–36
Coventry, 58, 70, 75, 238
Cracow, 125, 257
Cranmer, Thomas, 270
Cuenca, 206

Dalmatia, 26, 97
dance, 37, 123; of death, 51. *See also* morris
    dance
Dante Alighieri, 49
Dati, Goro, 55–57

Datini, Margherita, 14–16, 33
Davis, Natalie Zemon, 92, 101, 186
day, liturgical significance of the, 55–57, 74–78
dead and dying, rituals for the, 44–52, 71–72
Della Casa, Giovanni, 121–22, 127, 167, 270
Della Torre, Alvise, 106
Delumeau, Jean, 15
Denmark, 249, 258
Devon, 196
diabolism, 218
Dijon, 28
dining rituals, 126–32. See also food, manners
divorce, rituals of, 41–44
Dominicans, 159, 176, 212
Dorothea, Queen of Denmark, 258
Dorothea's day, St., 63
Dortmund, 116
drama and ritual, 64–65, 68–70, 86, 88, 92–93, 123, 136
dreams, 122
Du Cange, Charles Du Fresne, 30
Duccio di Boninsegna, 234
dueling, 141–44
Duffy, Eamon, 60, 161, 197–98
Durkheim, Emile, 3, 16, 73

Easter, 58–61, 63–66, 162
Eastern Europe: Reformation in, 199–204; style of manners in, 126
Eastern Orthodoxy. See Orthodox churches
Edict of Thessaloniki, 58
Edward VI, King of England, 196–98, 259, 270
effigies in rituals, 62–63, 102, 251–53
Egidio da Viterbo, 166
Ehem, Marx, 187–88
Eliade, Mircea, 73
Elias, Norbert, 117, 120, 138, 257
Elizabeth I, Queen of England, 196, 246, 259
Ely, 32, 190
Emmanuel College, Cambridge, 176
emotions and ritual, 2, 13–16, 121–22, 156
Endingen, 110
Enlightenment and ritual, 269–74
England, 67, 72, 96, 108; beliefs about caul in, 26; communion in, 161–64; coronations in, 249–50, 259; Corpus Christi in, 69–70; death rituals in, 44; divine kingship in, 243, 250; elimination of feast days in, 76–77;

eradication of feuds in, 141; fertility rituals in, 39; heresies in, 6; iconoclasm in, 190; manners in, 125–26; Reformation in, 195–98; youth-abbeys in, 27
entries, ceremonial, 239–46; 255–56
Epiphany, 58, 61
Erasmus, Desiderius, 48, 93, 127, 135, 150, 167, 178; on manners, 119–20; satire on ritual, 168–69
Essen, 65
Esslingen, 190
Este family, 259–60
Este, Alfonso d', 99
Estonia, 95, 202
Eucharist, 7, 8, 147–50, 207; Catholic Reformation and the, 205–6; Corpus Christi processions and the, 67–70; theories about, 158–76. See also communion, host, mass
exorcism, baptism as an, 21
extreme unction, 155, 170
Extromission theory of vision, 192–93

Fabian and Sebatian, Sts., 62
Farel, Guillaume, 188
Fat Tuesday. See Carnival
Feast of Fools, 95–96
Feast of Holy Innocents, 95. See also Epiphany
Feast of Lights, 62
Felix and Regula, martyrs, 234
Ferrara, 108, 242, 246
fertility rites, 15–16, 39–41, 61–63, 93
Festival of the Twelve Marys, 62–63
flagellation, 64–65, 161, 206–7, 210–11
Florence, 13, 74–76, 87, 89, 157, 233; baptism in, 23; bigamy case in, 32; ceremony book of, 240; funerals in, 48–49; marriage ceremonies in, 33–35; ritual violence in, 111–13
Flynn, Maureen, 64, 207
food: rituals of consuming, 81–83; the host as, 160–61. See also meat
France, 71, 89, 96; Catholic Reformation in, 204, 206; Corpus Christi processions in, 69; courtship in, 132–36; death rituals in, 44; decline of ritual system in, 270–74; divine kingship in, 243; dueling in, 143; godparentage in, 22; manners in, 123–24; prayer books in, 164; revolution in, 273–74; royal rituals in, 249–57; Wars of Religion in, 86, 165, 191; youth-abbeys in 27–29
Francis of Assisi, St., 61

François I, King of France, 143, 205, 251, 257
Flandrin, Jean-Louis, 89, 129
Frederick II, Holy Roman Emperor, 244
Frederick III, Holy Roman Emperor, 242
Friuli, 24–26, 106–108, 143, 218
Fugger family, 187–88
funerals, 46; of French kings, 251–53

Galateo, 121–22, 127, 131
gangs. *See* youth-abbeys
Gargantua, 96–97
Geertz, Clifford, 4, 230–31, 233
Gennep, Arnold van, 19–20, 21, 30
Geneva, 99
Genoa, 104, 245
Gentilcore, David, 209
George III, King of England, 272
George, St., 75, 96, 238
Germany, 72, 89, 96; Catholic Reformation in, 204; Corpus Christi in, 68–69; feast days in, 62; manners in, 127–28; Peasants' War in, 191; Protestant Reformation in, 185–91; unction of kings in, 249; youth-abbeys in 27
gestures, 117, 119
Gévaudan, 106
Ghent, 243
ghosts, beliefs in, 51
giants, 96–97
Giesey, Ralph, 251
Gilmore, David, 105
Ginzburg, Carlo, 1, 9, 221
Gluckman, Max, 4, 90
God. *See* communion, Eucharist, host, mass
godparents, 21–22
Goffman, Erving, 247
Golden Legend, 61
Good Friday, 64, 74
grace, 156, 170
Great Schism, 6
Greene, Thomas, 167
Gregory XIII, Pope, 74
Guazzo, Stefano, 132
Guelders, 242
Guerre, Martin, 99
guilds, 69
Guinefort, St., 25

Halloween, 71
Hamburg, 138
Hammer of Witches (Malleus Maleficarum), 219–20
Handelman, Don, 4
hands in rituals, 30–31

handshake, 125–26
Harvard, John, 176
hats, 125, 131
Hebrew calendar, 57–58
Henry II, King of France, 40, 143
Henry III, King of France, 105, 257
Henry IV, King of France, 252–54
Henry VII, King of England, 70
Henry VIII, King of England, 77, 93, 196, 197, 259
Heraclides, Jacob, 199–200
Herald, office of, 240
hermeneutics, 8, 150–51, 168, 170
Hildesheim, 190
Holland, manners in, 125–26
Holy Innocents, Massacre of, 61
Holy Roman Emperor, 247
Holy Week, 61, 64–65, 189, 207
Holy Year, 57
honest dissimulation, 120–22
host, cult of, 159–65, 215–16. *See also* communion, Eucharist, mass
hour, ritual significance of, 78–79
Hsia Po-chia, R., 214
Huguenots, 103. *See also* France: Wars of Religion in
Huizinga, Johann, 136–37
humanism, 167–70
Hungary, 27, 199
Hus, Jan, 149, 165–66. *See also* Bohemia, Utraquists
Hutten, Ulrich von, 169

Iceland, 26, 106
iconoclasm: in Orthodox lands, 199–204; Protestant, 185–98
illness: magical causes of, 217; ritual cures for, 161, 212
images, ritual uses of, 13–14
incarnation, doctrine of, 158
infants, baptism of, 20–27
interregnum rites, 248–56
Ireland, 7, 26, 48, 204
Italy: beliefs about caul in, 26; Catholic Reformation in, 204, 206–7, 210–11; Corpus Christi processions in, 69; death rituals in, 44; dueling in, 141; godparents in 22; manners in, 131; youth-abbeys in, 27
Ivan the Terrible, Tsar of Russia, 202, 229, 258

James I, King of England, 246, 250, 270
Janarius's day, St., 75
Jansenism, 271–72
Jeanneret, Michel, 131, 132

Jesuit Order, 123, 180, 207, 272
Jews: the week as conceived by, 72–74;
    ritual execution of, 110; alleged anti-
    Christian rituals of, 152, 213–16
Joachim of Fiore, 166
Joan of Arc, 254
John the Baptist, St., 20, 75–76, 233;
    decapitation of, 74; nativity of, 70
John of Damascus, 191–92
John the Evangelist, St., 14
Joseph, St., 101
Judaizers: in the eastern European sense,
    201–202; in the Spanish sense, 208
Juliana of Liège, 67, 148
Julian calendar, 60–61
Julius II, Pope, 244–45, 261
Justina's day, St., 75–76

Kantorowicz, Ernst, 250
Karlstadt, Andreas, 173, 177, 185–86
Kaufbeuren, 190
Kertzer, David, 3–4, 231
Kibbey, Ann, 175
king's touch, 255, 270, 273
king's two bodies, 250–55
kingship: desacralization of, 272–73; rituals
    of, 246–62
Kinser, Samuel, 86, 245
kiss in ritual, 30–31, 33–34, 108, 125, 134,
    164
Klapisch-Zuber, Christiane, 33
Koenigsberg, 89

La Boétie, Etienne de, 270
Ladislaus IV Vasa, King of Poland, 125
Langhe, 104
Languedoc, 48
Lateran Council, Fourth, 171
Le Goff, Jacques, 31, 49, 55
Le Roy Ladurie, Emmanuel, 85
Lebrun, Pierre, 270
Leipzig, 65
Lent, 58, 63–64, 81–84, 118
Leonardo da Vinci, 193
Lepanto, battle of, 75
Levack, Brian, 217, 221
Lévi-Strauss, Claude, 4, 126
Liège, 161, 180
lies, 121–22, 142–43
Liguria, 27, 106
liminality, 19–20, 27, 51, 90, 97, 248
lit de justice, 253–55
Lithuania, 201, 203–204
liturgical cycles, 57–72
Livonia, 202
Lollards, 166. See also Wycliff, John

Lombard, Peter, 155
London, 5, 70, 94, 109, 197, 239
Lorqua, Ramiro de, 110
Louis IX ("The Pious"), King of France,
    249
Louis XII, King of France, 245
Louis XIII, King of France, 253–54
Louis XIV, King of France, 247–48,
    254–57, 262, 273
Louis XV, King of France, 272
Low Countries, beliefs about the caul in
    the, 26
Lucaris, Cyril, 200–1
Lucca, 237
Lünig, J. C., 247
Lupercalia, 62
Luther, Martin, 97, 149, 166; death of,
    44–45; on baptism, 177; on death
    rituals, 52; on marriage, 31, 35; on the
    Eucharist, 172, 174–75
Lutherans, relations with the Orthodox,
    199–200
Lyons, 28, 99, 102–3, 180

Magdeburg, 187
magic, 216–23
maleficia, 217–23
Malleus Maleficarum, 219–20
mannerism, 131–32
manners, 84, 117–44
Mantua, 259
Marburg Colloquy, 175
Marcourt, Antoine, 163
Mardi Gras. See carnival
Marie de Médicis, Queen of France, 253
Mark, St., 75, 233–34, 237
market-place, rituals of the, 42–43
marriage, 31–44; as a sacrament, 155, 170;
    of the sea, 235–37; satire of, 98–104
Mary, Queen of England, 196, 197, 259
Mary, Virgin: devotion to, 192; feasts of,
    61–62, 71, 101; patron of Siena,
    234–35. See also Assumption of the
    Virgin, Candlemas
masculinity, concepts of, 28–29, 105
masks, 101
Masonic lodges, 271
mass, 148, 164; for the dead, 271;
    institution of the, 159–60; reform of
    the, 185–86. See also communion,
    Eucharist, host
mattinata, 27, 99. See also charivari.
matza, 214–16
May Day, 78, 83, 93, 101
meat, 81–83, 85–86, 88–89, 127–30, 162
Meissen, 98

Melanchthon, Philipp, 185–86
Memmingen, 190
merchants' time, 55–57
Methodism, 152, 272
Midsummer, 70, 83, 94–95, 118, 137, 239
Milan, 75, 79, 180, 233, 240
military parades, 238–39
Modena, 260
Modern Devotion, 167
modernism, 269–70
Moldavia, 199–200
Montaigne, Michel de, 45, 122, 165, 167
Montenegro, 106
Montespan, Madame de, 45
Montpellier, 87
More, Thomas, 139
Morelli, Giovanni, 13–16, 23, 33, 55, 192
morris dance, 70, 93, 94
Moscow, 89, 229
Muchembled, Robert, 132–33
Munich, 110–11
music in festivity, 37, 157
Muzio, Girolamo, 141

Nalle, Sara, 206
Nallo, Florie, 99, 102–3
naming, 22–23
Naples, 75, 87, 112–13, 244
nativity cycle of feasts, 58
Nebra, 190
Nelli, René, 134
New England, beliefs about caul in, 26
Nicholas, St., 234
Nicholas of Cusa, 165
Nikon, Patriarch, 202
Norwich, 238
Nuremberg, 65, 87, 89, 93
Nussdorfer, Laurie, 260

Oberman, Heiko, 172, 174
Oecolampadius, Johannes, 173
ordination, 155, 170
Orkneys, divorce rituals in the, 42
Orthodox churches, 60, 199–204
Orvieto, 148
Otranto, 41
Ottoman Empire, 199, 201
Ottonian Empire, 249
Oxford, 70, 77
Ozouf, Mona, 273

Padua, University of, 90
pageants, 238–39
Palm Sunday, 63, 156, 229, 242–45, 258
Pappenheimer family, 110–11, 222–23
Paris, 45, 109, 137, 205, 237, 245, 251–53

parishes, Catholic Reformation reliance on,
    209–12
Parlement of Paris, 253–54
Partridge, Loren, 237, 244
Pascal, Blaise, 270
Passover, 72, 213–16
Patriarch of Constantinople, 200–1. See also
    Orthodox churches
Patron saints, 233–35
Paul, St., 20, 62, 170
Paul IV, Pope, 261
Paulinus of Nola, St. 61
Pax-board, 108, 164
Peace of God, 108
penance, 155, 170, 206–9
Pennsylvania, 125
Pentecost, 58, 65, 67, 94
Peter, feast of the chair of St., 63
Peter the Great, Tsar, 203, 258
Peter of Prague, 147–48
Petrarch, Francesco, 244
Peyer, Hans Conrad, 234
Peyretier family, 103
Philip IV, King of Spain, 262, 270
Philip the Good, Count of Burgundy, 243
Philip and James's day, Sts., 93
Phythian-Adams, Charles, 60
Piedmont, 101, 210–12
Pilgrimage of Grace, 77
pilgrims 147, 151, 169
pillages, ritual, 259–62
Pius IV, Pope, 179
Pius V, Pope, 179
Platonism, 119
play, 81–83
Poland: manners in, 117, 124–25, 131,
    134–35; Reformation in, 201, 203–4;
    royal ceremonies in, 247, 249, 250,
    257–58
Polotsk, 202
Portugal, 71, 204
posture, bodily, 122–24
Prato, 14
Praybook Rebellion, 196–97
prayers for the dead, 46, 50–51
presence and representation, theories of,
    7–9, 93, 151–53, 165–81, 270. Also see
    Eucharist, Real Presence,
    transubstantiation
priests, ritual functions of, 155–56, 160,
    163, 180, 271
processions, civic, 237–39
Prodi, Paolo, 260
progresses, ritual, 245–46
prostitutes in rituals, 29, 108, 138
Protestants. See Reformation, Protestant

protocols, diplomatic, 241
Provençal romances, 134
punishment, ritual 108–13, 138–40, 207–9
Purgatory, 49–50, 71
Purification of the Virgin. *See* Candlemas
Purim, 86
Puritans, 77, 176

Quakers, 118, 125

Rabelais, François, 93
rape, 28
Ravaillac, François, 253
Real Presence, doctrine of, 147–50, 172, 189. *See also* Eucharist
Reformation, 6–7
    Catholic, 151–53; as a ritual process, 204–12; in France, 271; on sacraments, 155–58, 178–80, 204–5
    Protestant, 151–52; as a ritual process, 185–98; eliminates feast days, 76–77; on baptism, 20, 176–78; on death rituals, 52; on marriage, 35–38; on the Eucharist, 158–76; royal rituals after, 258–59
regal ceremonies, 246–62
Reinburg, Virginia, 163–64
Rej, Mikolaj, 117
representation. *See* presence and representation, theories of
Reuchlin, Johannes, 170
Rheims, 248–49, 252, 255, 273
rites: of enactment, 247–48; of malevolence, 212–23; of passage, 16, 19–52, 153, 241, 248; of role reversal, 89–90; of satire, 97–104; of supplication, 66–67; of vassalage, 29–31; of violence, 104–14; of weather, 157
ritual: decline of, 269–74; definitions of, 1–9; origins of term, 167
Roch, St., 25
Rogation days, 66–67, 94
Romania, 27, 95
Romans, 85–86, 92, 113
Rome, 87, 90, 244–45, 248, 260–61
Roper, Lyndal, 35
Rossiaud, Jacques, 28
royal ceremonies, 246–62
Rubin, Miri, 68
Ruggiero, Guido, 217
Russia, 26, 140, 229, 258; icon veneration in, 201–203; manners in, 129, 131
Ruthenia, 26
Ruzante (Angelo Beolco), 88

sabbath: origins of, 72–74; witches', 220–23
Sacks, Oliver, 2–3
sacraments, 155–58; biblical sources of the, 170–71; Catholic Reformation and, 178–80, 204–5; Protestant Reformation and, 158–78. *See also* baptism, confirmation, Eucharist, extreme unction, marriage, ordination, penance
safety valve thesis, 90–92
Saint-Denis, 251, 252, 255
Saint Gallen, 190
Saint-Pol, Constable of, 110
Saint-Rambert-sur-Loire, 103
saints, cults of, 104–105. *See also* names of individual saints
Savonarola, Fra Girolamo, 46, 74, 166
Savorgnan, Antonio, 50, 107–8, 114
Scandinavia, 93
Schwartz, Regina, 72, 175, 176
Schwenckfeld, Caspar, 178
Scipio Africanus, 244
Scotland, 27, 71, 106
Scribner, Robert, 157, 186, 187, 189, 190
seasons, liturgical, 57–72
Selden, John, 17
Serbia, 23, 26
Seville, 87, 109
sexuality: and magic, 218, 222–23; in ritual, 81–83, 89, 93, 97, 132–36, 149; of Christ, 158–59
Shakespeare, William, 93, 132, 270
shame, 135, 136–44
Shils, Edward, 269
Shrove Tuesday. *See* Carnival
Sicily, 95
Siena, 108, 234–35, 238
Simon of Trent, 213–14
Sixtus V, Pope, 180, 261
Skye, isle of, 42
sorcery, 218
Spain, 71, 96; Catholic Reformation in, 204, 207–9; Corpus Christi in, 69; court rituals in, 257; Holy Week in, 64, 207; manners in, 123–24; marriage in, 32; youth-abbeys in, 27
Spencer, Herbert, 269
spinning-bee, 133, 189
Spinoza, Baruch, 270
sports, ritual antecedents and elements of, 105, 123, 138, 140
Starn, Randolph, 237, 244
Steinberg, Leo, 158
Stephen of Bourbon, 90
Stoicism, 119, 270

Storace, Giovan Vincenzo, 112
Strocchia, Sharon, 45
Sunday, 34–35, 58, 73
Sweden, 26
Switzerland, 27. *See also* Calvin, John;
    Geneva; Zürich; Zwingli, Ulrich
Szamowska family, 134–35

table fork and manners, 129–30
Tableaux vivants, 238–39
Tallard, 188
Tenenti, Alberto, 46
Teresa of Avila, St., 159
theater states, concept of, 152–53, 230
Thiers, Jean-Baptiste, 270
Thompson, E. P., 42, 58
time, ritual constructions of, 8, 55–79
Tissirand, Etienne, 102–3
Tocqueville, Alexis de, 270
Toledo, 208
Torre, Angelo, 210–11
Touch. *See* King's touch
Toulouse, 32, 135, 206
Transubstantiation, 147–50, 171. *See also*
    Eucharist
Transylvania, 199
Trent: Council of, 38–39, 48, 151, 178–80,
    204–5, 210–11; persecution of Jews in,
    213–14
Trèves, 242
Trexler, Richard, 74, 240–41
Trier, 180
Trieste, 63
Trinity Sunday, 67
triumph, ritual form of, 240, 244–45, 258
Turin, 239
Turner, Victor W., 4, 20, 90
Tuscany, 101

Udine, 24–25, 106–8
Ukraine, 146, 203
Ulm, 189
Urban, St., 157
Urban IV, Pope, 67, 148
Urban VI, Pope, 165
Urban VIII, Pope, 261, 262
Utraquists, 166. *See also* Bohemia; Hus,
    Jan

Valentine's day, St., 63
vassalage, 29–31
Vattimo, Gianni, 151

Venable, Peter, 151
vendetta, 27, 106–8, 138–39, 162
Venice, 62–63, 75, 89, 104, 109, 123, 180,
    233–34, 259; beginning of year in, 58;
    bridge battles in, 105; Carnival in,
    87–88, 137; civic rituals in, 235–37;
    Corpus Christi in 69; dogeship in,
    250–51; Easter in, 64–65; godparents
    in, 22; marriage of the sea in, 66; table
    fork introduced in, 130
Versailles, 256–57
Vigarello, Georges, 123
Vikings, 248
Villach, 107
Villani, Giovanni, 113
violence: in rituals, 85–86, 102–4; shame
    of, 136–44. *See also* rites of violence
Virgin Mary. *See* Mary, Virgin
virginity, symbols of, 38
Vladimir, Grand Duke, 201

Wales, 32, 41–42
Walter of Brienne, Duke of Athens, 111–13
Wandel, Lee, 193
Weber, Max, 185, 269
week, liturgical significance of the, 72–74
Westminster, 248
Whiting, Robert, 196–97
Whitsun. *See* Pentecost
William III, King of England, 270
Wilsnack, 165
witchcraft, 110–11, 152, 216–23
Wittenberg, 97, 173, 185
wives, ritual sale of, 42–44
women: churching of, 24; fertility rituals
    for, 39–40; rites of passage of, 27;
    rituals of, 101, 136, 159, 205, 217–18
Woodstock, 94
Wycliff, John, 165, 166

year, liturgical construction of the, 57–72
York, 32, 70, 238
youth-abbeys, 27–29, 99–101, 104–5,
    139–40, 210
Yuval, Yisrael Yaakov, 214–15

Zerbavel, Eviatar, 56, 73, 78
Zürich, 172–73, 234
Zwickau, 90, 190
Zwingli, Ulrich, 166; on baptism, 177; on
    images, 192–94; on marriage, 31; on
    the Eucharist, 172–75